African
Connections

THE AFRICAN ARCHAEOLOGY SERIES

The **African Archaeology Series** is a series of volumes intended to present comprehesive and up-to-date summaries of current research on the African cultural past. The authors, who range from paleoanthropologists to historical archaeologists, all are presently active in their disciplines, work in Africa, and detail the results of their ongoing research interests. Though the essential subject matter of each volume is drawn from archaeology, they are equally dependent upon investigation of the historical and anthropological records as well. The authors understand the diversity and depth of African culture and history, and endeavor to explore the many sources of the African experience and the place of the African past and lifeways in the broader world. At the same time, while intending to reach an audience beyond specialist confines, the series permits Africanist scholars the opportunity to extend authoritative information beyond the narrow limits of the monographic site report, in order to transform their field results into more general syntheses, giving context and meaning to a bare bones archaeological record, exploring and utilizing new techniques for explaining, as well as comprehending the past.

Series Editor
Joseph O. Vogel (University of Alabama)

Books in the Series:
I. Chapurukha M. Kusimba, *The Rise and Fall of Swahili States* (1999)
II. Michael Bisson, S. Terry Childs, Philip de Barros, Augustin F. C. Holl, *Ancient African Metallurgy: The Socio-Cultural Context* (2000)
III. Innocent Pikirayi, *The Zimbabwe Culture: Origins and Decline of Southern Zambezian States* (2001)
IV. Sibel Barut Kusimba, *African Foragers: Environment, Technology, Interactions* (2002)
V. Augustin F. C. Holl, *Saharan Rock Art: Archaeology of Tassilian Pastoralist Iconography* (2004)
VI. J. D. Lewis-Williams, D. G. Pearce, *San Spirituality: Roots, Expression, and Social Consequences* (2004)
VII. Peter Mitchell, *African Connections: An Archaeological Perspective on Africa and the Wider World* (2005)
VIII. Andrew B. Smith, *African Herders: Emergence of Pastoral Traditions* (2005)

Submission Guidelines:
Prospective authors of single or coauthored books and editors of anthologies should submit a letter of introduction, the manuscript, or a four- to ten-page proposal, a book outline, and a curriculum vitae. Please send your book manuscript or proposal packet to:

The African Archaeology Series
AltaMira Press
1630 North Main Street, #367
Walnut Creek, CA 94596

AFRICAN CONNECTIONS

An Archaeological Perspective on Africa and the Wider World

Peter Mitchell

ALTAMIRA
PRESS

A Division of Rowman and Littlefield Publishers, Inc.
Walnut Creek • Lanham • New York • Oxford • Toronto

ALTAMIRA PRESS
A Division of Rowman & Littlefield Publishers, Inc.
1630 North Main Street, #367
Walnut Creek, CA 94596
www.altamirapress.com

Rowman & Littlefield Publishers, Inc.
A Member of the Rowman & Littlefield Publishing Group
4501 Forbes Blvd., Suite 200
Lanham, MD 20706

PO Box 317
Oxford
OX2 9RU, United Kingdom

British Library Cataloguing in Publication Information Available

Library of Congress Cataloging-in-Publication Data

Mitchell, Peter, 1962–
    African connections : an archaeological perspective on Africa and the
wider world / Peter Mitchell.
        p. cm. — (The African archaeology series)
    Includes bibliographical references and index.
    ISBN 0-7591-0258-9 (cloth : alk. paper) —
    ISBN 0-7591-0259-7 (pbk. : alk. paper)
    1. Africa—Antiquities. 2. Africa—Relations—Foreign countries.
    3. Africa—History. 4. Africa—Civilization. 5. Human evolution.
    I. Title. II. Series.

    DT13.M58 2004
    960—dc22   2004016679

Printed in the United States of America

∞™ The paper used in this publication meets the minimum requirements of
American National Standard for Information Sciences—Permanence of Paper
for Printed Library Materials, ANSI/NISO Z39.48–1992.

Contents

We carry within us the wonders we seek without us: there is all Africa and her prodigies in us.

—THOMAS BROWN,
Religio Medici (1643),
Part 1, Section 15

Illustrations

Tables

Sidebars

Foreword

WHAT ARE AFRICA'S links with the rest of the world? How ancient are they and what is their significance? And how can archaeology shed light on these questions to illuminate the many fancied myths, untested speculations, and academic hypotheses about these links and the flow of people, things, and information into, and out of, Africa?

The practitioners of archaeology, bound by the rules of academic inquiry, attempt to describe and explain things that, for the most part, happened long before anyone thought that the trivialities of everyday life were worthy of note. Our professional interest extends beyond describing and cataloging modes of subsistence, residence, or technology to attempt, as well, to explain how things came to be in the distant past. At one time or another, professionals have utilized simplistic explanations like migration, diffusion, or acculturation arising from contact with a foreign, superior culture. The use of such explanatory modes was long the norm, rather than the exception, in the history of Africanist archaeology. Latterly, however, as more subtle means of explanation have come to the fore, speculative commentators, less bound by the formalities of academic discourse, have also stepped forward to offer alternative views of the value of the African past. As a result, the place of a supposed "dark continent" in the cultural history of the world and its connections with the world has popularly, as well as academically, been constructed along a scale ranging from marginal to critically pivotal to the great movements of history.

It is therefore useful to have a scholar like Peter Mitchell not only dissect some of the foibles of past explanations, but also offer a serious estimate of the state of our knowledge of the connectivity of events and cultural processes occurring on the African continent and in the rest of the world from the perspective of archaeology and its ancillary disciplines. In order to do this, he has not only digested a far-ranging literature on the

African past, synthesizing a general history of Africa's connections with people and things off the continent, their impact on the developmental history of human communities there, and the effects of contact with Africa and Africans on people and events elsewhere, but also endeavored to clear away some of the obscuring cobwebs of past explanation.

Clearing the explanatory obscurities of past investigators and commentators is not always a simple task. Archaeology is an essentially political process. Like its arch coconspirator history, it often describes not so much the past, or even what we remember of the past, but what we wish the past to have been. Its explanatory fashions, fads, and follies, for better or worse, range from highly disciplined academic science to uninformed speculation embedded in a matrix of prevailing opinion. While archaeology is subject to development, the infusion of new concepts, and change, it, too, still often reflects ideas formed outside its prevailing investigative methodologies, or forms those methodologies in ways that conform to certain kinds of cultural expectation. We need only remember the opinions that the archaeology of James Bent and his contemporaries brought to Great Zimbabwe more than a hundred years ago, the persistence of the Hamitic myth past the middle of the twentieth century, the argument that the Swahili city-states were the product of migrations along Africa's East Coast, or the long political debate over the first appearance of Bantu-speaking populations south of the Limpopo River to understand a few instances of archaeology's use of faulty premises supported by conventional wisdom.

Sometimes these opinions or debates are held long after archaeology has found more satisfying and testable solutions or they are reshaped to satisfy some other political purpose; Randall-MacIver solved the "mystery" of Great Zimbabwe early in the twentieth century, but objectors to his solution can be found today. Similarly, the Hamitic race may be dead in anthropology, but the corpse has risen from its grave in another, more politically tinged discussion, citing otherwise long-discredited sources. Africa, but not only Africa, has a long history as a center for such arguments staged between academic archaeology and those desiring a different kind of history.

Sub-Saharan Africa, the home of substantial autochthonous polities, once the equal of their contemporaries elsewhere, was, for example, viewed quite differently when met by the industrialized West in the nineteenth century. Nineteenth-century imperialists themselves required a different view of the continent and its inhabitants than that to be encompassed in the vision of twentieth century nationalists. Subsequently, at the same time that a generation of late twentieth century archaeologists and anthropologists forged a new perspective on African culture and history, a growing cadre of Africanists of African origin seriously questioned the descriptions of earlier observers as insensitive and unresponsive to the core of the African cultural and historical experience. Though their criticisms are undoubtedly true, attempts to gild the lily are often as fictive as the reconstructions they seek to supplant. The socialist utopia at Great Zimbabwe envisioned by Mufuka is as misguided in its way as his contemporaries Bruwer and Hromnik, and their reliance on foreign invaders, are in theirs. Fortunately, Mitchell deals with many of these arguments, debates, and fancies in his far-reaching discussion of the real evidence of the links between Africa and the world. Reading Mitchell, one realizes that the continent and the people living there were never the passive receptacles of foreign influences as they were, so often, depicted during the colonialist period, but they were instead active participants in their own destinies, innovating here, absorbing new ideas there, and everywhere adapting to changing social and cultural environments.

The ebb and flow of appreciations of the African career has been suggested in the foregoing. At one time or another, the continent has been depicted as an empty vessel requiring filling from elsewhere; equally, there are those who would claim the origin of most things culturally significant as the creation of African invention. Obviously, these are dichotomous poles that far overreach the realities of the African past. As Mitchell explains, throughout much of history Africa, as a geographic location in the center of the Old World, was in a unique position to participate in interaction spheres that stretched from the Far East to western Europe, as well as, late in its career, affecting and being influenced in return by the New World. Here and there, as we have seen, observers have exaggerated the relative give and thrust of these interactions: once imparting too great an African influence, while at others attributing too small an effect. It is fair to speculate that, since the time that early humans left the African continent to settle the Earth's many and varied environs, they have been handy in the creation of interaction spheres, of greater or lesser dimension, not only adapting people to one place or another, but also drawing upon distant resources and ideas to enrich their existence, all the while sending forth local commodities and other ideas. It is this mutual give and take of material culture, people, perceptions of their surroundings, and concepts of society, technology, and worldview that has shaped humanity into the form we know today. And significantly, Africa has been a player in this production from the very beginning, sometimes looming large to fill the center stage, sometimes being a lesser player on the margin, or offstage altogether. But Africa is not unique in this role, since the same characterization can be made of everywhere else, and of every other population, at one time or another. It is this understanding that this book assists in developing. Africa was at once a critical link in the creation of humanity, a passive observer, and a mutual partner in change.

At present it is politically convenient, in some quarters, to regard Africa, its people, and their cultural history in a unitary fashion, as if there were somehow an African "nation-state," conversant with a single worldview. Obviously, this is not the case, nor was it ever so in the past. The variety of cultural expression on the continent—ranging from simplistically appearing hunter-gatherer bands to highly complex state-level societies—raises the question of which of these are purely indigenous and which imported from elsewhere. Posing the essential problem of understanding Africa's links with the rest of humanity during its career on Earth, Mitchell explores some basic technologies of African life—metallurgy and food production—setting them in historical perspective in regard to our present knowledge of their development on the continent and linkages with events elsewhere. The history of Africa's commerce and trade and their relationships to links with others are also explored, along with the development of African states. Consideration of the roots of the slave trade delves into matters of slavery within traditional African society, as well as the basis, organization, and differences between the Atlantic trade and the cross–Indian Ocean and trans-Saharan links that took slaves to Islamic lands. These are all important issues that Mitchell treats in an exhaustive and balanced fashion, presenting a comprehensive demonstration of Africa's linkages and the role of Africanist archaeology in gathering the evidence of them.

Joseph O. Vogel

Preface

No man is an island.

—JOHN DONNE, 1624, Devotions upon
Emergent Occasions, *Meditation XVII*

O PEN AN ATLAS and look at the world (figure P.1).
Africa lies at its center, with Europe to the north, the
Middle East at its northeastern edge, and the rest of
Asia across the Arabian Sea and Indian Ocean. To the west, beyond the
Atlantic, lie the Americas and beyond them the Pacific. But though Africa
may be at the center of the world, and surely lies at the heart and origin
of the human evolutionary story, its more recent past, and particularly its
connections with other continents, have been neglected in grand historical narratives. Sidelined, except where ancient Egypt is concerned, Africa
is excluded from, or only fleetingly acknowledged in, most general discussions of the emergence of food production, the development of centralized political systems, or the origins of urban societies. Where it is
taken into account, it is all too often as a passive victim or recipient of the
attentions of others, a process often seen as culminating in the iniquities
of the trans-Atlantic slave trade, European colonization, postcolonial
"underdevelopment," and ongoing "globalization."

There is, of course, a degree of hyperbole in what I have just written,
and few would now agree (at least openly) with the notorious words of
Lord Dacre that, before European contact, Africa had no history, merely
the endless gyrations of barbarous tribes (Trevor-Roper 1963, 871). That
this is so is partly because of the efforts of those who have produced major
syntheses of the African past, from the magisterial, if now dated,

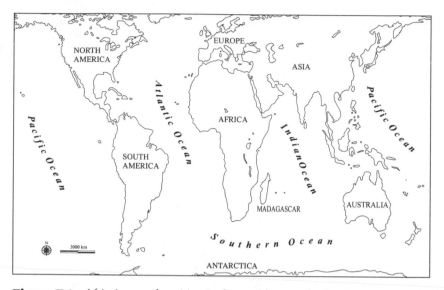

Figure P.1. Africa's central position in the world mapped using Peter's Projection to represent relative landmass size as fairly as possible.

Cambridge History of Africa and its UNESCO successor, to the single-volume treatments of Davidson (1991), D. Phillipson (1993a), Iliffe (1995), Reader (1998), Connah (2001), Ehret (2002), and others.[1] The contributions of journals, including the *Journal of African History* and *African Archaeological Review*, research institutes (such as the British Institute in Eastern Africa), and societies (like the Society of Africanist Archaeologists) have been central to rewriting Africa's past, underpinned by the individual efforts of numerous historians, historical linguists, anthropologists, and archaeologists, African and non-African alike. And yet Africa and its connections with the rest of the world are still too little acknowledged in most general syntheses of world history or prehistory, once the initial excitement of human origins is over. Given just five chapters out of forty-six for the last 10,000 years, compared with Europe's twelve, in an encyclopedia that is now more than 20 years old (Sherratt 1980), Africa beyond Pharaonic Egypt still rates only 5 percent of the coverage for the same period in one of archaeology's most popular textbooks (Fagan 2001), and a mere two pages (plus map!) in one of its competitors (Wenke 1999).

Contributing to the righting of this imbalance is among this book's ambitions. The strategy adopted is to focus on the last 10,000 years, during which climatic conditions were, very broadly, similar to those of today.

The emphasis is on looking at how, during this time, Africa's inhabitants interacted with those of other landmasses, not merely as consumers or dependents, but as equal partners in exchange and active donors of goods, ideas, and people. It is archaeology's expansion since 1960 that allows us to question the biases of an earlier era and dispense with models that once saw Africa, particularly sub-Saharan Africa, as passively following influences from elsewhere. Working alongside cognate disciplines such as paleoenvironmental research, historical linguistics, and the study of oral histories, archaeology provides a new basis on which to write an account of Africa's precolonial past, one that pays due attention to the continent's dynamic interactions with the rest of the world. At the same time, focusing on those interactions may help archaeologists working elsewhere to broaden their own perspectives through an acquaintance with African research (Stahl 1994; S. McIntosh 1999a). From the origins and spread of systems of food production and metallurgy, through the organization of trade and exchange, the growth of larger, more politically complex societies, the expansion of world religions, and the impact of slavery, to the effects on each other of colonizer and colonized, African archaeology can increasingly contribute not just examples, but also its own insights to broader theoretical debates. Indicating how this can be done is another of this book's ultimate goals.

But while to an Africanist this agenda has the undoubted benefit of addressing one aspect of Africa's marginalization within the general narrative of human history, it runs the risk of simultaneously reinforcing the traditional social evolutionary model that African data and experience can help us question. There is, in fact, little reason to accept that Africa's historical development must necessarily be constructed in the image of that of Europe and of those societies (in the ancient Near East and Pharaonic Egypt) that the West privileges as its cultural ancestors. Yet, as Stahl (1999a, 44) reminds us, a research emphasis on "trade, towns and states is consistent with a progressive developmentalist perspective that is alive and well in African archaeology." The mere replacement in models of cultural change of simplistic ideas of diffusion or migration by trade with partners based on or beyond the peripheries of the continent will do nothing to address these biases. Indeed, in many cases local and regional networks of interaction were essential to the development of those longer-distance, continent-linking exchanges that still attract disproportionate interest. At the same time we must bear in mind the impact of the distant and the new at the local level and in the realm of the everyday, for it was here that new subsistence staples such as maize and cassava, the development of cash crop economies, such as cocoa, and the introduction of new kinds of artifacts and belief systems affected individuals and effected, or did not effect, social change. Among the questions that we can then ask are: Can we detect any general patterns in the ways in which connections between African societies and those in other parts of the world have been structured? Are distinctive types of communications, transactions, or exchange identifiable? What role has Africa's physical geography played in framing these interactions? And what degree of continuity can be traced in them over time? To allow readers to check the evidence on which my own answers to these questions have been made and have ready access to the sources that I have consulted, I have deliberately opted to exclude from the bibliography unpublished conference papers or contract archaeology reports. For the same reasons I have also tried to keep references to graduate theses to the essential minimum.

Structure

Where to draw boundaries in studying Africa's past has never been straightforward, and I first consider how the idea of "Africa" has come about and how far it is useful to distinguish Africa as an entity or to separate areas south of the Sahara from those to its north. Next I review the resources, material and intellectual, involved in the interactions between Africans and non-Africans and look at how archaeological thinking about these exchanges has developed. To situate these observations within a physically tangible context, I introduce key features of Africa's geography and ecology, emphasizing how they can define various frontier areas, or "interfaces," between Africa and the rest of the world. Though this book's main theme is the last 10,000 years, chapter 1 concludes with a background sketch of the expansion beyond Africa of the genus *Homo*, the more recent spread of anatomically modern humans, and the evidence for contacts between Africa and Eurasia during the late Pleistocene.

With chapter 2, I move on to examine the development and spread of the diverse systems of food production practiced in Africa before the bridging of the Atlantic and Indian Oceans. African populations developed many ways of producing food from indigenous resources, while benefiting from and contributing to the range of domesticated plants and animals available elsewhere. In discussing these topics I also consider some of the constraints that disease, geography, and climate imposed on the expansion of these systems. I look too at how the African record compares with the situation in other world regions as regards recognizing cultivation when plants do not exhibit morphological change, experiments in rearing species that were subsequently not retained under close human control, and the extent to which plant and animal species were domesticated across broad zones rather than in just a few localities.

The next four chapters examine several of the interfaces between Africa and the rest of the world, beginning with the Nile Valley and the Red Sea. Ancient Egypt and its successors have often been treated so distinctly from the rest of Africa as to make one wonder whether they were located on the same landmass. Without adopting the Afrocentric position of Diop (1967), one concern of chapter 3 is to establish the African basis for the distinctive features of Pharaonic civilization, while still explaining the different (but how different?) cultural trajectories followed along the Nile Valley. A related question is how far interactions between Egypt, Nubia, and southeastern Sudan, and the physical constraints and opportunities of moving along or beyond the Nile, structured and created the patterns we observe. Here it is important to recall that the Nile is but one of northeastern Africa's waterways. Stretching southeast for almost 2,000 km, the Red Sea is another, and written sources have long alerted us to how it was used by the Egyptians and others to gain access to exotic luxury goods. Archaeological evidence is now starting to illuminate both these north–south contacts and the antiquity of east–west movements between Africa and the Arabian Peninsula. The two-way exchange of domesticates, the development of one of Africa's great early civilizations, that of Aksum, and the still more recent spread into Africa of Islam are just three of the topics to which those movements are relevant.

The Red Sea provides a gateway to East Africa and the Indian Ocean. This was home to a complex system of international trade long before the Portuguese entered it and forms the subject matter of chapter 4. New research hints that these networks may be significantly older than previously thought. The antiquity in Africa of ultimately Southeast Asian domesticates such as chickens and bananas is one topic that I consider, the colonization of Madagascar by Indonesian migrants some time in the late first millennium cal. B.C. (sidebar 1, page 22) a second, and the accumulating evidence for a pre–Iron Age African presence on offshore islands like Zanzibar and Mafia a third. But the chapter's main thrust is to look at how archaeology tracks the growth of connections between Africa's eastern coast and the lands on the other side of the annual monsoon system, in Arabia, the Persian Gulf, India, and beyond. These connections were vital to the development of Swahili civilization and the introduction of Islam to this portion of the continent. How far they should be held responsible for the growth of complex societies farther inland is another issue, along with the disruption and transformation of older trading systems after European entry into the Indian Ocean in 1498.

Islam and trading systems intimately associated with its spread are not just a feature of Africa's eastern shores. Indeed, if the Red Sea is a gateway to the Indian Ocean then it also bisects one of the world's great deserts, which stretches from the arid expanses of Arabia in the east through to the Atlantic Ocean in the west. It is easy to see this desert as an impediment to human movement, not least when, during parts of the Pleistocene, it was even larger and drier than today. Conversely, a significantly more benign ecology during the early Holocene facilitated the initial expansion of livestock keeping, only for increasingly arid conditions to encourage the outward movement of people and their animals. But the Sahara is more than a barrier. Chapter 5 thus considers it as the focus of an international trading system once uniquely associated with the expansion of Islam. I show how archaeology demonstrates that urban communities had developed within and south of the Sahara long before the Arab conquest of North Africa. The impacts of Islam and trans-Saharan contacts on the inhabitants of the desert's southern shore, the Sahel,[2] and on those of the forests yet farther south, as well as the significance of contacts with tropical West Africa to the peoples of the Maghreb, also demand attention.

Europe's entry into the Indian Ocean was from the west, and chapter 6 turns to Africa's other, Atlantic coastline. Excepting the colonization of the Canary Islands and of Bioko, the historical emphasis here is comparatively recent. The main focus is the different forms taken by European movement and expansion and the impacts that they had. Slaves were widely sought out, but we should not forget the importance of gold, ivory, and pepper, and all this before the widespread initiation of plantation-based cash crop economies in the nineteenth century. Stress is placed on the active role of Africans in choosing what they wished to adopt by way of new goods, crops, and technologies, along with the limited opportunities for European colonization, still less political domination, before the mid-nineteenth century.

Slavery of the kind touched on in chapter 6 removed millions of Africans from their homeland, and in chapter 7, I consider this forced expansion to the Americas and the Indian Ocean in greater detail. One question to be asked of the archaeological evidence is how enslaved Africans related to each other, to their enslavers, and where present, to indigenous peoples; another question is how, and how successfully, Africans maintained their own identity in the face of attempts to destroy it, and how important longstanding African traditions were in this. Here we touch on the ways in which people resisted enslavement, and we can inquire more broadly into what forms this resistance took. Though most of the archaeological work relevant to these questions has been undertaken in the Americas, the scope of this chapter is deliberately set wider to emphasize the value of comparative study.

To conclude the book, chapter 8 reviews the material covered, identifying the main themes that emerge and considering how the archaeology of Africa's interactions with other parts of the world demonstrates the truly global interest and concern of the continent's past. I examine too what general patterns can be discerned and emphasize the value of comparing between the regions into which I have otherwise divided the book. Finally, the challenges confronting archaeological research in Africa today, the contribution that it may, perhaps, be able to make an African "renaissance," and the opportunities for developing distinctively African forms of archaeological research are also considered.

Notes

1. Since the original manuscript of this book entered production several other works of synthesis have appeared. Two of particular note are Connah (2004) and Stahl (2004).

2. In West Africa a distinction is sometimes drawn between the Sahel, lying immediately to the south of the Sahara, and the more extensively wooded Sudan, or Sudanic belt, still farther south. As this differentiation is less generally made when discussing areas such as Niger and Chad and to avoid any possible confusion with the modern Republic of Sudan, I have opted to employ Sahel alone when referring to the broad band of arid to moist savannas between the Sahara and the West African/Equatorial forest zone.

Acknowledgments

ANY BOOK, and particularly perhaps one with a scope as large as this one, reflects the input of many people. For the initial suggestion and their continuous encouragement, including comments on the text, I should like to thank Joe Vogel and Mitch Allen, the staff of AltaMira Press who helped see it through to publication, especially Monica Riley and Terry Fischer, and Sam Challis, who produced all the maps.

Many colleagues took the trouble to comment on draft chapters or, in some cases, earlier versions of some of the arguments presented here. I may not always have taken their advice, but I am nonetheless grateful for their suggestions and corrections of fact. For their assistance here I should like to thank Larry Barham, Nick Barton, Yvonne Brink, Jeremy Coote, Matt Davies, Vivian Davies, Anne Haour, Tom Huffman, Tim Insoll, Ken Kelly, Kevin MacDonald, John Mack, Susan McIntosh, David Phillipson, Innocent Pikirayi, Andrew Reid, Garth Sampson, Ann Stahl, Marijke van der Veen, Gavin Whitelaw, and Andrew Wilson. Several of these individuals also helped by contributing illustrations, and I have acknowledged them and other colleagues who were kind enough to assist in this way in the text.

This book also draws on—and, I hope, benefits from—contacts with many other Africanists over the years. David Phillipson first interested me in African archaeology as an undergraduate and has been of immense support to me and other British-based Africanists. Teaching with him in the Cambridge of 1982–83 were John Alexander, Graham Connah, and Francis van Noten, all of whom opened my eyes to other parts of the continent. That process continued in Oxford under the supervision of Ray Inskeep, who encouraged me to take on this project and provided important insights in its initial stages; it is a great sadness that he died before its completion. Through him my own fieldwork and research have concentrated in southern Africa and I am grateful to all my colleagues there, but especially to John

Parkington and the other members of the Department of Archaeology at the University of Cape Town and to David Lewis-Williams, Karim Sadr, Ben Smith, and Lyn Wadley at the University of the Witwatersrand. John Sutton kindly hosted a visit several years ago to Kenya and Tanzania, while George Abungu helped organize a trip to the Lamu Archipelago. Ken Kelly deserves thanks for allowing me to participate in his excavations at Savi, thereby introducing me to West African archaeology. Pierre de Maret and other contributors to the International Certificate in African Archaeology, as well as the organizers of and participants in successive conferences on African archaeology in Los Angeles, Poznán, Cambridge, and Bamako, expanded my horizons further, with Steven and Melanie Brandt and Susan McIntosh facilitating a truly enjoyable visit to sites in Mali. Proving the worth of conferences still further, the 1992 SAfA meeting at Los Angeles also introduced me to Kit Wesler, a colleague with a great facility for the kind of wide-ranging, intercontinental comparative study of which African archaeology still stands in need if its voice is to be heard beyond the confines of the Africanist community itself. Working in Oxford I have also been fortunate to benefit from teaching in an environment where able students are not in short supply: Sam Challis, Luiz Costa, Matt Davies, Will Ellerby, Marcus Starling, and Chris Wingfield in particular helped me change my mind on many things, while Anne Haour, John Hobart, Fumiko Ohinata, and Brian Stewart helped doctoral supervision to get off to a flying and very pleasurable start. Finally, I should like to thank all those other colleagues who are now working in African archaeology from within the United Kingdom; the growth in our numbers and the collegiality displayed at recent meetings augur well for the future of the subject.

This is the second book I have written since my daughter was born. To Chiara, Gloria who made her and so many other things possible, and—for reasons best known to ourselves—Cesare, many thanks for your support, comment, and distraction.

CHAPTER I

Introducing Africa: Definitions, Routes, Resources, and Interactions

Societies grow and thrive as they successfully interact with their neighbours.

—SHERRATT 1999, 33

T HIS CHAPTER PROVIDES the background for the rest of the book. The first question considered is, What is Africa? To answer this I look at the term's origins and how it has come to be applied to the entirety of the continent. Next I examine the degree to which Africa can be considered to be a coherent whole and how far the frequent separation of sub-Saharan Africa from the rest of the continent is warranted. Attention then turns to the continent's physical geography and how its climate, physiography, and ecology constitute the frontiers through which African populations have interacted with each other and the wider world. These interfaces have been, and continue to be, framed by what Africa produces and what its inhabitants have sought from abroad, as well as by the organizational and logistical structures through which these resources were exploited and moved. Discussion of the material, social, and technological bases of Africa's connections with the rest of the world forms the third part of this chapter.

From here I move to how archaeologists have thought about these connections. Early speculations that emphasized the passive receipt of external influences were closely linked to European colonial conceptualizations

I

of Africa as a "dark" and "timeless" continent where little changed except through contact from outside. Such ideas, which long influenced Africanist scholarship, still cast a shadow today (M. Hall 2002). For archaeologists their rejection encouraged several projects geared specifically toward examining the impacts of long-distance trade, colonial activity, and world religions. (Thinking only of sub-Saharan West Africa, examples include Robert et al. 1970; Posnansky 1976; S. McIntosh and R. McIntosh 1980; Devisse 1983; Insoll 1996, 2000; Berthier 1997; DeCorse 2001a; and Stahl 2001a). Current archaeological research employs several models to help frame interaction between one society and another, and I examine some of these ideas, highlighting those considered later on. Finally, I look at Africa as the continent of origin of both hominids and anatomically modern humans and the extent to which connections with Europe and Asia are traceable through the last stages of the Pleistocene.

Where and What Is Africa?

The answer to the question of where and what is Africa might be thought self-evident, but things are, as so often, more complex than they first seem. A fundamental reason for this is expressed by Appiah (1995, 23):

> Most people in the continent have lived in societies that defined both self and others by ties of blood and power. It would never have occurred to most of the Africans in this long history to think that they belonged to a larger human group defined by a shared relationship to the African continent.

Consciousness of belonging to "Africa," rather than to communities defined by religion, language, ethnicity, or political allegiance, came out of reaction and resistance to the experience of colonialism and its aftermath (Mazrui 1986). "Africa," in other words, as an entity both whole and differentiated from other major landmasses is very considerably a European invention. For the Classical Greeks *Libya* was already one of the world's three known continents. Roman authors took up this idea, sometimes extending the name of one of their provinces, *Africa* (roughly modern Tunisia and Tripolitania), to the whole continent (Mudimbe 1988, 1994), the southern (broadly, sub-Saharan) portions of which they knew as *Aethiopia*.

Exploration of Africa's Atlantic coastline during the fifteenth century and the slow accrual of information about its interior that followed were one facet of Europe's late medieval expansion (J. R. S. Phillips 1988). Confronted with cultural differences on a previously unimaginable scale,

Europeans first differentiated between themselves and those whom they encountered on the basis of religion: Christian as opposed to Muslim or pagan. But however keen to seek allies in Prester John's Ethiopia and however favorably impressed by some of the polities with which they traded, the Portuguese came armed with papal bulls and a heritage of crusading activity that saw them claim ownership of the lands they "discovered." Though actual colonization, as opposed to the establishment of fortified trading posts, was a considerably later phenomenon, the sense of European superiority implicit in such claims was quickly combined with economic imperatives and translated into a developing trade for slaves, most notably for use in Europe's American colonies (chapters 6 and 7). From the sixteenth century onward, and culminating in the "Scramble" of the late 1800s (Pakenham 1991), Europeans of all nationalities increasingly constructed their own sense of self-identity and self-worth in opposition to the lifestyles and cultural practices of people elsewhere in the world, no longer defined by religion but by increasingly tight linkages between notions of primitiveness, race, and geographical location. Museums, including those exhibiting African artifacts, and the developing disciplines of archaeology and anthropology played important parts in this exercise (Coombes 1997).

As part of this process, "Africa" was increasingly equated with "Black Africa" (Mazrui 1986), an identification that formalized the distinction between "sub-Saharan Africa," inhabited predominantly by people of negroid physical stock, and areas farther north. There, by contrast, the inhabitants were "white" (Arab or Berber), Islam predominated, not traditional religions or syncretic combinations of the two, and connections across the Mediterranean with Europe could be emphasized, as witnessed by the establishment of Greek and Phoenician colonies along North Africa's shoreline and its subsequent incorporation into the Roman Empire. Nineteenth and early twentieth century European settlement was more or less explicitly seen as a renewal of the same process, with archaeology duly invoked in its support (Liverani 2000a, 17–18).

At one level of analysis the entire Mediterranean basin does indeed form a coherent whole (Abulafia 2003), and in a long-term perspective it is the comparatively recent advent of Islam, its contraction back into the Maghreb, and the latter's colonial history that crystallized the distinction here between Africa and Europe.[1] But to admit these points should not confine North Africa to a compartment that excludes or downplays its connections with the much larger landmass to its south. Judged across the last 10,000 years, its commonly touted Mediterranean orientation might even be considered a phenomenon that only truly *began* in Classical times (cf. Cazzella 2001) and was never complete. In the Predynastic period, for

3

example, and for much of the following millennia, Egypt and Nubia drew on a common cultural tradition, participated in a shared political economy, or both. Pharaonic Egypt drew too on a heritage from pastoralist communities whose expansion played out across the desert *and* the lands to its south (and north?) long before the Garamantian polity served as a conduit for traffic across the Sahara. In both cases, the spread of Islam strengthened and facilitated already old Nile-long and transdesert connections.

While archaeological research can undoubtedly support these propositions, it has also frequently been carried out in ways that reinforce North Africa's separation from the rest of the continent. One instance of this is the continuing use of an originally South African terminology that subdivides the Stone Age into Earlier, Middle, and Later components. Devised explicitly to replace imported European terms (Goodwin and van Riet Lowe 1929), this system spread rapidly across Africa *south* of the Sahara, but further north, in the Maghreb, Libya, and Egypt, archaeological industries remain grouped within the Paleolithic divisions—Lower, Middle, and Upper—employed in Europe and western Asia. One could argue that this accurately reflects the quite real isolation of regional populations during much of the Pleistocene, when the Sahara was frequently larger and more arid than today, but a contrary view is that it reflects nothing more than "scholarly tradition and geographic distance" (Klein 1999, 407), the former grounded ultimately in the early twentieth century development of a white South African nationalism (Schlanger 2002). The persistence in post-Paleolithic archaeological thinking of distinctions between tropical "black" Africa and the continent's north similarly owes much to convention, the dominance of the Classical literary tradition, and the physical impressiveness of Pharaonic and Roman ruins. Rather than claiming that Egypt or the Maghreb have "long had such diverse connections with the Mediterranean and South-West Asia" (Connah 2001, 14) as to justify or require their continued separate treatment, it is the emphasis traditionally placed by Europeans on the archaeology of their own "ancestors" that is in play here, whether those ancestors are thought to be Tutankhamun or St Augustine.

This is far from subscribing to notions that all African populations share a single heritage, that this derives from ancient Egypt, or that the Egypt of the Pharaohs was the principal source of European civilization. Long advocated by Senegalese researcher Cheikh Anta Diop (1967), these propositions have been taken up by the broader Afrocentric movement in the United States (Asante 1987), while, with different motivations, Bernal (1987, 1991) has controversially emphasized a range of supposed cultural borrowings from Pharaonic Egypt in Classical and Bronze Age Greece. Few of these claims, including those about the supposedly negroid racial character of the ancient Egyptians (Diop 1981) or the transmission from Egypt to other parts of Africa of specific technologies or whole populations, withstand sustained scrutiny (Lefkowitz and Rogers 1996; MacDonald 2003; North 2003). More critically, such arguments merely buy into Africa's historical definition, by Europeans, as a single landmass equated with an arbitrarily, color-defined racial group and understood through overly simplistic correlations of "race" and "culture." Not only that, but they imply that Africa's cultural attainment *must* be measured in European terms along a unilineal, evolutionist continuum (Stahl 1999a) and that its past should be explained in a hyperdiffusionist manner that pays scarce attention to the actions or histories of non-Egyptian Africans (Appiah 1997).

One way forward from here is to emphasize not the uniformity, but rather the diversity, of African cultural experience (Appiah 1995). To do so is not to deny the importance of widely shared cultural values and traditions where these exist, as among Mande-speakers in West Africa (R. McIntosh 1998) or Bantu-speaking peoples in the equatorial forest (Vansina 1990), the Great Lakes region (Schoenbrun 1998), or southern Africa (Huffman 1989). Rather it is to underscore the importance of moving beyond a simple cartographic definition of Africa to one that views Africa as a historically constituted entity, composed of networks of multiple connections, differing in their spatial extent, antiquity, and scale of social, political, and economic complexity. Such connections invariably have strong local roots, but the routes that link them also frequently move beyond the African landmass per se. Together, these connections constitute the frame of reference within which this book is written.

Africa's Geography

Deserts, rivers, coasts, and seas. To understand how these helped constitute Africa's connections with the rest of the world, we need to glance at the continent's geography, beginning with an outline of its main physical characteristics. First of these is its antiquity, for much of Africa's geological structure took shape in the earliest stages of earth's history, while its present geographical form reaches back to the breakup of the Gondwanaland supercontinent 100 million to 200 million years ago. With a relatively unindented coastline and only one significant peninsula (the Horn, essentially modern Somalia), Africa is surrounded by water on all sides, though the isthmus linking its northeastern corner to Southwest Asia was cut by the Suez Canal as recently as the 1850s. The contrast with Europe or East Asia is striking and constrains access to Africa's interior, as well as contact between its different parts. Another difference is that except off its southernmost tip Africa's continental shelves are narrow, limiting fishing opportunities and ensuring that changes in world sea levels have had minimal effects on the creation or loss of coastal plains. Offshore islands are few, small, and generally volcanic in origin, except for Madagascar, a large subcontinental fragment with its own Gondwanaland origins.

Reaching to almost 36° N and 35° S, Africa spans the Equator to roughly equal extents, though its northern part is substantially larger and more extensive in east–west orientation (figure 1.1). Climatic zones and biomes are little affected by topography since much of the continent consists of shallow basins or plateaus separated by scarcely evident watersheds. However, the Great Escarpment, which in places measures 3,000 m, is an important barrier in parts of southern Africa. Both it and the geologically older Cape Fold Mountain Belt impeded European settlement of the interior in the eighteenth and early nineteenth centuries. At the continent's opposite end, the Atlas Mountains extend over 2,000 km and have several parallel ranges interspersed with plateaus and valleys. Not so difficult to cross, they protect northwestern Morocco and the north of Algeria and Tunisia from desiccating Saharan winds, contributing to the higher, more reliable precipitation that these areas experience relative to those further south.

Perhaps the most striking of Africa's mountains are those flanking the Rift Valley System that stretches 5,000 km from Botswana's Okavango Delta as far as Turkey, dividing midway into separate eastern and western sections that reunite in Ethiopia in the north and Malawi in the south. Still affected by seismic and volcanic activity, the Rift features towering escarpments and volcanoes, as well as massive troughs within which lie two of the continent's greatest bodies of freshwater, Lakes Malawi and Tanganyika. Lake Victoria, which is even larger, occupies the area between the eastern and western rifts at their northern edge. The northern part of the Rift Valley is also filled by water, but in this case the salt water of the Red Sea, which splits Africa from the geologically similar Arabian Peninsula. Continuing north as a series of hills, a rugged escarpment separates the highlands of Ethiopia and Eritrea from the coast, but this is broken by several passes, access through which has historically been more a matter of politics than of geography. Major gorges, like that of the Blue Nile, offer pathways west from these highlands toward the Sudanese Nile Valley.

If today Africa has few significant bodies of freshwater, except those of the Rift Valley and the greatly shrunken Lake Chad, it more than makes up for this with the might of its rivers. The longest is the Nile, which rises a little upstream of Lake Victoria to drain north and join the Blue Nile at Khartoum. From there it proceeds onward to issue into the Mediterranean,

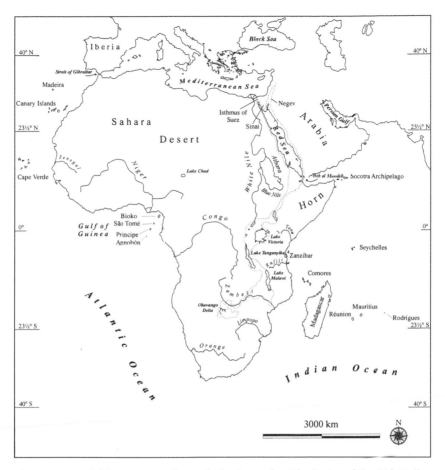

Figure 1.1. Africa: topography and physiography. The limits of the Rift Valley System are represented in dotted outline.

accepting no further input save the Atbara on its 6,600 km journey. Of Africa's other great rivers, three stand out. The first, the Congo, drains much of the equatorial rainforest before debouching into the Atlantic. The Niger also flows into the Atlantic, but has a geography suggesting less commitment to its final destination. Rising in the Guinea highlands only 250 km from the sea, it flows northeast to nudge the Sahara before veering southeast to empty at last into the Bight of Benin. Finally, the Zambezi, with headwaters lying close to some of those of the Congo, moves south and southeast, draining much of south-central Africa before flowing into the Indian Ocean. Smaller rivers include the Senegal and the Gambia in West Africa, East Africa's Rufiji and Tana, and the Limpopo and Orange (Gariep) of southern Africa, but none has had the historical importance of the four I have described.

None of these giants is navigable for any great distance. Cataracts and waterfalls limit unimpeded upstream movement from the coast to no more than 500 km (1,500 km along the Nile). Extensive stretches of navigable water do, however, exist farther inland, especially in the Congo Basin, where they have been used by reconnoitering archaeologists (Eggert 1993), and along the Niger, where the Inland Delta's seasonally flooded marshlands facilitate water transport (R. McIntosh 1998). The swamps of the Sudd, on the other hand, are frequently cited as constraining movement along the Upper Nile (Welsby 1996, 58),[2] but perhaps this is too Egyptocentric a standpoint, encouraged by the paucity of local archaeological research (Robertshaw 1987). Even so, Africa's waterways, though vital in linking sections of the continent with each other, can fairly be said to offer only limited access to its interior. Another challenge to movement across and beyond the continent is posed by its climate.

Africa is the quintessentially tropical continent—three-quarters of its landmass falls between the Tropics of Cancer and Capricorn. As a result, temperatures are generally high throughout the year, though moderated in places by altitude and desert nights. Areas of permanent snow and ice survive only on East Africa's highest mountains and are now shrinking rapidly in response to global climatic change. High temperatures and abundant insolation also make for high loss of water through evaporation, and many soils undergo extensive desiccation in the dry season. Rainfall is essentially monsoonal, with high temperatures creating low-pressure areas into which humid air is drawn from both the Atlantic and Indian Oceans. The Inter-Tropical Convergence Zone marks the boundary between humid air over these oceans and dry, descending air in the easterlies of continental high-pressure cells. The Inter-Tropical Convergence Zone oscillates north and south during the year, reaching 15°–20° N in February–August and 8°–16° S in the following semester (Adams et al. 1996). Rainy seasons of variable length result: single 3-month-long seasons near the two Tropics and two each year closer to the Equator, experienced with a shorter, more variable break between them in West Africa than in East Africa. Even on the Equator itself, seasonal contrasts in rainfall are evident. Droughts, frequently severe, plague much of the remainder of the continent, with the driest regions left largely untouched by the Inter-Tropical Convergence Zone; aridity is further exacerbated along the Namibian, Angolan, Moroccan, and Somali coasts by cold off-shore currents. Only at Africa's southwestern and northern margins is the influence of the Inter-Tropical Convergence Zone replaced by that of onshore-moving midlatitude depressions.

The result of all this is a largely symmetrical distribution of climatic and ecological zones (figure 1.2). The boundaries between them are, for the most part, gradual, except where topography creates sharp distinctions. Africa's northern littoral has a winter-rainfall climate and scrublike Mediterranean vegetation, trending into drier, steppelike conditions to the south. Farther toward the Equator the Sahara occupies some 19° of latitude from the Atlantic to the Red Sea; rainfall is extremely low and erratic, temperatures very high, and vegetation sparse. Only the Nile and such mountains as the Ahaggar, Aïr, and Tibesti break the expansive dry stony plains and dunefields to create locally more moderate, wetter conditions. Beyond the desert one enters the first of a series of steppelike vegetational zones that become increasingly wooded on moving south, turning first into savanna and finally into relatively moist woodland below about 11° N. Like the Sahara, the various zones to its south run almost the entire breadth of the continent, but in northeast Africa they are interrupted by the highlands of Ethiopia and Eritrea, on the higher reaches of which montane grassland and patches of afromontane forest are found; drier wooded steppe and subdesert continue around the southernmost part of these highlands into the Ogaden, Somalia, Kenya, and northern Tanzania.

A narrow band of forest-savanna mosaic lies along the northern fringe of the tropical rainforest, which itself falls into two fairly distinct regions. The smaller runs down to the Atlantic shoreline from Sierra Leone in the west to Ivory Coast in the east, at which point (the Ghana-Bénin Gap) drier, savanna-woodland vegetation largely replaces it. Farther east, the forest resumes in southern Nigeria, expanding outward through southern Cameroon and into the Congo Basin. The sequence of forest-savanna mosaic, moist woodland savanna, and dry woodland savanna repeats itself on the far side of the forest, with the latter supporting the greatest diversity and density of large mammals, including elephants, source of the ivory that was traded out of Africa through both the Atlantic and Indian Ocean coasts. Beyond, semiarid subdesert vegetation occupies the Karoo biome of Namibia and South Africa, but true desert is restricted to a narrow coastal strip in Namibia and southern Angola. Distinctively southern African are two other biomes, the highland grasslands of South Africa's interior, which extend eastward into Lesotho, and the Mediterranean-like climate and vegetation of the southern and southwestern Cape, home to a multitude of endemic plants and animals. Madagascar too has its own distinctive biota, living in rainforest along its eastern side, but in progressively more arid savanna and woodlands further west. This is but a brief sketch of a highly complex reality, and more detailed treatments are

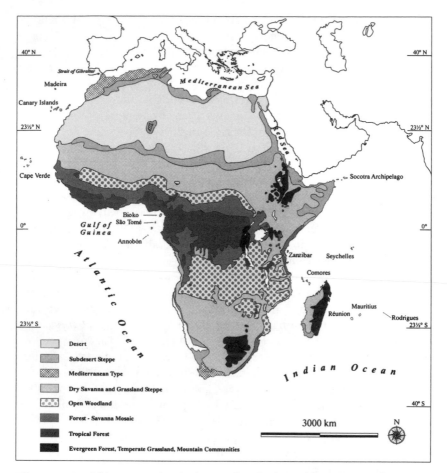

Figure 1.2. Africa: vegetation (redrawn after Cooke and Butzer 1982, figure 1.6).

numerous. Suffice it to add that the situation just described reflects the climatic situation of today and ignores the environmental changes and accelerating anthropogenic effects that are important on time scales of decades to millennia (e.g., Hassan 2002). I draw attention to these as necessary in the chapters that follow.

One element has been left unmentioned, Africa's seas. Four are of concern, the Red and Mediterranean Seas and the Atlantic and Indian Oceans. Together they envelop the continent, save for the Isthmus of Suez, each divisible into smaller bodies of water and each extending beyond Africa's confines to offer possibilities for uniting its peoples with those of other continents. Again, I investigate this in greater detail where needed but, as a general comment, maritime connections have sometimes been hindered by the relatively small number of navigable estuaries and the scarcity of protected bays offered by Africa's smooth coastline. Opportunities for Africans themselves to develop maritime skills have also been constrained, at least on the Atlantic coast, by the relative lack of offshore islands, though lagoon and estuary networks from Bénin to Gabon saw a flourishing commerce (Nzewunwa 1980). More significantly, the pattern of currents and winds differs markedly between Atlantic and Indian Oceans. While the latter features regular seasonal monsoons that can be used to sail from East Africa to Arabia and India, the prevailing winds off Africa's west coast long kept sub-Saharan and Mediterranean navigators apart. Only when the Portuguese fully understood the Atlantic's winds and currents in the fifteenth century was this problem resolved. By contrast, movement across the Mediterranean and Red Seas involves much smaller distances (the Strait of Gibraltar is 14 km across, the Bab el-Mandeb 30 km). Possible harbors are also relatively numerous on both African and non-African coasts, so long as suitable water and food can be obtained.

Pulling these observations together, how can we best define the networks linking Africa's regions with each other and with the world beyond? The choice is inevitably arbitrary, and recent studies of interaction within the Mediterranean (Horden and Purcell 2000; Abulafia 2003) and along Europe's Atlantic façade (Cunliffe 2001) emphasize how larger zones of contact are made up of overlapping, smaller microscale and mesoscale contacts that vary in extent and intensity over time. Pursuing the main theme of this book, Africa's connections with the rest of the world, directs our attention to its interfaces with Europe, Asia, and the Americas. Hence the choice of the Indian Ocean as the theme of chapter 4, the Atlantic for chapter 6, and of the two together as the backdrop for chapter 7. As Mazrui (1986, 29–34) pertinently observes, the fact that the Red Sea component of the Rift System is filled with water, not dry land, has made this another defining element in Africa's continental definition. Challenging the decision to divide rather than unite the similar geologies, vegetations, faunas, and historical experiences of Arabia and northeastern Africa, the Red Sea contributes to chapter 3. It does so along with the Nile, for here, as well as in selecting the Sahara, with its two-way connections north and south, as the theme for chapter 5, I opt to incorporate Africa's Mediterranean coastline into the wider story, rather than to separate it out from the rest of the continent. How successfully this is achieved can also be gauged from chapter 2, which includes in its discussion of Africa's systems of food-production the expansion of Middle Eastern-derived domesticates into Egypt, Cyrenaica, and the Maghreb.

These, then, are the webs of connection that I examine, grounded in smaller-scale patterns and in African soil, but providing the basis for interaction with areas beyond Africa. What form those exchanges took is the next topic I discuss.

The Basis of Interaction: Resources and Technologies

Africa is, without question, a continent rich in resources. For present purposes these can be summarized as the minerals and metals, plants and animals, people, manufactured goods, and ideas that have moved into, across, and outside the continent throughout the past 10,000 years or so. The first of the groups just mentioned is perhaps the easiest with which to begin, because Africa's geological history has concentrated many metals and other minerals in quite specific locations (figure 1.3). Gold, for example, was exploited in precolonial times mainly in the desert east of the Nile, Ethiopia's highlands, the Zimbabwe Plateau, and two major West African sources, the Akan and Bambuk-Bure goldfields (Holl 2000). Copper ores, on the other hand, concentrate in Mauritania, Niger's Aïr massif, the Niari area of Congo-Brazzaville, the Copper Belt of Katanga and northern Zambia, and several locations in southern Africa. All these areas saw extensive indigenous mining activity, with copper and gold moving both within and without the continent (Bisson 2000). Tin was less heavily exploited; South Africa's Rooiberg Mountains and Nigeria's Jos Plateau are the two best known areas, but only the former provides evidence of precolonial export overseas (Grant 1999). Iron ores, in contrast, are more ubiquitous, though this is not to say that large-scale production did not develop (De Barros 2000) or that iron was not also sometimes exported abroad (Kusimba and Killick 2003).

Reuse of metal, frequently by mixing objects of different origin, makes sourcing the provenance of gold, copper, copper alloy, or iron artifacts problematic, though the Igbo-Ukwu bronzes demonstrate what can be achieved (Chikwendu et al. 1989; Craddock et al. 1997). Other materials, including obsidian, a highly desirable, ultrasharp volcanic glass, are easier to source. In this case a range of physicochemical techniques tracks its movement from specific quarries in Kenya and Ethiopia, from whence some crossed the Red Sea (Zarins 1990). Chlorite schist from Madagascar (Wright 1993) and rock crystal, perhaps from Tsavo, Kenya (Horton and Middleton 2000), are other minerals with potentially well-defined origins. Salt, on the other hand, is almost invisible archaeologically, though a physiological necessity for many tropical agricultural populations. Extracted from vegetable sources and seawater, brine springs, and quarries, it was

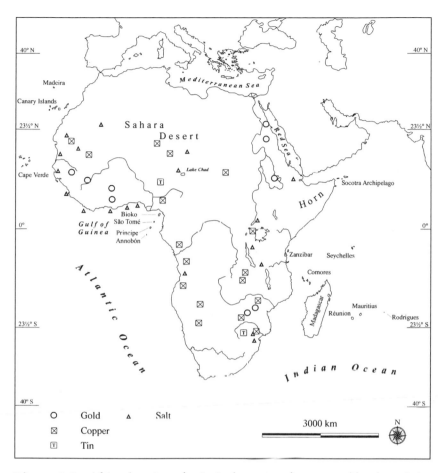

Figure 1.3. Africa: location of principal sources of copper, gold, salt, and tin.

widely exchanged. But it is the rock salt deposits of the Sahara that have attracted most attention because of their role in furthering and sustaining intercontinental trade networks (Lovejoy 1986; Alexander 1997).

Today many in the West think of tropical Africa as a paradise for wildlife, and plants and animals and their products are among the other resources that we must consider. In chapter 2 the emphasis is on the two-way movement of domesticates. Coffee, sorghum, millet, guinea fowl, and donkeys are some of those domesticated in Africa but now also grown or kept elsewhere; sheep, goats, camels, horses, wheat, barley, chickens, bananas, rice, some kinds of yam, maize, and cassava are among those with extra-African origins. Critical for the subsistence of those who used them and adding greatly to the diversity of African and non-African cuisines and transport systems alike, their transmission between people was itself a negotiated transaction, a form of exchange. Wild plant and animals have been at least as important. A far from exhaustive list might include the arena animals exported to Roman Italy, the ivory (of both elephant and hippopotamus origin) traded across the Sahara and the Indian Ocean, animal skins, aromatic resins (obtained from the mysterious land of Punt by the Egyptians more than 3,500 years ago), and the mangrove poles sent from East Africa to Arabia until the 1980s (Horton and Middleton 2000). Nor should we forget the movement of stimulants such as kola, one of the few narcotics permitted by Islam, qat, cannabis, tobacco, and the spirits that lubricated the Atlantic slave trade. As well as the two-way flow of intoxicants, there has been the exchange of disease, plague and smallpox entering Africa from Eurasia, for example, (Posnansky 1987; A. Smith 1989; R. McIntosh 1998), yellow fever migrating thence to the Americas (Porter 1997, 464).

Critical to many of the networks linking Africa to the wider world was a range of manufactured goods. In the case of the Atlantic slave trade, guns and textiles were important, but we should not forget that this was but one route through which knowledge of firearms and of how to make them spread or that information about new technologies has often been even more critical than craft products themselves: the debate over whether iron smelting was independently developed in sub-Saharan Africa (Holl 2000) and the possibility that knowledge of pottery was transmitted from North Africa to early agricultural communities in the Levant (Ehret 2002) illustrate how important such information can be. While ceramics survive extremely well in the archaeological record, the same is not true of cloth, and most of our information on its movement is historical in nature, though sufficient to suggest how important textiles were in many of Africa's international trade networks. Glassware, leather items, and artifacts and ingots of metal flowed along the same routes, but it is the exotic pottery and much more common, more widely distributed glass beads of Malayo-Indonesian, Chinese, Indian, Middle Eastern, and European origin that loom largest in the archaeological consciousness by reason of their durability, ease of source determination, and capacity to provide more or less tightly constrained dates for the contexts in which they are found. Cowrie shells, though scarcely modified from the form in which they were supplied, also deserve mention here for their use as money in many parts of tropical Africa since at least the twelfth century (Hogendorn and Johnson 1986). Other kinds of shells were also employed as currency, along with copper and iron ingots, copper bracelets, and raffia cloth (Bisson 1975;

Herbert 1984; Vansina 1990), but many functioned as special-purpose money within restricted spheres of exchange (Bohannan 1959). We should not automatically assume that coins struck by North African, Aksumite, or Swahili rulers were invariably different in this respect.

All these items and the knowledge that they imply were moved by people, but people, their beliefs, and their languages are also relevant to our inquiry as commodities or phenomena connecting Africa to the rest of the world. One obvious instance I have already noted, the slave trade across the Atlantic instituted in the sixteenth century (DeCorse 2001b). But this is just one of the ways in which people were forcibly relocated beyond their area of origin, and slavery had a long ancestry and took many forms within African societies themselves (Mies and Kopytoff 1977). Before and after the trans-Atlantic trade, slaves also formed an important element in the trading networks that spanned the Sahara or connected East Africa with the Persian Gulf (Lovejoy 2000). As they were moved long distances within and beyond Africa people took with them their genes and a surprising share of their cultural inheritance: chapter 7 examines the archaeological evidence for this diaspora, which continues to manifest itself through language, folktales, music, and religion (such as the Voudou of Haiti or the Candomblé of Brazil). Three world religions, Judaism, Christianity, and Islam, have themselves been introduced to Africa from outside, finding both receptive and hostile audiences, but always developing distinctively local forms, many with archaeologically visible consequences: the famous mud-mosque architecture of the Sahel and the rock-cut churches of Ethiopia are but two examples. Reforming movements within these religions have also spilled outward beyond the continent, not least in the case of the Almoravid and Almohad jihads of the early second millennium. And finally, Africa has been both a giver and receiver of languages, some written, others only spoken (figure 1.4): if Arabic was introduced with Islam, Malagasy from Indonesia, and, for a time, Latin, Greek, and Punic from the northern and eastern shores of the Mediterranean, then other languages have moved in the opposite direction. Reconstructions of early forms of the Afroasiatic family, to which Arabic, Hebrew, Ancient Egyptian, Amharic, Berber, and numerous other languages all belong, suggest, for example, that it originated in an area extending from the Middle Nile to the Red Sea and south through Ethiopia's highlands (McCall 1998). Much later came the export of African-derived languages such as Gullah that were brought to the Americas as a result of the Atlantic slave trade (R. Brown 2002).

As well as what has connected Africa to other parts of the world, this book is also concerned with the archaeological evidence for how those connections have been structured. Foremost among the technologies that

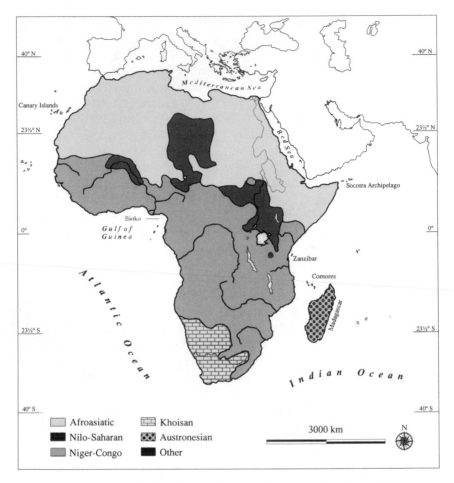

Figure 1.4. Africa: distribution of indigenous language families ca. 1700.

have sustained interaction are those relating to transport, though the use of wheeled vehicles did not penetrate beyond the Sahara. Pack animals, with their greater versatility for covering variable terrain, were more important, as in much of preindustrial Europe (Bulliet 1992). Four species were commonly used: cattle, donkeys, camels, and horses. Pack oxen, like horses, are depicted in Saharan rock art and were used sporadically as far as South Africa, where they were also ridden (A. Smith 1992). But donkeys and camels have historically been more significant as beasts of burden, in part because of their enhanced capacity for enduring thirst. First domesticated in northeast Africa, donkeys were used in Egypt before the

First Dynasty (Gardiner 1961, 393–94). Able to carry loads of more than 50 kg, to survive without water for 3 days, and to move at 40 km per day, they assumed considerable importance in areas unsuitable for camels, as well as among some East African pastoralists (Clutton-Brock 1997). Despite their recent associations, camels have a history that long antedates the arrival of Islam. Capable of carrying 150 kg, moving over 2,000 km in a month, and going without water for days (Reader 1998, 267–68), they were present across northern Africa 2,000 years ago, perhaps before (Liverani 2000a). Horses nonetheless remained significant farther south, becoming a major military force in the Sahel (Goody 1971) and being imported as prestige items by elites far to the south within the environmentally unsuitable tropical rainforest (Law 1980). Linguistic evidence hints at their introduction south of the Sahara some 3,000 years ago (Blench 1993a), but the earliest firm osteological evidence dates to the mid-first millennium (MacEachern et al. 2001). Lastly, we should note that Africa's elephants, though used in war and display by Carthaginians, Greeks, and Kushites alike, never played a role comparable to that undertaken by their more docile Asian cousins, posing instead a considerable threat to the livelihood of African farmers (Reader 1998, 252–56).

Looking at Africa as a whole, the general pattern is one in which domestic livestock, whether as draft animals or beasts of burden, contributed little to the movement of goods or people south of the Equator or in rainforest areas to its north. Reasons for this, and the corresponding restriction of the plow to North Africa and the Ethiopian-Eritrean highlands, are complex, but three are readily apparent: the prevalence of disease (chapter 2), the excessive energy costs of keeping draft animals in the absence of suitable fodder crops (Ward et al. 1980), and a widespread emphasis on long-fallow systems of cultivation (Starkey 2000). Instead, people-power dominated, but human porters can carry fairly limited quantities (15–20 kg) and even then have to be fed and housed en route. As the Aztecs, who completely lacked suitable domestic animals, also found (Berdan 1975), this restricts what people can carry over distance to lighter or highly valuable items, in the African case often gold, ivory, cloth, glass beads, and salt. One solution was to use slaves, who themselves could be sold at journey's end, but whole communities (such as the Nyamwezi) sometimes also took on the role of professional carriers (Cummings 1973).

As elsewhere in the preindustrial world, constraints on land-based transport made movement by water attractive. Within Africa canoes plied rivers, lakes, and coastal lagoons, carrying 20–30 metric tons in some cases along the Niger. An 8,000-year-old wooden dugout from Dufuna, northeastern Nigeria, more than 8 m long demonstrates the long antiquity of African watercraft (Breunig 1996). Similar, if larger, vessels were presumably used to settle Bioko, and perhaps the Canaries, but references to sewn boats in the *Periplus of the Erythraean Sea* suggest that this distinctively Indian Ocean technology, which includes the famous dhow (figure 1.5), is at least two millennia old along Africa's eastern seaboard (Casson 1989). Africa's overseas connections also depended on the state of maritime technology and knowledge available to European, Middle Eastern, Indian, Indonesian, and Chinese sailors, something I discuss further in chapters 5 and 7. Finally, for all these forms of transport, the structures of physical and political geography offered opportunities for growth and enrichment to those occupying middleman locations at places where lines of movement converged or goods had to be transshipped; the great trading centers of the Middle Niger and the Swahili seaboard are classic illustrations of such situations.

This comment emphasizes that, as well as looking at how people and goods moved, we should consider the social and economic structures within which their movement took place. This is a vast topic, but a few broad statements are possible. Firstly, we must note that exchange can take numerous forms, not all of them the purely commercial actions with

Figure 1.5. A dhow of a type used in long-distance trade along the East African coast (courtesy and copyright the British Institute in Eastern Africa).

which the modern world is most familiar. Indeed, some of the clearest descriptions of what anthropologists call gift exchange, a balanced, but frequently delayed, reciprocal exchange of goods the purpose of which is as much social as economic, come from Africa (e.g., Wiessner 1982). Typical of many small-scale societies, these systems probably contributed to the growth of many of the networks that I examine.

Even where trade is extensive—and the annual movement of commodities such as salt in West Africa was measured in thousands of metric tons—it may remain embedded in what at first seem noneconomic institutions. One example is provided by the existence of so-called trading diasporas, widely scattered, but interlinked, communities of particular ethnic affiliation whose common origin provides a basis for mutual confidence and continued business. In West Africa the Hausa provide one well-studied example of such a diaspora (Cohen 1969), the Soninké or Wangara another (Curtin 1975). In both cases commonality of religion strengthened the ties that bound traders together. Indeed, a primary reason for Islam's initial adoption south of the Sahara may have been so that indigenous traders could ensure their equal treatment by Muslim merchants, an equality that extended to protection from enslavement (Insoll 2003a). Nor should we forget that Islam's history in Africa identifies other means by which innovations can spread: migration, as witnessed by the settlement of Arabian Bedouin in Egypt and Sudan (Adams 1977, 554–57); the regular movements of pastoral nomads, like the Tuareg; and the significance of state control over large areas in sponsoring or guaranteeing the safety of trade.

The degree to which substantial settlement of Muslim outsiders took place in either East or West Africa has been a matter of debate, reviewed in chapters 4 and 5, but it seems unlikely that it involved more than immigration by a few individuals, however influential, or the establishment of foreign traders in their own residential quarters. Early European settlement on the West African coast followed a similar pattern, initially confined to small trading "factories," fortified as much against European competitors as local polities, frequently trading at the total discretion of their rulers, and often the focus of cosmopolitan, but fundamentally African, adjacent communities. Larger-scale colonization was a patchier phenomenon, constrained by disease and the strength of indigenous polities until well into the nineteenth century. But this is not to say that colonial exploitation and the imposition of systems of tribute, what Horden and Purcell (2000) refer to as a "command economy," were installed solely by modern Europeans. Egypt's exploitation of parts of Nubia in the Middle and New Kingdoms (Morkot 2001), Rome's extraction of cereals and olive oil from its North African provinces (Mattingly 1995), and Omani-run plantation economies on the East African coast (Horton and Middleton 2000) are but three examples to the contrary.

Thinking about Interaction

Archaeological thought about these many kinds of interaction has changed considerably over the past 100 years. In the early twentieth century a near universal emphasis on external influences, rather than independent invention, as the principal mechanism of cultural change (Trigger 1989) combined with a limited, racist vision of African cultural achievements to suggest that "Africa has never invented anything, but has only received from others" (Ankermann 1905, 55). With the notable exception of Pharaonic Egypt, already appropriated as ancestral to Europe's own past, African societies were viewed as frozen relics of European prehistory. It was thus little wonder that physically impressive monuments were ascribed to outside influences, not indigenous populations. Attributing Great Zimbabwe and similar stonewall structures in southern Africa to the Phoenicians or ancient Arabians is a notorious example of this tendency (Bent 1892; R. Hall and Neal 1902), and its successful challenge by careful archaeological observation and excavation had little immediate impact (Randall-MacIver 1906; Caton-Thompson 1931). Instead, migration and diffusion were invoked, drawing in part on widespread indigenously African attributions of exotic origins to ruling elites (Folorunso 2003). Frobenius's (1913) assignment of Ife's brass sculptures to colonizing Greeks, Delafosse's (1912) summoning of Near Eastern immigrants as founders of the kingdom of Ghana, and the Abbé Breuil's (1948, 1949) identification of Minoans and Sumerians in Bushman rock paintings are but a few of many examples. Though diffusion was indeed the dominant archaeological paradigm worldwide in the beginning and middle of the twentieth century, we should not lose sight of the fact that, consciously or unconsciously, this emphasis on outside contacts lent support to contemporary European political control of the African continent.

One particularly popular vehicle for migrationist explanations was provided by the invention of pastoralist "Hamites," to whom were attributed stone and earthwork monuments in East Africa (Huntingford 1933) and the formation of states as far afield as West Africa and Zimbabwe (e.g., Irstam 1944). Bearing a political philosophy of divine kingship, their origins were variously placed in Pharaonic Egypt (Seligman 1930) or within a Nilotic substratum from which the former had arisen (Frankfort 1948). Even Stone Age sites were drawn within the same ambit (Cole 1954). The emphasis placed by later research on the supposed advantages for a successful agricultural economy of iron-working technology gave impetus to another migrationist school of thought (Oliver 1966). In this case the close relationships between Bantu languages do partly support explaining their distribution and that of archaeologically attested iron-equipped, food-producing communities in terms of actual movements of people. However, despite Africanists' continued fondness for invoking such movements from linguistic, and now also genetic, data, the links postulated between ceramic styles, settlement organization, language groups, gene frequencies, and "tribes" need careful scrutiny and assessment (MacEachern 2000). In the Bantu case, alternative explanations for the expansion of these languages and of new technologies, including food production, still receive too little attention (M. Hall 1987; Vansina 1995).

But it is in explaining the development of sociopolitical complexity and large, urban settlements that greatest attention has been paid to outside influences. Even as the Hamitic myth was discredited,[3] what may fairly be called the "colonial paradigm" (Shaw et al. 1993, 22) continued to stress trade with North Africa or across the Indian Ocean as the prime mover in state formation and urban development south of the Sahara (Kirkman 1954; Clark 1962; Chittick 1974, 1984). Such diffusionist explanations only began to fall from favor in the 1960s, confronted by the twin challenges of an independent, radiocarbon-based chronology and new interpretations that focused once more on evolutionary models of social change, often expressed in functionalist, systemic terms (sidebar 1). One difficulty with diffusionist explanations had been that they were hopelessly vague (what, after all, was "diffusion"?), another that similarities between artifacts in different archaeological contexts were identified with far too little care (Renfrew 1973). The growing diversity of physicochemical techniques capable of characterizing raw materials by their point of origin offered a sounder empirical basis for pinpointing objects that had moved. In turn, different "falloff patterns" connecting finds to source seemed to provide a means of identifying different sorts of exchange mechanism, whether down the line, redistributional, or market based (Renfrew 1975). Much remains to be undertaken in this field, and the high costs of sourcing analyses can be prohibitive, especially for African-based scholars, but this continues to be a fast-moving field (e.g., Jourdan et al. 1999; Insoll and Bhan 2001) in which some studies question whether specific kinds of exchange are, indeed, inferable from purely distributional data (Merrick and Brown 1984). A second challenge to diffusionism came from the massively intensified fieldwork programs undertaken since the 1960s, some of which specifically targeted the effects of long-distance trade on local communities (Posnansky 1976). It has become apparent that models that saw urbanism and social complexity in areas like the Sahel or the Swahili coast as simple, unthinking responses to external, Arab stimuli cannot be sustained

---

SIDEBAR 1

Dating

For much of Africa during the period covered by this book written sources are few or completely absent. Radiocarbon dating therefore underpins the chronologies that archaeologists have developed, but its use requires caution. To begin with, all radiocarbon "dates" are really mean figures that have a specified probability of lying within the range expressed by the accompanying standard deviation. Because individual samples may also be contaminated, consistent patterns of dates are therefore preferable to individual determinations and using two standard deviations preferable to the normal one (S. McIntosh and R. McIntosh 1986a). Furthermore, because atmospheric production of the radiocarbon isotope fluctuates over time, radiocarbon years cannot be equated directly with calendar years. Calibration, using tree-ring dating, is required, and at some periods the effect is to increase, not diminish, the range of uncertainty within which a particular dated sample lies. This is particularly so in recent centuries for which typological studies of imported or locally made ceramics and tobacco pipes are significantly more reliable. In this book I try to overcome these problems by using dates calibrated by the INTCAL98 program (Stuiver et al. 1998). Calibrated dates (noted by "cal.") and dates derived or estimated from historical sources are both expressed relative to the Christian calendar. Where reference is made to particular centuries or millennia without using the letters B.C., A.D. should be understood.

(R. McIntosh and McIntosh 1981; Horton 1987a). In their place have come more subtle appreciations of the potential that interactions with other societies hold as catalysts or intensifiers of already immanent social change.

One such model is that of Coquery-Vidrovitch (1969), who argues that control over long-distance trade was crucially significant in the formation of African states. Taking an abundance of land and low agricultural productivity as her starting point, she proposes that complex societies could not evolve in Africa by exploiting agricultural surpluses. Rather, it was manipulation of long-distance exchange networks that could extract sufficient revenue, an idea developed further in Ekholm's (1972) analysis of the political structure of the kingdom of Kongo. Valued as tokens of wealth and status because of their exotic origin, consequent scarcity, and removal from traditional social controls, access to prestige goods provides emerging elites with means of distinguishing themselves from others while simultaneously rewarding followers. Taken up in a widely canvassed "epigenetic" model for the evolution of civilization (Friedman and Rowlands 1978), this idea has been applied in numerous archaeological contexts, including the controlled distribution of imported textiles and glass beads by elites of the Zimbabwe Tradition (M. Hall 1987; Loubser 1991). More recently, Blanton et al. (1996) have also considered the role of prestige goods, arguing that they provide one of two main routes to the development of more hierarchical, complex societies, the other being a more corporate, communal strategy in which power is diffuse and shared, prestige goods are unimportant, and control over ritual knowledge, including fertility, forms the mainspring of political action. Robertshaw (2003) uses both models to understand the development of the state in Uganda, but it remains unclear if African case studies neatly pattern into one or other camp (S. McIntosh 1999b).

As well as being vulnerable to competing polities, societies with prestige goods economies are frequently thought to be at the mercy of their exchange partners. They may also be understood to be exchanging important, perhaps irreplaceable, raw materials for mere trinkets designed to sustain an elite few. In the African context this has been thought a prelude to the "underdevelopment" of African economies that is argued to have been a distinctive feature of colonialism (Rodney 1972). Such dependent relationships have also been formalized in another widely applied model of intersocietal interaction, that of the "world system." As developed by Wallerstein (1974, 1980), this was a means of understanding the emergence of the modern global capitalist economy as an ever-larger, self-contained social system grounded in a division of labor between an advantaged core and politically, militarily, technologically, and economically weaker peripheries, linked through intermediate gateway communities or "semi-peripheries." Wallerstein himself argued that before capitalism such systems were either highly unstable or developed into unitary *political* systems (or "world-empires"). He also insisted that such systems dealt only in staple goods, not luxuries.

Archaeologists have applied Wallerstein's ideas rather more adventurously (e.g., Schneider 1977; Rowlands et al. 1987; Champion 1989; Sherratt 1993), helped by his emphases on systemic, dynamic change, trade, and relatively familiar spatial concepts (Schortman and Urban 1987). To do this, they have reformulated his original work to allow for the flow of the prestige goods (preciosities) that attract so much archaeological attention and have expanded beyond the narrowly economic to include the symbolic dimensions of what is exchanged (Blanton and Feinman 1984). But difficulties in precisely locating world systems in time and space persist, mere demonstration that goods moved within cycles of growth and contraction being insufficient. At the very least, inequalities in technology, craft production, and sociopolitical development seem necessary, but whether these are applicable if one partner is not already organized at a state level is uncertain (Harding 2001). And where one party *is* technologically or sociopolitically significantly more complex than the other, we must guard against assuming that relationships were invariably one-way. As Wolf (1982) is at pains to point out, "the people without history" were as much actors in the creation of their own destiny as the Europeans whom they encountered, a theme that in African archaeology resonates especially strongly in so-called revisionist accounts that emphasize the dynamic interactions of Kalahari Bushmen with the wider world (Wilmsen and Denbow 1990; cf. Solway and Lee 1990; Sadr 1997).

Recognition that there is more to intersocietal interaction than "trade" is now widespread, and its study must encompass not just staple commodities and prestige goods but also those social and ideological patterns that leave behind less tangible, but no less real, evidence. One model that seeks to do this is that of peer-polity interaction. Instead of assuming that relationships between societies must be those of domination and subordination, this focuses on those of more equal footing (Renfrew and Cherry 1986). Interactions between such polities may take many forms, but two are of particular interest, competitive emulation and symbolic entrainment. The first of these terms refers to the ways in which polities seek to outshine each other, for example, through building bigger and better monuments—but for all to play this game, it helps if the monuments share a common style, that is, if all polities follow much the same rules. Symbolic entrainment illustrates another way that this may happen, through a convergence of iconography and ideology that also helps leaders legitimize their status vis-à-vis each other (Schortman and Urban 1987, 72). Ceremonial exchange of valuables and marriage partners can serve the same goal, and development of a shared language may make interaction yet more effective. Wright (1993) argues that peer-polity interactions of this kind contributed to the growth of Swahili civilization and its associated trading networks.

One way of pulling this discussion together is offered by Sherratt's (1995) "interactionist approach," which focuses on how societies structure their interactions through material culture that is used to send social signals, whether in the form of cosmetics, jewelry, clothing, the commodities and skills used to make them, new or ostentatious forms of drinking, eating, and drug-taking, or the ideologies that justify, employ, or embody them. This emphasis on the social meaning of what is exchanged creates the basis for a narrative that is simultaneously alert to the historically specific and the processual, because "new modes of consumption and their material needs drive trading activities, which lead both to local intensification of production for exchange and to the emergence of wider systemic structures" (Sherratt 1995, 14). At the same time it pays attention to underlying spatial and geographical structures, such as the configurations of climate belts, seas, and patterns of resource distribution, the subject matter in other words of the preceding section. Core-periphery relations form part of this story, but they are not the whole of it. Along with peripheries we must also consider "margins," areas that did not undergo structural transformation but remained disengaged from processes of differentiation and specialization vis-à-vis cores, as well as "nuclei," areas of innovation that had not yet begun to be maintained by flows of products from those surrounding them (Sherratt 1993, 6–8). This model offers more nuanced insights into how processes of innovation and interaction develop historically and into how core and periphery mutually constitute and give shape to each other: teleological assumptions about the central roles of cores grounded in their later preeminence can, and must, be avoided. Instead, we should look for potentially complementary systems of interaction, the scope for growth inherent in the areas connecting them, and the possibility that other exchange systems were truncated or diverted as they reoriented (or were forcibly redirected) toward expanding cores and their systems of value (Sherratt 1995, 17–21).

Another concern has to be the divide too readily drawn between what Horden and Purcell (2000) term "high" and "low" commerce. This is not identical to Wallerstein's (1974) distinction between staples and luxuries, for both commodities and preciosities can be subjects of "high" commerce. Rather, it relates to the temptation to focus on those aspects of interaction that are organized, controlled, and manipulated by the politically and economically powerful, those who, not so coincidentally, also figure prominently in the historical documents with which archaeologists frequently seek to compare or correlate their excavated evidence. Defining trade routes and labeling resources as "high" commerce can obscure other patterns of redistribution (Horden and Purcell 2000, 365–66), all the more easily where exotic imports fit into developmental models of societal evolution, provide chronologies, and speak to long-distance connections rather than seemingly long-lasting isolation. Glass beads in the southern African Iron Age are but one example of an item that falls into these categories but may also have circulated through non-elite hands (M. Hall 1987; Loubser 1991; Denbow 1999; Wood 2000). Indeed, while "high" commerce draws attention away from smaller-scale, more utilitarian, less elite-controlled exchanges, it should not be forgotten that the needs of the many may have bulked larger than the preciosities of the few: West Africa's salt trade, to which I have already alluded, and Beach's (1994, 72) comment on the importance of imported cotton clothing on the Zimbabwe Plateau exemplify this point, as do the words of Ann Stahl (1999a, 44) cited in the preface. Shipwrecks, the archaeology of which is a growing concern in southern and East Africa, make the same point at a very human and historically specific scale, for alongside official consignments, they may also document the smuggling of other goods by private individuals (Werz 1999). Other connections take the form of interdependent relationships between groups pursuing different subsistence specializations, such as pastoralists and agriculturalists or pastoralists and hunter-gatherers. The ethnographic literature of Africa is full of such instances and also documents exchanges that seek to distribute wealth in the form of cattle as a means of minimizing losses to disease, drought, or raiding (A. Smith 1992). Whether with "other" ethnic groups or with members of one's own, the effect is to create ties that further facilitate the spread of other goods, technologies, and ideologies. In short, many of the networks of "high" commerce that I discuss probably grew out of, or latched onto, smaller patterns of connectivity that themselves took many forms (sidebar 2).

SIDEBAR 2

Local African Networks: Southeastern Southern Africa

Farming societies in South Africa's Thukela Basin in the first millennium cal. A.D. provide one example of the extent of internal African exchange networks onto which extracontinental contacts were later mapped (figure 1.6). These communities were linked to each other, we may presume, by marriage, and this probably involved transfers of bridewealth between different lineages. As well as small-scale exchanges between individual communities that may have evened out differences in production, discovery of masks probably used in communal initiation ceremonies suggests that people regularly came together for ceremonial purposes (Loubser 1993). Some villages also show evidence of specialized craft activities, including production of talc schist ornaments and, perhaps, iron smelting (van Schalkwyk 1994–95). Ivory and copper moved directionally toward others that were the residences of important chiefs (Whitelaw 1994–95), while within, and certainly beyond, the limits of farming settlement there were two-way exchanges with hunter-gatherer groups. Movement of iron, pottery, and ostrich eggshell beads can be demonstrated archaeologically, while that of ochre, skins, cereals, feathers, and bushmeat is suspected. Acquisition by farmers of hunter-gatherer women, vocabulary, and religious practices and beliefs was also underway (Mitchell 2002a, 292–97). The distributions of seashell ornaments, ostrich eggshell beads, and distinctive stone artifacts show that these hunter-gatherers were themselves part of interaction networks extending well into South Africa's interior (Mitchell 1996, 1999). Though farther south than the area of principal interest to those participating in the developing trans–Indian Ocean trade, glass beads and fragments of Middle Eastern pottery could still penetrate KwaZulu-Natal in the ninth century cal. A.D. (Whitelaw 1994–95). Future archaeological research will probably show a similarly broad range and complexity of intra-African interactions in those areas farther north from which skins, ivory, and gold were exported on an accelerating scale in succeeding centuries (Pikirayi 2001; Mitchell 2002a).

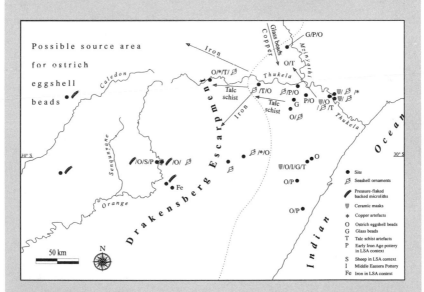

Figure 1.6. Southeastern southern Africa showing the distribution of archaeological finds at relevant sites of the first millennium as discussed in sidebar 2. The dotted line shows the approximate maximum inland penetration of agricultural settlement during the first millennium cal. A.D.

The Pleistocene Background

To conclude this chapter I look briefly at Africa's external connections in the long period before that which forms my chief concern (figure 1.7). As Darwin (1871) predicted, paleontological research confirms Africa as humanity's continent of origin (Klein 1999). Among the earliest archaeological sites outside Africa is Dmanisi in Georgia. Dating to 1.7 million years ago, it has produced pebble tools and several fossils, some assigned to the otherwise uniquely African taxon *Homo ergaster* (Gabunia et al.

Figure 1.7. Africa's Pleistocene connections, showing key sites and areas outside Africa mentioned in the text. The extent of the Rift Valley system is indicated by the dotted lines.

2000). Lying due north of the Rift Valley, its location, and that of another early site, 'Ubeidiya in Israel, suggest the Isthmus of Suez as the route by which *Homo* first left Africa, facilitated perhaps by the longer persistence of savanna in what is now the eastern Sahara (PRISM 1995). Movement into tropical Asia probably occurred around the same time, if dates apparently associated with *Homo erectus* fossils in Java are accepted (Milliken 2002). Lack of exploration in southern Arabia makes it impossible to say if this involved dispersals across the southern end of the Red Sea and the Gulf at a time of lower sea level.

For hominids to enter Europe several routes were available, with entry by land via Russia and Ukraine an ever-present possibility. Others depended on the lowering of sea levels during glacial periods or the capacity to cross open water. The Bosporus-Dardanelles–Sea of Marmara channel, which bisects Turkey, disappeared repeatedly during the Pleistocene, opening a dry land crossing from Anatolia into the Balkans. The Strait of Gibraltar, on the other hand, was never closed, though it certainly narrowed at times with islets appearing within it. Given the ferocity of its currents, this may not have sufficed to permit movement north from Morocco unless these were weaker at lower sea levels or boats were used, a possibility raised by stone artifacts in 0.8 million-year-old contexts in Flores, an Indonesian island apparently never connected by land to its neighbors (Morwood et al. 1999). Turning back to the Mediterranean, a final route, via Malta from Tunisia to Sicily, would have involved a still longer sea crossing, but geomorphological and paleontological evidence leave even this question open (Manzi 2001). Whichever routes were used, recent reviews make it unlikely that temperate Europe was settled significantly before 0.6 million years ago, although hominids were (intermittently?) present in the northern Mediterranean Basin at least 200,000 years before this (Milliken 2002).

Initial dispersal from Africa was far from the end of the story, and repeated movements beyond, and perhaps also back into, the continent can be suggested, though through much of the Lower Pleistocene Sinai and the Levant may have been as much barriers to movement as corridors (Milliken 2002, 29). Acheulian artifacts at Gesher Benot Ya'aqov, Israel, dated to 0.75 million years ago, are nonetheless, strikingly similar to those from sites of the same age in Africa (Saraguti and Goren-Inbar 2001). The earliest Acheulian assemblages in Europe also broadly resemble coeval occurrences there (Klein 1999, 339). Later exchanges are also evident: Middle Paleolithic Amudian/Pre-Aurignacian assemblages, for example, occur in both the Levant and northern Libya (Klein 1999, 429). Even if the Mediterranean did constitute a major barrier to population exchange

(Hublin 2001), such contacts, and a "short" chronology for hominid settlement in Europe, support a common derivation of western Eurasia's Neanderthals and archaic forms of *H. sapiens* in Africa from *H. heildebergensis*, a successor species to *H. ergaster* (Rightmire 2001). This common ancestry may have been even more recent if similarities between the Middle Paleolithic and Middle Stone Age artifacts found after 0.25 million years ago truly reflect another northward dispersal from Africa in the late Middle Pleistocene (Foley and Lahr 1997; Foley 2001).

Paleoanthropology has recently made enormous strides in understanding the origins of our own species, *H. sapiens*. There is now broad agreement that anatomically modern humans evolved first in sub-Saharan Africa, only subsequently expanding into the rest of the world (Klein 1999, 503–11). This view is supported by early dates for anatomically modern fossils south of the Sahara, the restriction to Africa of specimens that provide plausible ancestral forms, and genetic evidence from contemporary populations that humans are surprisingly similar the world over, but that some components of their DNA, including its mitochondrial portion, exhibit clear distinctions between sub-Saharan groups and those from elsewhere; the likeliest explanation for this is that the former have a longer history of evolutionary divergence. Eurasian hominids, on the other hand, including the Neanderthals, show no sign of evolving toward the modern condition. The idea that anatomically modern humans spread into Eurasia, and ultimately still farther, from an African birthplace is frequently termed the *Out-of-Africa 2* hypothesis of modern human origins. *Out-of-Africa 1*, in contrast, refers to the earlier dispersal of *H. ergaster/H. erectus,* although we have already seen that the situation was probably more complex than this.

Fossils from Qafzeh, Israel, demonstrate that anatomically modern humans had moved out of Africa before 90,000 years ago. The Isthmus of Suez was once again a significant dispersal route, for both people and other African mammals (Tchernov 1992), though supporting archaeological evidence in the form of assemblage similarities is not yet evident (Vermeersch 2001). A second route may have been across the Bab el-Mandeb Straits, which would have become dry land, or at least significantly narrower, at low sea levels. There is little hard evidence to support this possibility, but the fact that modern humans colonized Australia by 60,000 years ago, the presence of Neanderthals in northern Iraq and Uzbekistan, and the relative ease of eastward movement along the Indian Ocean coast (provided food and water were available on its Arabian shores) warrant its consideration (Petraglia and Alsharekh 2003). Europe, on the other hand, was apparently not settled by anatomically modern humans until 40,000–45,000 years ago. The tall, linear physique of these early Upper Paleolithic people confirms their relatively recent tropical origin, and their movement into Europe seems to have been from the southeast (Trinkaus 1981; Klein 1999). That Neanderthals survived longest in Iberia (Bocquet-Appel and Demars 2000) suggests that the Strait of Gibraltar did not form a second entry point for their expansion through the Mediterranean Basin.

There is, indeed, remarkably little sign for trans-Mediterranean contacts during the Pleistocene, and firm evidence for human settlement on, or visits to, islands unconnected to the mainland at low sea levels comes only from its very end, except in the case of Sicily (Cherry 1990; Chilardi et al. 1996; Peltenburg et al. 2000). Earlier suggestions that North African assemblages like the Iberomaurusian or Capsian derived from, or gave rise to, others in western Europe have been comprehensively refuted (Close and Wendorf 1990; Sheppard 1990). Nor have many similarities been detected between the artifact records of the Horn and southwestern Arabia before 10,000 years ago (Clark 1978, 70; Petraglia and Alsharekh 2003). Only via the Isthmus of Suez did African populations maintain contact with those of southwest Asia. The earliest Upper Paleolithic tradition in Cyrenaica, for example, resembles broadly contemporary assemblages in Lebanon, though Hiscock (1996) argues that it developed from local Middle Paleolithic antecedents. More securely, Ahmarian blade-based assemblages occur in the Levant, northern Sinai, and Middle Egypt, and some 20,000 years later distinctive ways of making microlithic tools point to a North African origin for the Mushabian complex of Sinai and the Negev (Bar-Yosef 1987); slightly later, Nile Valley shells reached Natufian groups in Israel and Ounan stone projectile points occur in both the Negev and the eastern Sahara (Bar-Yosef and Belfer-Cohen 1989). With these exceptions, the Pleistocene record, as currently understood, is marked more by hominids moving out of Africa than of continued exchanges of people, goods, or ideas between Africa and its neighbors. That, for the moment, seems to be very much more the story of the last 10,000 years.

Notes

1. This is, I freely admit, a western Mediterranean, if not European, standpoint. Much of North Africa, including Egypt, remained under Turkish rule or suzerainty well into the nineteenth century, and it is undeniable that the Ottomans came closer than any other power in reuniting the Mediterranean world once ruled by Rome. In this respect the distinction between Africa and Europe that we identify

today was, in much of the Mediterranean, a product of the slow collapse of Ottoman rule.

2. Their very name comes from the Arabic *sadd*, meaning "block" (Trimingham 1949, 2–3).

3. Discredited academically though it may be, the Hamitic hypothesis remains alive in current political discourse in parts of East Africa where it has, with genocidal consequences, reinforced the claims of ruling elites to exotic, foreign origins and supported ethnic distinctions (C. Taylor 1999). Elsewhere, versions of it have been used by African historians in a critical dialogue with European ideas (Zachernuk 1994).

CHAPTER 2

The Development
and Spread of African
Farming Systems

Man shall not live by bread alone.
—THE GOSPEL ACCORDING TO ST LUKE 4:4

A T THE START of the period this book examines, few if any of Africa's inhabitants exploited domesticated plants or animals. Today virtually all depend upon them for their livelihood. This chapter sketches out how this situation came about. The general format is chronological and procceds in a largely north–south direction. I pay particular attention to the implications that this patterning holds for how the development of food production in Africa articulated with comparable processes in Eurasia. I also consider some of the ways in which Africa's experience adds to our general understanding of how and why farming has supplanted hunting, gathering, and fishing as the mainstay of the modern world.

African Systems of Food Production

Among the most important characteristics of African farming is its diversity. Harlan (1982) distinguished four principal crop complexes, each with its own suite of staples and associated food plants (table 2.1). One, the Near Eastern Complex, is completely exogenous. Wheat, barley, lentils, chickpeas, and flax are its chief crops. Requiring winter rainfall or, failing

Table 2.1. Principal African Crop Complexes (after Harlan 1982; only major species shown)

	Near Eastern		Ethiopian	
Cereals	*Hordeum* spp.[1]	Barley	*Avena abyssinica*	Ethiopian oats
	Triticum spp.[1]	Wheat	*Eleusine coracana*	Finger millet
			Eragrostis tef	Tef
Legumes	*Cicer arietinum*[1]	Chickpea		
	Lens culinaris[1]	Lentil		
Others	*Olea europaea*	Olive oil	*Catha edulis*	Qat
	Linum usitatissimum[1]	Flax	*Coffea arabica*	Coffee
	Phoenix dactylifera	Date palm	*Ensete ventricosum*	Enset
	Vitis vinifera	Grape	*Guizotia abyssinica*	Noog

	Savanna[2]		Forest Margin[4]	
Cereals	*Digitaria exilis*	Black fonio	*Brachiara deflexa*	Brachiara
	Digitaria iburua	Fonio		
	Oryza glaberrima[3]	African rice		
	Pennisetum glaucum	Pearl millet		
	Sorghum bicolor	Sorghum		
Legumes	*Voandzeia subterranea*	Bambara groundnut	*Lablab purpureus*	Hyacinth bean
	Vigna unguiculata	Cowpea		
Tubers			*Dioscorea* spp.	Yams
			Plectranthus esculentus	Hausa potato

(Continued)

Table 2.1. Continued

	Savanna[2]		Forest Margin[4]
Tree crops	*Acacia albida*	White acacia	*Cola* spp. — Kola
	Adansonia digitata	Baobab	*Elais guineensis* — Oil palm
	Butyrospermum paradoxum	Shea butter	
Others	*Colocynthus citrullus*	Watermelon	*Hibiscus esculentus* — Okra
	Lagenaria siceraria[5]	Bottle gourd	

Notes

1. Also grown extensively in the northern highlands of Ethiopia/Eritrea.
2. In many areas of southern and eastern Africa pearl millet and sorghum have been largely replaced by an American introduction, maize (*Zea mays*).
3. Also grown in the West African forest zone, though originally a savanna grass.
4. Crops of ultimately Asian (*Dioscorea* spp. yams; *Colocasia esculenta* taro; *Musa* sp. bananas and plantains) and American (*Manibot esculenta*, cassava; *Zea mays*, maize) origin are now staples in much of the area in which the Forest Margin Complex is found. Other Asian introductions include rice (*Oryza sativa*), sugarcane (*Saccharum officinarum*), and coconut (*Cocos nucifera*).
5. While the young fruit is edible, this is widely grown as a container, not a comestible.

this, irrigation, it was restricted historically to the Maghreb, Libya's Mediterranean coast, Egypt, Nubia, Eritrea, northern Ethiopia, and isolated Saharan oases. Only in colonial times was it introduced farther south, chiefly into South Africa's winter-rainfall region. The Savanna Complex, on the other hand, is indigenous. Of several domesticated grasses, sorghum and pearl millet are the most important and widespread, though African rice dominates in parts of West Africa. Legumes, watermelons, and bottle gourds also feature. So too do tree crops, such as shea butter and baobab, which, though not planted or morphologically domesticated, are protected as sources of oil, food, or even water. Sorghum and pearl millet are adapted to fairly dry conditions, with millet the most drought tolerant of the pair, and in West and Central Africa's wetter, more forested zones, the Forest Margin Complex replaces them. African rice is important from Senegal to Ivory Coast, but this is really a tuber and tree-crop complex, and farther east yams dominate. Other key species include cowpeas and tree crops that once again are encouraged, not domesticated. They include kola (a stimulant) and oil palm (a source of edible oil, alcohol, and construction materials). The Ethiopian Complex is found only there and in neighboring Eritrea. Its distinctive taxa include tef, noog (source of an edible oil), finger millet (also grown with Savanna Complex grains in eastern and southern Africa), coffee, qat, and a variety of oats that is more properly a commensal than a domesticate. Several Near Eastern crops, including wheat and barley, are also grown, whereas in the southern highlands the staple is a banana-like plant, enset. Superimposed upon this already complex situation are food plants of ultimately Southeast Asian or Latin American origin—bananas, taro, cassava, peanuts, maize, and so on—the impacts of which I consider in later chapters.

Alongside this complex series of associations goes a similarly varied set of agricultural techniques. One distinctive practice is that of *décrue* farming, in which crops are planted in mud as floodwaters recede so that they grow without requiring rain or irrigation. The technique is now found mostly in the Niger and Senegal floodplains but was once common in Egypt; specific cultivars may be chosen for short-flooding or long-flooding regimes (Harlan 1982). Another strategy is that of transplanting, in which seedbed-raised sorghum or pearl millet seedlings are relocated to flooded areas after the land dries out and its grass is burned off. For most of Africa's farmers, such cultivation traditionally proceeded by hand using a hoe and digging stick; as already indicated, disease and lack of fodder limited livestock numbers in many areas, hindering the spread of plow agriculture beyond the Near Eastern and Ethiopian Complexes, though the utility of this technology is doubtful where shallow top soils have low natural fertility or lateritic soils might harden to the point of uncultivability

(Ehret 2002, 136). Long-fallow systems, extending in some areas into genuine shifting cultivation that forced settlements to move every few years,
are also typical, though by no means uniform. Varied strategies of agricultural intensification demonstrate as much and supported locally high
population densities (Widgren and Sutton 2003).

Though brief, this sketch should at least fix some of the associations
encountered later on. Others could be mentioned, and it is typical of

---

SIDEBAR 3

Africa's Other Animals

Cattle are the African domesticate par excellence, but they were not
alone. For donkeys, the quintessential pack animals, domestication
occurred somewhere in the broad region between Cyrenaica and
Somalia (Eisenmann 1995); linguistic evidence suggests it may have
happened more than once (Blench 2000a). Donkey caravans were an
important component of Old Kingdom Egyptian transport technology and the species had spread into the Levant by that time. The
guinea fowl, that favorite of formal dinners, was domesticated in the
Maghreb, or perhaps the Sahel, in the early first millennium B.C. There
are historical references to it in Greece by 400 B.C., and it was widespread in the Roman Empire (Mongin and Plouzeau 1984), though
its comparative uncontrollability encouraged partial substitution by
chickens in Africa. Cats probably domesticated themselves through a
commensal association with farmers, but this process may have taken
place in the Levant, where their wild progenitor also occurred, rather
than in Egypt (Clutton-Brock 1997). The situation with dogs and pigs
is more obscure. Both wild boar and wolf inhabited early Holocene
North Africa so some degree of genetic admixture is conceivable, but
both were probably first domesticated in the Near East (and, for dogs,
still more widely; Crockford 2000). Dogs are now ubiquitous across
the continent, probably spreading largely through associations with
herding, though their osteological similarity to jackals makes this difficult to track unless precisely the right faunal elements are present.
Pigs, which were domesticated in Egypt by 5000 B.C. and raised extensively in the pre-Islamic Maghreb (Gilman 1975), occurred as far
south as central Sudan and southern Ethiopia; less certain is whether
they were present in West Africa's forest-savanna zone before the
initiation of maritime contact with the Portuguese (Blench 2000b).

African systems of food production that they include not just plants that are sown or planted, but also many that are gathered. Hard-and-fast divisions between "farming" and "gathering" are arbitrary impositions upon the reality of what people actually do. Tree-crop management and the importance of wild-grass harvesting in the Sahara (Harlan 1989) and the Inland Niger Delta (S. McIntosh 1999c) illustrate this. Indeed, being uncultivated, such high-yielding cereals require little labor input and are extensively traded (Gast 1968). Trapping animals that visit fields or gardens is another example of how conventional boundaries between "wild" and "domesticated" resources blur, but of animals kept by people just three—cattle, sheep, and goats—dominate. They occur in association with all the crop complexes described (figure 2.1). Donkeys, horses, camels, and pigs, on the other hand, are geographically much more restricted (sidebar 3). Chickens, with their Southeast Asian origins, I consider in chapter 4.

African Origins for African Cattle: Early Pastoralism in Northern Africa

As global temperatures rose and ice sheets melted during the late Pleistocene, Africa's Inter-Tropical Convergence Zone shifted north, bringing monsoonal rains to the southern Sahara. The area occupied by desert consequently diminished, replaced by savanna, or at least subdesert, habitats populated by a wide variety of animals. People recolonized the same areas, engraving or painting species like hippopotamus, crocodile, and elephant utterly out of place there today (Coulson and Campbell 2001). They probably moved into the Sahara from several directions, including the Sahel and the Maghreb, not just from the Nile Valley, and show significant variations in toolkit style and composition (MacDonald 1998a). A new technology was pottery, which was widely adopted across the southern part of today's Sahara 8000–9250 cal. B.C., millennia before its production in the Near East. Well made, extensively decorated, and almost always locally produced, it was nevertheless strikingly rare at first, suggesting its initial function may not have been storage or cooking (Close 1995). Used in these ways, however, it probably did expand the diet, making some foods more palatable, minimizing the effort expended in cooking others. Haaland (1992) may thus be correct in seeing causal connections between its adoption, increased use of wild grains, greater permanence of settlement in one place, and ultimately, population growth.

Pottery occurs from the start of the resettlement of Egypt's Western Desert ca. 8500 cal. B.C., but rainfall remained very low, with occupation focused around temporary lakes. Sites near two of these—Nabta Playa

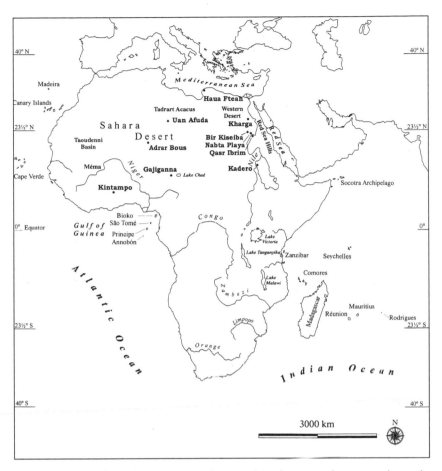

Figure 2.1. Africa showing sites discussed in the text relevant to the early domestication and spread of domestic livestock.

and Bir Kiseiba—have yielded bones of large bovids firmly assigned to cattle, not buffalo, although they do not show morphological changes indicative of domestication (Gautier 2002). Instead, the argument for this is ecological because the sparse wild fauna suggests a low-biomass, arid environment in which cattle could only have existed with human help (Wendorf and Schild 1980, 1994). Paleobotanical data reinforce the case for rainfall well below the levels at which wild cattle could have flourished (Neumann 1989; Close and Wendorf 1992), though if people and cattle were present only seasonally this may have been less of a constraint than it at first seems. Such scenarios have not, however, gone uncontested

39

because the Nabta fauna may be so impoverished that it cannot represent a real ecology (A. Smith 1986a, 1992; Muzzolini 1989). Furthermore, if water was really so scarce, so too presumably was grass, in which case what did the animals eat? More compelling archaeozoological evidence is needed finally to dispel these doubts.

Cattle remain rare in Western Desert faunas until 5800 cal. B.C., but the case for their independent domestication in North Africa, rather than introduction from Southwest Asia, is considerably strengthened by the earliest dates from the latter region (ca. 7500 cal. B.C.; Gautier 2002) and by genetic research. The mitochondrial DNA (mtDNA) of modern breeds indicates that Indian and Euro-African cattle separated hundreds of thousands of years ago. More importantly, it places a last common ancestor for African and European cattle around 22,000–26,000 years ago, well before any conceivable domestication event (Bradley et al. 1996). The morphological distinctiveness of Pharaonic Egyptian cattle supports the case for separate African domestication (Grigson 2000), while mtDNA analyses hint that this was followed by rapid expansion and diversification (Bradley and Loftus 2000).

One trigger for domesticating cattle may have been their desirability as a source of fat. Highly prized by hunter-gatherers for its nutritional value and taste, fat is rare on African ungulates, except on cattle (and eland) which store it, even in dry years. Perhaps then, people domesticated cattle to maintain access to a fat-rich resource as water and pasture diminished in increasingly arid conditions (A. Smith 1986a). However, fat can be accessed only by killing the cow, and the scarcity of cattle bones on Western Desert sites suggests this happened rarely. Instead, cattle may have been used as living reservoirs of milk and blood, tappable on demand for protein, fat, and liquid (Close and Wendorf 1992). The difficulty here is that most adult humans cannot digest the lactose in milk and some time must have elapsed before lactose tolerance became prevalent, though the dominance of the gene responsible for this may mean that this period was not long (Simoons 1973). In any case, fermented milk products (cheese, butter, yogurt, and so on) avoid the problem. Less widely addressed in the literature is the evolution of the capacity for regular milk production in cattle themselves because this is not characteristic of the wild form. Wendorf and Schild (2002) therefore suggest transport of water or housing as additional possible uses for the earliest cattle.

Situating these developments within a broader paleoenvironmental context helps us understand them better. Though the early Holocene saw conditions improve to the point at which people could use this part of the Sahara, at first this would only have been possible seasonally or opportunistically. Cattle may have been domesticated to facilitate this expansion into the desert, presumably in the Nile Valley, although they remain stubbornly absent there at this time, except as clearly wild animals (Gautier 2002). The Nabta–Bir Kiseiba area may also have occupied a crucial ecological position: far enough south to receive some rain, but only in small, highly variable amounts. Domestication may therefore have helped diversify people's subsistence base in the face of recurrent droughts. More pronounced arid episodes ca. 7570 and 6800–6500 cal. B.C. probably encouraged this process further, as well as cattle keeping's initial expansion beyond the Western Desert. Ephemeral campsites may mark this (Gabriel 1987; Close 1990), but dates are few and cattle keeping remained geographically restricted until 5800 cal. B.C. (Hassan 2000).

People in the Western Desert also exploited a diversity of food plants. At Nabta itself stone-built houses, storage pits, and wells suggest a more sedentary lifestyle after 7570 cal. B.C., supported by gathering fruits, tubers, and grasses, including sorghum (Wasylikowa et al. 1997). A similar pattern is evident elsewhere into the fifth millennium cal. B.C. (e.g., McDonald 1998; Barakat and Fahmy 1999), but by then cattle had been joined by sheep and goats, a topic considered later. Farther west, wild grasses were also important in the diet of people living in the Tadrart Acacus region of southwestern Libya (Barich 1992); early Holocene occupation of the Sahara may have concentrated in such central massifs. Certainly, areas in the far west, such as Atlantic Mauritania and northern Mali, were apparently unoccupied before 5800 cal. B.C. (Petit-Maire and Risier 1983), seriously bringing into question the validity of lumping early ceramic-using, hunter-gatherer-fisher communities together under the rubric "Aqualithic" (S. McIntosh and McIntosh 1986a; MacDonald 1998a; *pace* Sutton 1974). How far any had begun cultivating the cereals they were eating is questionable, as I show below. So too is the assumption that they spoke early versions of Nilo-Saharan languages, a conclusion reached from distributional correlations (Sutton 1974) and reconstructions of terms for activities thought to be detectable in the archaeological record (Ehret 1993). However, these reconstructions remain unconfirmed (Blench 1993b; Bender 1996; MacDonald 1998a), while proposed dates, founded in glottochronology, must be viewed with caution because of "the large degree of guesswork involved" (Ehret 1993, 115). Far more tangible is evidence for the confinement and feeding within Uan Afuda cave (Tadrart Acacus) of Barbary sheep (*Ammotragus lervia*). Accompanied by evidence of storage in pits and baskets, the adoption of pottery, and increased use of wild grasses, this looks like another strategy for coping with more arid conditions 6800–6100 cal. B.C. (Cremaschi and Di Lernia 1999). Interestingly, and for reasons considered at the end of this chapter, this did *not* lead to domestication. Instead, the expansion of pastoralism was based on cattle and two new domesticates of non-African origin, sheep and goats.

The Expansion of Livestock Keeping: The Sahara, the Sahel, and East Africa

Despite claims to the contrary (Muzzolini 1993), wild sheep and goats are absent from North African faunas. They did, however, occur widely in Southwest Asia, where genetic and archaeozoological data point to sheep being domesticated at the northwestern apex of the Fertile Crescent, goats in the Zagros Mountains (B. Smith 1998); both were present in the Levant by 7500 cal. B.C. and in Gaza by 5800 cal. B.C. (Hassan 2000). Goats and sheep are known from Egypt's Red Sea Hills ca. 5800 cal. B.C. (Vermeersch et al. 1996), while goats are documented in the Western Desert soon thereafter (Gautier 2002); dispersal across the Red Sea from southern Sinai is possible (Close 2002). Observations from Wadi Allaqi (Sadr et al. 1994), Haua Fteah (Klein and Scott 1986), and the Tadrart Acacus (Cremaschi and Di Lernia 1999) suggest sheep and goats occurred widely west of the Nile by 6,000 years ago. Less clear is whether the broadly contemporary, or perhaps slightly earlier, expansion of cattle keeping into Chad and southwestern Libya proceeded independently of this and whether new breeds of cattle arrived from Asia at the same time (Gautier 1987), but it may be significant that sheep and goats are better adapted to arid conditions than cattle. Dispersal of all three species was probably less a "wave of advance" and more a leapfrogging process that included diffusion of domestic stock among hunter-gatherer communities. It was no doubt encouraged by recurrent arid episodes, as well as less severe interannual rainfall fluctuations, and produced diverse interactions between groups with livestock and those without (Hassan 2002). Expansion probably began in particularly favorable circumstances as northward movement of the Inter-Tropical Convergence Zone and southward movement of the Mediterranean rainfall regime temporarily "pinched out" much of the desert (Close 1990). Indeed, the scarcity of seventh-millennium cal. B.C. radiocarbon dates in much of the Sahara indicates that the preceding drier phase created a widespread hiatus in occupation such that subsequent pastoralist settlement was less a frontier situation, more colonization of an uninhabited niche (A. Smith 1992). Thereafter, the pattern of climate change saw aridification take hold first in the north and east of the Sahara, helping to drive a dynamic of southward and westward expansion by livestock keeping groups (Hassan 2002).

Sheep and goats grew in importance after another arid episode ca. 4900 cal. B.C. (Hassan 2002). From about this time, there is also evidence of complex patterns of ceremonial behavior in the Western Desert

(Wendorf and Schild 1998), including construction of stone circles and other megalithic structures and burial of cattle beneath stone tumuli, signs perhaps of the initiation of that key role afforded them by many African peoples. Such practices suggest that increased effort was being put into binding communities together, perhaps as a way of coping with an increasingly marginal environment. Emigration was another option, and the appearance of livestock in the Nile Valley and northern Niger may not be unrelated (Hassan 2000). Wild food plants, including sorghum, were also gathered, but there is no firm evidence for their cultivation. Harvesting wild grasses is shown in Saharan rock art, but it is livestock that dominate the imagery here, especially cattle, which are shown being herded and sometimes milked (Muzzolini 2000; figure 2.2). That both light-skinned and dark-skinned individuals are depicted may imply that the region's inhabitants drew on populations to both north and south for their ancestry (A. Smith 1992). Physical anthropological evidence supports the rock art in placing a Maghreb-derived, Proto-Berber population in the central Sahara by 2500 cal. B.C. (MacDonald 1998a).

Around 3200 cal. B.C. the Inter-Tropical Convergence Zone shifted south, provoking serious, and more permanent, aridification (Hassan 2000). While this presumably encouraged people to seek pastures for their herds elsewhere, it simultaneously opened new areas to them. Though not the only disease affecting African livestock, trypanosomiasis (sleeping sickness) threatens cattle in particular. A southward shift in the 500–750 mm isohyet would have produced a corresponding relocation of its vector, the

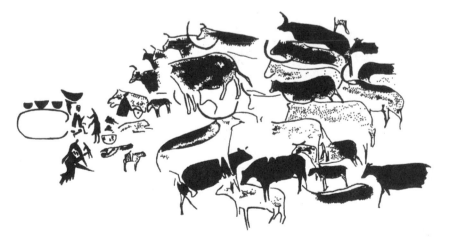

Figure 2.2. Painting of a pastoral encampment, Teshuinat, Tadrart Acacus region, Libya (redrawn after Muzzolini 1986, figure 52).

43

tsetse fly (*Glossina* spp.), which prefers bush to grassland. Dates from sites in Mali (MacDonald 1996), Kenya (Marshall et al. 1984), and northeast Africa (Marshall 2000) show that southward movement of people and animals occurred over a broad front. Similarities in material culture support movement from the central Sahara into the Niger Bend (A. Smith 1992), from Sudan into Kenya (Barthelme 1985), and perhaps from Nubia eastward into Eritrea and Ethiopia (Barnett 1999). Currently available evidence for the domestication of African cereals suggests that the societies involved in this process were pastoralist-foragers, not mixed farmers. Indeed, the archaeology of what is frequently called the Pastoral Neolithic implies that this situation continued in East Africa into the late first millennium B.C., perhaps later in some areas (Marshall 2000). Following an initial "trickle" when few domesticates are identifiable (Bower 1991), a much larger "splash" is evident around 1200 cal. B.C., perhaps linked to the establishment of a bimodal rainfall pattern capable of supporting year-round milk production (Marshall 1990). Yet, despite intensive field research and the reconstructions of historical linguists (Ehret 1998; Schoenbrun 1998), the only cultigen recovered remains the bottle gourd, known more as a container than for its edible fruit (Bower 1991). This is, however, alarming only if we make the mistake of thinking, in Eurasian terms, that pastoralism can exist *only* where its practitioners have access to agricultural produce (Monod 1975). African archaeology and ethnohistory amply demonstrate the contrary (A. Smith 1992), and in the Pastoral Neolithic case the carbohydrates that stable-isotope analyses show were consumed (Ambrose and De Niro 1986) were presumably wild. Their procurement perhaps formed part of the complex set of societal interactions implied by the diverse ceramic styles, varied lithic technologies, mortuary rituals, and movements of obsidian that constitute the East African record at this time (Bower 1991; Gifford-Gonzalez 1998).[1]

On the opposite side of the continent, the same period marks the introduction of domestic livestock into West Africa beyond the Sahel. Sheep and goats certainly occur on Kintampo sites in Ghana, cattle possibly so (Stahl 1994). Bifacial arrowheads recall Saharan examples, material culture again supporting the zoological evidence. Northern Kintampo communities in Ghana's savanna zone also cultivated pearl millet, a cereal of ultimately Saharan origin (D'Andrea et al. 2001). More southerly communities, living where pearl millet could not grow, used tree crops like oil palm and *Canarium*, and perhaps also yams. Above all, however, Kintampo is a particularly well-studied instance of a widespread set of related changes involving greater sedentism, use of pottery, elaboration of material culture, and new subsistence patterns (Stahl 1994). Although microlithic quartz assemblages suggest some hunter-gatherer communities survived until the end of the first millennium A.D. (MacDonald 1998a), socioeconomic intensification of this kind probably provided the starting point for increasing commitment to food production across West Africa's forest zone. Out of this came not only the Forest Margin Complex described previously, but also the further expansion of agricultural economies in a process, partly linked to the spread of Bantu languages, that ultimately brought food production to Africa's southern tip.

Domesticating African Cereals: Absence of Evidence or Evidence of Absence?

Although grown in Africa for 7,000 years and present in Saharan oases by 900 B.C. (van der Veen 1992), wheat and barley had their southward expansion blocked by aridity or the shift to a summer rainfall regime.[2] In sub-Saharan Africa, therefore, other cereal crops were cultivated. Understanding their domestication is difficult and complicated by the scarcity of relevant plant remains. Reasons for this lack of preservation include rapid nutrient recycling in tropical environments and mechanical disintegration in soils that alternate repeatedly between wet and dry (Young and Thompson 1999). Infrequent charring (perhaps because crop processing by-products were not disposed of in fire?) may also have contributed, but another factor is that macroplant fossils have been too rarely sought. Instead, linguistic and botanical studies have sustained discussion. Now, however, new research programs are producing results that may transform understandings of the circumstances in which cultivation of sub-Saharan cereals began (figure 2.3). They may also cast new light on a related issue, when and how they first spread into Eurasia.

Haaland (1996) argues that focusing solely on morphological domestication is too limiting a strategy for understanding the origins of cultivation. In part this is because several features of cultural interest typically associated with farming communities may predate the appearance of such evidence in the archaeological record. Examples include ceramics and sedentism, pointers perhaps to profound changes in the organization of gender relations and the wider community (Haaland 1992). A second reason is that it is now well established that sorghum at least will *not* undergo the morphological changes that identify it as domesticated if harvested by stripping the grain from the stalks or beating it into baskets (Harlan 1989). And yet sorghum impressions (all morphologically wild in status) are plentiful on early Holocene potsherds in Nubia, grindstones are numerous, and settlements occur in alluvial settings with heavy clay soils, contexts well suited for growing sorghum (Haaland 1996), whether for food or beer (Fernandez and Tresseras 2000). The conclusion drawn from

45

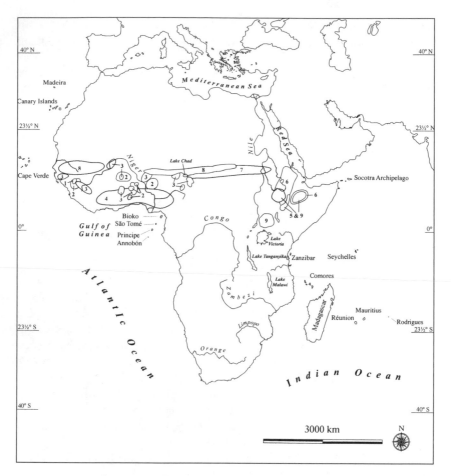

Figure 2.3. Africa showing the likely areas of origin of major indigenous staple crops (redrawn after Harlan 1982). (1) *Brachiara deflexa*; (2) *Digitaria exilis* and *D. iburua*; (3) *Oryza glaberrima*; (4) *Dioscorea rotundata*; (5) *Musa ensete* and *Guizotia abyssinica*; (6) *Eragrostis tef*; (7) *Sorghum bicolor*; (8) *Pennisetum glaucum*; (9) *Eleusine coracana*.

these observations is that sorghum has been cultivated for far longer than the morphological evidence shows.

Because wild sorghum varieties are widespread in tropical Africa, genetic isolation would have been needed to allow altered harvesting practices to operate effectively as selection pressures to bring about detectable morphological change (Stemler 1984). Here we confront some interesting observations, because the oldest claims for morphologically domesticated sorghum, pearl millet, and finger millet all come from southern Asia! Commonly cited among such finds are pottery impressions of sorghum from Bronze Age sites in Yemen and Oman (Constantini 1984, 1990) and actual grains of sorghum, the two millets, and two legumes (cowpeas and hyacinth beans) from first and second-millennium B.C. sites in Pakistan and India. Here Weber (1998) suggests that finger millet was introduced first, becoming a key crop by 2000 B.C. as part of a summer-rainfall package subsequently joined by sorghum and pearl millet. Fuller's (2003) more recent appraisal confirms the presence of pearl millet, sorghum, and the two legumes by the mid-second millennium B.C., but suggests finger millet is present only from around 1000 B.C. One of the difficulties in assessing these claims is that several are based on ceramic impressions rather than actual charred grains; another, that finger millet can be confused with indigenous Indian cereals (Fuller 2001; cf. Weber 2001); a third, that no African plants found in Asia have yet been directly dated. Overinterpretation has certainly occurred, and the Arabian evidence in particular, though initially expressed with caution (Cleuziou and Constantini 1980), has been seized upon with undue abandon and should be discounted.

The introductions of these crops to southern Asia could have come from sustained or episodic, direct or indirect contacts with Africa. It is possible to begin constructing a model for such contacts by linking the presence of Red Sea marine shells in Neolithic graves at Kadero (Krzyzaniak 1991) to similarities in the material culture of the Middle Nile Valley, southeastern Sudan and Eritrea (Fattovich et al. 1984; Marks 1987). Contacts across the Red Sea certainly existed before 2000 B.C., and communities in Yemen maintained connections as far as the eastern side of the Arabian Peninsula (Edens and Wilkinson 1998). There Oman, which exported copper into an early Mesopotamian-centered "world system," had its own exchange ties to the Harappan civilization of Pakistan and western India, but Indian connections with Yemen, or even with the African side of the southern Red Sea, seem a more likely vehicle for the dispersal of African crops given their absence from Oman itself (Fuller 2003, 264). A pendant of East African copal resin found in Mesopotamia and dating to 2500 B.C. indicates the spatial scale of Bronze Age exchange networks, even if as no more than mere "trickle trade" (Meyer et al. 1993).

The South Asian evidence clearly supports the thrust of Haaland's (1996) argument. It is true that DNA evidence from exceptionally well-preserved sorghum grains at Qasr Ibrim, Nubia, suggests that morphologically wild sorghum from the first millennium B.C. and two domesticated races dating to the last 2,000 years are genetically identical, implying a relatively recent domestication event in Sudan (Rowley-Conwy et al. 1999). However, the genetic sequences examined actually exhibit very little variability (Fuller 2003, 253). That the oldest published evidence for domesticated sorghum in Africa is of late first millennium B.C. age (Stemler and Falk 1981) is therefore probably no more than an artifact of the limited recovery and identification of relevant botanical remains. While sorghum was certainly sufficiently important to be represented on Meroitic temples in the decades either side of A.D. 1 (Welsby 1996), it, pearl millet, cowpeas, hyacinth beans, and even finger millet had all probably been domesticated in Africa many centuries before.

These arguments are supported by the admittedly largely atemporal linguistic and botanical evidence for a longer history of cereal cultivation south of the Sahara (Ehret 1982; Harlan 1993). More convincingly, they are encouraged by recent paleobotanical finds (table 2.2; figure 2.4). Fully domesticated pearl millet grains from Burkina Faso are, for example, directly dated to 1035–916 cal. B.C. (Neumann 1999), others from northern Ghana to 1740–1130 cal. B.C. (D'Andrea et al. 2001). Accelerator dates for sherds from Nigeria bearing impressions of the same species are similar in age (Klee and Zach 1999) and broadly contemporary (MacDonald et al. 2003), or even slightly older (Amblard 1996), in the case of examples from Mauritania. The onset of drier conditions may provide an environmental rationale for these developments, and perhaps significantly it is pearl millet, the most drought-resistant cereal and one that is generally preferred over sorghum for its taste and nutritional value, that currently has the oldest record of domestication.

Another scenario envisages cultivation developing as part of intensifying exchange relations between interacting specialists, each pursuing their own subsistence orientation (R. McIntosh 1998). Data from Mali's Taoudenni Basin (Petit-Maire and Risier 1983; Holl 1998), interactions between the Dhar Tichitt and Méma areas farther south (MacDonald 1999b), and the contrasting subsistence profiles of Kadero and some of its contemporaries (Krzyzaniak 1991) suggest this situation prevailed in many areas; foragers may even have moved north into the Sahel to participate in it (MacDonald 1997). Particularly neat demonstration that cultivation was only one of several strategies comes from three sites in the Chad Basin: one saw domesticated pearl millet replace wild grasses after 1000 cal. B.C., a second its gradual supplanting by wild rice, and a third its consistent subordination to wild cereals. Sorghum, moreover, though now the most common cereal, was a second millennium introduction (Breunig et al. 1996; Klee and Zach 1999). These observations strengthen Andah's (1993) suggestion that *Brachiara deflexa* and fonio (*Digitaria* spp.) were once more widely grown in West Africa, only to be relegated to subsidiary or local roles by the expansion of sorghum and pearl millet, and emphasize that many pathways were pursued before reaching today's situation,[3]

Table 2.2. Major cereals domesticated in Africa: area of likely origin and early dates for evidence of morphological domestication

Cereal	Area of likely origin (Harlan 1982, 1993)	Chronology date (bp)	Comment	Location	Reference
African rice (*Oryza globerrima*)	Inland Niger Delta	c. 2200 - 1850	[1]	Jenné-jeno (Mali)	S. McIntosh and McIntosh (1988)
Finger millet (*Eleusine coracana*)	Highlands of Ethiopia, Kenya, Uganda	1290 ± 50	[1]	Kadzi (Zimbabwe)	Pwiti and Mvenge (1996)
		c. 1200 - 1400	[1]	Magogo (South Africa)	Maggs and Ward (1984)
		c. 1000	[1]	Deloraine (Kenya)	Ambrose (1984)
Pearl millet (*Pennisetum glaucum*)	Sahara, but note Tostain (1998) for the closest genetic similarities between wild and domesticated varieties being in southern Mauritania and the Lake Chad region	3500 ± 100	AMS date[2]	Dhar Tichitt (Mauritania)	Amblard (1996)
		3460 ± 200	AMS date	Birimi (Ghana)	D'Andrea et al. (2001)
		3260 ± 40	AMS date[2]	Djiganyai (Mauritania)	MacDonald et al. (2003)
		2930 ± 60	[2]	Gajiganna (Nigeria)	Neumann (1999)
		2840 ± 49	AMS date	Ti-n-Akof (Burkina Faso)	Neumann (1999)
		2430 ± 70	AMS date	Kursakata (Nigeria)	Neumann (1999)
Sorghum (*Sorghum bicolor*)	Sahel, specifically Sudan/Chad	1970 ± 127	[1]	Meroë (Sudan)	Stemler and Falk (1981)
		1705 ± 60		Jebel Tomat (Sudan)	Clark and Stemler (1975)
		c. 1850	[1]	Qasr Ibrim (Egypt)	Rowley-Conwy (1991)
		c. 1850	[1]	Jenné-jeno (Mali)	S. McIntosh (1995)

(Continued)

Table 2.2. Continued

Cereal	Area of likely origin (Harlan 1982, 1993)	Chronology date (bp)	Comment	Location	Reference
Tef (*Eragrostis tef*)	Northern highlands of Eritrea and Ethiopia	c. 2000 c. 2000	1 1, 2	Lalibela (Ethiopia) Hajar bin Humeid (Yemen)	Barnett (1999) van Beek (1969)

Notes

1. Stratigraphic association
2. Ceramic impression rather than charred grain or seeds

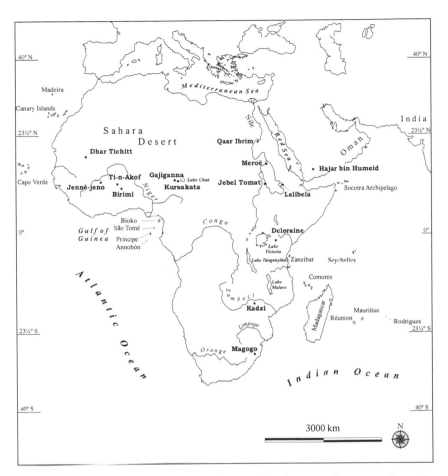

Figure 2.4. Africa showing sites discussed in the text relevant to the early domestication and spread of domestic cereals.

a classic demonstration of the principle of equifinality. Whether archaeology can convincingly show that one of these involved cultivation of *wild* cereals before morphological domestication remains moot.

Development and Spread of Food Production in Equatorial and Subequatorial Africa

If the Savanna Complex is poorly known, reliable evidence for its Forest Margin cousin scarcely exists. Its staples pose particular problems because oil palm is neither cultivated nor morphologically domesticated, while yams are virtually unrecoverable, though advances in identifying charred soft tissues and phytoliths (Piperno 1988; Hather 1991) and a broadening of horizons beyond traditional fixations with cereals (D. Phillipson 1993a, 115) offer hope. Oil palm kernels recur on ceramic Later Stone Age sites from Ghana to Cameroon and south into Gabon and Congo, but we remain unable to archaeologically confirm, or disconfirm, their linkage with yams (Stahl 1994). Whether early access to plantains could have facilitated agricultural settlement also remains just a tantalizing prospect for now (chapter 4). Poor preservation make hunting and herding equally elusive, but sheep and goats reached southern Cameroon by 500 cal. B.C. and the Great Lakes area by early in the first millennium cal. A.D. (van Neer 2000). Understanding farming settlement of Africa's rainforests thus depends heavily for now on linguistic evidence, in particular studies of the Bantu language family, which, originating along the Nigeria-Cameroon border, extends across most of subequatorial Africa. Sutton (1994–95) consolidates recent research on the expansion of farming across this area.

Vansina's (1990, 1995) work is fundamental in indicating that Proto-Western-Bantu speakers hunted, fished, kept goats, and grew oil palm and yams, initially without knowledge of iron. This fits archaeological residues dating to within the period 300–1200 cal. B.C. in Gabon and Congo-Brazzaville (de Maret 1986; Denbow 1990), but partly overlapping dates for iron working are difficult to understand (Eggert 1993).[4] Farmers initially moved along the coast, perhaps taking advantage of forest fragmentation under more arid conditions during the first millennium cal. B.C. (Schwartz 1992). However, by 775 cal. B.C. they were already using rivers to access the interior (Eggert 1993). Expansion of both Bantu and farming (not necessarily always synonymous) may have proceeded through assimilation of, or take-up by, indigenous foragers, as much as by demographic growth (Vansina 1995). It is thus important to note that suggestions that equatorial forests were previously uninhabited because of a dearth of accessible protein or carbohydrate (Headland 1987; Bailey et al. 1989) are difficult to sustain. Even in the Ituri itself, where such arguments were first made, occupation is evident through the Holocene (Mercader et al. 2000). Cameroon (Lavachery 2001), Gabon (Clist 1995), and Congo-Brazzaville (Elenga et al. 1994) provide similar findings. Vansina (1994–95) and Bahuchet (1993) reinforce the case for preagricultural forager rainforest occupation on linguistic grounds.[5]

Beyond 10° S, Forest Margin Complex economies found their expansion constrained by increasing aridity (Vansina 1994–95). That terms for cereal agriculture and cattle keeping in Angola's Western Bantu languages are all of Eastern Bantu origin supports a scenario in which these domesticates replaced earlier, less successful root-/tree-crop economies (Vansina

1994–95). Cattle were certainly present near Luanda by 900 (Lanfranchi and Clist 1990) but perhaps arrived considerably before this. Even so, and testifying to the key role of cereals, farming economies did not penetrate much beyond the 500-mm isohyet because insufficient and unreliable rainfall made dependable harvests impossible.

Speakers of Proto–Eastern Bantu, Bantu's second main division, apparently spread eastward along the equatorial forest's northern periphery, ending up around the Great Lakes. Linguistic reconstructions suggest they acquired cattle, sheep, and cereals there, the first two possibly from Pastoral Neolithic groups, but perhaps all three from communities not yet identified archaeologically (Schoenbrun 1998). Direct botanical and faunal evidence is again virtually lacking, but Urewe pottery, iron-smelting debris, and pollen sequences demonstrative of land clearance place farmers in the Interlacustrine area by 500 cal. B.C. Urewe is the earliest known component of the Chifumbaze Complex, which includes almost all early farming iron-using communities in eastern, south-central, and southern Africa (D. Phillipson 1993a). Their spread was rapid, facilitated perhaps by a conservative colonization strategy ("hopping" from one favorable location to another), as well as recurrent droughts, loss of soil fertility, and community fission (Jones 1984; Vansina 1995). The subsistence strategies of southern Africa's early farming communities are rather better known than those of other areas. They depended on pearl millet, finger millet, and sorghum as staples, supplemented by legumes and melons and combined with herding, hunting, and gathering; regional variation exists, but cattle, sheep, and goat were present from the start (Mitchell 2002a). The cereals' temperature and precipitation requirements (Huffman 1996a) helped confine these early farmers to savanna environments, with declining summer rainfall placing a limit to Chifumbaze settlement at 33.5° S (Nogwaza 1994). Mid-second millennium communities settled the interior's highveld grasslands, but there too increasing aridity prevented further movement west (Maggs 1976). Instead, southern Africa's arid western third was home not only to hunter-gatherers, but also to herders, historically speakers of Khoe languages, thought to have initially obtained livestock from farmers in northern Botswana or southwestern Zambia (Mitchell 2002a). Initially just sheep occur. Perhaps incorporated into otherwise largely unchanged forager lifeways, they reached the Cape (back into their *Ur*-Mediterranean-type habitat) by 2,000 years ago. Cattle were acquired later, and development of the large pastoralist communities encountered by Europeans after 1488 may have been the work of a few centuries (Sadr 1998). Research continues apace on this question and on the archaeological identity of those from whom sheep were first obtained: dates for cattle and Chifumbaze assemblages in southern Zambia of the terminal centuries B.C. (D. Phillipson 1989), though suggestive, need confirmation, just like linguists' claims for the presence in the same region of non-Bantu-speaking farmers (Ehret 2002).

Trans-Mediterranean Connections in North Africa

While adoption of the Near Eastern Complex is well attested in Egypt, research on early food production in the Maghreb remains limited (figure 2.5). Sheep and goats occur in Algeria's Aurès Mountains ca. 5400 cal. B.C., but cattle, which are initially rare (Roubet 1979), need their domesticated status reassessed (Gautier 1987). Hard evidence for cultivation is lacking before the first millennium B.C., even if pottery and ground-stone tools encourage some researchers to apply the term *Neolithic* (Muzzolini 1993). The situation recalls that of the western

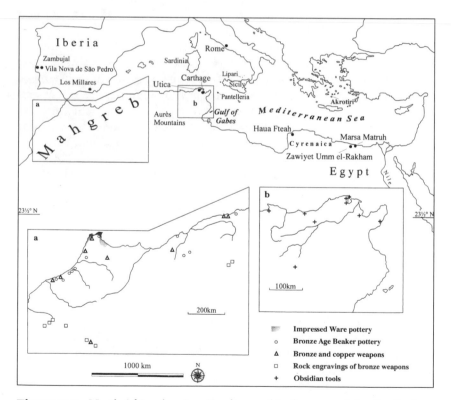

Figure 2.5. North Africa showing sites discussed in the text and the distributions in the Maghreb of Impressed Ware, Iberian metalwork, Beaker pottery (a), and Pantellerian obsidian (b) (redrawn after Camps 1982, figures 8.7, 8.8, and 8.17).

Mediterranean's European shores where integration of pottery, sheep, and goats into hunter-gatherer lifestyles may have preceded cultivation and domesticated cattle and pigs by at least 2,000 years (Lewthwaite 1989; cf. Zilhão 2000). If the same pattern prevailed in North Africa—and we should check that it does not result from a bias in favor of excavating rock shelters instead of open-air sites—then it reinforces the desirability of considering the westward expansion of the Near Eastern Complex in a framework that *avoids* seeing the Mediterranean as a divide. It also makes us ask what encouraged more intensive commitment to farming: climate change, increased demographic pressure because of immigration from the Sahara, development of exchange ties with such immigrant groups, or some combination of these factors? Comparison with developments in the Sahel might prove illuminating.

Two broad "Neolithic" traditions are evident in the Maghreb. On the high plains of northern Algeria and Tunisia the Neolithic of Capsian Tradition has stone tools suggesting continuity from earlier hunter-gatherer communities, another parallel with western Europe. Entirely coastal in location and found principally in northwestern Morocco is the Mediterranean Neolithic, which dates 7000–4400 cal. B.C. (Lubell et al. 1992). Here again sheep and goats are the only definite domesticates, with cattle and pigs of uncertain status. The term "Mediterranean" alludes to more than just geographical position, as ceramic motifs, including *Cardium* shell impressions, recall the Impressed Ware found along that sea's northern shores from Andalucía to Sicily. Trans-Mediterranean connections (see figure 2.5, insets a and b) are also attested by participation in networks transmitting obsidian from the islands of Lipari and Pantelleria to Tunisia and northeastern Algeria. Offshore fishing (Souville 1958–59) suggests that the Maghreb's inhabitants could have visited these sources themselves, and moved yet more widely by sea. Although obsidian forms only a tiny component of North African lithic assemblages (Camps 1982), such contacts raise the possibility that sheep and goats, and perhaps other elements of the Near Eastern Complex, entered the Maghreb by sea from Europe, rather than by land from the east, where the arid hinterland of the Gulf of Gabès may have hindered movement. Looking the other way, however, we know so little that transmission of innovations from North Africa into Europe cannot be excluded (Whittle 1996, 290). It also seems unlikely that farming was simply spread across the North African littoral by an intrusive Near Eastern–derived, Afroasiatic-speaking population (McCall 1998; Barker 2003 [*pace* Cavalli-Sforza et al. 1994]).

In the third and fourth millennia cal. B.C., renewed trans-Mediterranean contacts are evident, this time in the form of copper artifacts of Iberian manufacture and sherds of Beaker pottery from near Oran as well as the

Moroccan coast (Harrison and Gilman 1977). Later bronze weapons, again of Iberian type, are more common and constitute the subject matter of poorly dated rock engravings in the Atlas Mountains (Alaoui and Searight 1997). Parallels between Maghrebi stone-built tombs and others in Spain, Italy, and Malta can also be identified, but neither they nor their associated pottery necessarily require migration for their explanation, still less movement into, rather than out of, Africa (Leighton 1999 *pace* Camps 1982). Indeed, evidence for trans-Mediterranean connections is little greater in North Africa than in Iberia, where ivory and ostrich eggshell occur at Copper Age sites like Los Millares, Vila Nova de São Pedro, and Zambujal. However, their small amounts caution against assuming use as prestige goods to differentiate status (Whittle 1996, 349); precisely the same caveat should hold when interpreting exotic artifacts in North African contexts.

If the western Maghreb remains poorly known, so too do Tripolitania and Cyrenaica. Haua Fteah is a key site where sheep and goats first appear ca. 5400 cal. B.C.; dates for cattle are uncertain (Klein and Scott 1986). Egyptian references to metal-working peoples who presumably lived in Cyrenaica (but cf. Nibbi 1993) require that they engaged heavily in livestock rearing, while mention of "towns," the massive Nineteenth Dynasty fortress at Zawiyet Umm el-Rakham (Snape 2003), and the sheer numbers who later infiltrated Egypt all suggest herding must have been closely integrated with cultivation of cereals and other crops (O'Connor 1993a). Herodotus (IV 172) records precisely such an economy in the fifth century B.C., and simple lack of research is the most likely explanation for the absence of substantiating archaeological observations (Barker 1989). A variety of imported Aegean products at Marsa Matruh do, however, imply its use as a Bronze Age port of trade (White 2002); frescoes from Akrotiri interpreted as depicting the arrival of Minoan ships on the Libyan coast might support this (Marinatos 1974).

Yet apart from this one site and Egypt itself, North Africa shows little sign of participating in a "Bronze Age world-system" (in the sense of Sherratt 1993). If Maghrebi populations did realign themselves toward the Mediterranean as the desert dried this is scarcely evident (*pace* Insoll and MacLean 1995); enduring isolation punctuated by occasional trans-Mediterranean, southward, and eastward contacts seems an apter characterization. This is all the more striking given Mycenaean and Cypriot interest in Sicily, Lipari, and Sardinia (Dickinson 1994). Was this, as Sestieri (2002) suggests, not only a matter of economic geography, but also of physical conditions, given that the prevailing currents and winds favor east–west movement from the Levant and the Aegean to Spain via Sicily, rather than by a North African coastal route? Was it also because comparable levels of socioeconomic complexity were required for sustained trade, and these were lacking in North Africa? Or was it because the rest of North Africa could offer little not available more readily from Egypt, though Hayward (1990) suggests ivory as an export channeled through Libya, Richardson (2000) gum, *silphion,* and ostrich eggshell or feathers as additional products? In any event, parallels exist with the first millennium B.C. when Greek activity again concentrated in the north and central Mediterranean. Cyrenaica, virtually the only exception, saw five Greek colonies established in the seventh and sixth centuries B.C. Primarily agricultural settlements, they later engaged heavily in trade as well, notably in *silphion,* a plant of fabled medicinal value (Law 1978). Farther west, Phoenician colonization was similarly sparse, reinforced by the scarcity of readily exploitable metals along the North African littoral and emphasizing Carthage and Utica as way stations established en route to the rich ore mines of Iberia (Aubet 2001). Only as Carthage asserted its independence did trading sites multiply, tapping into the Maghreb's ivory, skins, metals, and cedar. How precisely such trade, along with political and military interactions, promoted the growth of urbanism and centralization within indigenous states like Mauretania and Numidia is little known, though royal funerary monuments document eclectic mixtures of Greek, Egyptian, and Punic tastes (Brett and Fentress 1996). Comparisons with similar processes on the periphery of Etruscan and Roman activity north of the Alps remain even more elusive (Cunliffe 1997). The eventual result, however, following Carthage's destruction (146 B.C.), was the same: incorporation into the Roman Empire (sidebar 6, page 144).

Patterns in the Emergence and Spread of African Systems of Food Production

This is far from being a comprehensive review of the history of African food production; several topics are addressed with woeful brevity. Yet I hope it provides a useful background to the chapters that follow and indicates that right from the start of the Holocene Africa's interactions with the rest of the world, and the evidence cited for them, are crucial to understanding the continent's past. Two studies emphasize this well: on the one hand, the strengthening case for an indigenous African domestication of cattle, on the other the controversy surrounding the domestication of sub-Saharan plant staples and the key role of South Asian evidence in requiring that at least some were grown in Africa long before the earliest dates that we yet possess for them there. In concluding this chapter, I consider some of the broader patterns that may be detectable in the growth of African systems of food production.

One convenient starting point is Africa's geography, particularly its north–south axis, which parallels that of the Americas[6] and differs from Eurasia's mostly east–west orientation. Animals, plants, and people moving from one latitudinal zone to another necessarily contend with differences in rainfall seasonality and quantity, habitat, and disease prevalence (Diamond 1997; figure 2.6). The impact of this simple observation on the spread of farming in Africa is readily apparent. Examples include the confinement of the Near Eastern Complex to the Middle Nile, the Ethiopian-Eritrean highlands, and areas north of 20° N; the suggestion that tsetse infestation initially constrained southward movement of cattle herders from the Sahara;

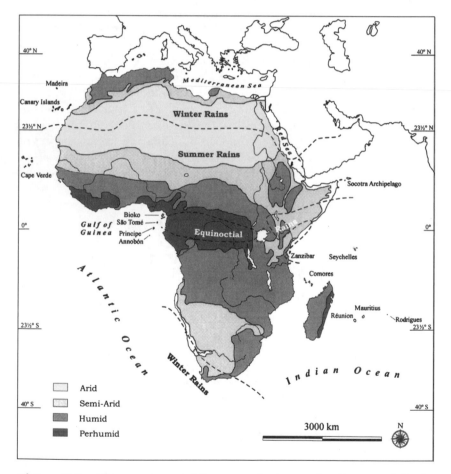

Figure 2.6. Africa: major rainfall patterns (redrawn after Butzer and Cooke 1982, figure 1.7).

the limited possibilities of the Forest Margin Complex for early farmers set-tling in Angola; and their inability to colonize South Africa's western third where summer-rainfall crops could not grow. On the other hand, it is impor-tant to note that some habitats extend over many degrees of latitude, per-mitting readier access to new areas than might first seem likely: the rapid movement of early farmers along the Indian Ocean coast from Kenya to KwaZulu-Natal comes to mind (D. Phillipson 1993a). Nor can we forget that east–west movement is facilitated *within* latitudinal zones. Desperately underresearched, the possibilities of movement from the Chad Basin to the Nile Valley, and beyond in both directions, should not be ignored, not least when thinking of the dispersal of technologies, including new food resources, among them sorghum and pearl millet. Recent work in Sudan's Wadi Howar, which helps connect the two areas just named, points sug-gestively to a reorientation of contacts from north/south to east/west around 4000 cal. B.C., the time when the *Leiterband* ceramics found there extend westward as far as Mali and cattle keeping first became a major economic pursuit (Jesse 2000; Keding 2000).

Partly mapping onto latitude, disease has recently come to the fore as a significant factor in understanding the expansion of African food-production systems (figure 2.7). Gifford-Gonzalez (2000) identifies several major livestock diseases endemic to sub-Saharan Africa. Trypanosomiasis is, in fact, among the least deadly because its impacts can be mitigated by reducing the brush cover that tsetse flies require, shifting pastures sea-sonally to avoid infested areas, keeping sheep and goats, but especially goats, rather than cattle, or employing dwarf, humpless cattle breeds tol-erant of the parasite. Other infections are more serious: bovine malignant catarrhal fever, corridor disease, and East Coast fever, which are hosted by wildebeest and buffalo, may all produce a mortality rate of 90 to 100 percent on initial exposure. Though strategies exist to combat these threats, their impact on livestock-keeping communities expanding into new habitats cannot be underestimated. The halt to the southward move-ment of livestock in East Africa ca. 1200 cal. B.C. and the fact that sheep expanded from the Zambezi to the Cape well ahead of cattle may reflect the existence in both eastern and south-central Africa of overlapping wildebeest and buffalo populations—a situation of double jeopardy for herders. The model clearly needs refinement. It does not, for instance, take into account new data, like the apparent presence of Pastoral Neolithic pottery (as yet without livestock) in southern Tanzania (Chami and Kwekason 2003) or possible fluctuations in wild game distributions. However, it does provide powerful insights into some of the constraints affecting the dispersal of cattle, raising the question, did similar restric-tions affect the expansion of other domesticates, plant and animal alike?

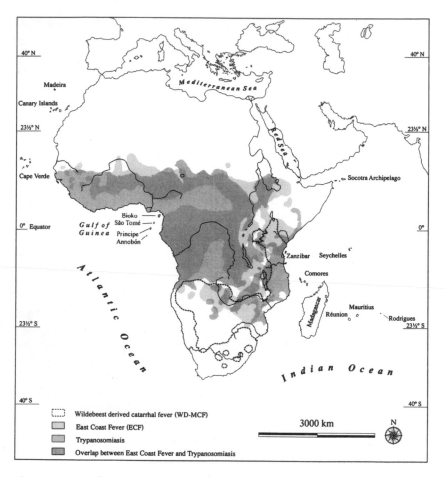

40° N

Madeira

Canary Islands

23½° N

Cape Verde

0° Equator

Mediterranean Sea

Red Sea

Socotra Archipelago

Bioko
São Tomé
Príncipe
Annobón

Gulf of
Guinea

Zanzibar   Seychelles

Comores

Atlantic

Ocean

Madagascar

Mauritius
Réunion
Rodrigues
23½° S

23½° S

40° S

Indian   Ocean

40° S

40° N

23½° N

0°

Wildebeest derived catarrhal fever (WD-MCF)

East Coast Fever (ECF)

Trypanosomiasis

Overlap between East Coast Fever and Trypanosomiasis

3000 km   N

Figure 2.7. Africa: major disease barriers to the spread of domestic livestock south of the Sahara (redrawn after Gifford-Gonzalez 2000).

The high mortality rates produced by African horse sickness, another sub-Saharan endemic epizootic, suggest that they did (Clutton-Brock 2000).

The impact of these diseases is, of course, so grave because horses, cattle, sheep, and goats are foreign to sub-Saharan Africa. But a wealth of antelope and other ungulates are not. Why were they not domesticated? A common answer is that they were so plentiful that the need did not arise (Reader 1998), but this is to accept a quite crude kind of demographic pressure argument for the origins of food production and, in any case, does not explain why cattle, rather than hartebeest, oryx, or some other bovid, were domesticated in northeast Africa. That attempts were made seems likely: Uan Afuda's Barbary sheep suggest as much, likewise perhaps representations of tethered giraffe in rock engravings from Jebel Uweinat (van Noten 1978) and elsewhere and of tamed gazelle and even hyenas in Old Kingdom tomb reliefs in Egypt (Brewer et al. 1994). In the Egyptian case, at least, such depictions may not show reality, but rather support the king's claims to control and tame the disruptive forces of the cosmos (Kemp 1989; cf. Dupuy 1988 for a similar argument in respect of tethered giraffe engravings in Niger). The Barbary sheep evidence, on the other hand, seems unquestionable (Cremaschi and Di Lernia 1999).

But if attempts were made to domesticate sub-Saharan ungulates, they were unsuccessful. The reason for this is something frequently overlooked by proponents of predominantly "ecological" or "social" models that purport to explain how food production developed (Rowley-Conwy 1986): it takes two to tango. Plants and animals, in other words, are not a tabula rasa on which people can do whatever they please. Of fifty-one bovid taxa native to sub-Saharan Africa, not one was domesticated. The reason surely lies in their behavior as much as in the absence of relevant resource imbalances or cultural pressures. Analysis of their social structure shows, in fact, that only two (eland and buffalo) even approximate to the requisite pattern, one that is hierarchical, nonterritorial, permissive of stable multimale associations, not disposed to immediate flight, and ready to breed in captivity (Diamond 1997). In short, for Africans to take up animal husbandry cattle, pigs, and donkeys were virtually the only indigenous options, and all occurred wild only within and *north* of the modern Sahara.

The case for cultivated plants is less well made, but three points are telling. First, Africa south of the Mediterranean has few large-seed grasses, the kinds likely to be foremost among candidates for domestication, though the case of tef shows this is not always determinant (Blumler 1992). Second, no significant food plant is indigenous to Africa south of the Equator. Third, even where African crops were domesticated, they were frequently superseded by higher-yielding Indonesian and American crops once these became available. Though this process is most visible with maize and cassava, it holds true too of the spread, adoption, and diversification of plantains, bananas, and even yams. Taken together, the limited productivity of many African food plants probably did affect the buildup of large, sedentary communities south of the Sahara and the possibilities for social complexity that they held, but we should not be unduly pessimistic in this regard. Cattle held potential for wealth accumulation and manipulation since at least 2000 B.C. (MacDonald 1998b), while the densely populated, earthwork-building urban societies of southern Nigeria were presumably founded upon a long history of cultivating yams with oil palm (Connah 2001).

Precisely where Africa's plants and animals were domesticated remains obscure. Cattle appear first in Egypt's Western Desert, and genetic and archaeological evidence might support the case for a quite focused domestication event. But for other domestic animals, no such precision exists. Turning to food plants, Harlan (1971) argued that domestication proceeded through multiple experiments across a broad front in a "noncentric" pattern. Though consistent with the interest taken in sorghum, pearl millet, and other grasses by hunter-gatherer-fishers and pastoralists alike across the Sahara and the Sahel during the early to mid Holocene, this has yet to be confirmed by hard evidence. Perhaps the dates now becoming available for pearl millet support it, but the model seems at variance with the picture emerging for plant domestication in better-studied regions. Thus DNA analyses pinpoint quite specific domestication localities for maize (Doebley 1990), beans (Gepts 1990), and several Near Eastern crops (Zohary 1996). Were Africa's crop complexes truly different? Recent genetic work with pearl millet that suggests wild populations in southern Mauritania and the Lake Chad region are closest to the cultivated form (Tostain 1998), and comparable studies placing the domestication of cowpeas in southeastern Nigeria (Vaillancourt and Weeden 1992), suggest the answer is probably no. However, even if Harlan's original hypothesis were partly sustained, food production in subequatorial Africa clearly depended almost entirely upon introduced resources.

Overstating diffusion and migration and positing overclose relationships between language and subsistence have undoubtedly hindered our grasp of the history of African farming systems, contributing to a view of the continent as an archaeological cul-de-sac (Stahl 1984). The reality was certainly more complex than a relentless "wave of advance"—new ideas about the spread of Bantu languages (Vansina 1995) and the partly drought-induced punctuated expansion of livestock keeping across northern Africa (Hassan 2002) attest as much. The historical fragility of associations between one ethnohistorically associated taxon and another are increasingly evident in many parts of the continent, as in the Chad Basin where diverse paths were forged in combining and recombining "wild" and "domesticated," "indigenous" and "exotic." Nevertheless, collectively those paths do seem to have enunciated general patterns, crudely describable in north–south terms and more specifically grounded in the availability and nonavailability of species suitable for domestication, the ecology of disease, and the basic layout of the continent. How that geography contributed to Africa's most distinctive farming complex, that of the Ethiopian-Eritrean highlands, forms part of the next chapter.

Notes

1. Since this chapter was completed I have been able to access Hildebrand and Marshall (2002), which provides a more up-to-date and comprehensive synthesis of the archaeology of livestock-keeping by East Pastoral Neolithic communities.

2. Other factors include the fact that sorghum photosynthesizes more efficiently in arid conditions with high temperatures and light intensities, even though it cannot be used to make bread and is toxic if fed to livestock, except immediately after seed ripening (Cappers 1999). Note, however, that Nachtigal (1967, 654) observed wheat and barley being grown at Kukawa, the capital of Bornu, only 13° north of the Equator, in the nineteenth century.

3. Some of these pathways were long. At Gajiganna in Nigeria's Chad Basin, where cattle, sheep, and goats occur from ca. 2100 cal. B.C. and domesticated pearl millet at ca. 3000 cal. B.C., all the stone tools were made on raw materials imported from up to 200 km away (Breunig et al. 1996). Such connections presumably facilitated the spread of domesticates and knowledge of them in ways that we as yet only dimly apprehend. Furthermore, aridity-induced discontinuities in occupation in many areas of the Sahel in the first millennium cal. B.C. make tracing such pathways even harder (Breunig and Neumann 2002).

4. Arguments over the exotic or local origins of sub-Saharan iron working and other metallurgical technologies are examined in chapter 5. Suffice it to say here that the part of iron agricultural tools in explaining the spread of farming beyond the Equator has certainly been overstated.

5. Interestingly, debate in another great equatorial forest, Amazonia, is reaching a similar conclusion (Politis 2002).

6. Maize, domesticated first in west-central Mexico and thus a tropical crop, spread fairly early to Andean South America and north into the American Southwest. The mainstay of a cereal-legume complex including beans and squash, its take-up across eastern North America was slow, perhaps because varieties had to be developed that could withstand lower temperatures and shorter growing seasons (B. Smith 1998). In both North and South America these factors ultimately set boundaries beyond which maize could not spread. To take just one example, was second millennium farming settlement of southern Africa's temperate highveld similarly dependent on new varieties of sorghum and pearl millet or merely a fortuitous climatic upturn (Mitchell 2002a)?

CHAPTER 3

The Nile and
Red Sea Corridors

What exactly is Africa?

—O'CONNOR AND REID 2003, 2

ONLY IN THE northeast is Africa physically attached
to another landmass, and it is there that its earliest
state societies developed. This combination of historical primacy and location frames many discussions of the relations
between Egypt and its neighbors, but is only one of the themes addressed
here. Northeastern Africa's mountains, deserts, and savannas are tran-
sected by two broadly north–south trending features, the Nile Valley and
the Red Sea (figure 3.1). The first of these, and specifically the part termed
Nubia, has been called a "corridor to Africa" (Adams 1977). A similar
designation is applicable to the Red Sea, which connects Africa to Arabia
and both to the Mediterranean and Indian Ocean worlds. In this chapter
I look at the role connections along these corridors played in the cultural
trajectories pursued in Egypt, Sudan, and the Ethiopian-Eritrean highlands.
Links beyond these regions into Africa and Southwest Asia, and the eventual impact on northeastern African populations of successively introduced world religions thus form an important part of the discussion.
Implicit throughout is the question that heads this chapter, how far these
areas have an African, rather than Asian or Mediterranean, heritage, and
what has been the impact of their connections with those other parts of
the world.

Figure 3.1. Location of sites and other places discussed in chapter 3.

Gift of the Nile?

If Herodotus (II 5) termed it the gift of this wholly African river, Egypt has also frequently been isolated inside a Near Eastern–Mediterranean cocoon, its relations with the rest of Africa reduced to those of a colonial exploiter. Reasons for this include Pharaonic Egypt's own accounts of its interactions with its African neighbors, an overemphasis on monuments and texts in much of Nubian archaeology, the still limited research carried out elsewhere in northeastern Africa, Egypt's nineteenth century imperialist ventures in Sudan, and Europe's appropriation of Pharaonic civilization as ancestral to its own (O'Connor 1990). And yet archaeology shows that the origins of Ancient Egyptian society lay in the complex interactions between long-established populations along the Nile, the Saharan herders whom we encountered in chapter 2 and, in a few specific ways, the inhabitants of Palestine, Syria, and Mesopotamia. Furthermore, the developments out of which the first Egyptian state grew were common to a much longer section of the Nile Valley than that lying north of the First Cataract.

From the start, agriculturally based societies along the Nile reflect contacts with the Levant, not just in rearing sheep and goats, but also in growing wheat and barley, two Southwest Asian crops. Distinctively shaped stone artifacts and ceramics strengthen these connections, but ground stone axes, tabular flint tools, and other kinds of arrowheads point too to the presence of Saharan elements (Hassan 1988). Strong similarities between the Badarian pottery found in Upper Egypt from 4000 cal. B.C. and other rippled, burnished, black-topped ceramics from the eastern Sahara reinforce this conclusion (Hassan 1997, 406), while ceramic sourcing and Predynastic-like stone tools from Libya's Acacus region point to contacts in the opposite direction (Di Lernia 2002). The need to maintain distant connections as an insurance mechanism against drought, settlement along the Nile by pastoralist populations escaping periodic, and intensifying, arid spells, and their merger with long-established riverine communities, who themselves perhaps moved seasonally into adjacent grasslands (T. Wilkinson 2003), may explain such patterns. Badarian-like ceramics and similarities in burial practices also show that Egypt and Nubia shared a common cultural outlook at this time (Wengrow 2003). Kadero, a fifth millennium cal. B.C. village near Khartoum, is one example of this, its grave goods already documenting considerable social differentiation and access to exotic items from the Red Sea and the eastern Sahara (Krzyzaniak 1991). In fishing and keeping livestock too it was comparable to contemporary Egyptian communities, its emphasis on collecting (growing?) sorghum a divergence due to its location within the summer-rainfall belt.[1] Along the Lower Nile, where wild cereals were few, sorghum and millet absent, and hunter-gatherers emphasized roots and tubers, wheat and barley were perhaps adopted to counteract the adverse consequences on wild plant and fish stocks of unpredictably high, low, or short-lived floods. Domesticated cereals not only could be stored, but were also more flexible in their planting locations. In addition some southern Levantine populations probably relocated to Egypt as a result of an abrupt arid episode across the eastern Mediterranean ca. 5800 cal. B.C. (Rossignol-Strick 2002); ornaments of stone and shell certainly traveled through the Levant from the Red Sea and Sinai, and earlier exchange networks reaching as far as the Nile are likely (Bar-Yosef and Belfer-Cofen 1989).

To the connections even earliest Egyptian farmers maintained beyond the Nile was soon added copper from the Eastern Desert and Sinai (Midant-Reynes 2000). Excavations at Maadi near Cairo have produced the widest range of copper items, including axes, as in contemporary Palestine. Hundreds of Syro-Palestinian pots and similarities in flint industries, house form, and burial practice reinforce this connection (W. Hayes 1964; Caneva et al. 1989). Maadi's inhabitants probably traded with the Levant using donkey caravans (Caneva et al. 1987), but ships were also used. At one port, Buto, north Syrian pottery and clay cones similar to those used to decorate temples in Mesopotamia expand the evidence for foreign contacts (von der Way 1987). What significance do these connections have for understanding the processes leading to the establishment of a single Egyptian state ca. 3100 B.C.? Emery's (1961) idea of an all-conquering "Early Dynastic Race" of Mesopotamian origin is certainly outmoded, but the late fourth millennium B.C. did see the gradual adoption through much of the Delta of a material culture similar to that of Upper Egypt. Insofar as this reflects extended cultural or political influence, one motivation may have been securing access to foreign trade, including the Lebanese cedar needed for large boats able to control the Nile and move goods along it (Bard 2000).

Competition between emerging chiefdoms in Upper Egypt, where the scope for agricultural expansion was much reduced relative to the Delta, was very likely important in the gradual unification of the Lower Nile Valley. Inventing an ideology of rulership that legitimized the establishment of elites and their privileged access to resources was critical to its success (Kemp 1989). Much Pharaonic iconography, including the king's characterization as a "strong bull" and the importance of bovine deities (Frankfort 1948), draws upon ancient pastoralist roots, an origin reinforced by Late Neolithic ceremonialism and cattle burials at Nabta Playa (Wendorf and Schild 1998) and rock engravings in the Eastern Desert (T. Wilkinson 2003). Exotic preciosities and ideas also displayed and reinforced status. As one example, consider the contents of Tomb 11 at Hierakonpolis's Locality 6, dating to just before the First Dynasty: turquoise from Sinai, Ethiopian obsidian, Anatolian silver, and Afghan lapis lazuli (Adams and Friedman 1992). As well as moving upstream along the Nile, such items could have been introduced via desert wadis from the Red Sea coast. Artistic motifs characteristic of Early Bronze Age Elam, rather than Mesopotamia's own Uruk culture, may support this: a victorious human figure shown between two beasts and the distinctive niched palace façade (*serekh*) later used to frame kings' names and decorate Early Dynastic royal tombs (H. Smith 1992). Here then, in a much more nuanced way, may lie the truth behind Emery's "Early Dynastic Race."

Lower Nubia participated in the same processes of expanding exchange and social differentiation during the fourth millennium B.C. Elite individuals buried at Qustul used much the same symbolism of rule, so much so that B. Williams (1986) suggested that Egyptian kingship originated there, a conclusion now rendered unlikely by earlier examples of royal iconography in Egypt proper (Baines 1995). Raw materials obtained from the Eastern Desert and farther south that could be exported to Egypt, such as ivory, ebony, and pelts, may have fuelled the Qustul polity's growth, but Lower Nubia's narrower floodplain constrained its agricultural, demographic, and political potentials compared with its Upper Egyptian neighbor. Pottery and stone vessels of Egyptian origin in graves confirm intensifying trade in the late Predynastic period (Takamiya 1994), and cultural transfers *from* Nubia *to* Egypt are suggested by cattle burials like those from Qustul at Hierakonpolis's Locality 6 royal cemetery (Hoffman 1982). However, once united, Egypt aggressively sought more firmly defined frontiers, closer control over valued imports, and reduced competition from once powerful neighbors, provoking a population collapse in Lower Nubia (T. Wilkinson 1999).

Egypt at the Fulcrum of Asia and Africa

A prime function of Egyptian kings was to subjugate foreigners, controlling the political and ideological potential for disorder that they embodied (Kemp 1989). More prosaically, access to valued goods was also desired. I look at how these actions were pursued along Nile and Red Sea corridors in a moment, concentrating here on Egypt's position at the fulcrum between Asia and Africa and its place within the wider Mediterranean world. I. Shaw (2000) summarizes the position for the pre-Muslim period, and I identify only some key features here. State-sponsored trading expeditions into Palestine were one enduring strategy, sometimes supported by a permanent Egyptian presence, as at En Besor during the First Dynasty. Aromatic oils and resins were important imports, direct mining of Sinai's turquoise and copper a later development. From 2700 B.C. Egyptian interests focused on the Lebanese port of Byblos and the import of cedar, resins, oils, and later copper; shipborne cargoes may have been twice as fast as land-based caravans (T. Wilkinson 1999, 162). Byblos remained key to Egypt's Levantine trade for centuries, its rulers taking Egyptian titles and using Egyptian artifacts in their burials (Markoe 2000). Until the mid-second millennium B.C., military operations to obtain goods or deter hostile neighbors were relatively unimportant, though forts to control Egypt's northeastern frontier are known from the Twelfth Dynasty. Excavations at Tell el-Dab'a show an Egyptianized Asiatic population already resident in the eastern Delta around 1800 B.C., well before this site developed into Avaris, the capital of one of the polities into which Egypt fragmented a century later. Ruled by the Hyksos, a dynasty of Asiatic origin, Avaris was vastly bigger than any contemporary Palestinian city, dominated Egypt's northern half, and maintained trading ties with the Levant, Nubia, and Minoan Crete (Bourriau 2000).

The introduction of the horse and chariot were two lasting consequences of Hyksos rule, both spreading west and south from Egypt in succeeding centuries. Another, after Ahmose I, first king of the Eighteenth Dynasty, conquered Avaris and expelled the Hyksos, was a greatly enhanced Egyptian involvement in the power politics of the Near Eastern–Eastern Mediterranean world. Minoan-style frescoes in the Eighteenth Dynasty palace at Avaris are one indication of this. Continued trade with the Bronze Age Aegean is also indicated by later tomb frescoes at Thebes and by Egyptian (or Egyptian mediated) products in Greece. Examples include hippopotamus ivory (Krzyzkowska 1984) and the African ebony from the famous Ulu Burun shipwreck (Bass et al. 1989). More directly, the New Kingdom Pharaohs sought prestige and tribute from developing an empire in the Levant: glass, metal, and wooden objects of Syrian manufacture became status symbols for high officials, and the worship of Syrian deities, such as Astart, was heavily promoted once Egypt's original competitor, Mitanni, became an ally. It and other states sought Egyptian gold and political support, as revealed in the diplomatic correspondence preserved in the Amarna letters, but from 1340 B.C. Egyptian control withered in the face of Hittite attacks, finally disappearing following the still poorly understood incursions of the Sea Peoples ca. 1200 B.C. (I. Shaw 2000).

While Egypt remained involved in international politics, it now did so from a much weaker position, not least because of internal political disunity. Briefly occupied by the Assyrians, it remained exposed to external conquest, passing successively, with only brief flourishes of independence, under Persian, Macedonian, and ultimately Roman rule (Bowman 1996). It was, however, during the last millennium B.C. that Egypt exercised some of its most enduring impacts on its Mediterranean neighbors. The ninth and tenth centuries B.C. saw renewed Egyptian influence on Phoenician art, especially in ivory and metalwork, influence transmitted westward to Greeks and Etruscans by Phoenician traders (Markoe 2000). Greek mercenaries formed a major component of Egypt's army during the Twenty-sixth Dynasty (664–525 B.C.), as well as the later struggles for independence from Persia. Archaeologically this is reflected in at least two large forts east of the Delta and by inscriptions as far south as Abu Simbel (J. Boardman 1999). Greek commercial interest in Egypt was channeled through a largely Greek settlement, Naucratis, in the western Delta, founded in the late seventh century B.C. Excavations have emphasized sanctuary areas, but there is good evidence for local production of faience statuettes and vases that were widely traded across the Mediterranean (figure 3.2), and for the exchange of silver coins and bullion for Egyptian corn. More indirectly, and without falling into line behind Bernal (1987, 1991), the initial development of Greek stone architecture, including the

Figure 3.2. An Egyptian-made aryballos (a small jar used to store oil or perfume) bearing the cartouche of the Pharaoh Apries (ruled 585–570 B.C.) from the Lipari islands, Italy (courtesy and copyright the Ashmolean Museum, Oxford).

Doric order, and colossal stone sculpture were certainly influenced by Egyptian examples; so too features of Greek and Etruscan polychrome painting (Barker and Rasmussen 1998, 259; J. Boardman 1999).

If foreign rulers, especially the Egyptian-based Ptolemies (322–30 B.C.), employed traditional Pharaonic iconography and built major temples as at Edfu and Philae, a growing degree of cultural syncretism also developed (Bowman 1996). The well-known encaustic portraits on Roman period mummy cases show this in art. In religion it is most striking in the hellenization of some Egyptian gods, the officially sanctioned development of the cult of Serapis, and the extent to which his worship and that of the goddess Isis spread across the Greco-Roman world; frescoes from Pompeii are just one indicator (Witt 1971). For the Romans, Egypt was a vital grain source, with more than one million metric tons dispatched annually to Rome in the early first century. Our knowledge of grain production comes largely from papyri, not archaeology, but the material evidence is stronger as regards Egypt's other attractions. First, it supplied three of the Roman world's major decorative stones: Aswan granite and porphyry and granodiorite from the Eastern Desert. The two last were first exploited in Roman times, and the granodiorite from Mons Claudianus is almost wholly restricted to a few major monuments in Rome itself. Excavations have focused on the quarries, forts, wells, and associated settlements that procured stone from there and nearby Mons Porphyrites, moving it by cart 120 km to the Nile and thence downstream to Alexandria (Peacock and Maxfield 1997). Egypt also gave the Greco-Roman world seaborne access to the products of the Indian Ocean. Evidence from excavations at the ports of Berenike and Myos Hormos as diverse as inscriptions (Sidebotham and Wendrich 2001–02), exotic foodstuffs (Cappers 1999; van der Veen 2003), and teak (Vermeeren 1999) documents contact with southern India, from which resident Tamil-speaking merchants derived. In return Roman Egypt exported the wine and gold of Tamil poems, the glass and ceramics found at Arikamedu (Begley 1996), and the silver of which the elder Pliny complained (Pliny's *Natural History* XII.84).

During the mid-first millennium, Egypt remained a key grain supplier for both the Eastern Roman (Byzantine) Empire and its Islamic successors, a role it played once again under Ottoman rule. In between, it was itself a major power within the same region, its Fatimid (969–1171), Ayyubid (1171–1250), and Mamluk[2] (1250–1517) rulers exploiting their pivotal position between African, Mediterranean, and Red Sea–Indian Ocean commercial systems (Hrbek 1977). Control over much of the Levant, though temporarily interrupted by the Frankish Crusader states (1099–1187), strengthened their position still further by including ports that were termini for land-based routes stretching east into Mesopotamia and Iran. So too did suzerainty over the Muslim holy cities of Mecca and Medina and the prestige, and pilgrim traffic, that went with it, but it was the disruption caused by the Mongol invasion of the Middle East in the mid-1200s that finally left the Red Sea, with Egypt at its apex, as the vehicle for up to 80 percent of the spice trade to the Indies from the thirteenth to sixteenth centuries (Curtin 1984, 121). The many mosques, religious schools, and other public buildings of medieval Cairo demonstrate Egypt's wealth and power during this period and themselves reflect stylistic influences from Iraq, Armenia, and Byzantium (Creswell 1952–59). Archaeological work has concentrated on al-Fustât, the earliest Muslim settlement at Cairo. Though constrained by later overburden and the site's enormous size, the scale of the city's planning, including water and sewage systems, is evident; so too the rapid development of glass, ceramic, and textile industries, which exported to Europe and the Middle East (Kubiak 1987; Scanlon 1994). As we shall see in chapter 4, they were joined by objects made in Egypt using ivory and rock crystal imported from East Africa.

Nubia: Corridor, Cul-de-sac, Colony, or Competitor?

A much earlier source of ivory was Nubia. Sometimes termed a corridor between the Mediterranean and sub-Saharan Africa (Adams 1977) or a cul-de-sac for Egyptian penetration of the African interior (Alexander 1988), Nubia was in fact a region with long-lasting cultural traditions of its own (O'Connor 1993b; Welsby 1996, 2002). While firmly rejecting the view that only by absorbing civilization from its neighbors could Nubians "detach themselves from the wholly primitive world of Black Africa" (Adams 1977, 20), economic, political, and cultural interactions with Egypt and the rest of Sudan have nonetheless been a constant feature of Nubian history. Here I look at the forms some of these interactions took.

Historically and prehistorically Nubia's population concentrated in three core areas of greatest agricultural potential, Lower Nubia, the Dongola Reach (base of the Bronze Age Kerma polity), and the Shendi Reach (homeland of the Meroitic state). Connecting these areas was the Nile, but six successive cataracts impede travel along it (figure 3.3). In addition, while downstream movement is aided by the current and upstream navigation by the prevailing northerly wind, the latter fails along the reverse bend between Abu Hamed and Debba. To circumvent the cataracts, boats had to offload and transport goods by land, though the Egyptians constructed canals at the First Cataract and a slide for dragging boats around the Second. The difficulties posed by the cataracts and the marked clumping of population along the river encouraged use of overland routes, initially with donkeys, but later using camels (Manzo

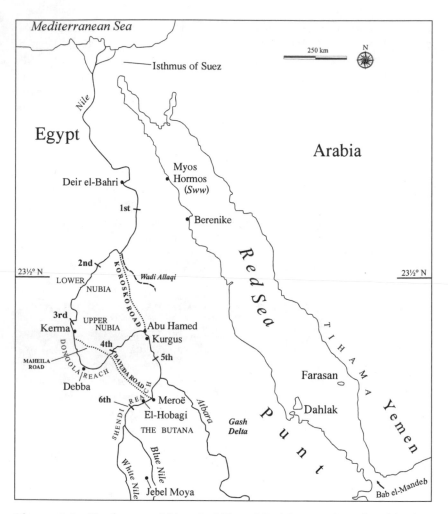

Figure 3.3. Northeastern Africa: the Nile and Red Sea corridors identifying key geographical features relevant to movement by land and sea and the likely location of Punt. The six cataracts of the Nile are numbered and dotted lines indicate the major cross-desert routes of Upper and Lower Nubia.

1999). Two routes in particular have been important, the Bayuda Road from near Meroë to just downstream of the Fourth Cataract and the Korosko Road from the apex of the Abu Hamed Reach to the Wadi Allaqi, home to much of Lower Nubia's gold, and thence to the Nile. A third route, the Maheila Road, cuts out much of the Dongola Bend, while others extend out from the Nile and its last tributary, the Atbara.

If Lower Nubia was "not far behind Egypt in the process of state formation" (T. Wilkinson 1999, 176) during the fourth millennium B.C., its proximity to Egypt saw this trajectory curtailed on the latter's unification. Manzo (1999) identifies the primary Pharaonic motive as being to inhibit the development of polities that could control key bottlenecks in exchange routes or interfere with Egyptian access to desired products, but without necessarily requiring direct Egyptian control over producing areas. As well as copper and gold from the Nubian desert, these products included others from south (sometimes significantly farther south) of the Second Cataract: ebony, ivory, skins, slaves, ostrich feathers, and incense. Egypt pursued a range of strategies to secure these items: military action to ensure their continued flow; direct control, first seen in the Fourth Dynasty copper-producing settlement at Buhen; and using donkey caravans to bypass intermediaries and reach producing areas directly. By 2200 B.C. a major polity was developing centered at Kerma near the Third Cataract. Perhaps encouraged by Egypt at first as a trading partner (Morkot 2001), Kerma was later seen as a competitor. For this reason, as much as to control trade movements or because of architectural megalomania, the Twelfth Dynasty Pharaohs constructed a series of massive fortresses in Lower Nubia. Excavations show Kerma was a densely packed urban settlement (Bonnet 1992), and both temples and royal tumuli compare favorably with contemporary Egyptian structures in size (O'Connor 1993b). Interestingly, though some features (funerary temples, the major temple's pylon façade, etc.) suggest Egyptian influence, overall burial format and architecture are distinctly non-Egyptian or use Egyptian artifacts in novel ways, such as placing Pharaonic statues outside royal burial chambers; ceramics, figurines, and metalwork also reflect wholly local traditions (Török 1995). Trade in perishable commodities is indicated by a range of Egyptian storage and transport vessels (Bourriau 1991), but wealth in cattle, which were certainly of ritual importance, was probably also critical to Kerma's elite (MacDonald 1998b).

At its peak Kerma allied with the Hyksos and successfully invaded Egypt (Davies 2003),[3] paying the price for this when a reunited, resurgent Egypt conquered the areas downstream of the Fourth Cataract, beyond which another polity (Irem) survived or developed as a periodic opponent and trading partner (O'Connor 1987; Manzo 1999). Farther north, local elites Egyptianized, becoming mainstays of New Kingdom colonial rule and perhaps contributing to the development of the kingdom of Kush after Egyptian dominance ended (O'Connor 1993b; Morkot 2001). Kush's earliest royal tombs at El Kurru revived Kerman traditions of bed burials under round tumuli (Adams 1977, 256), and only after Kushite kings conquered Egypt in the late eighth century B.C., briefly uniting the whole Nile Valley downstream of Meroë, were Pharaonic rituals, such as mummification and the use of pyramid tombs, introduced. Though Egyptian iconography and religious beliefs are strongly evident throughout Kushite history, and Egyptian hieroglyphs were used into the first century, they were employed in distinctive ways, largely to legitimize royal rule and the status of subordinate elites. They should not be privileged to draw inferences about Kushite social organization because of outdated diffusionist views that emphasized the creative role of Pharaonic Egypt in Nubia's history and prehistory (Fuller 1997). Indeed, Pharaonic symbolism was complemented by both local traditions and influences from the contemporary Greco-Roman world (figure 3.4; Welsby 1996).

Meroë's very location at the upstream end of the Bayuda Road implies a significant expansion of overland movement compared with previous centuries, and this emphasis on cross-desert routes that avoided the worst navigational hazards of the Middle Nile has led to its identification as the first of the "empires of the steppes which arose in the wake of the cara-

Figure 3.4. Greco-Roman-inspired representations of two gods in the Lion Temple, Naqa, Sudan (redrawn after Lepsius 1848–59). That on the left represents Serapis, that on the right a deity wearing a radiant crown.

van trade" (Adams 1977, 305). Meroitic stockpiles of ebony and ivory are known, and gold and slaves are other likely commodities (Welsby 1996). Camels probably facilitated their movement, but the scale of their employment remains uncertain (Welsby 1996, 155). Nor should we assume that commercial exchanges operated on any scale. Edwards (1996, 89) notes the importance of Egyptian coarse pottery imports (to supplement local wares or, more probably, as containers for oil, wine, and dried foods) in Lower Nubia but otherwise argues that Meroitic trade with Egypt was "primarily concerned with small quantities of nonutilitarian 'luxury' products" distributed by interelite gifting and state-controlled embassies. This reinterpretation calls directly on anthropological studies of the role of preciosities in maintaining other African savanna states (Coquery-Vidrovitch 1969; Goody 1971) and demands a recontextualization of Meroitic civilization as part of Sudanic Africa, not just an appendage of Egypt (Edwards 2003). It stresses too the frequent mortuary contexts of imported goods, a use that both displayed and reinforced hierarchical distinctions and removed them from circulation, thereby maintaining demand. These goods, including jewelry, metalwork, glassware, wine and the vessels with which to store and drink it, olive oil, and perfumes of Mediterranean and Egyptian origin, were mostly retained in royal hands; lower-ranking elites had to make do with locally produced prestige bronze work, ceramics, and faience (Edwards 1996, 33).

An introduction with more far-reaching consequences was that of the *saqia*, an animal-powered wheel for lifting water first brought to Egypt from Mesopotamia in Ptolemaic times. The specially designed pots (*qawadis*) that it used are highly distinctive and recognizable in Nubia from the fourth century. More than doubling the vertical range of the *shaduf*, a more primitive, human-powered device for lifting water from one level to another, and substantially increasing the amount of cultivable land, the *saqia*'s advantages were partly offset by the fodder needs of the animals that powered it, but its introduction may have facilitated the development of a multiharvest cropping system; at Qasr Ibrim in Lower Nubia it broadly correlates to the post-Meroitic appearance of more advanced varieties of sorghum and wheat, sesame and pearl millet, a pattern of agricultural diversification with both southern and northern sources (Edwards 1996). One consequence may have been that local elites became more able to sustain themselves independently of connections with Meroë itself. Isolation from Roman Egypt, which was encouraged as desert nomads settled in Lower Nubia to establish ministates that were recruited as Roman clients, probably resulted in the loss of essential prestige goods, contributing to the breakdown of Meroitic power in the early fourth century (Edwards 1996). Another reason may lie in commercial competition from Aksum for ties with the Roman world, and direct military conflict between Kush and Aksum has been envisaged (Arkell 1961). Collapse was, however, drawn out. Fourth century tumuli at El Hobagi show continuities in elite burial rituals from Meroë and used imagery borrowed from Roman coins and medals as an additional source of political legitimacy (Lenoble and Sharif 1992).

Even such a brief sketch as this shows that Nubia was by no means always at the mercy of its neighbors, but instead more often than not politically independent, with strong, long-lasting cultural traditions of its own. Nor was trade with Egypt the only power basis of Nubian elites: control of animal husbandry and agricultural production was important to both Kerma and Meroë, ideological legitimation a concern central to all polities. If neither simply colony nor competitor, was Nubia then a corridor or cul-de-sac? Surely, Nile and overland routes connected Egypt and Nubia together, but the penetration of long-distance trade into southern Sudan seems more a feature of medieval and postmedieval times, fuelled by demand for slaves (Alexander 2001). Meroë probably never exercised political control much beyond Sennar, where Egyptian imports occur at Jebel Moya in mid-first millennium cal. B.C. contexts (Gerharz 1994; Welsby 1996). Certainly, Sayce's (1912) view that Meroë was the link between Egypt and Africa, particularly in the diffusion of iron working, cannot be sustained. The massive slag heaps at Meroë itself, where iron production may have been state controlled, are of late date (third to sixth century; Shinnie 1985), and iron working in Darfur did not derive from there (Muhammed 1993).[4] However, other kinds of contact west of the Nile should not be utterly discounted (see later discussion), and links east and southeast of the river were important from Pharaonic times, gaining added momentum when transformed into pilgrimage routes to Mecca. Neither cul-de-sac nor solely a riverine corridor, Nubia has for millennia been an active player in Africa's relations with other parts of the world.

Early Movements on the Red Sea

One of African archaeology's achievements in recent decades has been the expansion of fieldwork east of the Nile. This casts new light on a long-standing Egyptological problem, the location of the land of Punt (*Pwnt*), from which came gold, ebony, incense, and a host of other marvels (see figure 3.3). Rejecting its earlier identification with Somalia, Kitchen (1993) firmly locates Punt in northern Eritrea and adjacent areas of Sudan.[5] The ebony (*Dalbergia melanoxylon*) found in Pharaonic contexts occurs only here, along with one kind of incense widely used in Bronze Age Egypt and the Levant, Eritrean *Pistacia* resin (Serpico and White 2000). Punt was visited by Egyptians over some 1,400 years, between 2500 B.C. and 1100 B.C., until land-based routes from southern Arabia provided an alternative camel-using based route for importing aromatics (Manzo 1999). Temple reliefs at Deir el-Bahri dated ca. 1460 B.C. give the most detailed account, documenting the exchange of food and drink for myrrh, ebony, gold, precious woods, slaves, and ivory, but some of these items came via Punt, not from it (J. Phillips 1997). Nor was contact exclusively Egyptian led; slightly later tomb scenes show Puntites arriving in Egypt with similar goods carried on flat-bottomed rafts equipped with sails and a steering oar, ideal craft for coastal navigation given the Red Sea's coral reefs (figure 3.5; Bradbury 1996).

Reviewing this and other evidence of contacts along the Red Sea and between it and the Nile, J. Phillips (1997) and Manzo (1999) emphasize Fattovich's (1991) work in the Gash Delta, which has yielded small amounts of exotic pottery, including Egyptian and Arabian sherds. Kerman ceramics stand alone ca. 2300–1700 B.C., suggesting preferential access to the region's gold, incense, and ebony in a way that stresses

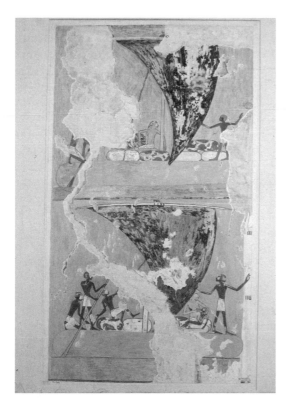

Figure 3.5. Puntite rafts, Tomb of Min, Thebes, Egypt (courtesy Jacke Phillips). The illustration is based on a photograph of a watercolor facsimile by N. de G. Davies held in the Ashmolean Museum, Oxford.

Kerma's role as a "link with a major part of the African continent" (Bonnet 1992, 623); clay seals from the key Gash Delta site of Mahal Teglinos that resemble others from Kerma reinforce this link, and attest to some considerable administrative complexity, complemented by possible status distinctions in burial evidence (Fattovich 1996). While the Kerma connection could have provided a motive for Egypt's Twelfth Dynasty renewal of direct maritime contact with Punt using the harbor of *Sww* near Quseir (Sayed 1983), New Kingdom Egypt may have developed direct overland contacts to southeastern Sudan, to judge from inscriptions at Kurgus and ceramics newly found near Meroë; in the sixth century, travel from the Red Sea coast to Aswan via the Gash Delta, the Atbara, and thence across the desert took less than a month and rare finds on both the Middle Nile and in highland Ethiopia hint that such crossings took place considerably earlier (J. Phillips 1997). If Sadr (1991) is correct in modeling the development of pastoralist adaptations in northeastern Africa as the "ranching industry" of early complex societies, then regular movements by such groups may have been another and enduring means by which goods and ideas were transmitted between the Nile, the Red Sea, and Ethiopia.

Obsidian is another signature of long-distance contact in this part of Africa. Ethiopian sources provided the small amounts found in the Gash Delta and from late Predynastic times in Egypt (Zarins 1996), but Ethiopian obsidian also moved across the Red Sea into southern Arabia beginning by the sixth millennium cal. B.C. and continuing into the Bronze Age (Francaviglia 1985; Zarins 1990). However, defining with greater clarity the intercultural influences prevailing between Middle Nile, southeastern Sudanese, Ethiopian, Eritrean, and Arabian populations remains difficult. Fattovich (1997) grouped apparently similar ceramics in Yemen and Eritrea within the Tihama Cultural Complex, and Edens and Wilkinson (1998, 92) go further to suggest an African origin for the initial introduction of pottery technology into Yemen. Recent work near Asmara now disputes some of these links and emphasizes that Eritrean rock art, supposedly similar to first to third millennium B.C. examples in Arabia, remains undated (Schmidt and Curtis 2001, *pace* Cervicek 1979). While such claims certainly do require firm evidence and more field research is sorely needed, sufficient evidence does exist to suggest that connections between the Red Sea and the Nile have been underplayed: as one example, seashells, including cowries of possibly Indian Ocean origin, occur from the Neolithic onward in Nubia and Egypt alike, perhaps signaling exchange networks influential in the movement of domesticated plants and animals (J. Phillips 1997; chapter 2).

Movement across the waters of the Red Sea itself is constrained by the strong northerly winds that blow for much of the year, making sailing against them difficult, especially in its northern half. This fact helps explain the longer-term success of Berenike over Egypt's other Greco-Roman port, Myos Hormos; Berenike was 300 km farther south, if more distant from the Nile. On the other hand, and especially south of Port Sudan, southerly winds prevail from October to May, facilitating two-way movement along the sea. Near-coastal "corridors" protected by coral reefs also offer calm water, so long as ships are not too deeply bottomed (Manzo 1999, 10). East–west crossings are shortest at the Red Sea's southern end, where distances are least and the Dahlak and Farasan Islands offer possible staging points, but in the Bab el-Mandeb Straits themselves currents are strong, and everywhere reefs demand exact knowledge of local conditions. This information was certainly available to Greco-Egyptian mariners in the early third century B.C. when the Ptolemies estab lished a series of ports on the African shore. Accessing incense, spices, and war elephants, the tanks of their day, were their principal motives, developing Myos Hormos and Berenike part of the same strategy (J. Phillips 1997). Archaeologically unknown, these southern Red Sea ports paved the way for direct contact between the Mediterranean world and India and East Africa (chapter 4). More immediate to our concerns here were the east–west contacts across the Red Sea that contributed to the development of the first states in Eritrea and highland Ethiopia.

Aksum and Its Predecessors

Ethiopia, wrote Ullendorf (1960, 23), "has always formed a bridge between Africa and Asia." We saw in chapter 2 why this may have been so in the early movement of African cereals into the Indian subcontinent, but it is also true of Ethiopia's own distinctive agricultural complex. Though tef is laborious to harvest, it is very nutritious and, like finger millet (with origins from central Ethiopia to northern Uganda), resists mold and insect attack far better than other cereals (D'Andrea et al. 1999). It was certainly cultivated in the Aksum region by the mid-first millennium B.C. (D. Phillipson 2000) and had crossed to Yemen, where it is still grown, by the first century A.D. (van Beek 1969). Wheat, barley, flax, and perhaps Near Eastern legumes were also grown by 500 B.C. (S. Boardman 1999), probably as additions to indigenous agricultural systems. In a still "lamentably incomplete" archaeological picture (D. Phillipson 1993b, 356; Barnett 1999), cattle bones in an early second millennium cal. B.C. context from Laga Oda (Clark and Williams 1978) provide the earliest, albeit tentative, evidence of food production. If cattle arrived with herders moving from Nubia via eastern Sudan into Ethiopia, then the presence of barley at Kerma and Mahal Teglinos would suggest that it (and plowing?)

spread along the same route. This might fit Ehret's (1979) argument that terms for wheat, barley, and plow were borrowed into Ethiopia's Semitic languages from a Cushitic source and must therefore predate the former's arrival in Ethiopia.[6] However, with no clear sense of when this might have happened, we should also consider contacts with Arabia *before* the arrival of Semitic languages as another possible origin for the Near Eastern components of Ethiopia's farming complex. Obsidian finds certainly demonstrate that contacts across the Red Sea are several millennia old, while the dominance of sorghum and similarities in architecture, material culture, and physical appearance attest to the strength of connections between the Tihama and Africa (Serjeant 1966; Zarins et al. 1981).

Such contacts have long been invoked to explain the development of Aksumite civilization. The "Pre-Aksumite" polity of D'MT,[7] most clearly evidenced by the massive temple at Yeha (figure 3.6), certainly reveals southern Arabian (particularly Saba'an) influences in royal titles, architecture, religion, and script. But none of this, or the possibly Yemeni origin of local iron-working technology (Mapunda 1997), demands the implantation of actual colonists, though this may have been involved, per-

Figure 3.6. Exterior view from the northwest of the temple at Yeha, Ethiopia, part of the Pre-Aksumite kingdom of D'MT (courtesy and copyright David Phillipson).

haps as part of a search for additional goods to feed into southern Arabia's trade networks with the Levant, Mesopotamia and Egypt. Schmidt and Curtis's (2001) recent work near Asmara confirms that the development of protourban settlements rested heavily on a successful local agricultural base, stressing the importance in this respect of humped zebu cattle, which have a much higher tolerance of heat, thirst, disease, and poor-quality grazing (figure 3.7). Ultimately of Indian origin, they spread westward after 3000 B.C. (Matthews 2002) and could have arrived in Eritrea via Egypt, Nubia, or southern Arabia. Whatever the case, and perhaps the latter is most likely, local elites, if not themselves Arabian in origin, certainly adopted an exotic Arabian veneer to enhance their status at home and abroad; post-D'MT employment of the disk and crescent as divine symbols and of Saba'an script may reflect continuity from the past, not renewed Arabian influence (Munro-Hay 1993).

The D'MT polity may have been short-lived and its connections with later Aksumite civilization are poorly known. Most of Aksum's own surviving monuments are of third to sixth century date (D. Phillipson 2003), but Greco-Roman sources show the state already existed in the early first

Figure 3.7. Zebu cattle in the Lamu Archipelago, Kenya. Note the swastika on the rump, an indication of Indian (Hindu) influence on the local Swahili community (courtesy and copyright Andrew Reid).

century. Fieldwork has focused there and at several major sites in Eritrea, including the ancient port of Adulis (D. Phillipson 1998). Much remains to be discovered about the processes leading to the emergence of a state capable of erecting the huge stelae and buildings already known. Aksum's subsistence base and local exchange networks both require further study.[8] Archaeology nonetheless confirms Aksum's participation in long-distance trade, and it is not unreasonable that this was crucial for its development. The city's location, 12 days' journey over a precipitous escarpment from the coast, was peripheral to the Red Sea, but probably important for accessing major exports. Of these, ivory was most significant, its value enhanced by the approaching extinction of Rome's North African sources. The size, availability, and carving properties of African ivory all favored its use over that coming from India, and Greco-Roman writers from the mid-first century author of the *Periplus of the Erythraean Sea* to the sixth century Byzantine traveler Kosmas Indikopleustes emphasize ivory as a crucial Aksumite export (D. Phillipson 1998). Excavation of the late fourth century Tomb of the Brick Arches shows how skillfully it was carved locally (D. Phillipson 2000) using the numerous stone tools from workshops on the city's outskirts (L. Phillipson 2000).

Rhinoceros horn, tortoise shell, and skins are among other Aksumite exports recorded by the *Periplus*, to which may be added the frankincense still produced to the city's south and, perhaps, slaves (D. Phillipson 1998). Gold from local sources was also exploited, with a possible workshop known at Adulis (Paribeni 1907). One use of gold was to mint sub-Saharan Africa's first coinage (Munro-Hay and Juel-Jensen 1995). That these gold issues were based on the Roman weight standard and inscribed in Greek shows they were targeted for circulation abroad, and their distribution gives a partial indication of the extent of Aksum's international connections; silver and bronze coins with Ge'ez inscriptions are more common on Aksumite sites themselves. We know from Kosmas Indikopleustes that Aksumite ships sailed to Sri Lanka in the sixth century (Wolska-Conus 1968–73), and some possibly Indian objects (particularly glass beads) from Aksumite sites hint at what they acquired. Of far greater interest must have been the spices for which the Greco-Roman world had such great demand (J. N. Miller 1969). Aksum probably engaged directly in their acquisition from the Indian subcontinent, and control over this trade and the local southern Arabian production of incense may lie behind its recurrent interest in dominating Yemen (Munro-Hay 1991), where excavations at Shabwa confirm Aksumite presence (Breton 1991); Aksumite pottery and a coin from Berenike allow us to draw the further inference that Aksumite traders carried both their own and Arabian and Indian Ocean goods north to Egypt (Sidebotham and Wendrich 2001–02).

In considering what Aksum gained in return, we should recall that foreign manufactured items loom larger in the archaeological record (and mind) than exported commodities that preserve less well and are harder to identify (D. Phillipson 1998). A frequent feature of Africa's relations with the outside world, this points up the importance of literary sources for complementing what excavation can offer. Specifically from Aksum itself, there is direct and (extrapolated from their containers) indirect evidence of Mediterranean glassware, metalwork, textiles, wine, and olive oil (D. Phillipson 2001). Recent finds at Beta Giyorghis just outside the city center include, for example, Egyptian/Palestinian glass, North African *terra sigillata* pottery, amphorae from Upper Egypt and Gaul, and other pottery of Syrian origin (Bard and Fattovich 1995, 1997). In some cases these imports stimulated local industries, including production, or at least reprocessing, of glass (D. Phillipson 1998, 80), and manufacture of copies of *terra sigillata* red-slipped ware (Bard et al. 1996). Imports were also reused in novel ways, amphorae, for example, to bury babies and their sherds to make spindle whorls. But as well as these commercial connections, there were less material influences. The use of Greek on coins and the institution of coinage itself we have already noted. Of far greater import, and the subject to which I now turn, was Aksum's conversion to Christianity.

Northeastern Africa and the Spread of World Religions

Only in Africa's northeast do all three major monotheisms—Judaism, Christianity, and Islam—survive from early times. Admittedly, the first of these is now represented in Egypt by only a tiny community, but its roots reach back at least to the seventh century B.C. when mercenaries stationed near the First Cataract built a local version of the Temple of Jerusalem (Kraeling 1953). In Ptolemaic and Roman times Alexandria was the principal concentration of Egyptian Jewry, home to the translators of the Septuagint, the first Greek version of the Old Testament, as well as the philosopher Philo. However, archaeological evidence of Jewish presence in both Egypt and Cyrenaica is restricted to inscriptions, ostraca, and papyri; no synagogues are known (Binder 1999). Much the same is true of later periods, but the incomparable Geniza archive shows just how important Egypt's Jewish population was during the tenth and eleventh centuries. Goiten's (1967–88) analysis reveals the extent of its mobility and involvement in a commerce that reached from Spain as far as India.

From soon after the Crucifixion, Alexandria's large Jewish population provided a ready home for early Christian activity. Most of Egypt was Christian by 400, but several features of the indigenous Coptic Church recall Pharaonic practice: offerings of food to the dead; a calendar of 12 30-day months and a supplementary period of 5 days; New Year visits to family graves carrying water and palm fronds; and representations of the Virgin with Child and the Archangel Michael that respectively recall Isis with Horus and the god Thoth weighing the soul of the dead. Most obvious of all is the survival of the ankh sign (the hieroglyph for life) in the Coptic Cross. Furthermore, given Egypt's historical and ultimately ecclesiastical primacy in northeast African Christianity some of these elements are also evident in Ethiopia and Nubia (Finneran 2002).

Egypt was central to the early development of Christian theology, witness the Gnostic tradition illuminated by the Nag Hammadi papyri (Pagels 1979), St Cyril's elaboration of the doctrine of the Incarnation, and the conflict between the two Alexandrian clerics Arius and Athanasius that eventually resulted in the Nicene Creed. As far reaching was the movement by reclusive ascetics into the desert from the mid-third century. Under St Anthony's inspiration, some of these individuals began to aggregate, though without formal rules. A more communal lifestyle with joint meals, work, and worship was initiated by Pachomius (ca. 290–346), enhanced by Shenouta, founder of the still surviving White Monastery at Sohag, and then exported to Rome's Near Eastern provinces under the leadership of St Basil. Egypt thus lies at the root of the Christian monastic tradition (Stewart 2002; figure 3.8), directly inspiring its spread into southern Gaul (Markus 1990) and early Christian Ireland (MacGinty 1983), and helping establish the basis for Christian hagiographical writing (Mathew 1966). Both kinds of monastic community are recognizable archaeologically in Egypt from their different spatial organizations (Finneran 2002), while pioneering new work is providing fresh insights into topics such as diet, independent of textual evidence (Harlow and Smith 2001).

The Roman Empire established Christianity as its state religion in 390, but was preceded in this by Aksum, making Ethiopia, next to Armenia, the oldest surviving (predominantly) Christian state in the world. Archaeology confirms that at the elite level, where it began, this conversion was rapid. Coins of King Ezana (dated to approximately 330–60) first showed the pagan crescent and disk, but were then struck with the Cross and Christian references. Royal tomb style also changed, with the erection of their accompanying stelae abandoned.[9] Ethiopian tradition records that the first Christian proselytizers came from Egypt. Both the liturgy and ritual of the Ethiopian Orthodox Church recall this, and until the mid-twentieth century it continued to be headed by a bishop appointed from Egypt. Ethiopia thus followed the Coptic Church in adopting Monophysitism after the Council of Chalcedon in 451. Features such as the use of red ink for divine utterances

Figure 3.8. A view over the interior of the Coptic monastery of Deir Anba Bishoi in the Wadi Natrun, Egypt. Founded in the fourth century, Deir Anba Bishoi dates back almost to the start of the Christian monastic tradition.

in Scripture and the employment of the sistrum at services hark back to Pharaonic practice (J. Phillips 1997). Still others, like keeping Saturday as well as Sunday as the Sabbath, ritual dancing before the Ark of the Covenant, and dietary prohibitions, follow Jewish tradition (Ullendorf 1956). These Old Testament influences may have been deliberately adopted as part of early medieval Ethiopia's self-identification with Biblical Israel, beleaguered by pagan and Muslim neighbors (Tamrat 1977), but within Ethiopia itself the Falasha, linguistically and racially identical to their Christian neighbors, are known to have followed an archaic form of Judaism.

Christianity's spread among the general Aksumite population was hastened by the arrival of additional religious teachers from Syria in the sixth century who also introduced monasticism. Archaeologically, this is reflected in the widespread appearance of clay crosses and the dominance of the Cross on later Aksumite pottery. Integration with pagan beliefs may have helped this process by siting churches and monasteries at already sacred locations (Hein and Kleidt 1999). Aksum's conversion played well with Rome, and the two allied against Persia in the late sixth century (Munro-Hay 1991); mirroring this alliance, the Byzantine-style basilica at Adulis used imported Anatolian marble to produce locally made liturgical furnishings in East Mediterranean style (Finneran 2002). More prosaically, a country church near Aksum preserves an imported late Greco-Roman amphora said to have been used by God to drink beer while overseeing early Christian residents (D. Phillipson 1998, 143)!

Propagated in Ethiopia by the Aksumite kings, Christianity remained key to their legitimacy and that of their successors, who developed a claim to Solomonic ancestry that made them relatives of Christ Himself. Aksum collapsed, perhaps quite suddenly, in a poorly understood process that began in the late sixth to early seventh centuries as first Persia and then Islam took control of southern Arabia, interposing themselves along the Red Sea's trade routes, something confirmed by a marked drop in the use of ivory in the Mediterranean world at this time (Cutler 1985). Environmental degradation (Butzer 1981) and shifts in the scale and intensity of monsoonal rains may also have been involved, leading to declines in urbanism, long-distance trade, and coinage comparable to those experienced in Europe after the collapse of the Western Roman Empire. However, Ethiopian Christianity and an Ethiopian state survived, in part because of the effectiveness of monasteries in preserving cultural traditions and converting pagan communities. Throughout the medieval period religious links were retained with Alexandria and Jerusalem, and by 1500 small Ethiopian communities existed there and in Cyprus, Rhodes, and Italy. Reflecting some of these connections, Coptic, Armenian, and Syrian influences are evident in Ethiopian religious paintings, and it has been suggested that the fabulous rock-cut church complex at Lalibela, which stands in architectural succession to the

---

SIDEBAR 4

Coffee

Writing as a confirmed devotee of espresso, I believe that coffee must surely rank high among Africa's contributions to the world. Native to Ethiopia's southern forests, *Coffea arabica* was originally chewed, not drunk, just like the robusta variety (*C. canephora*) that only became economically important from the late 1800s (Purseglove 1976). Crossing the Red Sea at some unknown date, reports of its brewing come first from Arabia in the late fifteenth century. Yemen (hence the term *mocha*) quickly became a production center, though coffee was also exported into Red Sea trade networks from Christian Ethiopia. Despite initial hostility against it as a stimulant, it spread rapidly across the Islamic world in the sixteenth century, reaching Venice around 1615 and soon becoming the fashionable drink of Europe too (Braudel 1981). Losing its domination of Europe's imports of spices after Portugal's entry into the Indian Ocean in 1498 (chapter 4), Egypt controlled the coffee trade from its position at the head of the Red Sea until the plant was successfully established in European colonies in Java, Réunion, and the Caribbean. Novel archaeological demonstration of its movement comes from the *Sadana* shipwreck, a vessel of 900 metric tons lost sometime after 1765, probably en route to Suez (figure 3.9; Ward 2001). Coffee and aromatic resin formed the bulk of its cargo, along with a consignment of Chinese porcelain specifically designed for Muslim taste (only one object bears an animal image). Sadana, the only well-studied example of several broadly contemporary Red Sea wrecks, illustrates the kind of insights into long-distance trade networks that underwater archaeology can provide. Thus far, however, the process by which coffee originally came into use remains obscure, even though some late Aksumite ceramic vessels resemble modern coffee pots (Wilding 1989).

Figure 3.9. Excavation near the junction of the floor timbers and first futtocks of the *Sadana* shipwreck, Egypt (photograph by Meredith Kato, courtesy of Cheryl Ward for the Institute of Nautical Archaeology).

monumental stone-building of the Aksumite era, was built as an earthly allegory of Jerusalem (Munro-Hay 2002).

Religious and political motivations combined as medieval Ethiopia's rulers sought alliances with Christian Europe against the threat of Muslim incursions (Northrup 2002). Pursuing information on how to access the spice trade free of Muslim middlemen (sidebar 4), Portugal initiated its own diplomatic contacts in the late fifteenth century and later allied with Ethiopia against the Ottoman Turks, who built forts on the Eritrean coast in the sixteenth and seventeenth centuries (Insoll 2003a, 83–84). Portuguese forces helped Ethiopia survive the attacks of Ahmad Grañ in 1541–43, but his depredations and incursions by Oromo cattle herders seriously weakened the Christian state. Continuing alliance with Portugal promoted, if it did not demand, Catholic proselytization and two rulers, Za Dengel (1603–4) and Susenyos (1607–32), even converted, though their overthrow led to Portuguese missionaries being expelled (Caraman 1985). Jesuit influence survives, however, in some sixteenth and seventeenth century buildings (figure 3.10), and some Catholic religious imagery was also adopted into Ethiopian art (Munro-Hay 2002).

Between Ethiopia and Egypt lay Nubia, and here another pattern of conversion is visible. Literary sources make plain that Christianity was adopted in the mid-sixth century by all three local kingdoms and at broadly the same date, as may have been the case among the Garamantes of Fezzan, much farther west (chapter 5). In Nobadia and Makuria, conversion was at Byzantine initiative. That the former followed Monophysite, the latter Melkite teaching on the nature of Christ[10] may reflect a deliberate attempt to sow discord between potentially troublesome neighbors, not just rivalries in the Byzantine court or local Nubian antagonisms; the southernmost state, Alwa, then became Monophysite via contact with Nobadia, leaving Makuria theologically isolated. Byzantine influence is evident in early church architecture (and fortifications) at its capital, Old Dongola (Welsby 2002, 33), but Melkite and Monophysite differences are not obvious in church design. Ultimately, Monophysitism prevailed, in part because the Arab conquest of Egypt in 642 cut direct links with Constantinople. Indeed, Nubian bishops were appointed from Alexandria and many clergy and monks may also have been Egyptian, factors that perhaps ultimately hindered the development of an organizational infrastructure capable of withstanding Islam once support from the state had disappeared.

Christianity had massive effects on Nubian life, ending millennia-long traditions of impressive tombs and grave goods. Indeed, no Nubian royal tomb can be identified for certain. Instead of uniting in a divine ruler, religion and state became more separate, though still mutually supportive,

Figure 3.10. The castle of Fasilidas, Gondar, Ethiopia, built in the mid-seventeenth century, possibly by an Indian architect, for Fasilidas, the emperor who expelled the Portuguese Jesuits from the northeast African kingdom. A roofed water cistern inspired by others of Jesuit design is located nearby (courtesy and copyright David Phillipson).

and organized religion more populist, not the preserve of the elite; that almost all settlements have churches attests to this. These initially adopted the standard Roman basilica plan, but then increasingly developed local features (Adams 1977). Syrian and Armenian influences on church design probably reflect continued contact with the Holy Land well after 642, and pilgrimages to Jerusalem continued into the fifteenth century. Nubia's religious art, including the impressive fresco paintings from Faras Cathedral (Michalowski 1967), developed locally from initial Egyptian and Byzantine inspiration and retained contact with Coptic art, but artists also clearly kept abreast of developments as far afield as Byzantium (Welsby 2002, 228). Nubian royal iconography too borrowed heavily from Byzantine models, while Greek remained the liturgical language (Adams 1977, 467).

Egypt's new Islamic rulers balked at conquering Nubia, concluding a perpetual armistice (*Baqt*) in 652 with the newly united polity of Makuria and Nobadia by which the Nubians were to deliver 400 slaves annually in return for cereals, wine, horses, and textiles. This treaty, unique in the early Muslim world, survived more or less intact into the thirteenth century, and trade encompassed more than just these items, even if ivory, skins, and wood are difficult to capture archaeologically. The long-distance connections of Alwa's capital, Soba, for instance, which may have come via Egypt or perhaps the Red Sea, included Islamic glass and glazed pottery, as well as rare Chinese porcelain (Welsby and Daniels 1991; Welsby 1998). The scale on which slaves moved north must, however, have been far greater than that envisaged by the *Baqt*, to judge from the numbers of African slave-soldiers in Fatimid armies, even if there is almost no archaeological record of this (Alexander 2001). Demography and climate suggest that most of these slaves came from beyond Nubia itself, raising the possibility that Christian Nubia's influence southward in Sudan was essentially destructive (Welsby 2002, 214). Nor did Mamluk and later Ottoman prohibition on the use of African slaves as soldiers curtail the slave trade. Instead, demand for domestic servants, mine laborers, and concubines remained steady, and Islam's southward expansion, with its attendant prohibition on enslaving Muslims, pushed the zone from which slaves were taken ever farther south (Lovejoy 2000).

Nubian Christianity survived at the periphery of Islam, largely dictating the nature of their mutual contacts, for some 600 years. Only in the thirteenth century did pressure grow significantly from Arab nomads encouraged to leave Egypt by its new Mamluk rulers. The Mamluks themselves increasingly intervened in Makuria's succession disputes after 1260, and within 100 years the kingdom had collapsed. Rump Christian principalities survived into the sixteenth century, when the southern kingdom of Alwa too passed under Muslim control. Physical conversion of churches into mosques was a drawn-out process and that of Nubian Christians to Islam not complete until the eighteenth century; even today some practices survive in popular religion and the Nubian language has not yet been superseded by Arabic (Welsby 2002, 258), although many Nubians now claim Arab ancestry to assert membership in the wider Islamic community (Adams 1977, 564). Archaeological fieldwork at Qasr Ibrim shows how the local church was turned into a mosque after this Lower Nubian fortress passed under Ottoman control and how houses were rebuilt to focus on the interior in accordance with Muslim ideas of domestic privacy (Insoll 2003a). Taking a longer view, Edwards (1999) makes a strong case for changes in Nubian ceramic traditions reflecting the advent of Islam, with elaborate Christian and pre-Christian pottery that was probably used to consume beer (and for the elite wine) replaced by more mundane wares once alcohol was prohibited. Qasr Ibrim's exceptional organic preservation supports this by recording the cessation of bicolor sorghum cultivation after the site passed under Muslim control, since it is this variety that is best suited to making beer (Rowley-Conwy 1989).

Elsewhere, comparatively little archaeological work has been undertaken on the Islamic period, despite Ethiopia's significance as a refuge for early Muslim converts during Muhammad's lifetime, the many Ge'ez words in the Koran (Insoll 2003a, 46), the region's interest for studying relations between Christian, Muslim, and animist communities, the importance of its ports for the pilgrimage to Mecca (hajj), and the degree to which Islam's expansion reunited Arabia to Africa (cf. Mazrui 1986, 29–34). Most research has focused on coastal sites like Suakin, Er-Rih, and Dahlak el-Kebir (figure 3.11), all of which became centers for exporting commodities such as slaves and ivory, as well as participants in trade networks spanning the Red Sea and Indian Ocean (Greenlaw 1995; Insoll 1997a, 2003a). Farther inland, the Gibe area (Abir 1965) is recorded as a major center for the exchange of local African products and goods from across the Muslim world, but the sites of its fairs, like the growth of those Muslim sultanates in eastern Ethiopia and northern Somalia that developed partly

Figure 3.11. Glass bracelet fragments from Dahlak el-Kebir, Eritrea (courtesy and copyright Tim Insoll).

on the back of trade, remain unstudied archaeologically. The expansion of the hajj is, on the other hand, implied by the wells, cisterns, and cemeteries at the Egyptian port of Aidhab, which are far more extensive than the local community could have needed. Increasingly, hajj pilgrims came from across the Sahel belt stretching west of the Nile as far as the Atlantic, something reflected at Aidhab by both Maghrebi and Egyptian ceramics (Insoll 2003a). To conclude this chapter, I therefore turn briefly to the contacts between Nile-based societies and those beyond the river in older, pre-Islamic times.

Beyond the Niles: Contacts between Egypt, Sudan, and Ethiopia and Other Parts of Africa

We saw in chapter 2 that Egyptian texts imply a substantial Bronze Age population in what is now Cyrenaica. These peoples posed a growing military threat to Egypt from the thirteenth century B.C. Their infiltration, encouraged by recruitment into the army, subsequently took hold, especially in the north of Egypt, ultimately establishing in power the Libyan-derived Twenty-Second and Twenty-Third Dynasties (945–715 B.C.). Interestingly, a distinctive Libyan identity survived for some time, reflected in names and chiefly titles and contributing to the development of a less centralized, quasi-federal form of government (J. Taylor 2000). In this we see something of a turning of the tables for since early in the Pharaonic state's history it had exalted in the military subordination of its neighbors, exploiting and administering the Western Desert's oases from ca. 2500 B.C. as bases for mineral exploration, overland trade with Nubia, and the control of smuggling. Kuper (2001) has recently argued that Egyptian interest, marked by stations equipped with water and other provisions, presumably transported by donkey caravan, penetrated more than 350 km southwest of Dakhleh and could have reached as far as Jebel Uweinat, more than 630 km west of the Nile. More critically, Kuhlmann (2002) considers that a wide variety of options may account for such finds. Certainly, there is as yet no evidence for the Pharaonic state seeking or maintaining contacts across the Sahara to Fezzan or the central Sahel.

West of the Nile, Meroitic influence is also conspicuously absent; isolated finds of Nubian origin in Darfur and supposed influences on pottery from Koro Toro, Chad, date to the late first and early second millennia (Trigger 1969), and the much earlier mid-first millennium B.C. Kushite fortress of Gala Abu Ahmed in the Wadi Howar seems to have been sited more to control north–south movements parallel to the Nile than those east–west from and toward it (Jesse 2003). On the other hand, the possible extent of connections between the Nile and the rest of Africa has been argued by Sutton (1991, 2001) in respect of the southeastern Nigerian site of Igbo-Ukwu, a poorly understood but richly equipped burial-cum-ritual complex of late first millennium cal. A.D. age (T. Shaw 1977; figure 3.12). The enduring puzzle of Igbo-Ukwu, which lacks any associated settlement context, is the basis on which its more than 160,000 glass and carnelian beads[11] and elaborate, extensive bronze work were accumulated. Though copper, tin, and zinc were all locally derived (Chikwendu et al. 1989), the weights of unalloyed copper bars conform well with Late Roman/Islamic standards and the beads are all of Egyptian (perhaps specifically al-Fustât) and/or Indian origin. Sutton (1991) notes that despite this no systematic comparison of Igbo-Ukwu's stylistic repertoire with those of North Africa or the Nile Valley has been attempted, in part because their art and archaeology still exist in separate disciplinary compartments from those of sub-Saharan Africa. Emphasizing that, whatever the specific reasons through which the Igbo-Ukwu material was collected and deposited, "everything had to be paid for" (Sutton 1991, 154), he provocatively discusses the possibility that silver, conceivably a by-product of local copper exploitation, and tin might have been exported first by river and then by donkey (and camel?) east through Chad to Christian Nubia, or

Figure 3.12. Bronze vessel from Igbo-Ukwu, Nigeria (copyright Thurstan Shaw Collection, University College, London, courtesy Kevin MacDonald).

northeast via the Chad Basin and Fezzan to Egypt. Specifically Nigerian products certainly seem more plausible than ivory or slaves, which could have come from anywhere south of the Sahara (*pace* Insoll and Shaw 1997), but why assume that just because Igbo-Ukwu has an enormous concentration of locally produced elaborate metalwork and imported beads it was closely involved in international trade itself, rather than acquiring them via political or economic mechanisms and on a more immediately local scale? On the other hand, as with recent work in Sudan's Wadi Howar (chapter 2) and Edwards's (1996) reevaluation of the political structures of the Meroitic state, Sutton's arguments have the great advantage of encouraging precisely the kind of breaking down of disciplinary boundaries that can but strengthen Africa's archaeology.

Scope for similar thinking exists in the opposite direction from the Nile. J. Phillips's (1997) analysis of interconnections between Nubia, Eritrea, Aksum, and southeastern Sudan is one example, and I have called on this several times. If there is little sign of Meroitic control south of Sennar, cattle herders had certainly entered southernmost Sudan by 2000 cal. B.C. and could be one donor for the livestock that began to trickle into East Africa from about the same time (A. Smith 1992). Another route, where trypanosomiasis and other diseases were less prevalent, would have been via Ethiopia. However, similarities in material culture between East African Pastoral Neolithic sites and possibly contemporary Ethiopian ones are "very limited" (Marshall 2000, 210), just as there is as yet no sign that iron working entered East Africa from a source in the Horn of Africa (Mapunda 1997). In these respects, and although domesticated livestock must, on zoological grounds, have had ultimately northeast African origins, the archaeologically poorly known borderlands of southern Sudan and southern Ethiopia appear for now to place a limit on penetration of Africa's interior from the Red Sea and Nile Valley corridors and their traffic. When and how this limit was transcended is the subject of the next two chapters.

Notes

1. Wheat and barley were grown in Lower Nubia by 3000 B.C., along with other Levantine domesticates like peas and lentils (Adams 1977, 125). Barley was subsequently grown in Upper Nubia during both the Kerman and Meroitic periods and by medieval times was present as far south as Soba. Bread made from wheat seems, however, to have been an early medieval introduction from Egypt (Rowley-Conwy 1989).

2. The Mamluks were prominent among Egypt's imports in medieval and postmedieval times, male slaves of ultimately Caucasian or Central Asian origin trained as soldiers and then freed, who ruled as a military elite.

Because their children could not become Mamluks, constant recruitment was needed and continued under Ottoman rule (Ayalon 1977).

3. Many of the Egyptian statues from Kerma itself may be the spoils of this or other attacks (Davies 2003).

4. A recent paper by Abdu and Gordon (2004) confirms, using archeometallurgical evidence, that the iron working tradition represented at Meroë is distinctive and different from those known in the Mediterranean Basin on the one hand and sub-Saharan Africa on the other. Its origins remain obscure.

5. Meeks (2003) argues for an alternative location somewhere in western Arabia, but his reasoning seems to me to be less than convincing.

6. The diversity of wheat and barley strains in highland Ethiopia, many of them endemic, supports a considerable antiquity for their local presence (BOSTID 1996).

7. The inscriptions recording its name are unvocalized, but it may have been pronounced Daamat (D. Phillipson 1998, 45).

8. Salt, which is still extracted in the Danakil Desert and traded on camelback, was probably of prime importance in these networks, as in recent centuries (Abir 1965).

9. The archaeologically attested collapse during erection of the last and biggest stela (Stela 1) may have hastened Aksum's conversion and was perhaps even deliberately instigated to that end (D. Phillipson 1998).

10. The Melkite doctrine that Christ has separate divine and human natures united in One Person was defined in 451 at the Council of Chalcedon and is held by the Greek Orthodox and Catholic Churches and their offshoots. The opposing Monophysite view is that Christ has but one nature, partly divine, partly human.

11. The carnelian beads found here and elsewhere in sub-Saharan Africa are enigmatic. Most were probably produced in the western Sahel, for which both documentary confirmation (Levtzion and Hopkins 2000, 86) and a possible production site near Gao (Gaussen and Gaussen 1988) exist. Others were probably imported ultimately from western India (chapter 7). Sourcing methods are being developed (Insoll and Bhan 2001).

Africa in the
Indian Ocean
World System

Oceans do not really exist: they are constructs of the mind.
—FERNÁNDEZ-ARMESTO 2001, 461

THE INDIAN WAS the first of the world's oceans to become interconnected through a series of long-distance, interlocking maritime exchange systems that penetrated far inland onto the surrounding landmasses. Chaudhuri (1985) and others sketch the historical development of this system as a whole, but our focus lies at its western edge with the actions of the inhabitants of Africa's eastern seaboard and hinterland. I look in turn at newly emerging evidence for the colonization of eastern Africa's offshore islands, the introduction of Southeast Asian domesticates, and the expansion beyond the Red Sea of those Greco-Roman trade links touched on in chapter 3. I next consider the archaeological background to the emergence of the Swahili civilization that integrated much of eastern Africa's coasts into a single mercantile and cultural community. Examining how that integration was achieved, I discuss the roles played by transoceanic trade, Islam, and political changes beyond Africa, as well as the effects of intercontinental trade much farther inland. Finally, I consider how this Swahili-centered system was altered and transformed when linked to the Atlantic world after 1498.

Eastern Africa in the Indian Ocean World

The reason it was the Indian Ocean, not the Atlantic or the Pacific, that first became an integrated whole lies in its geography, for "it is wind and current that unify bodies of water, not the land masses or islands round about" (Fernández-Armesto 2001, 461). In the Indian Ocean case, the unifying factor lies in the annual monsoon, meaning, in Arabic, "winds that change seasonally" (figure 4.1). Put simply, because continental air masses over Eurasia cool faster than the oceans during the Northern Hemisphere winter, high pressure develops, which pushes air south toward the Equator. The Earth's axial rotation deflects this air to the right so that it blows from the northeast. In the northern summer the situation reverses, with the stronger southwesterly monsoon moving across the Indian Ocean

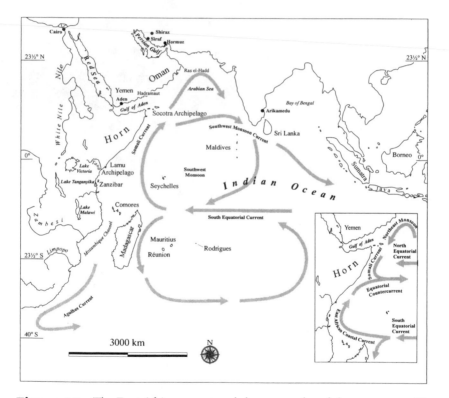

Figure 4.1. The East African coast and the geography of the monsoons. The main map shows the distribution of ocean currents during the Northern Hemisphere's summer (May to October), the inset shows the current reversal, operating from November to March.

to bring heavy rains to the Indian subcontinent, southernmost Arabia, and Ethiopia. Intimately connected to these movements of air are those of the sea, because the northeasterly monsoon carries water south along the Somali coast in winter, whereas in spring the warmer, southwesterly monsoon reverses this current so that it flows north and east. Finally, note that the main east–west Indian Ocean currents reverse direction every 6 months, facilitating voyages between India and Southeast Asia.

Compared with the Atlantic, which remained a barrier into the fifteenth century, the monsoonal system is ideally suited to linking distant shores. It is possible, for example, to voyage from Arabia, the Gulf, or western India to East Africa and back within a single year, moving with one monsoon in one season and the other during the next across what Pearson (1998, 36) aptly terms the "Afrasian sea." Such movements were facilitated from the seventh century on by the spread of Islam, which created a common system of law, culture, and religion across many of the Indian Ocean's shores, turning it into a Muslim lake (Chaudhuri 1985). The one catch in all this is that Indian Ocean sailors look inward as a function of landmass distribution and the monsoons, not outward onto the trade winds (Fernández-Armesto 2001, 483). Ultimately, this had massive consequences, as it was Europeans who entered the Indian Ocean from the Atlantic after 1498, not the reverse. The same cusp marks a change in the design of the ships traversing the Indian Ocean. Though little direct evidence survives, lateen-rigged, double-ended dhows (i.e., vessels pointed at both bow and stern) were probably employed for centuries as part of a wider range of boats that included square-rigged *mtepe*-style vessels for coastal movement; all were sewn together using coconut fiber cords, not nailed. Portuguese arrival precipitated the use of iron fastenings and the redesign of dhow sterns to a square form (Hourani 1995).

If eastern Africa (figure 4.2) looks out onto the possibilities I have described, not all of its coastline is equally well situated to take advantage of them. Initially arid with few harbors, from Mogadishu to the Kenyan border the coast becomes more accessible, if still exposed and fairly barren. With the Lamu Archipelago the first of a series of coral reefs occurs. Along with several drowned estuaries, they offer protected inshore waters with multiple harbors and inlets, while offshore islands provide freshwater and security from the mainland. In mangrove-free areas the shoreline's configuration—steep upper part and gently sloping lower section—facilitates access by local shipping, which can sail in at high tide and then come to rest on the foreshore as the tide recedes (Chittick 1977). Finally, at the far south of the Swahili world, beyond Maputo, southward currents and the absence of the monsoon conspire to limit the sailing range of those coming from farther north.

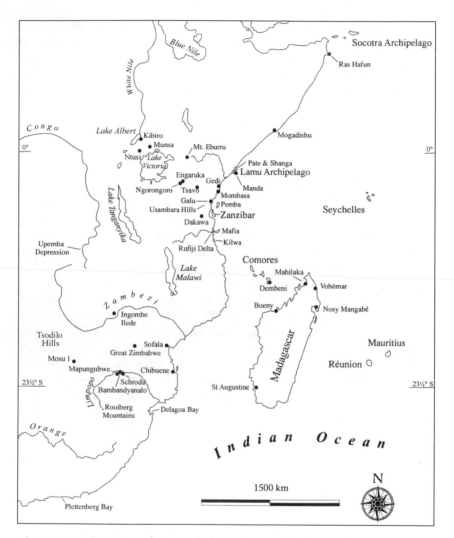

Figure 4.2. Location of sites and places discussed in chapter 4.

The character of areas inland of the coast is also quite variable, and by no means necessarily unattractive. Even its northern Kenyan and southern Somali stretch is ecologically diverse and home to a range of cultivators, pastoralists, and hunter-gatherers linked to the inhabitants of the Swahili towns discussed later in this chapter. Connections between the coast, its immediate hinterland, and the deeper interior were crucial to the evolution of eastern Africa's overseas ties, and movement inland was facilitated by rivers that drain into the Indian Ocean. If the Zambezi is in a class of its own, other rivers were also important in facilitating navigation or caravan movement into the East African interior. Damming, irrigation, and climatic change have all reduced water flow, but in the late nineteenth century boats could move 450 km inland along the Tana River (Kusimba 1999). Three final points deserve comment. First, resources attractive to long-distance trade are not uniformly distributed: gold, for example, is found only on the Zimbabwe Plateau, not farther north. Second, some locations benefit from advantageous positions vis-à-vis the monsoon system: the coastal current, for instance, turns east close to Lamu, making this an ideal finishing point for those voyaging from western Asia (Horton 1987a). Third, many of Africa's offshore islands have historically been important participants in the interaction networks I describe, and it is to these that I now turn.

Colonizing Offshore Islands, Introducing Southeast Asian Crops

Archaeologists have given considerable thought to island communities and the links between them (e.g., Waldren and Ensenyat 2002), but Africa has rarely been included in such studies. Recent finds suggest, however, that the time is ripe for reappraising this situation so that questions asked of island archaeology, such as human impacts on island ecosystems, the maintenance of interisland and island–mainland connections, and the development of distinctive insular cultural traditions, can also be asked of East African data. Four kinds of island may be identified. First are those lying close offshore that were very much part of the Swahili world—the Lamu Archipelago, Kilwa, Pemba, Zanzibar (Unguja), and Mafia. Once thought to have been occupied only during the past 2,000 years, new fieldwork is pushing their settlement back beyond the advent of Iron Age communities. Second, there is the island continent of Madagascar, separated from Africa for tens of millions of years, with its own unique Gondwanaland-derived flora and fauna and a substantial Indonesian basis to its population and culture. Filling the gap between these groups, geographically and perhaps historically, are the Comoro Islands; the Socotra archipelago occupies a not dissimilar position at eastern Africa's northern terminus, nearer to Somalia than Arabia but historically closest to Yemen.[1] Lastly come the islands of the Indian Ocean's African diaspora, Mauritius, Réunion, Rodrigues, and Seychelles, known perhaps to earlier mariners but first inhabited after European intrusion, their populations substantially implanted through plantation slavery.

Our understanding of the initial colonization of Africa's offshore islands is being rapidly transformed. Many of those immediately offshore were settled by the beginning to middle of the first millennium cal. A.D. by Early Iron Age societies that must have used sailing craft similar to recent dhows and had the skills to cope with deep sea channels and strong currents (Chami and Msemwa 1997; Chami 1999a). Excitingly, excavations at Machaga Cave, Zanzibar, indicate that Early Iron Age presence was preceded as early as 2500 cal. B.C. by stone-tool-using people, who exploited a largely wild fauna (Chami 2001a). What appear to be Later Stone Age artifacts are also now known from Mafia, again presumably preceding Early Iron Age settlement (Chami 2000). The full implications of these finds still need to be assessed, but they imply that centuries, if not millennia, before anything that could be remotely called Swahili, people living along eastern Africa's coast could move over open water and may have developed a thriving network of exchange in fish, agricultural products, and, later, iron (Chami and Msemwa 1997).

This earlier than expected colonization of the islands closer to the mainland raises the possibility that settlement of the Comoro Islands and Madagascar might also be older than conventionally thought. For the moment, however, this remains speculation, and the oldest archaeological finds are of first millennium cal. A.D. date.[2] Madagascar's inhabitants almost all speak Malagasy, the closest relatives of which occur in Borneo (Dahl 1977). Genetic evidence confirms a central Indonesian component to their ancestry, as do cultural similarities such as outrigger canoes (figure 4.3) and the practice of second burial (Mack 1986). However, these markers are not spatially congruent, and the story is complicated by the presence within Malagasy of a substratum of Bantu phonological features and vocabulary that implies Indonesian settlement on the African mainland before colonization of Madagascar (Dahl 1988), intense movement between Africa and Madagascar immediately thereafter, or independent settlement of the island by Africans. Genetic data support an eastern African contribution to Madagascar's population, and there are historical references to non-Malagasy speakers along the island's west coast, though no traditions of arrival from elsewhere. The undoubtedly African derivation of sustainable livestock numbers and the use of Bantu-derived terms to describe them reinforce the case for settlement from the mainland (Vérin 1986; Dewar 1996).[3]

But despite much searching, evidence of early occupation is still difficult to identify: early first millennium cal. A.D. hippopotamus bones cutmarked by metal tools are among the best evidence, and forest clearance and exploitation may be of comparable age, though most long-sequence sites have basal levels of the eighth or ninth centuries (Dewar and Wright 1993). Human impact was severe, converting forest into agricultural landscapes, introducing livestock, fragmenting natural communities, and pro-

Figure 4.3. Outrigger canoes in Madagascar (British Museum, Madagascar Project, 1984, courtesy and copyright John Mack).

voking the extinction of many mammals and large birds (Dewar 1984). All areas of the island had been settled before 1000, and the archaeology fits glottochronological estimates of some 2,000 years ago for the divergence of Malagasy's dialects (Vérin et al. 1970). How Indonesians reached Madagascar remains unclear: direct movement could have taken 4 to 6 weeks in May to October given the favorable easterly trade winds and currents at this latitude, but perhaps several shorter moves along the Indian Ocean's northern and western shores are more likely. It is also likely that the island may have been known for some time before its effective colonization, which might explain the pattern of dates previously mentioned. If so, then perhaps a lack of readily accessible products or inhabitants with whom to trade made it less attractive than other areas of the Indian Ocean (including the African mainland?) until the reenergizing of contacts between the East African coast and the Middle East in the eighth century (Mack 2000, 176). Sanskrit loanwords in Malagasy hint at continued contact with Indonesia after initial settlement (Adelaar 1989), and Arabic references to "Waqwaq" traders and pirates imply Indonesian presence off East Africa's coast into the twelfth century

(Chittick 1977). The Comoro Islands may have been staging posts in this "Waqwaq" trade with Southeast Asia (Allibert 1991–92). Intervisible, if separated by dangerous currents and winds, they are accessible from Africa using both summer and winter monsoons, as well as from Asia in summer. Eighth to tenth century sites, which provide the earliest evidence of human presence, have yielded Asian rice, millet, and livestock of presumably African origin, ceramics similar to those from Chibuene in Mozambique, and burials of negroid individuals, some of whom practiced tooth evulsion, an East African custom (Wright 1984).

Inextricably involved with Indonesian settlement on the western side of the Indian Ocean is the introduction to Africa of crops of Southeast Asian origin. Bananas and plantains (*Musa* spp.) are by far the most important of these, if virtually invisible archaeologically since they do not produce pollen, seeds, or tissues that lignify. Although protein and fat deficient, they have ten times the yield of yams and their cultivation needs less clearance and labor (Vansina 1990). Their impact in equatorial Africa has been enormous (figure 4.4). Several waves of introduction can be defined (figure 4.5; De Langhe et al. 1994–95), of which two are of greatest antiquity: the East African AAA group, with some sixty endemic, mostly banana, cultivars, and the African plantains of the equatorial rainforest, which show even

Figure 4.4. Banana plantation at Lwentuwa near Ntusi, Uganda (courtesy and copyright Andrew Reid).

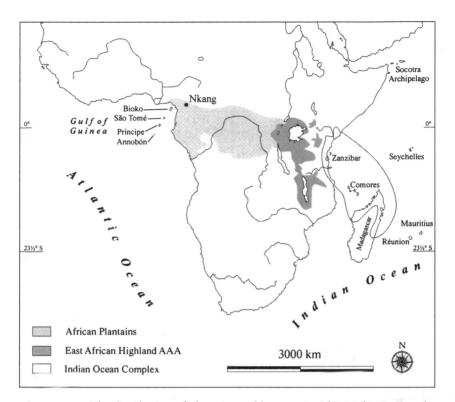

Figure 4.5. The distribution of plantains and bananas in Africa (after De Langhe et al. 1994–95).

greater genetic variability, all produced by somatic mutation. Distributions and genetics imply that the latter is the oldest group, with a time-depth of some 2,000 years. This is, in fact, probably a serious underestimate, since phytoliths identified as banana or plantain have been recovered from mid-first millennium cal. B.C. ceramics at Nkang, Cameroon (Mbida et al. 2000). Unless contamination or misidentification are involved (and there seems no sign of either, though Vansina (2003) raises doubts over the accuracy and size of the comparative sample employed), contact between Africa and Indonesia is the inescapable conclusion. Linguistic reconstructions of Proto-Malayo-Polynesian include many terms for outrigger canoe technology (Blust 1995), so there may be no navigational impediments to such an early date, even if contact was mediated via intermediate landfalls like India, a possibility enhanced by claims for Indian pottery on Mafia Island in the mid-first millennium cal. B.C. (Chami and Kwekason 2003).

Intriguingly, cultural lexical data suggest that bananas were known to Bantu-speakers *before* they came into contact with the ancestral Malagasy (Berchem 1989–90).

Cameroon is on Africa's western side, and drought and frost must have hindered *Musa*'s expansion inland from the East African coast, even though preexisting exchange networks, like those moving obsidian more than 200 km from Mt. Eburru, Kenya (Robertshaw 1993) or seashells 500 km inland to Tanzania's Ngorongoro area (Mutoro 1998), facilitated the diffusion of new crops and the skills to tend them. The initial introduction to Africa of bananas and plantains thus probably lies centuries before the Nkang dates, even if their similarities to enset, use of which was perhaps more widespread than today, encouraged their spread (Rossel 1994–95). Also of note is Nkang's location close to the presumed homeland of Bantu and its date, contemporary with the beginning of a significant increase in evidence for settlement of central Africa's rainforests. Did plantains fuel the population growth and expansion involved in the dispersal of Bantu languages (De Langhe and De Maret 1999)? Whether other Southeast Asian crops have a similar antiquity in Africa remains unknown, but the economic impact of taro, new yam varieties, and sugarcane was much less; historical references probably underestimate the antiquity of their presence on the continent (*pace* Wigboldus 1994–95). Another introduction, Asian rice (*Oryza sativa*), is the main staple of most Malagasy and known from the Comoros in the eighth or ninth centuries (Wright 1984) and Mahilaka on Madagascar itself from the tenth (Radimilahy 1998); when it arrived on the mainland is also uncertain. Lastly, chickens, another ultimately Southeast Asian domesticate, are depicted in New Kingdom Egypt, but probably remained rare there until Roman times. Uncertainly present in Meroitic art, their earliest firm dates south of the Sahara lie around 500 (MacDonald and Edwards 1993; Chami 1994). Rare bones in the Machaga Cave sequence, Zanzibar, claimed to be much older (Chami 2001a), are not yet directly dated and stratigraphic displacement from later deposits must be a possibility, but the Nkang banana phytoliths would no longer make a first millennium cal. B.C. presence surprising.

East Africa and the Greco-Roman World

One early historical source relevant to Indonesian presence in the western Indian Ocean is Pliny, who appears to describe the use of outrigger canoes in moving cinnamon to India and Arabia (J. N. Miller 1969, 156). Also from the first century is the *Periplus of the Erythraean Sea*, a navigational and commercial guide for Greco-Roman sailors trading in the Indian

Ocean (Casson 1989). Its author's prime interest lay in India, now directly reachable using the monsoons, the Greek discovery of which is attributed to Eudoxus of Cyzicus in 116 B.C. By 25 B.C. 120 vessels sailed annually to India and Arabia from Myos Hormos (Strabo, *Geography* II 5.12), but the timing of the monsoons meant that a return trip to East Africa took 2 years, more than double the time needed to reach India. The *Periplus* thus says little about East Africa, though much has been made of it by archaeologists and historians. The most convincing reconstruction of its itinerary identifies the island of Menouthias, the inhabitants of which used sewn boats and dugout canoes, with Pemba and locates its terminus, the port of Rhapta, around Bagamoyo. Apparently subject to a southern Arabian king, Rhapta exported ivory, rhinoceros horn, and turtle shell in return for iron implements, wine, grain, and glass stones (beads?). A century later, Ptolemy's *Geography*, though locating Rhapta farther north, shows an awareness of the coast as far as Cape Delgado (Horton 1990; but see Kirwan [1986] for an alternative interpretation). Until recently the only secure archaeological evidence reinforcing these accounts came from Ras Hafun, Somalia (ancient Opone), where two sites have been excavated. Lacking substantial buildings, they were probably ephemeral campsites used by sailors awaiting shifts in the monsoon to move on to India or East Africa; extracting dye from *Murex* shells is also likely (Horton 1996a). Ceramics suggest direct links to Egypt in the first centuries B.C. and A.D., followed by a decline in Roman trade and an increasing presence of visitors from the Gulf, especially in the third to fifth centuries (M. Smith and Wright 1988). That direct Roman trade with India was mostly a first century affair fits this pattern well. Confirmation of Greco-Roman interest farther south is also now becoming available. It takes the form of Egyptian glass, Middle Eastern glazed pottery, and eastern Mediterranean beads from sites in the Rufiji Delta (Chami and Msemwa 1997; Chami 1999b) and late Roman pottery from Zanzibar (Juma 1996; Horton and Middleton 2000, 32). Some of this pottery resembles that from Ras Hafun and could reflect direct Greco-Roman connections, but it may equally have arrived in East Africa via intermediaries. Though evidence of early first millennium Iron Age settlement of the coast is now emerging, the scale of intercontinental trade and local sociopolitical complexity remains to be established (*pace* inadequately substantiated claims for overseas export of iron—Schmidt (1995)—or state-level organization—Chami (2001b). Indeed, compared with the evidence for Roman trade with India, the finds so far are trifling, but there may have been some continuity in external contacts between the Greco-Roman period and the arrival of Islam. Sinclair (1991), for example, notes possible pre-Islamic (but perhaps only seventh or eighth century) sherds in the lowest levels at Chibuene, southern

Mozambique, and the two key Gulf cities trading with East Africa in the early Islamic period—Shiraz and Siraf—both have significant pre-Islamic occupation (Horton and Middleton 2000).

Origins and Development of the Swahili Trading System

Few African peoples have had their origins debated so intensely as the Swahili. The combination of strong nineteenth century Omani presence on the East African coast, their Muslim faith, and the occurrence of obviously Middle Eastern imports in ruined towns encouraged early European scholars to opt for an exotic origin in the form of colonizing Arab merchants, thereby divorcing the Swahili from both their hinterland and their African roots. Oral and written Swahili traditions that emphasize Persian or Arab ancestries reinforced this view, which in turn influenced pioneering archaeological work by Kirkman (1954) and Chittick (1974, 1984) and an initial research focus on stone-built mosques and houses (Horton 1987a). As Kusimba (1999) shows, several lines of inquiry have demolished this position, unequivocally concluding that the Swahili are African, however deeply involved in the broader cultural and trading systems of the Indian Ocean. Their architecture, for example, is distinctive (Garlake 1966), and some early Swahili settlements had gated, rectangular enclosures of the kind used ritually among the Mijikenda of Kenya's north coast (Horton 1987a). This observation gains added significance because the Mijikenda share a common linguistic origin with Swahili in the Sabaki family of Northeastern Bantu, and because almost all Swahili's Arabic loanwords, like many of their claims to exotic origin, reflect recent Omani colonization (Nurse and Spear 1985). Furthermore, Proto-Sabaki, which includes terms for boat technology, has a glottochronologically estimated origin of around 500–800 (Nurse 1983). This fits neatly with the age of the Tana Tradition ceramics that occur in the basal layers of many late first/early second millennium Swahili towns from the Lamu Archipelago to southern Mozambique, as well as offshore on the Comoros (Wright 1993; Horton and Middleton 2000). Significantly, Tana Tradition pottery derives typologically from local Early Iron Age ceramics (Chami 1994), although its precise origin remains contested (Chami 1998; cf. Helm 2000). Its widespread distribution may reflect the self-identification of many individual communities with an emerging economic system (Sutton 1998b), integrated as much by the spread of Swahili as a lingua franca as by simple expansion of a single ethnic group and varying in its sense and modes of self-definition through both time and space (cf. Pouwels 1987).

Our understanding of the growth of that economic system and its associated development of increasingly urban communities is greatly aided by contemporary historical sources—Arabic, Chinese, and Portuguese— and by local Swahili chronicles (Horton and Middleton 2000; Insoll 2003a). Visits to East Africa by al-Mas'udi ca. 915 (Freeman-Grenville 1962) and Ibn Battuta in 1331 (Gibb 1972) are particularly important eyewitness accounts for the period preceding European arrival. Both documents and archaeology make plain that Muslim trade with East Africa was underway before the Abbasid dynasty relocated Islam's capital from Damascus to Baghdad in the mid-eighth century, but that it grew significantly thereafter. In East Africa this is most evident at Manda, an excellent anchorage in the Lamu Archipelago with substantial quantities of eighth century early Islamic pottery (Horton 1987a). Nearby, initial occupation at Shanga (Horton 1996b) and Pate (Wilson and Omar 1997) is of similar age: significantly, this stretch of the coast was historically rich in elephants, mangrove forests, and ambergris and offered reliable monsoons for navigating across the Indian Ocean. Mangrove wood, much in demand in the Gulf as a building material, was extensively used at Siraf in the ninth and tenth centuries (Horton and Middleton 2000, 76). According to al-Mas'udi, ivory, on the other hand, was largely directed via Oman to India and China, whereas other exports included rhinoceros horn, then as now shamelessly used as both aphrodisiac and knife handle, and hawksbill turtle (*Eretmochalys imbricata*) shell, employed for inlay work. Not all of these items were exclusive to the Kenyan and Tanzanian coast, and by the early tenth century ivory was already being acquired from as far south as the Limpopo Valley. Turtle shell, on the other hand, was probably supplied from the Comoros, where glass beads, glass vessels, and glazed ceramics confirm participation in contacts with the Gulf (Wright 1984); house mice bones imply visits by large, long-distance ships (Wright 1992, 84).

Slaves have long been important in East Africa's Indian Ocean trade. In this early period, Arabic sources are widely interpreted to mean that large numbers were exported from East Africa's coasts for use on plantations and drainage projects in the southern Iraqi marshes (Horton and Middleton 2000, 73–75; but cf. Talhami 1977 for a more critical assessment). Pemba, if correctly identified with "Qanbalu," may have been conquered about 750 to provide an entrepôt for the slave trade and is the only Muslim community on the coast recorded by al-Mas'udi; it has produced ninth to eleventh century Gulf pottery (LaViolette 2000). Slaves must, however, have been obtained mostly from the African mainland: chains found at Manda and Shanga (Horton and Middleton 2000, 75) may attest to their export overseas, whereas Schmidt (1989) notes a late first millennium reduction in site numbers and the appearance of rudimentary fortifications in the Usambara Hills, 80 km inland, that may reflect slave raids on a previously densely settled area. Slaves continued to be taken in large numbers, to judge from Arabic chronicles, until the last and most violent of several revolts (868–83) and the decline of Abbasid power curtailed demand for their labor in Iraq (Afolayan 1998). Subsequent supply was more directed at domestic workers and concubines (Lovejoy 2000).

Coastal sites of this early period are generally small and agricultural with evidence of iron working and marine-resource exploitation, but by the ninth to tenth centuries some reached 5–10 ha and show enhanced proportions of imported ceramics. As well as the Lamu Archipelago sites already mentioned, examples include Unguja Ukuu on Zanzibar, Dembeni in the Comoros, and Chibuene, all with access to highly desirable local products, such as pearls, turtle shell, or ivory (Wright 1993). Gulf ceramics, some certainly made at Siraf and others paralleling the contents of merchant houses there, dominate the imported assemblages, but rare Chinese pottery is also found; some of the Gulf vessels may have been used to transport date syrup and other comestibles (Horton and Middleton 2000). Glass beads are more widespread, and potentially sourceable to place of manufacture (Robertshaw et al. 2003), but textiles remain frustratingly invisible, though well documented historically and ethnographically (Picton and Mack 1989). Another introduction, considered more fully later on, was Islam, but in this early phase it maintained only a sparse presence on the East African coast.

The Fatimid conquest of Egypt in 969 established a strong new Muslim state there, and the Red Sea resumed its former Greco-Roman importance as a route through which East African commodities reached the Middle East.[4] Direct voyages between Egypt and East Africa nonetheless remained rare for the same reason as in Greco-Roman times, the timing of the monsoons. Specific connections are evident in the glass vessels, Mediterranean coral, and Fatimid coins found on the Lamu Archipelago, Pemba, and Mafia, and perhaps the use of bird-topped parasols as royal regalia (Hrbek 1977, 85), but Red Sea/Mediterranean pottery is almost wholly absent, probably because of its bulk. The adoption, initially around Lamu and then, from the eleventh century, farther south as well, of the tradition of building mosques and other important buildings in *Porites* coral stone was probably another introduction from the (southern) Red Sea. Of items leaving East Africa, ivory continued to be a principal export. The late tenth through eleventh centuries witnessed a massive expansion of its carving throughout the Mediterranean world, and East African tusks were preferred to West African ones for their size and quality (figure 4.6; Cutler 1985). Rock crystal too was imported to Cairo and waste from its working

Figure 4.6. A late-medieval carved European ivory showing a man kissing a nun (courtesy and copyright Pitt Rivers Museum, University of Oxford). Such pieces, and others of a more obviously devotional nature, were frequently made from ivory originally imported from East Africa (Cutler 1985).

is known from the Lamu Archipelago. One likely source is in Tsavo National Park (Kusimba and Kusimba 2000), but northern Madagascar is also possible (Radimilahy 1998). Other recorded exports were gold, now emerging as a major trade item for the first time, and iron; al-Idrisi, writing in the mid-1100s, commented on the export of superior quality East African iron to India and the Gulf (Freeman-Grenville 1962, 20), and Kusimba and Killick (2003) interpret production of crucible steel at Galu, Kenya, in this light.

Buoyed by this expansion in trade, more hierarchical settlement patterns developed along the East African coasts from the eleventh century (Stiles 1992; Wright 1993). Massive expansion is evident at several sites, with Jongwe and Kilwa both exceeding 20 ha. Others, like Gedi and Mombasa, were established for the first time. Islam too was now adopted more widely. As Fatimid power waned, several interlocking networks emerged connecting East Africa with other parts of the Indian Ocean world. Ports like Hormuz remained important in the Gulf, their Indian and

Chinese ceramics closely matching those from East Africa. Yemen, and particularly the port of Aden, was another source of Chinese and Indian products, as well as the locally made "black-and-yellow" ware that reached the Swahili coast 1250–1350; ongoing work by Pradines (2003) and her colleagues in southern Arabia, Pakistan, and Kenya is explicitly designed to investigate these international connections on a comparative basis.

Gold looms largest in discussions of East Africa's exports at this period, its significance enhanced by its more restricted sources and consequent impact on the shape and form of the wider trading system. Finding a ready market in Europe, where gold coinage now became widespread, gold most probably passed through Kilwa, which controlled Sofala, the port at which the precious metal reached the coast. Kilwa grew rapidly at this time, keeping close religious and political ties with Yemen, striking its own gold coins, building new mosques, and constructing the palace complex of Husuni Kubwa (figure 4.7), the unique scale and nature of which argue for a Middle Eastern, or Middle Eastern–trained, architect (Sutton 1998a). As well as gold, ivory too continued to be traded, while textiles went from southern Somalia (H. Brown 1988) and Madagascar (Allibert 1990) to Egypt, the Gulf, and Arabia. Madagascar also supplied China with slaves

Figure 4.7. Husuni Kubwa, Kilwa, Tanzania (courtesy and copyright, the British Institute in Eastern Africa).

(Duyvendak 1949, 22–23) and exported gold, crystal, and vessels of chlorite schist. Succeeding late first millennium stations there, such as the island of Nosy Mangabé (Dewar and Wright 1993, 430), many of these commodities were funneled via newly established trading ports like Mahilaka, a massive 70-ha walled town with evidence of substantial craft production, as well as imported Near Eastern and Chinese glazed ceramics and Near Eastern glass (Radimilahy 1998).

The combination of growing saturation of European demand for gold and the Black Death[5] provoked massive deflation and depopulation across the Indian Ocean in the mid-fourteenth century, but the slump was not permanent. Renewed building activity is evident, for example, at Kilwa in the 1400s (Sutton 1998a) when direct trade between India and East Africa grew sharply, free from Arabian or Gulf intermediaries. Slightly later Portuguese observers recorded Indian merchants in several Swahili towns and foodstuffs, soap, indigo, and carnelian as major imports to the African coast, along with cloth, traces of which occur as far inland as Ingombe Ilede, Zambia (Fagan et al. 1969). The fifteenth century also witnessed the remarkable voyages across the Indian Ocean of the Chinese admiral Zheng He, who first reached the Swahili coast in 1421, taking giraffes as gifts to the Ming court. Though they do not seem to have been followed up, Chinese (or Arab) ships may have voyaged considerably farther south; Chinese maps originating in the previous century, which draw on Arabic originals for many place names, give surprisingly accurate representations of Africa's southern tip (Chang 1971; Poumailloux 2003).

The high visibility of Middle Eastern and Chinese imports, coupled with problems in pinpointing the eastern African origins of gold, ivory, or other commodities in the archaeological record, might encourage the idea that Africans played passive, stay-at-home roles in the Indian Ocean trading system (cf. Pearson 1998, 40). To be sure, some historical references, including one by al-Idrisi, could support this interpretation, and Chinese records reporting the arrival of East African "envoys" as early as the eleventh century need not imply that they got there in their own vessels, any more than the East African pottery dumped at Ras el-Hadd, Oman, after carrying water onboard ship demands the presence of African traders (Horton 1996b, 243). However, ninth century Omani records do envisage the possibility of African merchants arriving there (J. Wilkinson 1981), outrigger vessels from Kilwa, Mogadishu, and Madagascar were recorded in Aden harbor around 1232 (Horton and Middleton 2000), and early Portuguese records report the "Moors of Sofala" selling ivory and ambergris in Gujarat, western India (Kusimba 1999, 136). Africans also took an active part in Indian Ocean trade by working as guards on merchant ships and as mercenaries on land (Gibb 1972), while slaves of

African origin rose to positions of considerable political and military importance in medieval and early modern India (Basu 2003; Pankhurst 2003). More subtly, and more archaeologically, fourteenth century mosque furnishings and other carvings from Mogadishu and Kilwa made of Gujarati marble were surely either commissioned from East Africa or made there by specially recruited Indian craftsmen (Lambourn 1999). This second possibility matches suggestions that East African bead-drilling, metal-lurgical, and textile technologies show Indian influences from the tenth century (Horton 1996b) and that copper wire–drawing techniques too may have been introduced from across the Indian Ocean (Bisson 2000, 105).

Structures of Trade

This survey may "place the Swahili within the Indian Ocean world of trade and exchange" (Horton and Middleton 2000, 27), but we have still to consider how that trade was structured and in particular how the Swahili towns were able to obtain resources from the African interior. In recent centuries trust between Swahili merchants and traders coming from overseas was built by fictive kinship ties and the sponsorship of the latter by leading Swahili patricians. Ibn Battuta mentions such arrangements, and Horton's (1996b) excavations at Shanga identified possible guest rooms equipped with private bathroom facilities in the outer courtyards of some stone houses. Another dimension is offered by the "sea-walls" of Manda, originally tenth century but greatly expanded thereafter, perhaps to provide massive footings for masonry buildings such as factors' compounds (Chittick 1984). To facilitate the business dealings that no doubt took place in such structures, the first coins were minted locally in the ninth century, probably using a weight system linked to the Cairo dinar, the standard weight for Islamic coinage in the Indian Ocean (Horton and Middleton 2000).

Turning to the distributions of different kinds of goods, it is clear that more than a simple import-export system was in operation. Chittick (1977) makes this plain, differentiating African goods sought for export overseas (ivory, gold, skins, timber), goods imported from overseas for trade with the African interior (glass beads and cloth), goods imported for consumption in the coastal towns (fine ceramics and their contents, cloth), and those made there for trade with the interior (shell beads, cloth,[6] and perhaps salt). And to these distinctions we must add the "low" commerce (*sensu* Horden and Purcell 2000) of the many items moving, often over small distances, from one part of the Swahili world to another: grain, leatherwork, metalwork, textiles, paper, and so on (H. Brown 1988). These more complex definitions provide a better framework for the archaeological record. For example, imported Chinese porcelain and Near Eastern glazed ceramics are, on the East African mainland, almost wholly restricted to the Swahili coast.[7] Their ownership was largely exclusive to local patricians who, from the thirteenth century, displayed them on their tombs or in the same special *zidaka* niches in their houses in which other valuables—Islamic texts, rich textiles—were kept. The use of imported pottery in this way, rather than for eating (Donley 1987), is a good example of how artifacts can shift their meanings when they move from one cultural milieu to another (Appadurai 1986; N. Thomas 1991). Slaves too could be decommoditized once converted to Islam, or even freed, while cloth had uses as a medium of barter and status signifier, not just as a covering (Horton and Middleton 2000).

How coastal communities accessed goods from their hinterland and the African interior beyond varied. One means was by reciprocal exchange between groups practicing different subsistence strategies. For example, Yajima (1996) shows how coastal foragers in the Tana River area supplied honey, wax, ivory, rhinoceros horn, and skins to pastoralists and farmers in return for dairy and cereal products and to Swahili townsfolk in return for shell and glass beads, iron tools and weapons, and metal jewelry. Mutoro (1998) describes a comparable instance for the nineteenth century Mijikenda, and Kusimba and Kusimba (2000) demonstrate that such exchange systems, which mobilized products for consumption on the coast and export from it, could act as successful risk-minimizing strategies for hunter-gatherers living in marginal environments like Tsavo National Park. Specialized caravan trade, on the other hand, is not identifiable earlier than the eighteenth century. Except for gold, neither the commodities sought nor the scale on which they were traded abroad may have required deep, sustained penetration of the interior before then. Instead, glass and shell beads may have moved through multiple, shorter distance intercommunity exchanges that principally involved foodstuffs and spouses (Mutoro 1998). But are we in danger here of underestimating what was happening? Many items important historically in trade, such as salt, cloth, and ochre, are, for example, perishable. Consider too that Tana Tradition ceramics from Dakawa, 200 km inland in Tanzania, hint at links to coastal trading systems as early as the eighth and ninth centuries, specifically, so it is suggested, by exchanging ivory, skins, and slaves for the substantial amounts of iron smelted on-site (Haaland and Msuya 2000). Even farther inland, Mapunda (1995) reports Tana Tradition sherds from the shores of Lake Tanganyika, and Indian Ocean cowries (sidebar 5) occur in tenth through twelfth century graves in southern Congo's Upemba Depression (De Maret 1999). Down-the-line local exchange could account for all this, but in one case, that of the Zimbabwe

SIDEBAR 5

Cowries

One of the Indian Ocean's most characteristic products is the cowrie, the precolonial currency of choice in much of Africa. Of more than two hundred species, some trickled into Egypt and Nubia in Predynastic times (J. Phillips 1997), others the Near East, and, in the first millennium B.C., Europe (Reese 1991). But one species outperformed all others, the money cowrie (*Cypraea moneta*). Obtainable along the East African coast, where the Swahili trading station of Somana may have been one collection point (Duarte 1993), its principal source lay in the Maldive Islands. There the shells were particularly abundant and easy to collect from relatively pure stands, their sale permitting settlement of otherwise uninhabitable atolls. Impossible to counterfeit and without any other practical value, cowries could be traded accurately by weight, volume, and number, were difficult to break, and only slowly lost their color and luster (figure 4.8). As yet, cowries have no systematic archaeological corpus, but they were already circulating widely among farming communities in southern Africa in the first millennium cal. A.D. and were carried in bulk across the Sahara to the Sahel (9,000 km from their source!) in the eleventh and twelfth centuries (Levtzion and Hopkins 2000, 83; Monod 1969), moving farther south into the forest zone before Portuguese arrival. Egypt may have been one conduit, and the Geniza documents refer to them in passing as ornaments and trinkets destined for the Maghreb (Goiten 1967–88), but Mecca, Morocco, and Iran also acted as suppliers within the Muslim world. Once Portuguese, and later Dutch and British, ships could carry them from the Maldives, they were introduced to West Africa in amounts that eventually exceeded 100 metric tons (100 million shells) a year. Along the coasts of Togo, Bénin, and Ghana, in particular, cowries dominated as units of exchange or account in purchasing individuals for the Atlantic slave trade, with prices reaching 170,000 shells per head in the 1770s (Hogendorn and Johnson 1986). Valued also as jewelry, they were even carried across the Atlantic and employed in the Americas to help maintain a sense of African identity in slavery (Yentsch 1994, 303). Back in Africa, they declined in use in the early 1800s as the slave trade waned, but revived again with the export from West Africa of palm oil in the mid-nineteenth century. Only after that did hyperinflation, caused in part by the European introduction of another species (*Cypraea annulus*, from the coast of Tanzania), and colonial prejudice in favor of coined money lead to their disappearance.

Figure 4.8. Cowrie shells incorporated into a leather amulet box from the Yoruba region of southwestern Nigeria (courtesy and copyright Pitt Rivers Museum, University of Oxford).

Plateau and Shashe-Limpopo Confluence, it certainly does not. How can we understand this?

Contrasting Interiors: The Zimbabwe Tradition, Uganda, and Upemba

For more than a century, Great Zimbabwe has exercised a hold over the Western imagination (figure 4.9). Though attributions to the Phoenicians are thankfully banished from serious discussion, debate continues as to the role played in its development, and that of the wider cultural tradition to which it belongs, by long-distance exchange connections with the east East African coast. Finds from Chibuene (Sinclair 1991) hint at southern Africa's participation in the Indian Ocean trading system before the

Figure 4.9. The Great Enclosure at Great Zimbabwe, Zimbabwe, with some of the Valley Enclosures and the *dare* (open court area) in front of it. The photograph is taken from the Hill Complex.

seventh century, and it was certainly underway by the late first millennium when glass beads and seashells occur widely in areas of Early Iron Age agricultural settlement and glass could reach as far inland as southern Zambia (Vogel 1971). Between 900 and 1020 cal. A.D. imported finds concentrate at Schroda in the Shashe-Limpopo Basin, which has produced massive evidence of ivory working (Hanisch 1981). This neatly parallels al-Mas'udi's reference to the export of ivory from the east coast, and the many carnivores in the Schroda fauna (Voigt 1983) may reflect his further comment on the export of animal skins. A cache of standardized ivory bangles (made ready for sale?) from Mosu I, eastern Botswana (Reid and Segobye 2000), suggests that Schroda was tapping into exchange systems reaching far inland, ultimately as far as the Tsodilo Hills, where Iron Age villages were perhaps hubs for the integration of local hunter-gatherers into farmer-dominated political and economic networks (Denbow 1999; cf. Sadr 1997 for an alternative interpretation).

In the eleventh century cal. A.D., Schroda was succeeded as the principal settlement of the Shashe-Limpopo Basin first by Bambandyanalo and then by Mapungubwe Hill. Huffman (1996b, 2000) argues that relocation to Mapungubwe ca. 1220 cal. A.D., with its concomitant repositioning of the cattle pen away from the settlement's center and the innovation of the practice of elite residency on hilltops behind access-controlling stone walls, marks the establishment of new patterns of rulership based on class distinctions in southern Africa's first state-level societies. This may be to overstate familiar Western concepts at the expense of more communal types of authority, but differential access to exotic valuables is certain: tens of thousands of glass beads, some of types unknown elsewhere, as well as rare Chinese pottery, confirm this. No other southern African site can match such finds at this time or the gold-equipped burials from Mapungubwe Hill (Meyer and Esterhuizen 1994; Meyer 1998; Wood 2000). For reasons still unclear, Mapungubwe was eclipsed by Great Zimbabwe. This, by far the largest of more than 200 comparable stonewalled sites in and adjacent to the Zimbabwe Plateau, has produced a unique set of finds indicating contact with the Swahili coast: Chinese and Persian ceramics, glass, coral, cowries, and tens of thousands of glass beads, recovered in conjunction with masses of iron and brass wire and iron artifacts, including gongs (Garlake 1973). Other than glass beads, such finds are, virtually without exception, unique to Great Zimbabwe in the fourteenth and fifteenth centuries; along with its size, they attest to this site's preeminence within the Zimbabwe Tradition (Huffman 1986; Pikirayi 2001).

The Zimbabwe Plateau is the only part of eastern or southern Africa that could provide both ivory and gold, thus giving coastal traders greatest returns for their investment. Copper from northern Zimbabwe and copper and tin from northern South Africa were other attractions; some 18,000 metric tons of tin ore were extracted in precolonial mining in the Rooiberg Mountains, the scarcity of tin or bronze artifacts in southern Africa suggesting almost all was exported overseas (Grant 1999). The Shashe-Limpopo Basin was itself prime elephant country, and Bambandyanalo has produced considerable evidence for the hunting and working of ivory (Voigt 1983). Gold first appears in the local record at Mapungubwe, but there is circumstantial evidence that it was mined on the Zimbabwe Plateau in the late first millennium cal. A.D. (Swan 1994). Readier access to gold may be one reason why Great Zimbabwe transcended Mapungubwe (cf. Huffman 1996a), while the close early fourteenth century parallel between its expansion and Kilwa's florescence suggests the two were organically linked through the metal's export; significantly, all the Indo-Pacific glass beads found on the Zimbabwe Plateau seem to have entered southern Africa via Kilwa (Wood 2000). How were they and other imports then used? It seems likely that the answer lies in the concept of a prestige-goods economy, with southern African elites seeking to monopolize access to valued imports that offered greater possibilities of building power than cattle, the main traditional resource. Rare and not subject to natural increase, beads and textiles could be used to secure allegiance, expressed partly through providing tribute in the ivory and gold that could then be exchanged for more exotica (Loubser 1991).

Did this pattern set in motion southern Africa's exploitation by outside powers of the kind envisaged by core-periphery models, and can it alone account for the development of the Zimbabwe Tradition? The answer seems to be no. In the first case, mining and alluvial panning were both probably undertaken by peasant farmers in the agricultural off-season, whereas elephant hunting was a positive boon in safeguarding fields and settlements. Both, in a sense, were economically marginal activities that generated exchangeable by-products, African equivalents of the mass-produced beads and cloth for which they were traded (M. Hall 1987). In response to the second question, Swahili-derived preciosities were by no means alone as signifiers of elite power or the basis of it. The Zimbabwe Tradition was underpinned first by a successful agropastoralist economy, including perhaps control of the best lands for grazing and cultivation; faunal analyses suggest that control over cattle and preferential access to prime-age beef were elite prerogatives. There are hints too that iron working fell within their ambit and some evidence for the movement within the African interior, reaching up to the Zambezi, of salt, copper, and iron, all highly desirable goods for the majority of the population. Nor, though it is less tangible, should one forget the possible significance of ritual claims, for example, in ensuring rain, as a basis for power (Mitchell 2002a, 326–31). Power is, however, never certain or permanent, and competition by subordinates for access to trade with the coast must always have been a worry for Great Zimbabwe's rulers. It may have been among the factors that led to the site's eclipse in the late fifteenth century and the emergence of new polities, Mutapa in the northeast and Torwa in the southwest, which continued to trade in gold, ivory, and, in Mutapa's case, copper, first with the Swahili and later mostly with the Portuguese; imported ceramics and other finds at some of their capitals should not, however, obscure the continued importance of control of people and cattle as the foundations of elite power (Pikirayi 2001).

How does the interior of the rest of the Swahili coast compare with the Zimbabwe Tradition? Across most of East Africa's interior even comparatively well-studied sites like Engaruka, a complex of irrigation-using settlements northwest of Arusha, have produced only a few cowrie shells or glass beads (Sutton 1998b). Farther inland new research in Uganda's Interlacustrine area has focused on large earthwork sites that are, for the most part, of fourteenth/fifteenth century cal. A.D. date, although settlement at Ntusi began several hundred years before this (Reid 1996; Robertshaw 1997; Sutton 1998c). One craft undertaken there was ivory carving, hinting perhaps, along with rare glass beads and copper objects, at long-distance exchange networks. Water-pipe fragments for smoking cannabis, a plant of Indian origin but now widely diffused in Africa (Du Toit 1976), support connections, but not necessarily commerce, with the Indian Ocean coast (Sutton 1998c, 25). Glass beads in pre-earthwork elite burials at Munsa that date to between the tenth and twelfth centuries also show that access to extra-African goods is not just a recent phenomenon (Robertshaw 1997). However, while suggesting new forms of adornment and use as prestige items exchanged between patrons and clients in competitions for followers (Schoenbrun 1998), such items remain rare. They do not, as yet, speak to involvement in trade with the Swahili coast on anywhere near the scale of the Zimbabwe Tradition. Instead, expansion into a previously poorly settled frontier region, the need to accumulate labor for agricultural production, differential access to the best grazing and agricultural land, and manipulation of religious shrines and beliefs about healing and fertility probably underpinned the growth of more complex, if unstable, polities out of existing lineage structures (Schoenbrun 1998). Significantly, perhaps, glass beads are lacking from earthwork contexts themselves, and salt and iron were probably more important trade items, the former eaten by cattle and people, the latter used to make tools and weapons (Robertshaw 1999). Interestingly, development of extensive salt production at Kibiro on the shores of Lake Albert is contemporary with early second millennium expansion into the Interlacustrine area's central grasslands (figure 4.10; Connah 1996).

A similar story is evident in southern Congo's Upemba Depression where the excavated archaeological record consists almost wholly of burials, not settlements. Iron regalia and jewelry using copper imported from Katanga suggest that status differences comparable to those identified historically were apparent in the eight and ninth centuries, recognized more widely after 900 cal. A.D., and markedly more hierarchical after 1200 cal. A.D. (De Maret 1999). Although a few Indian Ocean cowrie shells appear alongside greater evidence of exchange with the Copper Belt from the tenth century cal. A.D., trade does not seem to have driven increasing social differentiation. More important were demographic growth fed by rich local fish and agricultural resources and the demands of organizing labor to exploit these successfully. Characterized from the thirteenth century on by increasingly standardized X-shaped copper ingots that came to serve as a multipurpose currency (Bisson 1975), long-distance trade then rode on the back of these developments, just as the later Luba polity depended on manipulating regalia and objects of power for its rulers' legitimacy, not their control of the growing export of ivory to Omani and Swahili traders (De Maret 1999).

Figure 4.10. The earthworks at Ntusi, Uganda. The Main Hill with the *Bwogero* (wide scraped depressions) in the middle ground (courtesy and copyright Andrew Reid).

The Spread of Islam

Sharply distinguishing all these interior regions from the coast is the fact that all known pre-nineteenth century mosques and Muslim tombs in eastern Africa are within 1 km of the shore (Horton and Middleton 2000, 48). This only emphasizes Islam's importance in the formation of Swahili culture and its overseas connections, but by what processes was the faith introduced, given that some level of trade with Arabia preceded Islam's innovation and that simplistic notions of immigrating Arab, Muslim traders can no longer be entertained? Both historical and archaeological sources make plain that Islam's introduction was complex and drawn out. The oldest excavated evidence comes from Shanga, where a sequence of seven timber structures underlay a small tenth century stone mosque (figure 4.11). Radiocarbon determinations, stratigraphy, and imported ceramics place the earliest of these structures at about 750. All seven buildings are interpreted as mosques from their location, general, and increasingly precise, alignment toward Mecca, association with burials in typically Muslim positions, and lack of non-Muslim religious activity (Horton 1996b); Donley-Reid's (1990) arguments to the contrary are unconvincing. Elsewhere on the coast, timber mosques preceded the eleventh century stone mosque at

Figure 4.11. The main mosque, Shanga, Kenya.

Ras Mkumbuu, Pemba, and may be present in the tenth century at Unguja Ukuu, Zanzibar (Horton and Middleton 2000), broadly contemporary with burials in correct Muslim orientation at Chibuene, southern Mozambique (Sinclair 1991).

There is then good archaeological evidence for an Islamic presence along the coast by 1000, probably introduced by traders and teachers, as well as by religious dissidents seeking refuge from Arabia or the Gulf (Wright 1992). Indeed, historical sources suggest that a noticeable Shi'ite presence persisted on the East African coast into the thirteenth century, and Shi'ite-associated inscriptions on coins from the early twelfth century Mtambwe Mkuu hoard could reflect this (Horton et al. 1986). Widespread Swahili patrician claims to originate in Shiraz may be related, given the domination of the Baghdad Caliphate 945–1055 by a Shiraz-based, nominally Shi'ite dynasty, and the earlier importance of Siraf and Shiraz in trading with East Africa. Siraf-style lettering on the mihrab of East Africa's oldest still-functioning mosque at Kizimkazi, Zanzibar, reinforces this link (Flury 1922), but we should not forget either that Fatimid Egypt, East Africa's major trading partner in the late tenth and eleventh centuries, was itself a Shi'ite state (Hrbek 1977). Today, however, and over recent centuries, most Swahili follow the majority Sunni version of Islam.

It seems likely that trade was once more instrumental in bringing this about, in this case as Yemen emerged as a major partner, because it was there in the eleventh century that prestige in matters of religion and Muslim law was first accorded to Sunni descendants of Muhammad (Horton and Middleton 2000); pilgrimages to Mecca by Kilwa's Mahdali rulers and their attendance at religious schools in Yemen also signal this connection between shifts in trade and patterns of religious allegiance (Sutton 1998a).

If Muslim presence is widely attested by 1000, it was probably thin on the ground. A non-Muslim burial and pig tusks from Period Ia at Kilwa (Chittick 1974) and consumption of lemur and tortoise in the ninth and tenth century Comoros hint as much (Allibert et al. 1990), and al-Mas'udi (clearly wrongly) even claimed that only Pemba had converted by 915 (Freeman-Grenville 1962). In fact, mosques only became more common and larger from the thirteenth century, presaging Ibn Battuta's visit of 1331, which provides the first reliable historical evidence for the coast's large-scale adherence to Islam (Gibb 1972). Later, when elaborated in the fourteenth and fifteenth centuries, many mosques were made smaller, perhaps as centrally located mosques became restricted to higher-ranking townsfolk (Wright 1992). Why, we may ask, did East Africans convert? Answers must inevitably be general and similar to those that can be provided for other parts of Africa, but being able to trade on more equal terms with overseas Muslim merchants, being taken more seriously as coreligionists and receiving protection from enslavement must all have been clear inducements, alongside any genuine spiritual experiences. Given these advantages, then, why did Islam not penetrate beyond the coast until the eighteenth and, especially, nineteenth centuries? Swahili monopoly of trade with overseas merchants is one reason, but very probably the Swahili also sought to keep Islam to themselves. They could thus continue to benefit from the absence of a single system of values—economic, religious, and legal—when exchanging the beads and cloth they made or acquired from overseas for the ivory, gold, and slaves that they exported or used themselves (Horton and Middleton 2000, 90).

Finally, we may ask if the Swahili practiced a distinctively "Bantu" form of Islam? With few exceptions, such as the importance accorded royal ancestors on some stretches of the coast (and kingship was by no means a political norm; Horton and Middleton 2000), there is, in fact, little sign of cultural syncretism—undated depictions of incense burners on tombs and mihrabs and recent veneration of spirits, often at ruined town sites, do not amount to much. Even if the characteristic pillar tombs (figure 4.12) do recall traditional non-Islamic mortuary practices elsewhere in East Africa, neither they nor the absence of minarets or madrassas need

Figure 4.12. An example of a pillar tomb, Gedi, Kenya. Such tombs were a distinctive feature of Muslim funerary practice along the Swahili coast and recall traditional non-Islamic funeral architecture elsewhere in East Africa.

imply anything more than a distinctively Swahili, but wholly orthodox, architectural pattern. The one area where syncretism is more strongly evident is Madagascar. There ports like Vohémar dating 1350–1550 have burials oriented in Muslim fashion, but accompanied (in contradiction of Muslim practice) by rich grave goods that included Middle and Far Eastern ceramics (Vérin 1986). Perhaps things were more orthodox at largely uninvestigated smaller coastal settlements in northern Madagascar. Some familiarity with Islam and Swahili loanwords still survives there, but Muslim influence penetrated much further, persisting in day and month names and divination practices. More puzzlingly, in southeastern Madagascar, where today knowledge of Islam is minimal, Arabic script has been employed since at least the sixteenth century to write Malagasy magicoreligious and historical texts (*sorabe*) that are still in use. Regrettably, while local Antaimoro people may be among the island's most recent immigrants, their exact origins remain unknown (Mack 1986).

The Emergence of the Swahili World

Whether considered as a "corridor" (Horton 1987b), a "trading wheel" (Sinclair 1995), or simply a community linked by commonalities of language, belief, and economic interest, the question remains as to how we should understand the emergence of the Swahili world that extended over 2,000 km, from Mogadishu to Mahilaka and Chibuene. To suggest this was simply the result of overseas stimulus is clearly false: the archaeological record is too complex, the African roots of language and culture too strong, the evidence of pre-Muslim offshore settlement and movement too compelling. To treat the Swahili as a cog to be slotted into a core-periphery model raises many difficulties and obscures the complexity of the exchanges in which they engaged, across the sea, among themselves and inland. Indeed, Wright (1993) concludes that the development of settlement hierarchies and urbanism did not proceed in direct response to changes in the scale or direction of intercontinental trade. Access to valued exotic goods that coastal leaders could use to display and enhance their own standing is, however, likely. Where successful, it probably fed upon itself as such leaders were empowered to accumulate additional resources for exchange. Participation in exchange systems, especially at the more local level, would also have offered ways of alleviating the risks posed by scarce or undependable agricultural resources, and some communities were surely positioned, by flukes of geography, in what were predisposed to become strategic positions within local and transoceanic networks (Kusimba 1999, 181). Reinforcing these ties were a shared language (KiSwahili) and regionally defined styles of material culture (Wright 1993; Chami 1998). Within the Swahili world itself, Islamic symbols (in language, dress, and ritual) and access to exotic goods provided the basis for elite identity and dominance and definition from, or association with, mainland neighbors and partners, African and non-African alike. Whether expressed in terms of peer-polity interaction (Wright 1993) or the establishment of corporate power strategies (Kusimba 1999; Robertshaw 2003), this interpretation may best capture the development of the Swahili-centered trading system that connected so much of eastern Africa with the opposite shores of the Indian Ocean.

Foreign Colonizations of Eastern Africa's Coasts

This system experienced a major new challenge when Europeans entered the Indian Ocean. Seeking cheaper, direct access free of Muslim intermediaries to the spices of the Orient that were essential for preserving food, and simultaneously intent upon propagating Christianity, the Portuguese finally reached the Indian Ocean and India in 1498. To seize control of key resources, particularly the exchange of Indian textiles for African gold and ivory that could then be used to buy spices, they sacked Kilwa, Mombasa, and Ungwana, imposed tribute, established strategic bases, and restricted maritime trade through a permit system. Though they succeeded in cornering 75 percent of Europe's spice imports in the late 1500s (Curtin 1984, 144), they had little impact on local eastern African commerce. Incursions from inland, including those of Somali pastoralists, posed at least as much difficulty for the Swahili towns (Kusimba 1999; Horton and Middleton 2000). Indeed, the Portuguese ultimately lacked the manpower to enforce control, despite constructing fortresses at several key locations. Fort Jesus, Mombasa, built in 1593, is the most impressive of these, its massive walls enclosing a central court and buildings that included a church (figure 4.13). Kirkman's (1974) excavations explored its constructional history, extending beyond the Omani conquest of 1698, and recovered a range of exotic and local ceramics, but without, perhaps, adding much to our knowledge of the site's inhabitants. Indeed, both onshore and offshore the Portuguese period remains little explored archaeologically, though Mombasa harbor has been recently surveyed (Forsythe et al. 2003). This follows excavation of the frigate *São Antonio de Tanna*

Figure 4.13. The sea wall of Fort Jesus, Mombasa, Kenya, built by the Portuguese in 1593.

wrecked there in 1697. Its combination of Indian earthenwares (reflecting the ship's base in Goa), African pottery for cooking and storage, Chinese and Thai ceramics, Portuguese cannon and wine bottles, and more than 200 ebony logs being carried as cargo amply illustrates the scope of Portuguese interests (Sassoon 1981). Much farther south, wrecks off the South African coast have also been investigated (Auret and Maggs 1982; Maggs 1984), along with the campsite where survivors of the *São Gonçalo* spent 10 months at Plettenberg Bay in 1630 (A. Smith 1986b). Their accounts, and those of other shipwrecked crews, provide important firsthand observations of South Africa's indigenous inhabitants.

Elsewhere, Portugal's presence remains little studied by archaeologists, even on Pemba, which was settled by Portuguese farmers (Horton 1997), who helped introduce a wealth of new, American-derived crops (Freeman-Grenville 1988). The one exception is in Zimbabwe, the principal focus of Portuguese gold-getting activity. By 1550 small trading communities were established at strategic locations along the Zambezi, which, despite its falls and rapids, gave better access to the highlands than the Save farther south (Pikirayi 2001). Others followed across northeastern Zimbabwe, hosting trade fairs (*feiras*) aimed primarily at accessing gold exports from the Mutapa state. Excavated examples have yielded Chinese and European pottery, glass and gold beads, lead shot, and gold dust (Garlake 1967). Much of this trade soon passed out of direct Portuguese control into that of local transfrontiermen, or *prazeros*, landholders in the Zambezi Valley who intermarried with Africans and adopted indigenous political structures and symbols; Newitt and Garlake (1967) describe the Massangano *prazo*, but texts, not excavations, record the shift from gold to ivory[8] and then, around 1800, to slaves as the major exports taken by the Portuguese. Farther south, tin was still extracted from the Rooiberg Mountains and, along with copper and ivory, was traded to Europeans calling at Delagoa Bay, a point to which I return in chapter 6.

Returning north two other factors had greater consequences than Portuguese attempts at domination. One was the sixteenth and seventeenth century spread, notably to the Lamu Archipelago and the Comoros, of Hadrahmi and Yemeni clans revered for their religious prestige who also established new commercial networks (T. Vernet 2003). The other was the military intervention of Oman along the coast. Invited to free the Swahili elites from the Portuguese and with an eye on the gains to be made from direct access to East African trade, Oman took Mombasa in 1698, but subsequently exercised only a loose suzerainty. Swahili patricians exploited this, and the earlier difficulties of the Portuguese in enforcing a commercial monopoly, to expand their control of trade networks capable of delivering ivory to Mozambique, mangrove timber to the Gulf, and slaves thence and to Arabia, especially Oman, and the Mascarene islands (chapter 7). Intermarriage with local communities in the interior and the recruitment of the children of those unions into patron-client relations with Swahili elites helped underpin and extend this system. By the early 1800s Euro-American demands were emphasizing cloves, ivory, copal (for varnishes and polishes), and ebony (for pianos). The growing value of these exports led Oman's sultans to reassert control over the Swahili coast, relocating their capital to Zanzibar in 1832. Colonization of strategic ports ensued, with slaves increasingly sought not just for export but also to work in a rapidly developing plantation economy geared to producing food, spices, coconuts (for copra and coir), rubber, sisal, and sugar (Lovejoy 2000).[9] Arab settlers from Oman and Hadramaut came to dominate many coastal communities, especially Zanzibar, and Swahili elites intensified their own claims to Arab ancestry as a response (Horton and Middleton 2000). By 1880 Omani and Swahili traders had opened up caravan routes hundreds of kilometers into the interior, building on the actions of mainland African populations, including the Nyamwezi of northern Tanzania and Yao of the Lake Malawi area. Their caravans, several hundred men in number, transported ivory and slaves to be sure, but also moved more "internal" goods that, in the Nyamwezi case, included iron, salt, grain, and livestock (Mutoro 1998). The complexity of Nyamwezi trade is further indicated by their use of coastal imports to buy copper in Katanga that was then exchanged at home for cattle and for the ivory taken to the coast (Gray and Birmingham 1970).

But however well documented historically, these developments are underexplored by archaeologists (but cf. Lane 1993; Insoll 1997b), even while the locations of some trading sites or the capitals of new, trade-based leaders are known and agricultural intensification to supply the caravan trade is attested (Anderson 2002; Insoll 2003a, 386–88). Nineteenth century conversions to Islam, which were substantial among the Yao for whom they facilitated the trade with the coast that brought higher status, and the presence of Muslim traders in inland polities like Buganda also lie uninvestigated, despite having brought new forms of dress, novel foodstuffs, and mosque construction (Insoll 2003a, 390–95). Even on the coast, where Omani presence survives in upstanding buildings, such as Zanzibar's stone town and nearby palaces (Horton and Clark 1985) and forts on Lamu, Kilwa, and Pemba, their reconstruction, where attempted, has typically had little archaeological input or consequence (Horton 1997).

As a contrasting case, colonial intrusion long had relatively minimal impact in Madagascar, despite the island's attractions to Europeans as a stopping-off point and for trade. Seventeenth century English and French attempts at settlement were halfhearted and repeatedly unsuccessful, hampered by disease and a Malagasy hostility only occasionally eased by marriage into local communities (Parker Pearson 1997). These failures have received little archaeological examination (cf. Parker Pearson and Godden 2002), and in only some areas are European trade goods plentiful—in the hinterland of St Augustine, for example, where elite burials used imported silk, gold, beads, and guns (Parker Pearson 1997), and at Boeny in the northwest (Vérin 1986). The latter was an important slaving port and exchange of slaves for guns and gunpowder a major European interest, largely for export to plantations on Mauritius and Réunion, though previous to this, in the sixteenth, seventeenth, and early eighteenth centuries, if not before, the island was also the principal source of slaves exported from the East African coast to Arabia and the Gulf (T. Vernet 2003). Slaves were obtained from raiding the Comoros and Mozambique, as well as from within Madagascar itself (Mack 1986). Intensified warfare and wealth gained from trade contributed to the development of more complex political structures, such as the Sakalava polity that dominated Boeny after 1697, but guns commanded ritual and status values as much as military ones (Berg 1985). Acquisition of cassava, one of several American crops introduced to Africa by Europeans (chapter 6), was probably also crucial, supplementing rice, especially in the central highlands. Here enhanced food production facilitated the late eighteenth century emergence of the Merina state, recognizable archaeologically in a four-tier settlement hierarchy, specialized frontier military establishments, and deliberate reorganization of the cultural landscapes of conquered territories (Dewar and Wright 1993; Crossland 2001). In ways that parallel its use by southern African rulers such as Khama III (Reid et al. 1997), the Merina elite subsequently adopted Christianity as their state religion, along with many material trappings of nineteenth century European culture, in a conscious effort at nation-building and modernization that nonetheless failed to halt French colonialism.

Notes

1. Surprisingly little systematic archaeological work has yet been done there. The date of its initial settlement by people is unknown, though Greco-Roman texts show it was inhabited by the late first millennium B.C. and there is some archaeological support for this in the form of dolmen-shaped graves similar to examples on the Arabian mainland (Shinnie 1960; Naumkin and Sedov 1993).

2. Burney et al. (2004) provide the most recent statement and discussion of the dating evidence for the human settlement of Madagascar. They provide compelling evidence from newly reported cut-marked bones and pollen sequences that human colonization had begun as early as 300 cal. B.C. and also discuss in detail the chronology of the ecological transformation of the island that this brought about.

3. Cattle, sheep, and goats were by no means the only introductions. Tortoises (*Kinixys belliana*) and rock doves (*Columba livia*), for instance, were brought across from Africa in the eleventh to thirteenth centuries (Rakotozafy 1996).

4. Chinese T'ang Dynasty pottery from Aqaba, Jordan, suggests that international seaborne commerce was already reaching the northernmost ports of the Red Sea before 900, so the argument for a post-Aksumite lull in its flow may be overstated (Whitcomb 1988).

5. This was the first of several late-medieval outbreaks of bubonic plague to affect the Old World, its bacterial agent spread by fleas infesting rats. Bones of *Rattus rattus*, a Eurasian species, occur at Mahilaka (Rakotozafy 1996) and on several first millennium cal. A.D. sites in southern Africa (Plug and Voigt 1985), establishing the presence of this unwelcome seaborne introduction centuries before the pandemic struck.

6. Cotton is another originally Asian introduction to sub-Saharan Africa and may have been brought to eastern Africa from across the Indian Ocean, though it was already known in the mid-first millennium along the Middle Nile and at Aksum (D. Phillipson 1998, 59). Spindle whorls document its local conversion to cloth at Kilwa by the twelfth century (Sutton 1998a) and in the Limpopo Valley 100 years later (Huffman 1971). Higher-quality textiles from overseas remained in demand, however, despite developing local production.

7. Chinese blue and white porcelain is also well attested in Madagascar and was again often found in royal or elite contexts.

8. Pearson (1998) cites estimated annual flows of these goods from ports under Portuguese control as 23–121 metric tons of ivory and 0.5–1.5 metric tons of gold in the sixteenth and seventeenth centuries. Cloth imports to the Zambezi Valley alone may have totaled almost three hundred thousand pieces *per annum* around 1600.

9. Substantially preceding these developments, T. Vernet (2003) presents evidence to suggest that slave-based agriculture may have existed on Pemba and Zanzibar since the late sixteenth century and that demand for slaves to work on plantations in Oman grew significantly from around 1650 or the later seventeenth century.

Africa's Other Sea:
The Sahara and Its Shores

*What ship would ever visit a port unless there was a
chance of a cargo to collect?*

—CONNAH 2001, 143

E XTENDING ACROSS Africa from west to east, the
Sahara is the world's largest desert and, for the lands to
its south, almost another encompassing sea, additional
to the Atlantic and Indian Oceans (Curtin 1984, 26). Like them it has
ports and trading emporia, preferred routes of movement, islands (oases or
mountain massifs), ships (for the last millennium and more, the camel),
and shorelines (reflected in the use of the Arabic-derived *Sahel* for the
grasslands to its south and north; Levtzion 1973). Indeed, the very use of
this term, cognate with the word "Swahili," emphasizes the similarities
between these "seas" and the potential for comparative studies of their
cultural histories and dynamics. The recognition that seas unite as much as
they divide identifies one of this chapter's major themes, how the Sahara
has helped integrate the lands to its north and south (figure 5.1). A second, which runs counter to older, historical interpretations, is the complexity of exchange and urbanism within both the Sahara and Sahel before
Islam's arrival in North Africa.

I first consider how the desert's geography affected the ease of human
movement within and across it. As observed in chapter 2, climate change
is a key variable here, but also critical have been the technological and
organizational skills of the Sahara's inhabitants, whether for living within

Figure 5.1. Location of sites and places discussed in chapter 5. The inset shows the maximum extent of the four most important Sahelian states.

it or procuring desired items from beyond its confines; consideration of irrigation, caravan organization, horses, and camels bears this out in what follows. Taking up the story after the desert attained its approximately modern size and condition, I proceed along largely chronological lines, beginning with the case for pre-Islamic trans-Saharan contacts, including the appearance of metallurgy in sub-Saharan Africa, new work on the Garamantian civilization of Fezzan, the antiquity of towns and trade south of the desert, and the adoption of the camel. Next I discuss the spread of Islam, the often neglected Mediterranean dimension of Africa's political, cultural, and trading ties, the reasons for which conversion took place, and the roles of religion and trade in establishing more centralized polities during the late first and second millennia. Finally, I show how both exchange partnerships and Islam penetrated West Africa's forest zone, before concluding with the impacts on the Saharan system of Iberian/Ottoman struggles, the Moroccan invasion of Songhay, and the opening up of Africa's Atlantic coastlands to European trade.

The Sahara: A Brief Introduction

The Sahara is not a uniform mass of bare sand. A northern zone begins at the 150-mm isohyet in which shrubs may be widely scattered but vegetation is dense in wadis and depressions. Beyond this lie a central zone largely devoid of perennial plant cover, where annual precipitation averages less than 10 mm, and a southern zone that includes savanna elements, such as trees (G. Smith 1984). Topographically, these zones are mosaics of sand dunes and gravel plains, punctuated by depressions, fossil river systems, and rocky highlands. Some of these massifs, notably the Ahaggar, Aïr, and Tibesti, receive sufficient rain to support pasture, fields, and relic communities of Mediterranean and savanna species (Newby 1984). Their presence recalls much wetter conditions during the early Holocene when the desert contracted to a minimum and much of it experienced rainfalls ten to fifty times those of today (S. McIntosh and McIntosh 1988). Since then the overall trend has been one of growing aridity, with approximately modern conditions reached about 4,000 years ago, although fluctuations continued (Brooks 1998). In consequence human settlement has concentrated into the massifs, or those rare oases where water flows naturally or lies close to the surface.

Pathways across the Sahara necessarily focus on moving from one source of water to the next, with four main north–south routes identifiable, each more than 2,000 km long from Sahel to Mediterranean (see figure 5.1). The first connects the Senegal and upper Niger Valleys via Mauritania's western desert to Morocco. The second links the Middle Niger, and important trading centers like Jenné and Timbuktu, with Morocco and Algeria, using the oases of Taoueddeni, Teghaza, and Sijilmasa as staging posts. Moving farther east, other connections (Agadez, Ghat, Ghadames) unite Hausaland and areas downstream of the Niger Bend with Tunisia. Broadly paralleling this, a fourth route joins the Chad Basin to Tripolitania, with Bilma and Murzuq important way stations. In addition, we must emphasize the importance of routes operating in an east–west direction and along a broadly northeast–southwest alignment connecting Egypt's Western Desert oases and the Nile Valley with the central Sahara and ultimately the Niger. In all cases communication tended to become funneled through a few gateway communities at either end.

Given the constraints of moving across the Sahara once desertification had taken hold, and especially before the adoption of the camel, one might ask whether it could have been circumvented by sailing up, or down, Africa's Atlantic coast. As I show in the next chapter, there are sound reasons for thinking this impossible with the maritime technologies available before the fifteenth century. Contact between areas on either side of the desert had, therefore, to mean passing through it.

Of Chariots and Iron

A longstanding focus for exploring the antiquity of such contacts, the chariot engravings found within the modern Sahara are probably of mid- to late first millennium B.C. age (Muzzolini 2000). Initially understood as evidence for prehistoric routes of movement, their distribution more accurately tracks the outcrops suitable for their production (Camps 1982). Though the vehicles shown would have been incapable of travelling long distances over rough terrain and could have carried little, their depiction does imply widespread knowledge of both wheel and horse, perhaps as status symbols and at least in the north where the engravings are most realistic (Mauny 1978; figure 5.2); ox-pulled carts suggest a second means by which goods could have been moved under favorable climatic conditions (Munson and Munson 1969). One recurrent mechanism for the dissemination of these new means of transport must have been the movements of herds—from more permanent settlement foci in oases, highlands, and wadis—to exploit seasonal grazing. The changing history of such pastoralist systems, though little known beyond Libya's Acacus region (Cremaschi and Di Lernia 2001), may lie behind the later crystallization of links between oasis and oasis across the northern Sahara (Herodotus IV 181–85).

The dimly apprehended nature of these connections gains added significance from the fact that it was during the mid-first millennium cal. B.C. that production of iron artifacts began south of the Sahara. Though the intractability of the available evidence (Andah 1979; Okafor 1993) has shifted most research on African iron working away from examining its origins, the possibility that iron smelting, and metallurgy as a whole, were introduced from across the Sahara is so germane to the themes of this book as to demand consideration here. A major difficulty is that the period in question sees a flattening of the calibration curve, compounding the problems of resolution and possible contamination inherent in radiocarbon dating (Woodhouse 1998). Leaving aside van Grunderbeck et al.'s (1983) wholly anomalous second, even third, millennium cal. B.C. dates from East Africa, iron working *was* unambiguously established in

Figure 5.2. Engraving of a horse-drawn chariot from Teshuinat, Libya (redrawn after Muzzolini 1986, figure 56).

Niger, Nigeria, and Cameroon around 500 cal. B.C. This age, and the completely different kind of furnace employed, render Meroë wholly implausible as a source for the technology (Tylecote 1975), leaving North Africa, or Egypt, the only external alternatives. However, excavations there show no evidence of iron working before 700 B.C., with most iron objects at least a century younger than that (Holl 2000, 8). Not only does this leave little time for the technology to spread across the Sahara and beyond, but notions of a broadly Carthaginian origin are also handicapped by the exceptionally limited evidence for Punic artifacts beyond the North African littoral, notably a Punic-style copper earring and sixth century B.C. western Mediterranean bronze brooch at Akjoujt, Mauritania (R. Vernet 1986), and a Carthaginian-like statuette from a stone tumulus in the Algerian Sahara (Lihoreau 1993).

One of the difficulties in accepting an indigenous origin for sub-Saharan iron working, despite these problems with its North African alternative, is the apparent absence of earlier metallurgical traditions out of which it might have developed. Two early sources of copper working are relevant here. In Niger's Agadez region the present consensus rejects Grébénart's (1988) Copper I phase because the so-called furnaces are no more than charred tree stumps in copper-rich soils (Killick et al. 1988), though two dates placing cold or hot hammering of native unsmelted copper between 2500 and 1500 cal. B.C. may be acceptable, as are others for smelting in the Copper II phase of the middle to late first millennium cal. B.C. A similar age for copper exploitation at Akjoujt, Mauritania, is unproblematic (Holl 2000, 10), but in neither region was early copper smelting substantial in scale: artifacts are typically small and found in otherwise stone tool-using contexts (S. McIntosh and McIntosh 1986a). We are faced, then, with a situation in which copper production within the Sahara appears to be no older than iron smelting to its south, at least on the available dates and with our present level of chronological resolution.[1] Speculation that sub-Saharan potters might accidentally have produced small amounts of iron when firing hematite-slipped pottery in a reducing atmosphere (Woodhouse 1998, 178–79) remains no more than that. Furthermore, and without diminishing either the inventiveness and technical mastery of sub-Saharan iron-workers (Schmidt 1996) or the richness with which iron smelting and forging were symbolically elaborated in African cultures (Herbert 1993), the likelihood that sub-Saharan Africa moved from stone to iron technologies without benefit of outside influence runs counter to the experience of other world regions where iron smelting developed, *if at all*, only after millennia of experience in working with other metals.[2]

To my mind, then, and aware of the extreme paucity of relevant data on either side of the argument, an ultimately trans-Saharan source has more to commend it than the hypothesis of independent invention. If a North African source is correct—and a pattern of unequivocal dates older than 700 cal. B.C. from anywhere south of the Sahara would refute this—then it demands evidence for movement within and across the desert. Transport of copper ore from Akjoujt right across Mauritania as far as the Middle Senegal Valley and of copper artifacts and pottery 400 km north of Agadez to Aïr shows that people were in contact over considerable distances at broadly the right time (S. McIntosh and McIntosh 1986a, 105). The intensification of aridity that brought profound changes to many Saharan settlement systems from the mid-second millennium cal. B.C. (Cremaschi and Di Lernia 2001) regrettably hinders the recovery of data that might contextualize such movements further. However, in one area evidence is now emerging for the true scale and antiquity of an indigenous Saharan civilization that may have laid the foundations for more systematic trade across the desert and, we may hypothesize, have played a crucial role in the southward transmission of knowledge of iron working.

The Garamantes

Centered on Fezzan's Wadi el-Agial, more than one hundred thousand burials, many now sadly looted, and hundreds of settlement sites attest to the former presence of the Garamantes. First investigated by Italian archaeologists during the colonial period, recent attention has focused on areas south of their capital (modern Germa; Liverani 2000b) and on broader settlement pattern and landscape studies (Mattingly 2003). Critical to the maintenance of a substantial population around Germa was a dense network of *foggaras*, underground galleries that tapped aquifers to the south of the Wadi el-Agial and led water out to the more depressed wadi center. Some are certainly of early first millennium age, but others could be several centuries older, since they were used in Egypt in the fifth century B.C. (Wilson 2003, 265). Crops grown with their aid, including emmer, barley, bread wheat, and grapes, belong wholly to the Near Eastern farming complex; there is no sign of sub-Saharan cereals in paleobotanical samples of Garamantian age (van der Veen 1992).

The antecedents of the Garamantes probably lie in the early first millennium cal. B.C. site of Zinchechra, with *foggara* technology crucially underpinning a massive demographic increase from the last centuries B.C. that transcended the limits placed on agricultural and pastoral activity by the Sahara's aridity (Wilson 2003). This in itself was no doubt both cause and effect of organizational changes within Garamantian society, but trade was probably also important in producing the wealth and power evident from the Wadi el-Agial's stone-built monuments and elite burials. Liverani (2000a, 20) astutely notes that, from a Saharan perspective, Fezzan lies in "the very center of a regional system," a far cry from the peripheral position to which Mediterranean-centered views condemn it. Treating oases as key agricultural and commercial nodes, he outlines the potentially pivotal position of the Garamantes in an interconnected network linking Fezzan with Tripolitania, Cyrenaica, Egypt, Darfur, Tibesti, the Chad Basin, Niger, and the Ahaggar. Later trade routes, the distribution of water sources, and Herodotus's account of the northern Sahara all provide support for this system. Hard evidence for the movement of goods comes, for now, largely from the Garamantian heartland itself, where rare Punic ceramics occur in late first millennium B.C. contexts (Mattingly 2003) and cemeteries and settlements of the first four centuries A.D. produce much larger numbers of Roman artifacts, including fragile glassware, fine ceramics, oil and wine amphorae, and even cast bronze statues; Mediterranean influence is also evident in the architecture of the more impressive mausolea, such as the Gasr el-Uatuat (figure 5.3), the adoption of the rotary quern and even the presence of a Roman-style bathhouse (Daniels 1989; Mattingly 2003).

Although several Roman military expeditions penetrated Fezzan in the early Principate,[3] Greco-Roman references to the Garamantes are limited. Literary evidence makes them the source of "carbuncles," unidentified precious stones, but other commodities are surely required to account for the

Figure 5.3. The Garamantian mausoleum of Gasr el-Uatuat, Wadi el-Agial, Libya (courtesy and copyright Andrew Wilson).

known quantities of Roman imports. Offering the Garamantian elite material rewards in the form of desirable high-status goods certainly makes sense as a security measure designed to ensure their collaboration in maintaining peace along the frontiers of Roman North Africa (Mattingly 1995, 74; sidebar 6). But there is likely more to the Garamantian phenomenon than this. Liverani (2000a, 20) argues that it only makes sense if it interfaced with areas both north and south of the desert. The most plausible Garamantian exports to the north are carnelian and ivory, both of which were worked in the Wadi el-Agial (Mattingly 2003, 38; 360), and slaves.[4] Elephants can have existed only much farther south, and Law (1967, 196) notes an isolated reference by the Roman author Lucian (*Dipsades*, 2) to the Garamantes hunting them in that general direction; ivory may have gained importance as North Africa's own elephants dwindled to extinction from the first century. Slaves are scarcely more visible, though Herodotus (IV 183) records Garamantian raids against neighboring groups, perhaps those living in the Sahara's central massifs. How many passed into the Mediterranean world is unknown and textual evidence meager (Snowden 1970; Mattingly 1995, 156), but this is not to say that none did so. Presaging recent Tuareg practice, the Garamantes almost certainly acquired slaves for their own use in constructing and maintaining *foggaras* and growing crops (Wilson 2003, 276).

Recent work near Ghat provides further evidence of the penetration of Roman imports. The site from which they come, Aghram Nadharif, is one of several strategically located on known caravan routes, and fragments of painted pottery resemble known Iron Age wares from Chad (Liverani 2000b). Beyond the Sahara, excavations at Jenné-jeno, Mali, have produced three glass beads, two of Roman and one of East or South Asian origin (Brill 1995); substantially more beads of broadly "Asian" origin come from early/mid-first millennium cal. A.D. graves at Kissi, Burkina Faso, due south of the Niger Bend (Magnavita 2003). Interestingly, excavations in the Wadi el-Agial suggest that glass beads may have been produced there by the Garamantes (Mattingly 2003, 358); dates and manufactured goods are also conceivable as commodities moving east, west, and south from Fezzan. If together such finds and speculations offer as yet only limited support for *trans*-Saharan connections in pre-Islamic times, perhaps undertaken through numerous individual exchanges, two additional lines of evidence require attention. The first concerns the possible antiquity of the movement of salt from within the Sahara. A nutritional necessity in cereal-based diets,[5] salt is also obtainable from plant ash or salty earth,[6] but Saharan sources have long been, and continue to be, essential for agricultural populations in the Sahel and the forests beyond. The problem here, apart from salt's archaeological invisibility, is how such a bulky substance was moved before the adoption of the camel. Such difficulties would have mattered less for the other trade item with probable pre-Islamic origins, gold. Found in several parts of West Africa, there are no Greco-Roman references to its trans-Saharan movement, but Garrard (1982) makes a strong case that the suddenness with which Alexandria and Carthage began minting in gold in the late third century, the preference for Roman North Africa's taxes to be paid in gold during the fourth and early fifth centuries, the continuous production of gold coins after Carthage's reconquest from the Vandals, and the speed with which Arab issues commenced at Kairouan in 698 all argue for access to a new, previously unexploited supply. Coupled with the notable finds of gold artifacts in Garamantian tombs (Mattingly 2003, 360) and Brooks's (1998) observation that the hyperarid conditions of the previous six centuries eased around 300, it seems by no means impossible that late Roman North Africa had access to West African gold, although source analyses have not yet confirmed this.

But how would gold have been transported across the desert? Horses are one possibility, as suggested by the chariot engravings and confirmed by seventh/eighth century skeletal remains from Aissa Dugjé, Cameroon (MacEachern et al. 2001), and other broadly contemporary ones from Akumbu A, Mali (Togola 1996). Remembering that horses would also

SIDEBAR 6

Roman North Africa

What of the Garamantes's northern trading partner? North Africa was among the richest, most urbanized parts of the Roman Empire (Raven 1993; figure 5.4), an integral part for more than 500 years of the same political and economic system as Greece, Italy, and Spain. Its wealth, reflected in public monuments and private dwellings, was grounded in the production of wheat and olive oil (especially in Tripolitania; Mattingly 1995). From around 100 it also supported a massive pottery industry distributing red-slipped tablewares throughout the empire (J. Hayes 1997); more exotic exports included ivory and animals for the amphitheater. Beyond Tunisia and eastern Algeria, direct Roman colonization was limited. Instead, local elites rapidly became indistinguishable in material terms from those elsewhere in the empire, but Punic survived into the fifth century, while Berber languages and pre-Roman patterns of social organization persisted in many mountainous areas, and beyond the frontier (Brett and Fentress 1996). Christianity took firm hold relatively early, probably

Figure 5.4. View of the Roman forum at Lepcis Magna, Libya (courtesy and copyright Andrew Wilson).

first implanted via the strong Jewish community evident from funerary inscriptions found at Carthage and Volubilis. By 300, pagan dedications had largely disappeared, and a century later most towns had churches, with Hippo home to one of Christianity's most prominent theologians, St Augustine (Frend 1978).

Roman control weakened from the late third century in the face of attacks by desert nomads, shrinking agricultural productivity, violent competition between local elites, and prolonged conflict between an indigenous, mostly rural Donatist church and more urban, increasingly state-supported Catholic congregations. By 442 the Vandals, a German tribe fleeing other barbarian invaders in Spain, had conquered the surviving province. Leaving few identifiable material remains, they ruled in the eastern Maghreb until Roman (Byzantine) rule was reestablished in 534. By this time, however, urban lifeways were clearly in decline; churches continued to be built, some exhibiting the new Byzantine practice of separating the altar from the congregation (Finneran 2002), but only Carthage saw secular monuments constructed on a significant scale. This weakening of Roman rule, urban life, and opportunities for trade probably contributed, along with the local abandonment of *foggara* irrigation technology, to the broadly contemporary decline of the Garamantes (Liverani 2000a; Mattingly 2003). Farther west, beyond the limit of Roman control, several Berber kingdoms emerged, retaining Latin, Christianity, and the use of Roman titles (Brett and Fentress 1996), but at least sometimes drawing on pre-Roman traditions for the architecture of their royal tombs (Kadra 1983).

have facilitated east–west contacts through the Sahel as far as the Nile, their use across the Sahara would surely have benefited from the climatic amelioration just mentioned. Horses have, however, long been displaced as the Sahara's prime pack animal by the camel. Native to and domesticated in Arabia, dung from Qasr Ibrim, Lower Nubia, documents the presence of *Camelus dromedarius* in northeast Africa before 500 cal. B.C. (Rowley-Conwy 1988), though it was perhaps known in Egypt much earlier (Caton-Thompson 1934). By Roman times camels were used in Tripolitania and Tunisia, more as draft than as pack animals at first, and the camel-keeping pastoralists who threatened Roman-Byzantine control of North Africa continued to fight on horseback (B. Shaw 1979). Bones from third/fourth century cal. A.D. contexts at Siouré, Senegal (MacDonald and MacDonald 2000), do, however, show that the camel spread rapidly through the Sahara itself, and at a date consistent with Garrard's thesis. Its impact has been profound, whether we emphasize its capacity for carrying loads of up to 150 kg, its consumption of coarse, salty plants inedible to other grazers, or its ability to go without food for several months and water for several days, tolerate very high temperatures, or withstand weight losses of up to 30 percent without affecting performance (B. Shaw 1979). In all these respects the camel is a desert animal par excellence, and this is to say nothing of it as supplier of hair, meat, milk, skins, and dung (for fuel). For people living in the Sahara, its adoption was transformative, for those seeking to move things across it, revolutionary.[7] One sign of this may be the famous fourth or fifth century tomb of Ti-n-Hinan in southern Algeria (Reygasse 1950), a signal perhaps that the Garamantes were not alone in profiting from early transdesert commerce.

The Early Development of Towns and Trade in the Sahel

For Africa north and south of the Sahara to be linked by trade required more than the availability of desert-adapted transport. Archaeological research in Mali over the past 25 years has radically changed understandings of the development there of urbanism and trade, demonstrating their antiquity and significance as local processes long before Islam's arrival in North Africa. What emerges is a complex system of exchange and interaction preadapted for elaboration and expansion into an effective trans-Saharan network.

Absolutely crucial have been excavations at Jenné-jeno, an extensive tell site in the western Inland Niger Delta (figure 5.5). Before the work there of Susan and Roderick McIntosh (1980; S. McIntosh 1995), the historical consensus was that urbanism and political complexity owed their origins to, and thus postdated, Muslim North African instigation of cross-desert caravan routes, a view succinctly dubbed the "Arab stimulus paradigm." Far from supporting this model, work at Jenné-jeno exploded it. To elaborate, though agricultural colonization of the Inland Niger Delta began only around 300 cal. B.C., when decreased rainfall allowed permanent islands to form above seasonal flood levels, population rose rapidly, initially centered on areas, like Jenné-jeno, combining good rice-growing soils with flood- and dry-season pastures. By 400 cal. A.D. Jenné-jeno occupied 25 ha, reaching a maximum size of 33 ha by the ninth century when it was the focus of a cluster of many other settlements, some at least pursuing diverse economic specializations. Fuelling this growth were the productivity of the Inland Niger Delta environment and opportunities for exchange. Jenné-jeno is, in fact, optimally located to link its own agricul-

Figure 5.5. Susan McIntosh explaining the stratigraphy at Jenné-jeno, Mali (courtesy and copyright John Hobart).

turally and aquatically rich hinterland (source of rice, fish, and fish oil) with savanna highlands to the southeast (whence came iron or iron ore) and the Sahara (origin of salt and copper). Connecting them was the Niger itself, navigable for most of the year as far as its farthest extension into the desert around 17° N (S. McIntosh 1999c). Such connections must reach back to the beginning of permanent settlement in the Inland Niger Delta, because iron and stone (for grindstones), which do not occur there, are present from Jenné-jeno's earliest levels; salt was probably always another essential import.

Jenné-jeno was not the only early urban complex in the western Sahel. Both the Méma region (Togola 1996) and Dia, reputed home of Jenné-jeno's first settlers (Bedaux et al. 2001), supported extensive settlements by 500, for example. However, nowhere until late in the first millennium A.D. is there evidence of social stratification in, for example, disparities in burial treatment, housing, or monument construction. This raises the possibility that societal integration was achieved by other means, specifically the cross-cutting obligations and powers of different ethnic and/or occupational groups, particularly those with access to occult powers, such as hunters and blacksmiths (R. McIntosh 1998). As noted in chapter 1, such *heterarchical* forms of organization pose a significant theoretical challenge to conventional archaeological understandings of urbanism predicated upon the exploitation of the many by a few who use their power to aggrandize and legitimize themselves through rich burials, elaborate monuments, and other symbols of status (S. McIntosh 1999b). Yet another challenge is set by the scarcity of evidence for subsistence intensification, even though late first millennium Jenné-jeno and its immediate environs supported many thousands of people (R. McIntosh 1998, 200; S. McIntosh 1999c). Instead, wild plant foods remained important and labor-intensive hydraulic technologies undeveloped, strategies that in fact make considerable sense given the highly variable timing, duration, and extent of floodwaters and rainfall.

The Inland Niger Delta was settled by farmers quite late in the Sahel's history of cultivation. Oral traditions of local Nono and Soninké peoples fit with similarities in its earliest ceramic assemblages to suggest that these first settlers came via the Méma from the Sahara's southern edge (R. McIntosh 1998, 160–61). Excavations there in the Dhar Tichitt and Dhar Néma region have, as mentioned in chapter 2, produced some of the earliest examples of domesticated pearl millet. Their context is a surprisingly extensive complex of settlements, many of them large, dating from the mid-second to mid-first millennia cal. B.C. (Munson 1980; MacDonald et al. 2003). Still comparatively little explored, their sheer scale and number suggest they may document the existence of hierarchically structured societies, perhaps based on differential access to wealth in cattle (MacDonald 1998b). Such an interpretation might, as MacDonald (1998b) argues, place these Mauritanian sites in comparison with those of the Middle Nile by way of sociopolitical organization, as well as with the social stratification implied by tumulus and megalith construction in southern Libya from the third millennium cal. B.C. (Di Lernia 2002) and Niger in the first (Paris 1996). Alternatively, might they not have been integrated in much more heterarchical ways, say between complementary economic specialists (Holl 1985), just as the McIntoshs have argued for Jenné-jeno? Either way, societies supporting large populations and inhabiting several tiers of settlement clearly have ancestries in West Africa reaching substantially further back than the settlement of the Inland Niger Delta itself.

I have already indicated that exchange was a vital component of effective human settlement of the Inland Niger Delta and that contacts within the Sahara itself extended over several hundred kilometers even before the adoption of the camel. By around 500 cal. A.D. the archaeological record starts to show more fully how those connections interlinked with exchange systems farther south. From Jenné-jeno itself the clearest signs are ornaments made from copper, the nearest sources of which lie 350 km southeast in Burkina Faso (S. McIntosh 1995, 391). Despite Garrard's (1982) arguments, there is no comparably early evidence of gold, but another definite sign of long-distance connection from Jenné-jeno is the presence of chickens by 850 cal. A.D., reflecting either cross-desert movement or, perhaps more likely, contacts eastward through the Sahel toward the Nile (MacDonald 1995). The massive extent of post-500 cal. A.D. iron production in the Méma (Haaland 1980) suggests this too was exchanged on a considerable scale, while new types of ceramics with distributions both far beyond and right across the Middle Niger also speak to the elaboration of novel ways for structuring intercommunity relations (R. McIntosh 1998). There is no question that the Middle Niger remains better known than other areas of the Sahel at this time, but there are reasons to think that it was far from alone. It is, for example, interesting to note that the extensive copper workings at Marandet in the Nigerian Sahara date back to the third century cal. A.D. (Grébénart 1993) and that the oldest known occupation at Gao, downstream of the Niger's bend and close to its junction with a major north–south route along the Tilemsi Valley, dates to the sixth. Gao was probably central to another pre-Islamic regional trading system circulating not just Marandet's copper but also iron from areas to its south and north, Saharan salt, and foodstuffs, some of which may have supplied salt production centers in the desert (Insoll 1996). The antiquity of some large settlements near Bura (Gado 1993) and the ubiquitous opportunities (needs?) for exchanges of pastoral and agricultural products and salt suggest that similar networks will be discovered elsewhere in the Sahel, though they may not have been universal; there is, for example, no sign of them in the Middle Senegal Valley before ca. 900 cal. A.D. (S. McIntosh et al. 1992). Elsewhere, however, as on the Middle Niger, they certainly can be shown to predate Islam's arrival in North Africa.

Islam and the Mediterranean Dimension of Trans-Saharan Trade

Islam's arrival began with the Arab conquest of Egypt, but its westward expansion was slow, the Byzantine city of Carthage falling only in 698, Tangier in 710. Some of the Maghreb's Berber inhabitants readily adopted the new faith and participated in the conquest of Iberia that began in 711. However, their ambiguous position as tribute-paying subjects precipitated major revolts against Arab rule, revolts exacerbated by doctrinal disputes within the Islamic community itself. As a result, both Morocco and Ifriqiya (roughly Tunisia and northern Algeria) were effectively independent of the Abbasid Caliphate by 800, with dissenting Kharijite[8] polities established at Tahert and elsewhere. Large-scale conversion of the Maghreb Berbers to Islam began only after this time, partly for protection from discrimination by the Arab elite, but while Berber survived the spread of Arabic in parts of Morocco and Algeria and a Jewish presence continued down to the present, both Christianity and Latin had disappeared by 1200 (Brett 1978).

As early as 663 an Arab expedition penetrated to Fezzan, converting the Garamantes to Islam and imposing a tribute of slaves (Brett 1978, 506). Shortly after the conquest of Morocco, another expedition raided south of the Atlas as far as "the land of the blacks" bringing back "as much gold as wanted" (Levtzion 1978, 639). That gold and slaves were known about before 750 reinforces the argument for their northward transmission for some time before this. Together, they remained the most important commodities exported from "the land of the blacks" throughout the succeeding millennium. A key role in their early acquisition was, according to historical sources, played by Kharijite merchants, including those based at Sijilmasa, virtually the only Maghrebi entrepôt of this age to have received systematic archaeological attention (J. A. Miller 2001). Savage (1992) argues that it was the dwindling of a potential slave supply within the Maghreb as the Berbers converted to Islam that encouraged the development of other sources and thus the (re)forging of trade links across the Sahara. At first the slave trade may have been at a fairly low level, and only in the late ninth century is there documentary evidence for North African armies using "black" slave soldiers (Brett 1978, 529). Shortly thereafter came two new catalysts to the growth in demand for West African products: the initiation of an independent gold coinage by Spain's Ummayad ruler, 'Abd al-Rahman III, and the need for Ifriqiya's new Fatimid rulers to finance the armies and propaganda network required to conquer, and then relocate to, Egypt. In part by attempting to dominate Sijilmasa, both sought direct control of the trans-Saharan gold trade.

I pursue shortly how archaeology illuminates the development of trade and the expansion of Islam from a south-of-Sahara perspective. For the moment I emphasize some of the ways in which Saharan and sub-Saharan Africa came to form part of a broader political and economic system spanning the Mediterranean. That they did so is in large part due to the long-lasting Muslim presence in the Iberian peninsula, reconquest of which by the surviving Christian states was only concluded in 1492. The Ifriqiyan-based domination of Sicily that began in 827, and persisted until the Normans seized Palermo in 1072, expanded Muslim political, economic, and cultural influence still further; in both regions substantial Islamic populations survived for some generations after they again passed under Christian rule, and the overall experience of this enduring but complex frontier situation provoked comparable sociopolitical responses on both its Maghrebi and Iberian sides, including the construction of new sacred landscapes focused around pilgrimage to sites linked with holy men (Bennison 2001). A further signal of this integration is the presence in Marrakesh, Rabat, and Seville of strikingly similar minarets dating to the late eleventh century. Their erection, along with other Andalucían architectural influences in the Maghreb (Messier 2001), reflects the unification of much of Spain and the Maghreb by the Berber-led Almoravid revival movement, which began in the mid-eleventh century and rapidly conquered Awdaghust and Sijilmasa (figure 5.6), the key northern and southern "ports" of West Africa's trans-Saharan trade. Sijilmasa's physical expansion, the construction of new irrigation facilities, and its first regular striking of gold coins attest indirectly to the growth in trade that resulted, further confirmation of which might come from potsherds of possibly Middle Niger origin that could represent the remains of containers used to import goods from across the desert (J. A. Miller 2001). Also based on nomad Berber confederations, a second revivalist movement, that of the Almohads, followed in the mid-twelfth century, again uniting the Maghreb and Muslim Spain under a single rule before it too succumbed to doctrinal disputes and provincial rebellions in the 1200s (Levtzion 1977).

These movements, and the political unity they sustained, stimulated still further the trans-Saharan transport of slaves and gold (confirmed by physicochemical analysis of surviving dinars; Messier 1974; figure 5.7).

Figure 5.6. View of Sijilmasa, Morocco (courtesy and copyright Jim Miller).

Figure 5.7. Gold dinar of 'Ali bin Yusuf, Almoravid ruler of Muslim Spain and the western Maghreb between 1106 and 1142 (courtesy and copyright the Ashmolean Museum, Oxford).

Indeed, it has been argued that the Almoravids deliberately targeted the Senegambian polity of Takrur, weakened Ghana,[9] and attacked Tadmekka to redirect the flow of trade to their advantage (J. A. Miller 2001). As trans-Saharan commerce grew and Europe itself began to experience the economic prosperity that marked the high Middle Ages, West African gold also crossed the Mediterranean in increasing amounts: beginning with Alfonso VIII of Castile in 1173, other European monarchs and city states struck the first gold coins minted outside the Byzantine Empire since the fall of Rome. The effect was that "North Africa with its supply of gold gradually became the driving force of the entire Mediterranean" (Braudel 1972, 467), with black Africans literally "driving" this commerce where employed as slaves on agricultural plantations in the Maghreb, Sicily, and southern Italy (Verlinden 1977). The wide range of raw materials and manufactured goods exchanged between the two sides of that sea is one sign of this (table 5.1), the establishment of Italian trading colonies in Maghrebi ports a second, and Christian European attempts at seizing those same ports a third.[10] But perhaps it is thirteenth century Tunisia's near-simultaneous diplomatic contacts with Norway and Borno that best attest to Africa and Europe's growing economic interlinkage (Fisher 1977, 255).

The Archaeology of Trans-Saharan Contact

Though numerous, Arabic sources for understanding trans-Saharan trade and its impact on the societies of the western Sahel during the late first and second millennia require contextualization if they are to be employed (Insoll 1994).[11] Their use has long affected how archaeological research has been conducted, focusing attention toward sites mentioned, or thought to be mentioned, in the texts, an emphasis that has only recently begun

Table 5.1. Trans-Mediterranean trade in the thirteenth to sixteenth centuries (after Levtzion 1977). Maghrebi exports with origins south of the Sahara are shown in bold. European exports that reached south of the Sahara are italicized.

From the Maghreb to Europe			From Europe to the Maghreb		
Carpets	Hides	**Ostrich feathers**	*Copper*	*Glass beads*	Perfumes
Coral	Horses	Salted fish	*Cowries*	Iron	Silk
Dried fruit	**Ivory**	**Slaves**	Dried fruit	*Metalware*	Textiles
Dyes	Leather	Sugar	Glassware	Paper	Timber
Gold	Olive oil	Textiles			

to be corrected. With these caveats in mind, what does archaeology offer for understanding the expansion of trans-Saharan trade? The answer is, a great deal.

Imports from North Africa

If Kharijite merchants played a key role in elaborating trans-Saharan trade during the eighth and ninth centuries few North African imports are recognizable in either the Sahara or the Sahel at this early date, though Devisse (1992, 197) reports Ifriqiyan glazed pottery at Tegdaoust (Awdaghust), Mauritania. Urban occupation began there in the late ninth century (Devisse 1983) and it is from 900 that archaeology suggests a "boom" in trans-Saharan trade. Tegdaoust is one of several sites within the modern Sahara that were major stopping-off places for caravans, as well as centers of local manufacture. Others include Koumbi Saleh (Berthier 1997) and Essuk/Tadmekka (Lhote 1951). Characteristic features include clusters of stone, brick, or mud houses, congregational mosques, cemeteries following Muslim burial rites, and North African imports that include glassware, glass weights, and pottery. These goods are most common at Tegdaoust, which was partly sustained by wheat (for the elite) and dried fruit from the Maghreb (Levtzion and Hopkins 2000, 68), and has also yielded considerable evidence for local copper, brass, and pottery production. Imports are noticeably rarer farther south at Koumbi Saleh, despite its traditional interpretation as the Muslim merchant quarter of the capital of the kingdom of Ghana. Both sites also have largely uninvestigated "pre-urban" deposits that probably reflect use of mud instead of stone for building; their excavation would no doubt go far to expand knowledge of pre-Muslim trans-Saharan exchange networks.

Moving south into the Sahel, three broad categories of evidence for trans-Saharan influence can be identified: imported goods, new technologies, and religious conversion. I look at each before considering how participation in trans-Saharan exchanges may have spurred the development of larger, hierarchically more complex political institutions. Objects of North African origin or manufacture are readily identifiable in the archaeological record, though many more are documented only historically (table 5.2). Insoll's (1996, 2000) analysis of the finds from Gao Ancien illustrates the range present from the tenth to the sixteenth centuries: North African and Andalucían glazed ceramics, including types like lusterwares known only in elite contexts in Spain; marble funerary stelae for some of Gao's first Muslim rulers made in Almería; a wide range of Maghrebi and Egyptian glasswares; North African metalwork, especially in copper and copper alloys, including brass, to which documentary sources add iron and steel weapons; and a range of ornaments, including carnelian and glass beads and cowrie shells. Comparable, but more limited, finds occur elsewhere. At Sincu Bara, a mostly ninth to eleventh century site in Senegal, for example, numerous copper and brass artifacts are accompanied by much rarer cowries, glass beads, and North African ceramics; analysis of the metalwork shows it to be compositionally close to finds from Tegdaoust and North African in origin (S. McIntosh and Bocoum 2000). From broadly the same time, North African goods and influence in the form of brass, glass beads, and rectilinear house forms appear in the Jenné-jeno sequence, a century or so after the first gold (S. McIntosh 1999c). More widespread, and found across the Sahel from the early second millennium, are cowries, reflecting their documented demand in the eleventh century kingdom of Ghana and their use as currency by at least the 1300s (Levtzion and

Table 5.2. The flow of goods across the Sahara as documented historically (after Insoll 1996, 62–63). Italicized items are those for which archaeological evidence exists.

To the Sahel from North Africa and the Sahara		From/via the Sahel to North Africa and the Sahara
Brass	Linen	Dyed goatskins
Cedar wood	Medicines	Ebony
Clothing (in wool and cotton)	Metalwork	Gold
Copper jewelery	Paper, ink, books	Gum
Coral beads	Pine wood (for tar)	Hide whips
Cowries	Saffron	Ivory
Fruit (including dates and raisins)	Salt	Skins
Glass, glassware and glass beads	Semiprecious stones	Skin shields
Glazed pottery	Silk	Slaves

Hopkins 2000, 83; 260; see sidebar 5, chapter 4). Farther east in Niger and Chad excavations have been too few, or remain insufficiently published, to add much to this picture, though trade with North Africa is attested at Azelik by 1400 (Bernus and Cressier 1991).

More sustained fieldwork would certainly revise and improve this picture, but so too would further analyses of existing evidence; glass beads, in particular, call for more detailed study of their sources, which may have included local production in the Sahel using imported scrap glass (Insoll 1996, 82). For the moment Tegdaoust and Koumbi Saleh, both located on key caravan routes within the Sahara, and Gao stand out for the exceptional quality and quantity of their finds, a pattern that suggests much of what was transferred into the Sahel, and then beyond, consisted of perishable or recyclable materials (salt, brass, and copper) where it did not take the form of beads. Gao's finds, in particular, may reflect interelite exchange with Almoravid Maghreb and Andalucía, rather than simple commerce (Farias 1990). Insoll (1996, 74–75) further notes that other sites with North African and Andalucían ceramics and glass are known as primary centers for production within the Sahara, copper at Azelik and salt at Teghaza. Known Sahelian towns, like Jenné-jeno, have tiny amounts of such goods at best, emphasizing their role as centers of regional exchange, rather than merely links in the trans-Saharan trade.

Among the new technologies with possible trans-Saharan origins was the production of cotton textiles.[12] Finds in the Middle Niger date to the eighth or ninth centuries cal. A.D. (MacDonald 1999b, 41) and spindle whorls of broadly the same age come from Dia (Bedaux et al. 2001) and elsewhere. The spread of cotton clothing was certainly facilitated by conversion to Islam, which "in practice, if not in doctrine" (Watson 1983, 41) prescribes that the faithful should be well-clothed, but it also created new possibilities for symbolic elaboration and status expression. Finds from Mali's Bandiagara Escarpment confirm, for example, its spread beyond any religious confines by the eleventh century, if not before (Bolland 1991). Though transforming Sahelian domestic economies and making the region a major source of textiles exported south into the forest zone (Johnson 1977), cotton was not the only new crop introduced. Cabbage and lentil seeds are known from tenth century cal. A.D. contexts at Niani (Filipowiak 1979), while Watson (1983, 82) records the import to the Sahel of North African oranges, limes, and taro. Dates can be added to this from excavations at Gao (MacLean and Insoll 2003), and van der Veen (1992) reports a complementary northward spread of sorghum and pearl millet into Fezzan.

After clothing and new kinds of food, another introduced technology was the use of fired brick to construct important buildings, for example, a tomb complex at Gao-Saney and a mihrab at Gao Ancien, both dating to between the late twelfth and thirteenth centuries. Fired brick and the decorative colored plaster employed with it at Gao were extensively used in the Maghreb and a fired brick mihrab is also known from contemporary Almería, source of Gao Ancien's royal tombstones, evidence that points to a trans-Saharan origin for these skills (Insoll 1996). Much farther east, North Africa is also the likely inspiration for the fired brick mosque and courtyard walls at Birni Gazargamo and other Borno sites (Seidensticker 1981; Hambolu 1996). Here, however, Tripoli, the principal terminus of Borno's slave trade, is the probable source, either via foreign artisans or local craftsmen who had visited North Africa (Gronenborn 2001).

Finally, there was literacy, a skill closely tied to conversion to Islam as it involved the use of the otherwise unfamiliar Arabic script and language. Fisher (1977, 321) argues that this helped the Sahel maintain "essential lifelines with the heritage of the Muslim heartlands," enshrining Islamic ideals and transcending local political boundaries through adherence to a broader civilization that viewed Cairo as one of its principal seats of learning. The Malian king *Mansa* Musa's famous visit there en route to Mecca in 1324 strengthened the western Sahel's feelings in this regard, and both books and religious scholars were imported from Egypt as a result (Hrbek 1977, 92). Such pilgrimages to Mecca are, in fact, recorded for several rulers from across the Sahel, but this obligation, incumbent on all Muslims, was also fulfilled by local clerics and ordinary people, who no doubt enhanced their reputation and prestige as a result (Fisher 1977, 324–28).

Discussion of the hajj inevitably broaches the wider question of Islam's expansion south of the Sahara. Archaeological evidence for this, in the form of mosques (figure 5.8) or appropriately worded inscriptions, is complemented by historical sources and oral traditions and reveals a complex picture. At least three patterns are discernible (Insoll 1996). One was that of rapid conversion and militant adherence to the new faith, a pattern recorded for the kingdom of Takrur in Senegal and, at least in its early date, implied by Muslim burials from Mammanet, Niger, that predate 880 cal. A.D. (Paris 1996). A second pattern saw Muslims, generally traders, living under the protection of pagan rulers, frequently in spatially distinct settlements, a system of dual towns recorded historically for the capital of Ghana and probably evident archaeologically at Gao Ancien, with its elite imports and structures, and Gao-Saney, with its slightly more northerly location and heavy manufacturing activity in textiles, metals, and glass beads (Insoll 1996). Such dual settlements no doubt had the benefit for local rulers of restricting their subjects' access to foreign traders

Figure 5.8. The main mosque (and market) at Jenné, Mali. The present building is an early twentieth century French-sponsored reconstruction of the mosque, the earliest version of which was probably founded in the thirteenth century.

and simultaneously constraining the latter's ability to meddle in local politics. Finally, there was the possibility, however fraught, of striking a compromise between Islam and traditional beliefs. At an elite level this is evident in many Sahelian states, and it involved practices such as retaining pagan rituals and royal seclusion alongside pilgrimage and support for Muslim scholarship. Only when Islam began to spread beyond court and urban circles did some Sahelian rulers feel strong enough to base their kingship on Islamic sources of authority, most notably in sixteenth century Songhay (Hunwick 1985) and the revivalist states of the late eighteenth and nineteenth century jihads. On a more popular plane, archaeology confirms the survival of indigenous beliefs long after conversion had supposedly taken hold, for example, in the non-Muslim burial forms practiced in early second millennium Dia (Arazi 2003), the consumption of dogs at Gadei (Stengroome 2000), and the post-1100 proliferation of terracotta statuettes across the Inland Niger Delta, manufacture of which may have continued as late as the eighteenth century. Indeed, their production and associations with burials, rainmaking, and household protection may even have been a reaction *to* the spread of Islam (R. McIntosh 1996a, 49).

Why then did West Africans convert? Genuine belief should certainly not be downplayed nor, as suggested in the following section by the cases of Takrur and Ghana, the possibility of force. Other reasons can also be suggested (Insoll 2003a). First, the opportunities of trading with Muslim North African merchants on the much more favorable terms awarded coreligionists, including, at least in theory, freedom from enslavement by fellow Muslims. Second, the attractions of using Arabic, literate Muslim officials and a fixed calendar (Goody 1971, 460) in developing state bureaucracies—al-Bakri, for example, notes that even though Ghana's king remained pagan most of his ministers were Muslim (Levtzion and Hopkins 2000, 80). Finally, there was the increased prestige afforded by external trading contacts, the manipulation of Arabic to write charms and amulets (Green 1986), and claims to Arab ancestry or descent from learned Muslims, a phenomenon observable among Tuareg (Brett and Fentress 1996, 215), Hausa (Haour 2003), and Wandala (MacEachern 1993) alike. That Islam was often adopted first in urban settings and spread in large part along commercial networks certainly confirms the role of trade, and perhaps the faith's assistance in integrating ethnically diverse urban communities, as key motors in its expansion (Trimingham 1968). Others, particularly rural folk, may have found less to value when set against their traditional beliefs; many now solidly Muslim areas converted only during the nineteenth century *jihads*, and much remains to be done to explain the differential penetration of Muslim-mediated long-distance exchange networks and Islam itself.

West African Exports and the Articulation of Trade

We saw earlier how a wide-ranging system of exchanges operated in sub-Saharan West Africa before the advent of Islam. Along with exchanges of agricultural produce, fish, iron ore, and manufactured goods went movements of copper and salt from within the Sahara and the northward export of gold from sources largely within the forest zone (figure 5.9). The size and significance of towns like Jenné-jeno and Gao depended in part on their occupying key locations along these trade routes, often where land-based movement from across the Sahara and the Sahel connected to riverine movement along the Niger, giving them a strategic intermediate position between north and south. Along with oasis towns like Sijilmasa at the northern termini of cross-desert caravan routes, Timbuktu is a classic example of such a setting and, like them, a critical link in the transmission of Islamic civilization. Founded supposedly around 1100, in a region with a long history of prior settlement (S. McIntosh and McIntosh 1986b), Timbuktu became the principal southern terminus of trans-Saharan trade by 1450, superceding

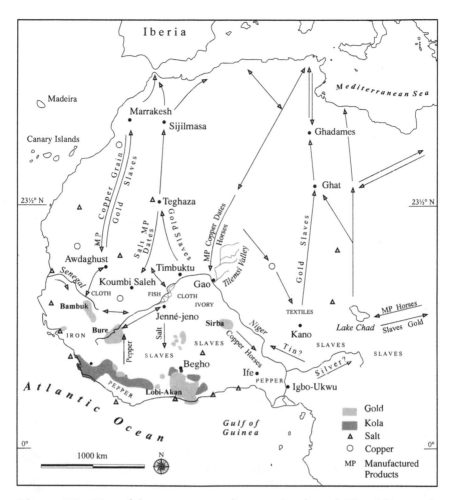

Figure 5.9. Map of the major commodities moving through West African and trans-Saharan trade networks in the beginning to middle of the second millennium.

Walata and Jenné-jeno (Gomez 1990), though this is not apparent archaeologically (Insoll 2003b). Its commercial importance derived from a location on the Niger's northernmost projection into the desert, as a result of which it relied heavily on imported foodstuffs, which in the case of sorghum reached as far into the desert as Tadmekka (Levtzion and Hopkins 2000, 85). Such goods, together with those involved in the broader trans-Saharan system, were moved along the Middle Niger in sewn-plank canoes, capable of carrying 20–30 metric tons. Transport south of the river used donkeys or human porters; movement north, camels. Salt was probably the principal commodity thus carried (figure 5.10), and Arabic references to its role as currency, royal treasure, and delicacy in the Sahel are numerous (Levtzion and Hopkins 2000). More extensive excavations at poorly known salt production centers such as Teghaza north of Timbuktu (Monod 1940), Awlil and Ijil in the western Sahara, or Kawar in Niger would no doubt add much to our understanding of its annual movements, which in the late fifteenth century could amount to 1.8 metric tons of salt for a single Jenné merchant (Fage 1977, 488)!

Another indication of the scale of cross-desert trade comes from the twelfth century "lost" caravan of Majâbat al-Khoubrâ, which was transporting thousands of cowries and a whole metric ton of copper and brass ingots (Monod 1969), but even this pales alongside Ibn Khaldun's record of caravans travelling between Egypt and Mali that counted twelve thousand camels (Hrbek 1977, 90). Such numbers illustrate how much this trade, in all its dimensions, required careful organization for it to flourish: caravans crossing the desert, for example, each had formally appointed leaders, muezzins, imams, and scribes, as well as guards. The uniquely valuable mid-thirteenth century archive of Tlemcen's Maqqari family (Levtzion 1977, 369–70) documents the importance of kinship ties in ensuring cross-desert trade, to which we can add those of shared religious allegiance.

Figure 5.10. Saharan salt on sale in a market at Mopti, Mali, 2001.

Though mostly thought of in Islamic terms, Jewish commercial communities too played a significant role, especially in bridging Christian and Muslim sides of the Mediterranean and in working the gold imported into Morocco. On occasion, Jews also joined caravans to the Sahel (Levtzion 1977, 449–50), and it is surely more than plausible that traders from Sahelian towns like Jenné-jeno and Timbuktu themselves traveled to, and perhaps had bases in, North Africa (R. McIntosh 1998, 237).

Although slaves and gold were the two principal sub-Saharan commodities moving through this system to the north, others were also involved, notably ivory (figure 5.11), civet for making perfume, and kola nuts. It would also be wholly wrong to think that the traffic in slaves was intended for North African or Mediterranean markets alone. Slavery has a long history within both the Sahara and the Sahel and is not wholly ended today. Tuareg society, for example, both profited from its role as a middleman in the trans-Saharan slave trade and employed slaves as agricultural laborers (Brett and Fentress 1996), and in eleventh century Awdaghust some individuals owned as many as one thousand slaves (Levtzion and Hopkins 2000, 74). Centuries later, extensive slave plantations were a feature of the Songhay empire (Lovejoy 2000, 32), if not of

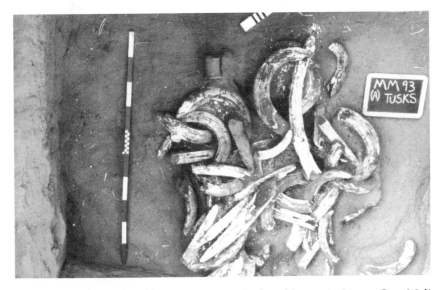

Figure 5.11. A cache of hippopotamus tusks found in excavations at Gao, Mali (courtesy and copyright Tim Insoll). A unique find, this cache confirms hints from historical sources that hippopotamus, as well as elephant, ivory was exported across the Sahara from West Africa.

earlier Middle Niger states. The uses to which the thousands of individuals transported across the desert to North Africa were varied (Alexander 2001). They included domestic service, concubinage, agricultural labor (notably on Moroccan sugar plantations in the 1400s), industrial workshops, and warfare (especially in the Maghreb from the fourteenth to seventeenth centuries). Last, but not least, salt mining in the Sahara also took its share. Total numbers crossing the desert numbered in the thousands every year, though in the centuries immediately before 1500 greater aridity and lack of access to New World sources of bullion perhaps favored gold as West Africa's major export (Brooks 1998).

Despite its scale, estimated by Austen (1979) as totaling almost 7,500,000 individuals between 650 and 1900, the slave trade left fewer signs culturally or physically than one might think. One reason must lie in the different dynamics of Islamic slavery compared with those of the trans-Atlantic system and specifically the encouragement offered by Islam to manumission and conversion (Lovejoy 2000). That the trans-Saharan trade favored women over men relative to the Atlantic one also helped promote assimilation through intermarriage (Lovejoy 2000, 26), and neither should we forget that some male slaves were made into eunuchs. Even so, some distinct communities do survive, like the Gnawa of Marrakesh, who retain beliefs in spirit control that have sub-Saharan origins (Braumann 1995); other black Africans of formerly slave status occupy marginalized positions within Saharan societies today (Segal 2002). While the western Sahel was certainly one source of slaves, and abandonment of sites around Dia may reflect the impact of slave raiding (S. McIntosh and McIntosh 1986a), it was far from its only export, and in fact traffic moved two ways; Mali's fourteenth century rulers are documented as *acquiring* Turkish and Ethiopian slaves from Egypt. In the central Sahel, where gold was absent, slaves were much more important, making this probably by far their larger source (Austen 1979). Indeed, the kingdom of Kanem-Borno appears virtually simultaneously with slave exports in ninth century Arabic sources, though still little investigated archaeologically (Gronenborn 2001). Later documents show Tripoli, and ultimately Egypt, Sicily, and Italy, as recipients of its slave exports (Levtzion 1977, 477). Written and excavated data (notably in northern Cameroon; MacEachern 2001) document the gradual expansion of this slave-raiding frontier, and Gronenborn (2001, 108) suggests that the appearance of glass and carnelian beads as grave goods in the fourteenth century southern Chad Basin may reflect their recorded use as currency to buy slaves.

As already indicated, metallurgical analyses confirm the historical documents and the inferences drawn from the massive post-900 increase in North African imports into the Sahel to identify West Africa as the source of the gold used for Almoravid coins. In fact, between the eleventh and seventeenth centuries, West Africa became the leading supplier of gold to the international economy, accounting at times for almost two-thirds of total world production (Hopkins 1973). With Mali's Sirba Valley gold workings only poorly dated to the fifteenth century (Devisse 1993, 357), the main sources of the metal lay on the upper headwaters of the Senegal and Niger river systems, or beyond the Sahel in the Lobi and Akan gold-fields of Ghana, for which the earliest dates are in the fourteenth and fifteenth centuries (Levtzion 1985; S. McIntosh and McIntosh 1986a). Obtained by Sahelian merchants, who went there exchanging their own and North African products, gold flowed into the trans-Saharan system through towns like Jenné-jeno, convincingly identified by S. McIntosh (1981) as the "Island of Gold" of Arabic scholars who remained ignorant of its true origin. From there the metal moved across the desert as dust, but also perhaps as ingots and wire to judge from a hoard from Tegdaoust (Devisse 1992). Its possession was certainly recognized as a key source of royal revenue within the states that emerged along the Middle Niger from the late first millennium, along with the duties levied on imports and exports of salt and copper (Levtzion and Hopkins 2000, 81; 174). Those goods, and the gold for which they were exchanged, linked the Sahel to the forests farther south, and it is to them that I now turn.

The Forest Dimension

Although ivory and slaves were obtainable within the Sahel, it is likely that they too moved north with gold from the forest zone into the pan-Saharan trading system. Another important forest product was the kola nut, a stimulant permitted by Islam, widely consumed within the Sahel, and valued at the extreme North African limit of distribution almost as highly as salt was farther south. Potentially of interest too for Sahelian merchants were copper (since some Nigerian mines were certainly being exploited in the tenth century cal. A.D.; Craddock et al. 1997) and tin, given that bronze was cast at Jenné-jeno in the late first millennium cal. A.D. (S. McIntosh 1995, 385). While salt was keenly sought after by forest-zone peoples, who also obtained it from marine sources, it has not left archaeological traces. Instead, we have evidence of other Sahelian, or trans-Saharan goods, foremost among them brass, the material from which the beautiful and technically highly skilled Ife and Benin "bronzes" of southern Nigeria were, in fact, made (figure 5.12). Widely recognized as a container, and signifier, of supernatural power (Herbert 1984) and imported both as ingots and actual basins, bowls, and other vessels, brass was reaching the Niger Delta by the fourteenth century cal. A.D. (Nzewunwa

Figure 5.12. A bronze plaque of early seventeenth or possibly sixteenth century date from Benin, Nigeria, showing the *Oba* sitting on a throne in the form of a kola-nut box. The heads of two Europeans appear to left and right above the *Oba* (courtesy and copyright Pitt Rivers Museum, University of Oxford).

1980, 247). Glass beads are a second archaeologically visible import, but were also recycled, if not made from scratch, at Ife in the early second millennium cal. A.D. (Sutton 1982). Other commodities passing south included horses, valued more as prestige symbols than for any military role within the forest zone itself, and cloth, another largely invisible item. How significant trade with the Sahel was in the development of complex societies in the forest zone, and notably in southern Nigeria, remains uncertain. Igbo-Ukwu (chapter 3) shows that external connections *of some kind* were already thriving by 900 cal. A.D., and Sutton (1997, 225) has further argued that the flow of brass into Ife requires more than a corresponding outflow of ivory and slaves, "the proverbial export staples of Africa," citing gold as a more likely possibility. However, for the moment the antiquity of Benin's earthwork systems (Darling 1984) and the deposits at Ife itself (T. Shaw 1978) suggest that local population growth, exchange networks, and competition were the most crucial processes.

Important in opening up areas beyond the Niger to participation in the trans-Saharan system was the expansion of Mande-speaking Dyula (Wangara) traders from the Sahel, a classic example of a trading diaspora (cf. Cohen 1969) whose members played a role analogous to that of the Berbers farther north. Like them they also helped propagate Islam. The clearest archaeological evidence of their presence in the forest zone comes from Begho, Ghana, an entrepôt where Akan gold was exchanged for salt, copper alloys, and cloth. Located at the tsetse-imposed southernmost limit for pack animals, where goods had to be transferred to human porters, Begho was inhabited by several economically specialized ethnic groups and had origins in the eleventh century (Posnansky 1976). As well as acting as a conduit for trade, it supported much local production in textiles, brass, ivory, and ceramics. The brass, North African brass vessels, and glass beads found there all have exotic origins, while ceramic weights conform to the Islamic *mitkal-uqiya* system; its Mande quarter, Kramo, is identifiable from the absence of religiously proscribed grasscutter (*Thryonomys* sp.) remains among its fauna and the drain tiles that imply flat-roofed houses of Sahelian type. Comparable sites include Kuulo Kataa (Stahl 2001a), Bono Manso (Effah-Gyamfi 1985), and a possible caravanserai at Yendi Dabarai (Ozanne 1971), but none shows the same quantity of finds. By the late 1400s Hausa and Borno trading diasporas too were active in Ghana and Burkina Faso, with Mande merchants reaching as far as the coast (Wilks 1962), where the Portuguese arrived at broadly this time (chapter 6). Reflecting this, Begho's later levels document access to European-derived trade goods and the shift to an Atlantic world economy in the sixteenth to eighteenth centuries (Wilks 1982).

State Formation in the Sahel

Thus far I have discussed the archaeological evidence for the kinds of goods passing through the trans-Saharan commercial networks of the past millennium and more without doing more than mentioning in passing the political context of those exchanges. It is now time to repair that omission, because associated with both trans-Saharan trade and Islam was a series of major states in the Sahel. One early signal of changes in the scale and complexity of political organization is the appearance of tumulus burials for individuals interred with gold jewelry, copper objects, including North African imports, horses, and sometimes (sacrificed) attendants. The well-known El-Oualadji tumulus dating 1030–1120 cal. A.D. closely parallels the documented burial rites of Ghana's kings (Levtzion and Hopkins 2000, 80–81), but even earlier examples are known in Mali's lakes region (S. McIntosh and McIntosh 1986a). Their first appearance broadly coincides with the evidence for more wide-ranging interactions previously noted, leading R. McIntosh (1998) to speak of a rapidly developing process of peer-polity interaction marked by flows of exchange, technological change, and shared symbols of power. Competition between polities (in the form of war or competitive emulation) becomes more evident in the early second millennium and was probably accelerated by the deteriorating climate that brought particularly dry conditions to the Sahel through much of the twelfth, thirteenth, and fourteenth centuries. In some areas, but not, for example, around Gao, one consequence was a noticeable decline in population density; two-thirds of sites around Jenné-jeno were abandoned soon after 1100 and comparable patterns are evident in the Méma. Compounding this, exotic diseases may have arrived with trans-Saharan caravans (R. McIntosh 1998, 246–49).

Ironically, therefore, the emergence of states in the western Sahel at least, though clearly associated with a boom in trans-Saharan exchange, appears to have gone hand in hand with a local demographic collapse. It seems likely that this in itself would have favored experiments with new religious and political ideologies, including the adoption of Islam. Ghana (the Wagadu of Soninké tradition), the first Sahelian state to appear in the historical record, does so around ca. 775. From the mid-tenth to mid-eleventh centuries it extended far north into the Sahara, controlling Awdaghust, but its capital may have been located close to the Niger, rather than at Koumbi Saleh, as traditionally supposed (R. McIntosh 1998, 257). Ghana's principal successor, Mali, was founded more explicitly on the marriage of traditional beliefs and practices with those of Islam and marks the emergence of what R. McIntosh (1998) terms the Imperial Tradition: states founded upon a warrior cavalry aristocracy, the borrowing of Islamic bureaucratic forms, religion, scholarship, law and regalia, and the transformation of traditional hunters' and blacksmiths' rituals and equipment into symbols of kingship. Mali was strongest in the late thirteenth and fourteenth centuries, during which two of its kings undertook the hajj. Thereafter, it too fragmented, succeeded from the mid-fifteenth to late sixteenth centuries by Songhay, focused farther downstream at Gao. As we have seen, Gao had clearly already gained a position of the greatest importance in trans-Saharan trade by the tenth or eleventh centuries and its kings converted to Islam ca. 1010, making it an early center for the spread of the new faith. Another lay in Senegambia, where, in a physically, ecologically, and culturally more uniform landscape than that of the Middle Niger, increased settlement pattern complexity and exchange do seem to go along with rich tumulus burials and the appearance of North African imports (S. McIntosh et al. 1992). There the key polity was Takrur, which also became Muslim, but in more militant fashion, in the early eleventh century and attempted the forcible conversion of its neighbors. As indicated above, the pattern in Songhay and Mali was one of a much more nuanced coexistence between Islam and traditional religion, including beliefs of divine kingship. Though little known archaeologically, Kanem-Borno (Gronenborn 2001), whose ruler also converted in the eleventh century, the city states of Hausaland (Haour 2003), and the more easterly Funj and Darfur sultanates of modern Sudan (Insoll 2003a) all apparently shared this latter trajectory.

Interestingly, while some of the early stages in the development of these polities are discernible archaeologically, there seems little sign of the great wealth and power recorded of the rulers of the Imperial Tradition. Ghana's capital, as we have seen, may still be unlocated. Insoll's (1996, 2000) excavations at Gao show very little sign of monumental building or foreign imports during Songhay's apogee, while even less was recovered from Niani, which its excavator, probably wrongly, claimed as the capital of Mali (Filipowiak 1979). Instead, as Conrad (1994) suggests, capitals may have been much more peripatetic, with power associated with individuals rather than a permanently located bureaucracy. The importance of mobility is evident in one of the principal components of the Imperial Tradition, the cavalry deployed by states right across the Sahel and the spatial correlation of those states with grassland areas suitable for horse keeping. Not only a crucial military force, horses were also potent markers of elite differentiation and status (Goody 1971; Law 1980). As well as helping rulers extract wealth from the ruled, horses dramatically extended the reach of slave raiding, encouraged perhaps by southward movement of tsetse infestation during the drier conditions prevailing ca. 1100–1500 (Brooks 1998) and the introduction from North Africa of improved breeds, stirrups, and saddles (R. Smith 1989). In addition, we should remember the effects they had in broadening people's geographical horizons. The two points neatly come together in the probably Mamluk derivation of the quilted cotton armor, mail coats, and iron helmets that first reached Hausaland around 1400 and continued to be imported from the Nile Valley into the twentieth century (Spring 1993). Archaeologically still little known, Hausaland reminds us that many innovations from across the desert quickly became indigenized, taking on local forms and variations. Its historical sources also make plain that despite the importance of trans-Saharan commerce, especially for elites, the fundamental basis of West African economies remained agriculture, pastoralism, metallurgy, and the exchanges that they required or made possible (Haour 2003).

The Trans-Saharan System since ca. 1500

The political and economic relationships that I have discussed underwent considerable change from the late fifteenth century. One reason for this was that Muslim control of the North African coast did not go uncontested. Portugal and Spain made repeated attempts, often temporarily successful, to seize key ports along the Maghrebi coastline during the fifteenth and sixteenth centuries, both to gain access to the termini of the trans-Saharan gold trade and to secure themselves from attack by the advancing Ottoman

Empire. Once the Portuguese had obtained direct access to West Africa by sailing south across the Atlantic, their interest in Morocco actually grew because they needed to secure the Moroccan trade goods desired by their new sub-Saharan partners, for example, horses in Senegambia and textiles in modern Ghana. The late 1400s and early 1500s, therefore, saw Portugal seize several key locations along the Moroccan coast, including Tangier, Agadir, and Safi, a control ultimately lost in 1578 to a resurgent Moroccan state; Redman's (1986) excavations at Qasr es-Seghir in northern Morocco best document this implantation of Portuguese, Christian life onto a Muslim settlement (figure 5.13). Spain's mostly sixteenth century attempts are less well known archaeologically, but were sustained until other pressures forced her to concede Ottoman domination of the North African seaboard in the 1580s, an event sometimes viewed as precipitating a final break in the unity of the Mediterranean world (Hess 1978), though perhaps heralding only a shift to a more fluid, maritime frontier of privateering and trade (Larguèche

Figure 5.13. The southern gate and city walls at Essaouira, Morocco. Essaouira's present defenses and city plan are the work of a French architect employed by Sultan Sidi Mohammed bin Abdallah in the mid-eighteenth century to develop an entrepôt for use by European merchants. Essaouira had previously been briefly occupied by the Portuguese in the sixteenth century, and the island of Mogador, scene of first millennium B.C. Phoenician and Carthaginian commerce, lies just 1 km offshore.

2001). The long struggle for control of the North African coast had several consequences for West Africa. First, it left Islam, not Spain, in command of the littoral, so that cross-desert communications remained open. Second, to avoid the main centers of Ottoman government, many pilgrims tended to move east from the western Sahel through Ghat, Ghadames, and Fezzan rather than north into the Maghreb. Third, it facilitated the southward spread of guns, which encouraged warfare, slave raiding, and aristocratic control of subject groups. Finally, it helped destroy the Songhay empire when Morocco's Sharifian rulers, to fund their jihad against Portugal, sought direct control over trans-Saharan gold by invading and conquering the western Sahel (Levtzion 1977, 412–15). One result was to promote increased conflict, political unrest, and the breakdown of the Imperial Tradition within the western Sahel (R. McIntosh 1998). Another was the continued northward movement of slaves, something that accelerated still further in the early 1800s when suppression of the Barbary pirates removed Europeans from the North African slave block. The trans-desert exchange of slaves for horses in particular proved resilient, however, not least to the competing attractions of the developing Atlantic market. As Webb (1995) so skillfully shows, it was also closely linked, in scale and organization, to the increasing aridity that prevailed after 1600: ecological crisis encouraged political violence and slaving as desert traders, pastoralists, and cultivators all saw their resource base imperiled.

Archaeological research has so far contributed little to understanding the Sahel's external relations during these recent centuries. Timbuktu, where accumulated sand inhibits access to lower levels, is one site that has received attention. Insoll's (2003b) excavations document access to Middle Eastern glass ornaments and European glass beads, as well as the historically known use of *Marginella* shells instead of cowries in the late eighteenth century. But this is not much, raising the possibility that the town's economic importance has been exaggerated. The local nature of the tobacco pipes found may, in fact, support Ozanne's (1969) conclusion that Timbuktu played only a minor role in diffusing tobacco smoking after Morocco's 1591 invasion of Songhay; introductions via Senegambia and Ghana were probably more important points of entry to West Africa (S. McIntosh et al. 2003). Elsewhere in the Sahel, but far to the west of Timbuktu, archaeologists have documented widespread changes in local ceramic assemblages during the seventeenth century that may reflect the disruption caused by slaving, for both Atlantic and (trans-)Saharan markets, political unrest, historically attested population movements, and drought (S. McIntosh 2001). At the Sahel's opposite extreme, free from the threat of foreign attack, newly introduced firearms actually strengthened the Borno monarchy, helping it obtain supremacy over neighboring groups and increase slave exports to Tripoli; so consolidated, its rulers were better placed to support Muslim clerics and themselves go on pilgrimages to Mecca, further institutionalizing Islam (Gronenborn 2001).

The spread of guns through West Africa was by no means only from North African sources. One immediate effect of Europeans circumventing the Maghrebi states by sailing down Africa's Atlantic coast was to divert part of the existing slave and gold trades to Arguin, where Sahelian merchants could now obtain North African imports more cheaply and directly from the Portuguese (Levtzion 1977, 450–52). Though Arguin was superseded as maritime contacts developed farther south along the coast, opening up the Atlantic seaways did not curtail the centuries-old movement of slaves and gold across and into the Sahara. Indeed, in both Senegambia (S. McIntosh 2001) and the central Sahel (MacEachern 2001) the two systems began articulating with each other. Well into the nineteenth century, demand remained strong at both ends of the trans-Saharan equation, in North Africa and within the desert for Sahelian and forest-zone products, and within and south of the Sahel for those of the Sahara and the Muslim shores of the Mediterranean.[13] The interdependent structures of trade examined in this chapter are thus good examples of Braudel's (1972) *longue durée* and of the enduring nature of long-distance connections within Africa and between it and the wider world.

Notes

1. Claims (Dupuy et al. 2001–02) that engravings in Mali's Adrar des Iforas region represent metal blades reminiscent of the Iberian-type Bronze Age weapons represented at some Moroccan rock art sites are intriguing. However, inferences that ideas or objects diffused south to initiate a local development of copper production in the second millennium cal. B.C. cannot be supported by the available chronology of Saharan copper smelting, or while the engravings themselves are only datable on vague stylistic grounds.

2. For the most comprehensive and recent assessment of the issues surrounding the appearance of iron metallurgy in sub-Saharan Africa, including a thorough analysis of the problems with the existing corpus of radiocarbon dates and their interpretation, see Killick (2004).

3. Greco-Roman knowledge of areas south of Fezzan was extremely limited, perhaps deliberately so by the Garamantes themselves. In the late first century, Maternus, a trader-cum-explorer, visited a country where rhinoceros was to be found, probably around Lake Chad (Law 1967 citing Ptolemy's *Geography* I 8–11). Otherwise, Herodotus's (II 32–33) account of a group of Nasamonian nobles from northeastern Libya who reached a crocodile-inhabited eastward-flowing river (inescapably the Niger) marks the limit, in antiquity and distance, of Classical exploration.

4. The possibility of a more deadly export is raised by Mattingly (2003, 372) when suggesting that Fezzan was a likely corridor for the spread of *falciparum* malaria into the Mediterranean; a (late?) Roman date for its introduction, at least to Italy, seems likely (Sallares 2002).

5. A daily intake of 12 g is sufficient, but where meat and dairy products are rarely consumed, supplements are needed. Livestock too require regular, and relatively large, amounts of salt.

6. Mattingly (2003, 359–60) notes evidence for Garamantian salt production in Fezzan.

7. Curtin's (1984, 21–24) observations on the bulk transport of dates by camel and their significance as a high-energy, easily preserved foodstuff suggest that the date-camel combination was not only important in exchanges across and within the Sahara, but also crucial in enhancing the viability of the nomad lifestyle that helped move commodities through the desert.

8. Contrary to both Sunni and Shi'a Muslims, Kharijites held the view that any Muslim, regardless of race or descent, could be chosen to lead the faithful. Theirs was therefore a much more egalitarian version of Islam.

9. The traditional view that Ghana was forcibly converted to Islam by an Almoravid invasion has been refuted by Conrad and Fisher (1982), although debate continues (Masonen 1995). Hrbek and El-Fasi (1992) suggest that the whole episode, including the well-known rebuilding of the main mosque at Ghana's putative capital, Koumbi Saleh, may reflect no more than the imposition of Sunni orthodoxy on a previously Kharijite community.

10. Motivated by economic, as well as strategic and religious, considerations, these attacks began with Norman assaults on Tripoli and Mahdiya in the mid-1100s, continued with St Louis's 1270 attack on Tunis, and revived with Portuguese and Spanish activity in the fifteenth century.

11. All were, for example, written by educated, often devout, men, who frequently saw themselves as racially superior to black Africans, were keenly interested in long-distance trade rather than local exchange, and were appalled by "pagan" customs; one might add that of those most commonly cited only Ibn Battuta (Gibb and Beckingham 1994) actually visited the Sahel himself. Though sharing some of these biases, note too that several important Arabic language indigenous histories were produced by local scholars *within* the Sahel and that oral traditions were widely maintained, if modified, by Islam (R. McIntosh and McIntosh 1981).

12. Unless it was introduced across the Sahel from the Middle Nile where cotton textiles are known in late Meroitic contexts (Welsby 1996, 160). Seeds and fibers occur much earlier in Lower Nubia ca. 3000 B.C. (Choudhury and Buth 1971) but in contexts suggesting use as fodder.

13. What Insoll (2003a, 309) terms "the last gasp of the trans-Saharan slave trade" is represented by still largely uninvestigated forts, trading centers, and political capitals in Chad (Huard and Bacquié 1964) and the Central African Republic (Cordell 1985).

Africa's Opening
to the Atlantic

*It would seem that European traders proposed, but that it
was African rulers who disposed.*

—OLIVER AND ATMORE 2001, 230

AFRICA'S ATLANTIC coastline is several thousand
kilometers long, and that ocean's winds and currents
connect the continent with Europe and the Americas
(figure 6.1). Although these connections have influenced much of the world
we see today (DeCorse 2001a, 10), their potential has only recently been
realized. Of the various islands offshore only Bioko and the Canary Islands
were occupied before European exploration of Africa's Atlantic seaboard.
Furthermore, just as sub-Saharan Africans did not navigate north toward
the Mediterranean, neither did Mediterranean sailors of Classical or early
medieval times succeed in moving any distance south. I first explore these
arguments and then outline the wider opening up of Africa's Atlantic coasts
that began with Portugal's fifteenth century voyages of discovery. Their
impact on the trading networks that the Portuguese, and then other
Europeans, sought to join and ultimately control is now being addressed
by a growing volume of archaeological studies. In West Africa, Ghana and
Bénin stand out, and at the continent's southwestern corner historical
archaeology is firmly established as a source of information on the
European-dominated settler communities of the Cape Colony. Though by
no means the only commodity Europeans sought, the traffic in Africans
enslaved and sold overseas is a dominating motif in both historical and

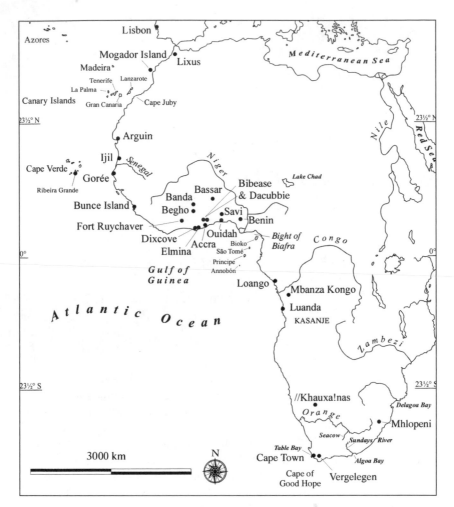

Figure 6.1. Location of sites and places discussed in chapter 6.

archaeological studies of Africa's Atlantic coasts. It, and the consequences for African populations of new technologies and crops, are among the other topics discussed as this chapter proceeds.

Atlantic Voyaging before the Portuguese?

Herodotus (IV 43) makes the earliest reference to the exploration of Africa's coasts when narrating the story of a Phoenician expedition that, to his own disbelief, apparently circumnavigated the continent in a voyage of 3 years' duration around 600 B.C. No archaeological evidence supports this, nor is any likely to be found, but the detail about the sun being on the right after rounding Africa's southern tip rings true, even though the mention of landing each autumn to grow (winter-rainfall) crops does not. Both Herodotus and other Greek writers recorded further attempts by Mediterranean sailors to move down the African coast, among them a voyage by Euthymenes of Massalia (Marseilles), who before 400 B.C. is said to have reached a large river (the Senegal?) with animals similar to those found in the Nile. Controversy surrounds this voyage and others, including the best known of all, that of Hanno of Carthage. The relevant document, the *Periplus of Hanno*, has been interpreted to mean that Carthaginian sailors reached as far as Cameroon (Law 1978), but there are good grounds for thinking it a forgery of the first century B.C. As Mauny (1978) goes on to argue, square-rigged ships of the Classical period were probably incapable of sailing back toward the Mediterranean once past Cape Juby, oar power alone being insufficient against prevailing northerly winds and currents. These negative conclusions are consistent with the geographically limited extent of archaeological evidence for Phoenician and Carthaginian activity along Africa's Atlantic coast (Aubet 2001). The southernmost point of such finds is the island of Mogador, just opposite Essaouira. Here Greek and Phoenician ceramics have been found dating back to the seventh century B.C., with tuna fishing the area's most likely attraction. More substantial Phoenician colonization is evident farther north at Lixus, again starting in the seventh century B.C. Located on the estuary of a river reaching up into the ivory- and ore-producing areas of the Atlas Mountains, it occupied one of the few sheltered harbors on Morocco's west coast and later became a flourishing Roman town.

If Classical sailors did not penetrate far down the West African coast, did they perhaps reach any of the islands offshore? The Canaries, as I show shortly, were certainly known to them, and there is a possibility that sailors blown off course in the fourth century B.C. reached Madeira, but without settling it (Cunliffe 2001, 10). Significantly farther west, a hoard of Punic and Cyrenaican coins found in the Azores in 1749 provides the merest suggestion of a landfall there too. Such knowledge as Europeans had obtained of the islands lying to Africa's west was lost, at least to our surviving literary sources, for several centuries following the fall of the Western Roman Empire. Subsequently, al-Idrisi, writing in the twelfth century, recorded a landfall by Muslim sailors on the Canaries (Levtzion and Hopkins 2000, 130–31). About the same time, Italian merchants were beginning to redevelop commercial ties with North African ports, including those of Atlantic Morocco. The Genoese were foremost in this, and in 1291 the Vivaldi brothers sailed south in an attempt to reach India. No knowledge of their voyage survives after they passed Cape Nun, and they were presumably shipwrecked or stranded farther south. Their explorations did, however, presage a rapid growth in European maritime activity off Africa's northwest corner, with another Italian, Lancelotto Malocello, rediscovering the Canary Islands ca. 1336. This event ultimately resulted in their conquest by Castile, but as early as the 1340s, return voyages from the Canaries to Europe may have stumbled across Madeira and the Azores (J. R. S. Phillips 1988). Settlement of all three archipelagos foreshadowed the much greater European expansion overseas generally associated with Columbus's voyage of 1492 (Crosby 1986).

The Canary Islands and Bioko: Africa's First Atlantic Islands

Conventionally considered by archaeologists apart, when considered at all, the Canary Islands and Bioko share several interesting features, despite their wholly different geographical locations. Alone among Africa's Atlantic islands they were settled long before European colonization by farming communities, who lacked knowledge of metallurgy, retained few links with the mainlands whence they had come, and put up considerable, if ultimately unsuccessful, resistance to European invaders. Hoping to excite a more meaningful comparative study, I consider them together here.

Comprising seven main islands and four smaller ones, the Canaries constitute an extended archipelago beginning 100 km west of Morocco's Atlantic coast, from which Tenerife's 3,715 m high Pico de Teide is visible. Although a substantial documentary record exists for them from the early fourteenth century, until recent decades little focused archaeological research has been undertaken; much earlier work is compromised by excessive attention to the supposed racial affinities of their prehistoric inhabitants (Del Arco Aguilar et al. 1992). Propinquity and surviving records of the islanders' speech in the fourteenth and fifteenth centuries indicate that the Canaries were settled from the Maghreb by people speaking a largely Berber-like language.[1] This was effected, probably in the first millennium cal. B.C. (Onrubia Pintado 1987), by an agricultural population equipped with a Near Eastern farming complex of sheep, goats, pigs, dogs, wheat, barley, and lentils. They also used stone tools, a technology retained until European settlement given the islands' lack of metal ores. Little is known in detail about Canarian social organization, but it appears to have been hierarchical, with considerable cultural diversity between what seem, in the fourteenth and fifteenth centuries, to have been largely isolated island communities (González Antón and Tejera Gaspar 1990).

Study of the islands' past has not gone unaffected by current politics, proindependence movements emphasizing Berber affinities at the expense of possible non-Berber elements, others asserting initial settlement from a "civilized" Classical North African source represented by Juba II, king of the Roman client state of Mauretania (Alvarez Delgado 1977; Eddy 1994). These tendencies are evident in the controversy surrounding the Zenata stone, an engraved object bearing an inscription apparently written in *tifinagh*, a Berber script still used today (Galand 1994). Further Libyco-Berber inscriptions and others written in a first century North African Latin script (Pichler 1995, 1996) do, however, indicate that the islands had contacts with the African mainland after their initial colonization. This is confirmed by excavations at El Bebedero, Lanzarote, that produced Roman potsherds and a few metal and glass artifacts, all of first to fourth century age. Most abundant are the remains of amphorae probably used to carry fish to salting stations on the Moroccan coast (Slayman 1997).

Medieval European interest in the Canaries focused on obtaining skins, tallow, plant dyes, and slaves, the latter a particular attraction given the depopulation the continent experienced from the Black Death soon after their rediscovery. During the fourteenth century, relations were generally conducted through trade, missionary activity, and raiding, but in the fifteenth this pattern shifted to one of outright conquest. Portuguese attempts having failed, by 1475 Castile controlled all but La Palma, Gran Canaria, and Tenerife, where rough terrain and guerilla resistance tactics delayed the final Spanish takeover until 1496. Castilian supremacy was based on a winning combination of several factors: superior military technology (ships, horses, metal weapons, a few firearms of poor quality); conflicts between Canarian groups themselves; cultural disorientation; ecological change as many new plant and animal species were introduced; and declining indigenous numbers brought about by slaving and new epidemic diseases to which the Canarians had no resistance. Their cumulative effect was such that by the mid-1500s few native Canarians survived other than those assimilated to the incoming Castilian population. The parallels to subsequent European colonizing strategies in the Americas are obvious and not coincidental (Tejera Gaspar and Aznar Vallejo 1992), but we shall see that they were not generally repeated along the mainland coast of sub-Saharan Africa.

Twenty-five degrees of latitude farther south, Bioko is the largest island in the Gulf of Guinea. Unlike São Tomé, Príncipe, and Annobón, it lies sufficiently inshore to have been joined to the mainland at times of low sea level. Evidence of pre-Holocene occupation is at best tenuous, but could be represented by a preceramic basalt-flake industry (Martin del Molino 1989; Clist 1998). Subsequent assemblages all feature pottery, which has similarities with ceramics known in Gabon, where Bioko's indigenous Bubi language also has links (Clist 1998; Ndong 2002). Oral traditions suggest multiple migrations, with new settlers initially using iron weapons to achieve dominance, though this technology was not sustainable given the island's lack of metal ores. Settlement was mostly coastal at first, spreading inland from the eleventh century cal. A.D. Despite a short-lived Portuguese presence in the 1520s and an attempted Spanish settlement in 1780, the isolating effect of the winds and currents prevailing off Bioko's southern and eastern shores, tropical diseases and active Bubi resistance left the local population unchallenged into the early nineteenth century. Only then did the introduction of iron and firearms help drive a process of centralization that, accompanied by immigration from the mainland and missionary activity, ended in the establishment of Spanish colonial control (Vansina 1990).

Much about Bioko's prehistory remains obscure. It is, however, possible to suggest that, like the Canaries, its size and closeness (32 km) to the African continent and the visibility of its tallest mountain, the 3,000 m Pico Basile, all conspired to make it a plausible "target" for mainland populations equipped with canoes of the kind in widespread use along the Gulf of Guinea's shores, lagoons, and estuaries by the fifteenth century (Nzewunwa 1980). In contrast, São Tomé lies 270 km offshore, visible only to ocean-going ships, just like Príncipe (200 km), and the much more distant Cape Verde archipelago (450 km). All were settled only after the Portuguese had mastered the complex winds and currents of the Atlantic (sidebar 7).

Africa and the Atlantic ca. 1400–1650

With few natural harbors, much of Africa's Atlantic shoreline is fringed by unwelcoming mangrove swamps or exposed, surf-pounded beaches. Still greater difficulties for navigation lie in the ocean's domination by the trade

SIDEBAR 7

Did Africans Cross the Atlantic before Columbus?

When European observers arrived off Africa's Atlantic coasts, the societies they encountered already had a long history of navigation. Fifteenth and sixteenth century African ships, though generally made from single logs and powered by oars or paddles, not sails, carried up to one hundred men, were readily maneuverable, and were a difficult target for European weapons. Is there, however, evidence that sub-Saharan Africans moved over the open sea before the 1400s? Arabic sources do, indeed, record that boats went north to take on salt from Ijil, Mauritania, but they were then constrained from going farther, despite awareness of the location of the Maghreb, by the same winds and currents that long prevented the southward movement of Mediterranean sailors (Thornton 1992, 15–16). Voyages west might, in principle, have been possible using the strongly westward flowing Equatorial Current, but there is no evidence for the existence of suitable craft and little likelihood that returning to Africa against the same current would have been possible.

Al-'Umari's account of a voyage by a Mali king westward into the Atlantic of whom nothing was heard again (Levtzion and Hopkins 2000, 263) is, if true, consistent with this view, but a considerable literature has grown up that presumes the contrary. Best known perhaps are the explorations of Thor Heyerdahl (1972). His papyrus boat, *Ra II*, an attempted reconstruction of vessels that might—there is little hard evidence—once have been used by the Ancient Egyptians, reached Barbados from Morocco in 1970. But the conclusions drawn from this are deeply suspect. Purported resemblances between Native American civilizations and that of Ancient Egypt are superficial and no assemblage of Pharaonic artifacts has ever been recovered from the Western Hemisphere. Van Sertima (1976, 1992) likewise identifies a purported voyage by Nubians or Egyptians as the inspiration for the Olmec and all subsequent Mesoamerican civilizations. As a recent review of his work concludes, the one difficulty in this argument, which receives enthusiastic endorsement from some Afrocentric quarters (e.g., Asante 1987), is that there is simply *no* credible evidence for pre-Columbian movements of people, animals, or plants between Africa and the Americas (Haslip-Viera et al. 1997). Regrettably, such writings offer historical reconstructions that fail to engage with archaeological method and evidence, while simultaneously propagating ideas of racial superiority and hegemony that only obscure the real complexity and significance of Africa's past connections with the rest of the world.

winds, a regular pattern of prevailing winds blowing in the same direction regardless of season (figure 6.2): northeast off Iberia and the Maghreb, southeast in latitudes linking southern Africa to Brazil. Between lie almost windless latitudes, the doldrums, while farther north and south are zones of westerlies. Local variations complicate the picture, but in essence the fixed nature of these systems posed the main challenge to successful voyaging along Africa's coast and east–west across the ocean itself. One crucial factor in mastering them was the gradual perfection, within the relatively safe

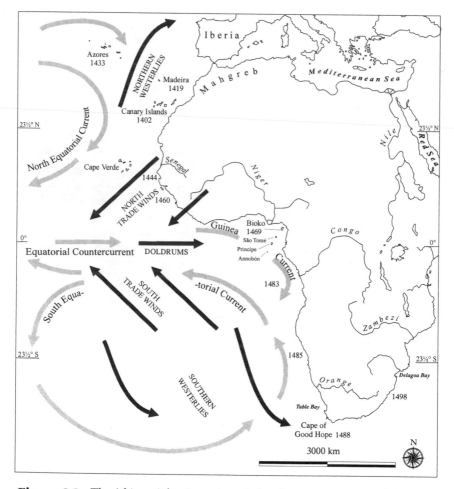

Figure 6.2. The African Atlantic: major wind and current systems and the dates of key points in the Portuguese voyages of discovery down the Atlantic coast and into the Indian Ocean during the fifteenth century.

laboratory afforded by the Canaries, Madeira, and the Azores, of the technique of sailing farther out into the Atlantic into the zone of westerly winds and using them to return to Iberia. Another came from the development of a more advanced ship design, the caravel, that was both robust and able to sail much closer to the wind. But neither of these factors, nor acquisition of the compass, estimations of latitude, or improved marine charts, sufficed alone. Rather, it was their gradual accretion by the societies of Atlantic Europe, with Portugal in the lead, and their combination with a competitive state system, missionary zeal, and the desire to win economic profits for state goals that spurred Europe's late medieval breakthrough into the Atlantic. Confirmed in the 1490s by Da Gama's discovery of a path across the southeastern trade winds around Africa's southern tip, Columbus's second trans-Atlantic crossing, and Cabot's voyage to Newfoundland, this breakthrough inextricably connected Africa with both Europe and the Americas (Fernández-Armesto 2001).

Seeking out the gold, slaves, and ivory that they already knew had sub-Saharan origins, Portugal's elite actively backed voyages of exploration down the African coast. As we saw in chapter 5, the post established at Arguin in 1455 captured an important share of West Africa's gold and slave exports for Portugal's own use and reexport within Europe. Within a decade the coast as far as Sierra Leone had been scouted and the Cape Verde archipelago settled on the lines already pioneered in Madeira and the Azores, including the use of enslaved African labor for plantation agriculture. The pace of exploration now accelerated, Diego Cão crossing the Equator to reach Namibia by 1483, Bartolomeo Dias rounding the Cape of Good Hope in 1488 and Vasco da Gama entering the Indian Ocean to begin Portugal's empire there only a decade later. Much of this exploration was undertaken by private entrepreneurs, a pattern followed in colonizing Cape Verde, where settlers were allowed to trade on adjacent coasts, intermarrying with local women and integrating into local politics to create a new society of European or half-caste traders and their African associates, at least as much African in outlook as Portuguese (Fage 1977; Brooks 2003). Though not invariable, a similar pattern was followed in Portugal's two other principal African colonies, Angola and, as we have already seen, Mozambique. In all three countries archaeological research should be able to contribute to understanding the development of these new Afro-Lusitanian identities.

Initially, Portugal's commercial interest focused on three areas, Ghana and the kingdoms of Benin and Kongo. Though it was Portuguese ships that linked them, the economics powering that linkage were, if anything, more African than European in origin. This is because on first entering sub-Saharan trading systems the Portuguese found themselves constrained by those networks and the expectations that they had generated. They had, for example, to import North African metal, textiles, and horses to Arguin and other trading stations farther south in Senegambia, areas already linked across the Sahara to the Maghreb and eastward to the Middle Niger, to access the gold and slaves that African merchants now brought there. A similar situation developed in the Gulf of Guinea and beyond, where, as well as acquiring pepper and ivory for their own use, the Portuguese moved slaves, beads, and cloth from the Bight of Benin to what soon became known as the Gold Coast.[2] The same goods were taken from southern Nigeria to Kongo and exchanged there for copper and ivory. Some of this copper may itself have been exchanged back to Benin, along with goods brought from Portugal and North Africa, such as coral, glass beads, and textiles. Only later did Portugal's trade broaden out from this multicornered system into a pattern of direct exchange in which slaves became increasingly important (Wesler 1998, 333).

Along the Gold Coast the principal focus of exchange quickly became the settlement of Elmina. Portugal's interest here was to obtain gold from the Akan goldfields and DeCorse's (2001a) fieldwork, which concentrated on the adjacent African settlement, shows that the ground plan of the stone fort the Portuguese built there in 1482 remains recognizable below its Dutch successor (figure 6.3). Intended to sustain Portuguese monopoly of European trade with the Gulf of Guinea, Elmina had already failed in this purpose by 1500, though the Portuguese alliance helped its inhabitants assert their independence from their neighbors. Shortages of manpower and funds, cumbersome administrative structures, and competition from traders of other nationalities increasingly turned Elmina into a loss-making venture for Portugal in the later 1500s, and, after earlier attempts, the Dutch took the post in 1637. Most of Elmina's archaeological record relates to the period of their presence, but remains of Portuguese churches are complemented by Iberian ceramics and glass vessels, including wine bottles, presumably destined for use by the small numbers of resident European traders and soldiers and/or exchange with Africans.

No large, centralized polities existed along the Gold Coast in the late fifteenth century, but this was not the case with the other two early centers of Portuguese activity. Of these, Kongo has received most attention, and I look at it first. Probably established in northwesternmost Angola in the 1300s, Kongo controlled the mouth of the Congo River when the Portuguese arrived (Hilton 1985). Its elite saw in them an opportunity for consolidating and expanding their own power and wealth and seized upon the possibilities for trade and technical assistance, including priests and craftsmen, that followed. Critical in this was the royal family's conversion to Catholicism in 1491, a process strengthened and extended when Afonso

Figure 6.3. Elmina Castle, Ghana. This photograph is taken from Fort St Jago, looking downslope.

I, an ardent Christian, became king ca. 1506. Following the arrival in 1512 of further missionaries and technicians, one of his sons traveled to Portugal and Rome,[3] returning in 1520 as Africa's first sub-Saharan Catholic bishop to play a crucial role in establishing and Africanizing the Church, a process aided by similarities between pre-Reformation Catholicism and traditional Kongo beliefs (Hastings 1994) and the Kongo nobility's recognition that Christianity, perhaps viewed as a powerful and exotic secret society, was the route to royal favor. Recent political instability and conflict have prevented archaeological excavation of Kongo's former capital Mbanza Kongo, but historical records indicate that by 1650 it included a dozen stone churches and a Jesuit college, along with the royal palace and a walled expatriate settlement (Thornton 2000). Within only a few years of European arrival, slaves began to substitute for copper and ivory as Kongo's main export, a process encouraged when Portuguese plantations were established on São Tomé. At first a royal monopoly, demand for slaves quickly outstripped local supply as Portugal lost interest in other goods. Kongo and resident Portuguese traders responded by sponsoring trading and raiding expeditions that ultimately reached far inland along the Congo River. Competition in exporting slaves from Angola and factional fights among Kongo's elite that were encouraged by subordinates' increasingly direct access to desirable imports gravely weakened the Kongo state by the mid-1600s.[4] Mbanza Kongo nonetheless retained a symbolic importance as the focus of sacred royal power (Thornton 2000). Catholicism too remained the religion of both state and people, contributing to Christianity's spread among enslaved Africans in the Americas. Potential archaeological evidence for its penetration in Kongo itself takes the form of stylized crosses and Christ-like and priest-like paintings, along with traditional geometric forms, in a rock shelter at Mbafo, Congo-Kinshasa, which also contained seventeenth century ceramics (Mortelmans and Monteyne 1962).

Whether a similar process might have developed in Benin is a moot point. *Oba* Ozalua did, in fact, dispatch an embassy to Lisbon in 1514 asking for both clergy and cannon, but the priests soon died and Benin was able to defend itself and expand against its neighbors without using firearms, becoming indifferent to European trade, demanding higher prices for its goods, and prohibiting the export of male slaves (Northrup 2002). In consequence the Portuguese turned attention away from Benin and toward Kongo and the Niger Delta as sources of slaves. From a material-culture perspective, an enduring legacy of their earlier contacts with Benin lies in some of the brass plaques for which it is famous; several contain cosmological references to European arrival from the sea, and they are complemented by brass statues of Portuguese and local soldiers carrying muskets (Ben-Amos 1980). While these brass works were produced for local consumption, another form of sculpture developed through contact between West Africans and Europeans in the sixteenth century had a different motivation: the spectacular "Afro-Portuguese" ivories of Benin and Sierra Leone, which often include European motifs, were deliberately made for export to Europe where they were collected by Renaissance elites (figure 6.4; Bassani and Fagg 1988).

Slaves and gold were at the top of the list of African desiderata from the earliest years of Portuguese exploration. Slaves were employed both in Europe and, increasingly from the mid-sixteenth century, the Americas, but Africa's Atlantic islands constituted a further important market. Sugarcane, the cultivation of which demanded a large and compliant workforce, was introduced to Madeira within 30 years of its initial settlement, as timber and other exports from its once virgin ecology declined (Crosby 1986). Between 1455 and the early 1500s, production soared from 70 to 15,000 metric tons a year, a growth built on using a substantial slave population to clear and terrace the island's steep terrain, maintain a complex irrigation system (Calvert 1978–79), and cultivate, harvest, and mill the cane itself. Though derived from multiple sources, including the indigenous Canarians, on both Madeira and the Canary Islands, where

Figure 6.4. A late fifteenth century Afro-Portuguese ivory salt cellar made by Sapi craftsmen in what is now Sierra Leone (courtesy and copyright Pitt Rivers Museum, University of Oxford).

sugarcane plantations were introduced in 1484, this labor force (or, rather, forced labor) was increasingly sub-Saharan in origin.

High rainfall and fertile volcanic soils encouraged the rapid expansion of sugar plantations to São Tomé and Príncipe, both of which Portugal settled in the late fifteenth century, initially to transit slaves onward to Benin and to supply ships returning to Europe or sailing to Brazil. Previously uninhabited, just like Madeira or Cape Verde, their settlement too must have impacted on local faunas and floras in ways we as yet only dimly appreciate. Constituting new areas for African settlement (however involuntary) and bringing together people from diverse cultural backgrounds, these islands also represent the first installment in the trans-Atlantic African diaspora, which forms the main subject of chapter 7. However, archaeological research that might explore the complex history of São Tomé and Príncipe, including the establishment on them of free-slave communities, has yet to be undertaken. Even on the slightly better known Cape Verde archipelago, which occupied another strategic location in sixteenth century Atlantic shipping lanes, it is limited to preliminary exploration of the cathedral and other buildings at the former capital of Ribeira Grande (Rodrigues 1997) and underwater excavation, largely for commercial sale (!), at a few of several hundred known shipwreck sites (Arqueonautas 2004).

A similar story holds for another area of Portuguese commercial penetration, Angola. This was already supplying slaves and ivory before the Portuguese established a settlement in 1575 at Luanda, a site chosen also for its access to the salt and *nzimbu* shells needed to obtain slaves from Kongo and areas upstream along the Congo River. Within a century European traders were present several hundred kilometers inland in Kasanje, whence caravans reached as far as the Lunda state in southern Congo-Kinshasa. By 1740 this system of trade, which made extensive use of indigenous polities as "broker states" that captured and traded on slaves to the coast, had connected to other caravan routes stretching east toward the Indian Ocean. Other Afro-Portuguese traders subsequently established themselves among the Ovimbundu kingdoms of the Angolan plateau, which exported slaves, ivory, wax, and ultimately rubber into the late nineteenth century. Even where slaves were not the main commodity passing along the routes thus established, they were often used as porters (Vansina 1962), something that was also true farther north in Gabon, where European trade focused on another area of indigenous political centralization around Loango. Here the Vili people supplied the raffia cloth used as currency in Luanda and acted as intermediaries in exporting ivory and redwood in return for salt and imported European goods, first to the Portuguese and then to the Dutch. Described by Vansina (1990) from historical sources, virtually no investigation of these systems and the sociopolitical changes that they precipitated has yet been attempted using archaeological evidence.

Africa's Atlantic Trade since 1650

From about 1650 trading networks and their associated economic and political repercussions underwent major changes, most notably in the arrival on the scene of organized trading ventures by a much wider variety of European nations and a massive increase in the volume of slave exports, almost wholly for American plantations. However, even though the slave trade looms large in academic works, popular imagination, and the chapter that follows this one, narrow concentration on this dimension of Atlantic commerce would be misleading. Not only did Africans export other goods, they also imported a wide variety of items, not always of European origin: commodities moved from one part of Africa to another by Europeans, Indian cottons, and American tobacco and rum were all involved in far from static systems of trade and cross-cultural influence (Alpern 1995; Northrup 2002). Furthermore, Europeans themselves had little direct involvement beyond the coast, save in Angola, the Cape, and Senegambia. Much of the Atlantic trade's impact was thus played out in purely African sociocultural contexts (DeCorse 2001c). Though by no means alone, DeCorse's (1992, 2001a) fieldwork at Elmina and that of Kelly (1997a, 1997b) in Bénin provide the most coherent archaeological accounts. Importantly, both projects show that access to European trade and the goods that it brought did not necessarily result in dramatic cultural changes but that Africans "adopted, transformed or rejected within [their] indigenous cultural traditions" (DeCorse 2001a, 16). Unsurprising as this conclusion should be—and it can be readily paralleled in northeastern North America (Wesler 1983; Bradley 1987)—it requires emphasis because, as discussed later, the argument has been made that Africans were forced into dependent exchanges of raw materials for cheap manufactures in a spiral of underdevelopment and exploitation (Rodney 1972).

As previously indicated, the bulk of the finds from Elmina relate to the seventeenth and later centuries. Numbering up to sixteen thousand inhabitants, Elmina was almost wholly an African settlement, with very few Dutch or other Europeans present, even in the castle's garrison. It thus provides an excellent, if exceptional, opportunity to investigate the creation of new lifestyles among a population largely independent of, but in close contact with, European merchants (DeCorse 2001a; figure 6.5). The settlement retained, for example, a densely packed, non-European housing pattern with few public spaces, but from the late seventeenth century many houses were built of masonry and by the 1800s some had tile or slate roofs rather than the more typical flat ones, themselves probably an innovation from the Sahel in the seventeenth century (DeCorse 2001a, 64). Internally, too, most excavated buildings retained indigenous arrangements of unspecialized rooms around a central courtyard, though the frequent use of stone flooring may be a European borrowing (DeCorse 2001a, 92). Excavation of food remains confirms that, despite access to a greatly expanded portfolio of (mostly American) crops, traditional soups and stews eaten communally by hand continued to be consumed, as they are today. Grinding stones and faunal remains virtually lacking in saw marks emphasize the persistence of a tradition of pulverizing ingredients and selling meat by weight, not by cut. For want of different foodstuffs and dependent on indigenous labor, local Europeans too probably ate a largely African diet. This may be reflected in the difficulty of attributing, to either Dutch or African sources, the faunal remains found in excavations at Fort St Jago, which the Dutch built higher up than and inland of the original Elmina Castle (Anquandah 1992a).

Turning from food to material culture, one consequence of European arrival off West Africa's coast was the introduction of virtually limitless supplies of brass: as but one example, a single Portuguese order from 1548 numbered in excess of one million copper or brass

Figure 6.5. View of the excavation of Locus A at the town site of Elmina, Ghana (courtesy and copyright Chris DeCorse, Syracuse University). Elmina Castle is visible in the background. The Locus A structure was probably begun early in the period of Dutch occupation of Elmina and was probably located near the market. The structure visible here is of nineteenth century date and contains several European-style features, but also incorporates remains of earlier buildings of possibly Dutch and Portuguese origin (DeCorse 2001a).

manilla bracelets (Teixeira da Mota and Hair 1988, 27). *Manillas* were mainly used as currency, but as already noted, copper and brass were valued above all in sub-Saharan Africa for their role as containers and signifiers of supernatural potency (Herbert 1984). Their import by Europeans facilitated a florescence of brass casting and manufacture of sheet brass vessels, though little direct evidence for either craft comes from Elmina itself. Interestingly, Elmina also shows little sign of local iron smelting and even before Portuguese arrival may have imported iron from farther inland. Subsequent to the development of the Atlantic trade, and as an integral part of the exchange networks that it helped build, evidence for iron and salt production, marine fishing, brass casting, and the reworking of glass beads does, however, increase along Ghana's central coast (DeCorse 2001a). Another response is reflected by changes in settlement pattern. Kiyaga-Mulindwa (1982), for example, interprets earthworks in the Birim Valley as defensive structures against slave raiding, and Anquandah (1992b, 1993) notes fortification of some sites and overall increases in site density in the Shai Hills, a known refuge area for the Dangme people as they retreated from Akwamu slave raids.[5] Though Akwamu tried to monopolize trade with Europeans, finds of imported goods and cowrie shells suggest this strategy was unsuccessful, and the Shai Hills' inhabitants also developed a thriving exchange in meat and ceramics with new settlements on the Accra Plains. Such polities, small and intensely competitive, acted as intermediaries between Europeans and Ghana's hinterland until subordinated in the early 1700s to the expanding Asante kingdom, which sought to monopolize trade on the Gold Coast, restricting other communities' access to overseas goods (Wesler 1983; Stahl 2001a).

In return for the gold and slaves that were the principal commodities exported through Elmina, what did Europeans introduce? Leaving food crops aside for the moment, DeCorse's (2001a) excavations show that an impressive 20 percent of Elmina's ceramic assemblage is imported. Limited in Portuguese times, this trade grew after 1637 to include a wider range of European wares and Chinese porcelains, providing a link here to Dutch trading colonies in eastern Asia and at the Cape of Good Hope. The pottery found spans a wide range, from ointment jars to jugs, but in the nineteenth century becomes simultaneously more common and less diverse, reflecting the creation of new European export wares tailored to African markets. Documents suggest that most of the glass found should reflect importation of alcohol, but though spirits, especially gin, were clearly imported on a growing scale during the period of Dutch presence, drinking glasses are also known. One use of spirits was in libations, and it is evident from grave forms and locations that there was substantial continuity in local religious beliefs into the late nineteenth century, reflecting limited Dutch interest in propagating Christianity. Along with glass beads and imported tobacco pipes, a final European import was firearms, trade in which seems to have taken off only in the late 1600s. Gun parts are, understandably, rare at Elmina or in other archaeological contexts, but gunflints are common, even if their interpretation is complicated by use, or reuse, as strike-a-lights; most of those at Elmina came from French and British sources. Collectively, and it is a sobering thought, all these items probably accounted for only a small fraction of what was imported to West Africa in the course of the Atlantic trade's heyday, most of which consisted of cloth, tobacco, alcohol, and metal (Feinberg 1989). The trade's complexities are also neatly illustrated by the fact that although a fifth of ships visiting Elmina in 1853 were American no more than a single stoneware sherd and a few glass fragments attest to this, most American trade being in either perishables or goods of European origin (DeCorse 2001a, 146).

Elmina is merely the best known of more than sixty fortified trading posts built along the Ghanaian coast by a bewildering variety of European nationalities (figure 6.6; van Dantzig 1980). Few have been examined archaeologically,[6] most studies emphasizing architectural history, conservation, and potential tourist development (Lawrence 1963; cf. DeCorse 2001c). Among those nations whose activities persisted into the mid-nineteenth century were the Danes, who eventually dominated commerce along the southeastern Gold Coast and ambitiously developed agricultural plantations after abolishing their own overseas slave trade in 1792. Examples include Daccubie (DeCorse 1993) and Bibease (Bredwa-Mensah 1994), where excavations document access by enslaved workers to British and Dutch pipes, gunflints, imported liquor, and rare European ceramics and beads. Northwest of Ghana excavations have been little more than exploratory of the potential of Bunce Island, an important slave-exporting station in Sierra Leone (DeCorse 1994), though a more intensive, interdisciplinary investigation has begun on Gorée Island, another such center in Senegal (Thiaw 2002, 2003a). Senegambia in general is of considerable interest in understanding the Atlantic trade's wider impact in West Africa

Figure 6.6. Interior view of Fort Batenstein just east of Dixcove, Ghana. This fort was built by the Dutch in 1656 nearby and in opposition to a Swedish fort at Butri. Fort Batenstein, like other Dutch possessions on the Gold Coast such as Elmina Castle, was ceded to Britain in 1872.

because of its centuries-old contacts across the Sahara (S. McIntosh 2001; Thiaw 2001). Systematic analysis of the glass beads introduced here, as elsewhere along the Atlantic coast, in payment for slaves and other commodities, both emphasizes African consumer choice and provides a potential dating tool for a period in which calibration problems mean that radiocarbon has only the most limited application (DeCorse et al. 2003).

Bénin is the other region of coastal West Africa to have received most attention. The Portuguese probably began trading here in 1473, and the area is a documented source of slaves in Brazil by 1560. As frequently happened elsewhere, exchanges were initially conducted from ship or on the beach, but "factories," that is, permanent if small trading posts, began to be created in the 1660s (Kelly 1997a). Among them were British, French, and Portuguese forts at Ouidah, from which as many as one million Africans may have been deported in chains, making it one of the largest slave-exporting centers of the late seventeenth to mid-nineteenth centuries (Law 2000). Ouidah's importance drew on its proximity to the shore, its role as a local fishing and salt-production focus, and its position within a lagoon system offering east–west access along the coast. Politically, however, it formed part of the Allada kingdom and, after the 1670s, of the Hueda state centered farther inland at Savi. Kelly's (1997a, 1997b) fieldwork here is notable in two respects. First, it emphasizes how much European traders operated in West Africa on local sufferance: the trading lodges permitted at Savi had to be adjacent to the palace and used traditional architecture, limiting interaction with local people while preventing traders from distancing themselves socially. In addition, Europeans were forbidden to fight among themselves, on land or at sea, even if their nations were at war elsewhere. Second, excavations illuminate aspects of a "Hueda ideology of contact" (Kelly 1997a, 355). The physical segregation of royal palace and trading lodges associated the Hueda elite with access to exotic goods, an association confirmed by the spatially restricted distributions of European and Chinese ceramics (figure 6.7), firearms, fine glassware, and imported alcohol. Even more tellingly, the palace compound used European bricks to floor at least nine rooms (figure 6.8), publicly demonstrating privileged royal access to an import denied local people and European residents alike, an import, furthermore, carried through 10 km of swampy terrain from the sea! Perhaps linked to this emphasis on elite control of access to European goods, only glass beads and tobacco pipes occur in commoner residential areas, and there are no examples of locally made ceramics imitating European forms (Kelly 2001). As with Elmina, Savi's contribution to archaeological study of the Atlantic trade owes much to its subsequent destruction without rebuilding, an event that took place when Hueda

Figure 6.7. Imported Chinese porcelain from excavations at Savi, Bénin (courtesy and copyright Ken Kelly).

was conquered by the expanding kingdom of Dahomey in 1727. Itself subsequently a major exporter of slaves, archaeological investigation of Dahomey's own past has only just begun (Monroe 2002).

Gradual suppression of the trans-Atlantic slave trade during the nineteenth century saw Euro-American demand for African products turn increasingly to raw materials and cash crops. Ironically, some of these were themselves produced by slave labor within Africa, notably the palm oil used from the mid-1800s to make soap and machine lubricants. Competition to supply this contributed to political disorders that encouraged formal European colonization in Ghana, Bénin, and Nigeria (Wolf 1982, 331), but palm oil plantations remain unstudied archaeologically. Cocoa production, which followed a different trajectory emphasizing small-scale cultivation by individual farmers, has also been little explored, though it too brought about significant new intergroup and interclass social relations (Wolf 1982, 342). Another theme still largely uninvestigated is the archaeology of European colonization as this expanded inland in the late-nineteenth-century "Scramble for Africa" (Pakenham 1991). The experience of historical archaeology elsewhere suggests this will prove a profitable vein to tap, something illustrated by Ogedengbe's (1998) study of a British colonial post in Nigeria and Vivian's (1992) argument that the

Figure 6.8. The brick floor at the palace at Savi, Bénin (courtesy and copyright Ken Kelly).

spread of Christianity may partly explain shifts observed in Akan funerary practices over the past 150 years. The most detailed case study of the impact of colonial economies comes from Banda, Ghana (Stahl 2001a, 2001b), close to the site of Begho, discussed in the last chapter. Here iron smelting and local pipe manufacture rapidly disappeared when European imports became cheaply available, but reworking of scrap to meet local demand continued much longer and pottery and cloth production survive today. Involved in this variability may be a tangled web of issues relating to the gender associations of artifact manufacture and use and the prestige of objects replaced and new. Farther east in Togo, De Barros (2001) has investigated the history of Bassar iron production. Initially this expanded to participate in widening trade networks and for self-defense against slave raids that were partly driven by European demands on Asante and its tributaries. Its later growth took advantage of German-imposed colonial peace and access to high-quality ores to compete successfully for a time with European imports. Both examples indicate the need to consider in detail the deeper historical changes wrought through the expanding Atlantic economy and their implications for using recent ethnographies as baselines for the remoter past (Stahl 2001b). The large-scale loss of able-bodied men and women to the Atlantic slave trade, in particular, which I discuss in greater detail later in this chapter and in chapter 7, is a clear case in point. The demographic burden that the trade created was borne by a range of societies, by no means always the same and by no means all at or even near the coast. Household reproduction must have been affected on both social and economic planes. As well as relocation in refuge areas, a strategy best exemplified in the Mandara Mountains of Cameroon (MacEachern 2001), impacts may have included the development of lineage structures as a means of limiting the impact of slaving where political authority was weak (Ekeh 1990) and the growth of what Kopytoff (1987) has termed "frontier societies"; if so, this would make two quintessential features of many African societies historical latecomers rather than historical constants, underlining the validity of Stahl's (2001b) argument about generalizing uncritically from the "ethnographic present."

The Southwestern Corner: European Settlement and Exploration in Southern Africa

Far to the south of the areas I have been discussing thus far a quite different set of interactions took shape between Africans and Europeans. The Portuguese rounded the Cape of Good Hope in 1488, occasionally trading with local Khoekhoe pastoralists for livestock in the ensuing decades. After the Viceroy of India's death in a skirmish in 1510, however, Portuguese vessels largely avoided the Cape, sailing directly to Mozambique. By the late 1500s English and Dutch vessels had replaced them in Table Bay, offering welcome supplies of iron, copper, and tobacco in return for sheep and cattle (Elphick 1985). Formal European settlement began in 1652 when the Dutch East India Company (or VOC, from an abbreviation of its formal Dutch name) established a revictualling station for ships sailing between Europe and the East Indies. Though European numbers still barely exceeded ten thousand by 1780 (Guelke 1989), the area of settlement grew rapidly. Only in the immediate vicinity of Cape Town was intensive farming feasible, and beyond this European settlers turned increasingly to extensive stock rearing and hunting in a largely uncontrolled process of expansion that saw them reach the Orange and Sundays Rivers by the time Dutch rule ended in favor of Britain in 1806. Favoring this expansion, compared with Europeans' experience elsewhere along the African coast, were substantively less complex indigenous economies, technologies, and levels of political organization, an absence of tropical diseases, and an ecology vastly more suitable for the establishment of European domesticates (Crosby 1986). In these respects the Cape Colony was much more similar to contemporary North America, and European expansion encountered successful long-term opposition only when it ran up against Bantu-speaking farmers from the late eighteenth century.

Much of the ever-increasing output of historical archaeology in southern Africa (Mitchell 2002a) comes from Cape Town itself, where ceramic inventories make plain the settlement's involvement in the wider world of Dutch international commerce and oriental porcelain was in common daily use (Klose 1992–93). Preliminary analysis of colonial foodways make the same point, with strong Malayo-Indonesian influences on ingredients and their preparation, although local drinking patterns remained more closely tied to Europe (Abrahams-Willis 1998). The VOC tried hard to monopolize trade with the Far East, but excavation of the *Oosterland*, wrecked in Table Bay in 1697, demonstrates that this was not always successful; the Chinese and Japanese porcelain recovered was almost certainly in private, not Company, hands. Other finds include tropical hardwoods, spices, and cowries, the latter destined for use by the Dutch West India Company in buying slaves at Elmina and elsewhere on the West African coast (Werz 1999), off which comparable wrecks have also been excavated (Sténuit 1977; L'Hour et al. 1989).

An important dimension of historical archaeology in South Africa is the cultural construction of colonial landscapes. Studies of Vergelegen, private residence of an early governor, Willem Adriaan van der Stel, suggest that its rigid symmetry and orderly layout were deliberately designed to impose Renaissance architectural ideas on an alien landscape, mimicking the country estates of Holland's metropolitan elite (Brink 1993; Markell 1993) and foreshadowing the impressive manor houses that rich Cape farmers increasingly built during the eighteenth century (figure 6.9; Brink 1997). Just as they, and the smaller farm buildings of more marginal agricultural areas, reflect an evolution of local architectural styles from a north European tradition (M. Hall et al. 1988), so too do nineteenth century British settlements in the Eastern Cape Province. Here both the creation of a distinctively British South African material culture and the imposition onto the landscape of an idealized "memory" of rural England are traceable (Scott and Deetz 1990; Winer and Deetz 1990).

The Cape Colony was a slave society, a situation arising from a labor shortage created by a small European population and initial difficulties in recruiting indigenous Khoekhoe farmworkers. Annual imports numbered no more than a few hundred, mostly from Madagascar, India, and Indonesia. As part of efforts to learn more about the underclasses of colonial society who go underrepresented in documentary sources, excavations at Vergelegen and the VOC Slave Lodge in Cape Town (Abrahams-Willis 2000) are beginning to show how slaves were able to maintain a distinctive material culture. Examples include Afro-Malagasy-like pit hearths for

Figure 6.9. The main building at Blaauwklippen, South Africa (courtesy and copyright John Hobart). Granted as a farm by the VOC governor Simon van der Stel in 1689, the present manor house dates to 1789. Its H-plan, thatched roof, gables, and three-sided porch are typical of many other Cape Dutch manor houses in the Western Cape Province.

cooking (Markell et al. 1995) and burials that follow neither Christian nor Muslim practice (Sealy et al. 1993). Stable-isotope studies showing contrasting childhood and adult diets help localize the origins of some enslaved individuals and of others probably brought to the Cape as political prisoners (Cox et al. 2001). Some of those detainees played important parts in the local establishment of Islam (Elphick and Shell 1989), while both slaves and so-called free blacks had other lasting impacts in traditional Cape cuisine and the development of the Afrikaans language.

South Africa was not, of course, uninhabited at European arrival, and Khoekhoe herders put up substantial military resistance to Dutch expansion in the late seventeenth century. Its failure, combined with loss of manpower and quality pasture lands to the settler economy, led, inexorably, to the gradual collapse of independent Khoekhoe communities in the southwestern and southern Cape. As an alternative to subordination and incorporation as farm laborers, some moved away from the Colony in a process paralleling the inland expansion of European settlers. J. Kinahan's (1996) work at //Khauxa!nas attests to partial acculturation by one of these groups, the Oorlam, to European architectural norms, alongside their continued use of more traditional dwellings. Farther north on Namibia's coast, Euro-Americans traded glass beads, tobacco, and metal for cattle, ivory, and other products. Here, as two centuries earlier in the Cape, increasing loss of livestock led eventually to the breakdown of indigenous exchange and social storage networks, precipitating general impoverishment, growing dependence on marine and wild plant resources, and scavenging or reuse of imported pottery, glass, and metal (J. H. A. Kinahan 2000). Farther south little archaeological work has been undertaken thus far on expanding "white" (*trekboer*) or "mixed race" (*Bastaard*, *Griqua*) pastoralist-hunter populations, a pity since there is considerable scope for their comparative study alongside Mozambique's *prazeros* or the culturally mixed Afro-Lusitanian communities of colonial Angola (Heywood 2002). Rock paintings (Vinnicombe 1976; Ouzman and Loubser 2000) and detailed work by Sampson (1994) and his colleagues in the Seacow Valley nonetheless document the active and innovative, if ultimately unsuccessful, resistance of Bushman hunter-gatherers to colonial expansion. That expansion, which accelerated after 1838, led within a few decades to European domination of all of southern Africa, a process reflected in many ways, including the frequent disappearance of traditional ceramics in favor of imported goods (S. Hall 1997) and the local development of archaeological research itself (Mitchell 2002b).

Transformations in Subsistence, Technology, and Demography: Africa and the Columbian Exchange

It would be untrue to characterize those parts of Africa considered here as wholly unaffected by the wider world before the arrival of the Portuguese (*pace* Thornton 1992, 13). Much of the forest zone inland of the Gulf of Guinea was, as seen in chapter 5, already linked to larger trans-Saharan networks, but even in the Congo Basin connections beyond Africa can be traced, long distance and indirect as they may have been. The widespread importance of plantains, Asian yams, and taro offers one example (chapter 4), cultivation of citrus fruits and sugarcane (a major crop on Bioko) another, even if the pathways of their introduction are obscure (Vansina 1990, 87). There is nonetheless no denying that the opening up of Africa's Atlantic coasts to Europe and the Americas had profound consequences for all three continents. To conclude this chapter, I look at three interrelated areas where those consequences were played out, those of subsistence, technology, and demography. Identifying such themes should, as Stahl (1994, 103) argues, act as a spur to archaeological research since all touch upon processes with profound and direct impacts on the lives of ordinary Africans.

Many of the staple food plants used by African peoples today were introduced to the continent as part of the so-called Columbian exchange (Crosby 1986; Alpern 1992), the movement of plants, animals, and diseases set in motion by Europe's colonization of the Americas. Documentary sources indicate that one major American crop, maize (figure 6.10), had been introduced by the Portuguese to Cape Verde by the mid-1500s, whence it spread within less than a century to São Tomé, the Gulf of Guinea coast, and Kongo, before continuing to expand through Angola and the Congo Basin. Needing little by way of new techniques but higher yielding than indigenous cereals, its ease of storage and transport in the form of flour was another advantage (Miracle 1965), even if high humidity and extra land clearance limited take-up in rainforest areas. With interests in the Indian as well as Atlantic Oceans, the Portuguese were also responsible for introducing Asiatic rice from the Swahili coast to West Africa (Portères 1962) and for bringing maize to eastern Africa; it is reported from the Mutapa state as early as 1561 and from European settlements on Pemba and Réunion in the seventeenth century. Little observed until the late 1700s, when it began to be a staple in much of Mozambique

Figure 6.10. Maize under cultivation, South Africa (courtesy and copyright Gavin Whitelaw).

and eastern Zambia, Swahili caravans then played an important part in its spread farther inland in East Africa during the nineteenth century.

Across much of equatorial Africa maize has been widely superseded by another Latin American import, cassava (manioc). A root crop, this was the best American food plant for rainforest conditions, though not confined to them. High yielding and readily propagated, its mature tubers store naturally underground but can also produce a "bread" that remains edible for several months. The downside is that cassava needs more labor than plantains for field clearance and processing, not least to remove toxic cyanogenic compounds, the concentration of which varies by variety (Purseglove 1969). Arriving in Angola after 1600, it reached central Zambia before 1850, expanding across the Congo Basin by 1900. Like maize, cassava was widely grown, sometimes using slave labor, around slaving ports to provision the European ships that took captives overseas (Vansina 1990; Carney 2001);[7] elsewhere, for example, in Nigeria, its spread may have been encouraged by outbreaks of disease that created labor shortages (Ohadike 1981).

Less transformative, but also widely taken up, was a wide range of vegetables and fruits, as well as tobacco (table 6.1). Not merely a garden crop, the latter was grown in plantations for export in several areas of Central Africa in the eighteenth and nineteenth centuries (Vansina 1990, 215). Tobacco is also, if only through the proxy evidence of the pipes used to smoke it, the one American import most easily traceable archaeologically. Forming an important dating tool (Ozanne 1962; cf. Shinnie and Kense 1989; S. McIntosh et al. 2003), both European and local pipe forms are known (figure 6.11). The former seem to have been imported only from the early 1600s, and since tobacco was introduced to the Sahel before then, its diffusion through West Africa is likely to have pursued both southward and northward paths, a possibility strengthened by similarities between Asante pipe forms and those known on the Middle Niger (Shinnie and Shinnie 1995; S. McIntosh et al. 2003).[8] Though tobacco may now be thought of as detrimental to health, the overall impact of the new crops was positive, expanding the range of African cuisine without necessarily altering how food was prepared and served (DeCorse 2001a, 115), although at least in some places perhaps associated with changes in the gender division of agricultural labor (Guyer 1991). From an overall demographic standpoint their contribution to increasing calorie production and bridging seasonal food shortages means that "it might be argued that the loss of slaves was compensated by the introduction of these crops" (Vansina 1962, 387). Certainly, the associations sometimes made between dynastic founders and their introduction, as in the case of the Kuba state, underline the significance of their impact (Oliver and Atmore 2001, 160).

Table 6.1. A partial list of American and African food-plants participating in the Columbian exchange (after Vansina 1990; Carney 2001; DeCorse 2001a).

Introduced from the Americas to Africa			
Avocado	*Persea americana*	Maize	*Zea mays*
Beans	*Phaseolus* spp.	Papaya	*Carica papaya*
Cacao	*Theobroma cacao*	Peanuts	*Arachis hypogaea*
Cashew nuts	*Anacardium occidentale*	Pineapple	*Ananas comosus*
Cassava	*Manihot esculenta*	Sweet potato	*Ipomoea batatas*
Chili peppers	*Capsicum* spp.	Tobacco	*Nicotiana tabacum*
Guava	*Psidium guava*	Tomato	*Lycopersicon esculentum*

Introduced from Africa to the Americas			
Castor bean	*Ricinus communis*	Peanuts	*Arachis hypogaea*[1]
Cowpeas (black-eyed beans)	*Vigna unguiculata*	Pigeon peas	*Cajanus cajan*
		Rice	*Oryza glaberrima*
Groundnut	*Voandzeia subterranea*	Sesame	*Sesamum indicum*
Kola	*Cola cuminata*	Sorghum	*Sorghum bicolor*
Oil palm	*Elaeis guineensis*	Watermelon	*Citrullus lanatus*
Okra	*Hibiscus esculentus*	Yams	*Dioscorea* spp.

Note

1. Peanuts, an originally South American crop, were introduced to North America from West Africa as a distinctively African variety, *A. hypogaea africana* (Carney 2001, 393).

Archaeological confirmation of changes in African farming economies remains, however, disappointingly limited. Stahl's (1999b, 2001a) excavations at Banda document reduced numbers of grindstones and increasing use of maize cob roulettes to decorate pottery from the late eighteenth century and the still earlier (seventeenth century) appearance of maize phytoliths, trends that probably reflect a gradual shift in emphasis from sorghum to maize, which was prepared by pounding in wooden mortars. Farther along the coast, maize was certainly present at Savi before 1727, but the admittedly sparse fauna shows neither pigs nor turkeys, both of which are documented European introductions by 1700 (Kelly 2001). It is, however, beyond the Atlantic in southeastern southern Africa that the impact of maize can be most clearly discerned archaeologically. Spreading south from Portuguese settlements, it quickly supplanted lower-yielding if more drought-resistant sorghum and millet during the 1700s, encouraged by abnormally high rainfall. Changes in population distribution (Barker 1988), increased site numbers, actual finds of maize cobs (Maggs

Figure 6.11. Locally manufactured fragments of tobacco pipes, Savi, Bénin (courtesy and copyright Ken Kelly).

1982), and the proliferation of larger, more deeply hollowed-out grind-stones (Huffman 1996a) all attest to its take-up. However, pronounced droughts and livestock diseases in the early 1800s then provoked food shortages in a condition of increasing political disorder, precipitated by competition to supply ivory and other commodities to European traders at Delagoa Bay.[9] The combination helped produce major structural changes among many southern African communities and the migration of some as far as Tanzania, a process traditionally termed the *Mfecane* (Mitchell 2002a).

Unlike the experience of Native Americans or the aboriginal peoples of Australia and the Pacific, contact with Europeans did not, on the whole, lead to massive epidemics among African populations. One reason may lie in the widespread presence of livestock throughout Africa, since many infectious diseases derive ultimately from transspecies transfers from cattle, pigs, and other domesticates (Mitchell 2003). But the absence of such virgin soil epidemics (except in the Canary Islands)[10] is itself testimony to how far Africans were *not* cut off from other Old World populations, an evaluation strengthened by the possible penetration of the fourteenth century Black Death to West Africa (Posnansky 1987, 16–17; R. McIntosh 1998, 248). On the other hand, the slave trade did have the unintended consequence of introducing yellow fever to the Americas, where it wreaked havoc among Native American and European populations who lacked the partial genetic resistance previously evolved by Africans (Porter 1997, 464).

If opening up the Atlantic brought Africa new food sources and little by way of new disease, its association with the transoceanic slave trade has made it a source of intense historical contention. Fage's (1969) argument that slave exports at most slowed population growth and led to little significant social change was countered by Rodney (1972), for whom they produced massive demographic losses and enduring economic and technological dependency upon Europe. More recently, this debate has continued, with Eltis (1987) developing the former position, Manning (1990) and Lovejoy (2000) arguing the latter. Archaeologically speaking, many more long-term studies that transcend the immediate centuries of European coastal presence are needed to contextualize the effects of Atlantic trade on African societies (S. McIntosh 2001), but some points can already be made.

First, and particularly before 1650, Africans more than held their own technologically: not only did Europeans offer nothing that was new, but the trade that took place was not in any way developed to satisfy basic needs or make up for production shortfalls. Instead, imports of metal and cloth went to satisfy the demands of prestige and fashion, probably accounting for only a fraction of African consumption (Thornton 1992, 45). The contrast in both quantity and necessity with Saharan salt imports into the Sahel and forest zone is telling. Furthermore, Africans *exported* manufactured goods as well as slaves and raw materials and not just the Afro-Portuguese ivories previously noted. A single early eighteenth century order from Sierra Leone was for 1 million mats, while Benin exported raffia to France, South America, and Angola still later; in Allada European cloth was even unraveled and reworked before being sold back to Europeans for use in the Caribbean (Thornton 1992, 52–53). Reference to Bénin reinforces the observation already made that for centuries, far from having organizational advantages, Europeans traded on African ground with African permission and consent, not despite them, a situation enhanced by the devastating impacts of tropical diseases on what was almost always a very small European presence until the late 1800s (Feinberg 1989). Northrup's (2002) study of African encounters with Europe draws similar conclusions: Africans acquired knowledge of European languages and customs not because they were "superior," but to build long-sustained relations that were to their own commercial benefit. Documented references to the acquisition of literacy, reflected in nineteenth century writing equipment from Elmina (DeCorse 2001a), support this, along with the presence in Europe of Africans who reached the continent not as slaves or freedmen but as ambassadors and scholars.

If Africans assertively structured their relations with Europeans, what of the suggestion that the trade in slaves was necessarily destructive? First, detailed studies show that more than 150 different kinds of goods were imported to the Gold Coast (Kea 1982); guns and alcohol were by no means the only imports. Second, in Ghana at least, imported liquor was principally consumed like indigenous beverages in socially restrained, symbolism-laden contexts (Akyeampong 1996). Third, the prime motive for acquiring guns was not participation in slave raiding for a European market but rather military need for safeguarding or expanding traditional polities. Slaves generated by such conflicts were their by-product, not their primary goal (Curtin 1975; Kea 1982). Indeed, in some important exporting areas, such as the Bight of Biafra, kidnappings, court judgments, and debt enslavement produced the bulk of those sold overseas, not warfare, and some states, including Asante, may have largely dropped their interest in the slave trade in the early 1800s when alternatives (gold in this case) sufficed to purchase needed guns. Far from being universalized weapons of destruction, firearms were typically confined to specialized military units and used as much in hunting, ceremony, and prestige or for self-protection as in aggressive warfare (Northrup 2002).

Nor were concepts of slave holding or slave exchange novel. As Lovejoy (2000) argues, among others, acquiring slaves through the various means just noted was a longstanding mechanism by which many African societies (or at least their elites) sought to enhance their numbers, resource base, wealth, and prestige in a situation where land was plentiful but labor scarce (Goody 1971). Not only were slaves exported for centuries before Europeans' arrival off the Atlantic coast (chapters 4 and 5), but in parts of the Sahel and Sahara indigenous agricultural and craft production had a substantial slave basis (Meillassoux 1991). There can, however, remain no doubt that enormous numbers of Africans were removed, unwillingly, from their continent of origin during the period on which this chapter concentrates and through the trading structures on which I have touched. Estimates vary, but figures of 400,000 for the period before 1600, 1.3 million in the seventeenth century, 6 million during the trade's heyday in the eighteenth, and a further 3.4 million during the nineteenth are plausible (Lovejoy 2000, 19). And to this total of more than 11 million we must add those who died during capture or transit. Why Africans in particular were so exploited and whence they came, what happened to them in the Americas, their principal destination, and how archaeology can address issues of resistance and cultural retention, innovation, and transformation within enslaved communities are discussed in chapter 7.

Notes

1. The term *Guanche* is commonly used to denote the prehistoric inhabitants of the Canary Islands but strictly refers only to those living on Tenerife (González Antón and Tejera Gaspar 1990). Hence my use of "Canarians" in what follows.

2. An interesting light on the principal products obtained by Europeans from West Africa comes from the names that evolved for various parts of its shores: Pepper Coast for Liberia, Ivory Coast for the country of that name, Gold Coast in modern Ghana, Slave Coast from Accra to Lagos, and Grain Coast in southern Nigeria (after its grains of malaguetta pepper).

3. A subsequent Kongo embassy to Rome, undertaken in 1606–08, is commemorated in frescoes decorating the Vatican Library (Northrup 2002, 38).

4. Ekholm's (1972) study of this process is a classic anthropological analysis of the transformation of prestige-goods systems and a model for many archaeological applications of the same idea (e.g., Frankenstein and Rowlands 1978; Friedman and Rowlands 1978).

5. DeCorse (1989) reports comparable changes in settlement pattern, including widespread fortification, in northeastern Sierra Leone during the eighteenth and nineteenth centuries, changes that local oral histories associate with self-defense from slaving.

6. Note, however, the pioneering investigations of Fort Ruychaver, another Dutch outpost in Ghana, by Posnansky and Van Dantzig (1976).

7. Regular supplies of traditional African staples (millet, rice, sorghum, yams, palm oil) were also produced on a substantial scale for onboard consumption, in part because some slave traders felt that this would improve survival rates across the Atlantic Ocean (Carney 2001, 383).

8. Multiple introductions could also hold true of other American crops; Portères (1955), for example, notes the possibility of a separate trans-Saharan introduction of maize to the Sahel from Spain via the Maghreb. Trans-Mediterranean contacts probably account too for its presence, with chilis, at Germa, Fezzan (Mattingly 2003).

9. The early penetration of European imports is indicated by the reworking of imported brass at Mhlopeni sometime between 1550 and 1680, substantially inland of the KwaZulu-Natal coast (Maggs and Miller 1995).

10. Claims that smallpox had massively destructive effects on aboriginal, especially Khoekhoe, populations in South Africa are debated (A. Smith 1989).

Out-of-Africa 3: The Archaeology of the African Diaspora

The archaeology of the post-Columbian African diaspora has the potential to be one of the most important kinds of archaeology in the world.

—Orser 1998, 63

SOME 1.8 MILLION years ago the first hominids exited Africa into Eurasia, a phenomenon generally termed Out-of-Africa 1. About 100,000 years ago we find the earliest evidence of anatomically modern humans beyond their continent of origin. Supplanting earlier hominid lineages in Europe and Asia, they also colonized wholly new continents in Australasia and the Americas, a process termed the Out-of-Africa-2 model of human origins. By the fifteenth century, descendants of those early African explorers had settled almost all inhabitable parts of the globe. In this chapter, I look at the renewed movement of Africans beyond Africa that gathered pace at that time, a process that one might call Out-of-Africa 3. Importantly, however, this, one of history's greatest migrations (Posnansky 1984), was almost wholly involuntary. Although similar processes had long operated across Africa's other frontier, it is the trans-Atlantic slave trade (H. Thomas 1997) that attracts particular attention for its scale, emphasized by its relatively compressed duration, and for the extent to which the descendants of its victims continue to constitute recognizable communities in the lands to which they were taken. I look first at the overall scale and spatiotemporal patterning of the trans-Atlantic slave trade and then at how archaeological data illuminate the experience of enslaved Africans in the New World, the maintenance of cultural continuities with African societies, the formation of new cultural identities, and the resistance of the enslaved to their enslavers. Collectively, it is these issues, and the contribution of the Atlantic slave trade's very structures to the formation of modern capitalism (Orser 1996), that underpin the quotation that begins this chapter. Because the trans-Atlantic slave trade did not stand alone, I also touch on the transportation of enslaved Africans to Europe and the new "Creole" island communities that were established in the Indian and Atlantic Oceans.

The Atlantic Slave Trade: Spatial and Temporal Dimensions

At the end of the last chapter, I cited figures for the numbers of Africans removed overseas through the Atlantic slave trade from the fifteenth to late nineteenth centuries. More than 11 million individuals were thus deported, just over half of them during the 1700s. These figures compare with rough estimates of 3.6 million and 1.9 million for the numbers of enslaved Africans taken across the Sahara and into the slave-trading networks of the Red Sea, Persian Gulf, and Indian Ocean, respectively, during the same period (Lovejoy 2000). Better studied and better documented, the figures available for the trans-Atlantic trade may overemphasize its importance, but there can be no question of the scale, or the enormity, of the movements that took place.

Estimates of the geographical origins of those people taken to the Americas suggests that almost half came from Atlantic Central Africa, fractionally more from the coasts and hinterlands of West Africa (Senegambia to Nigeria), and a small additional component from farther afield, including East Africa and Madagascar (figure 7.1). Many of those exported from particular stretches of the coast tended to reach specific colonial destinations, with Ghana, for example, the primary source for slaves used on Jamaica. Linguistically and culturally, West African slaves were commonly more heterogeneous than those from Atlantic Central Africa, who spoke Western Bantu languages and participated in a shared cultural tradition (Vansina 1990). Indeed, many came from just three regional clusters, centered among the Kongo, Mbundu, and Ovimbundu peoples. There is then, alongside older studies that emphasize the survival of specifically West African cultural practices in the New World, also tremendous potential in researching the cultural contributions of individuals from Atlantic Central

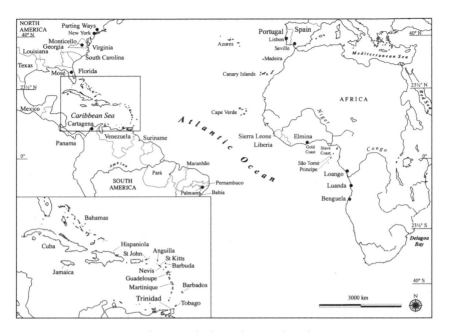

Figure 7.1. Location of sites and places discussed in chapter 7.

Africa (Heywood 2002), particularly where, as in South Carolina or Haiti, they formed the largest part of the total slave population.

To place the Atlantic slave trade in a longer historical perspective, we should recall that slavery was by no means unusual in late medieval Europe,[1] still less so in the Islamic world or sub-Saharan Africa. Africans formed part of the plantation labor force in the Mediterranean at the beginning of the fifteenth century, and Portugal, among other European states, sought slaves to reduce labor costs and compensate for the loss of workers to plague and migration from the countryside into towns (Wolf 1982, 111). Initially obtained by kidnapping, slave acquisitions grew quickly once trading ties were developed with indigenous polities. As remarked in chapter 6, many went to the expanding sugar plantations of Madeira, the Azores, and the Canary Islands, especially as the numbers of indigenous Canarians declined. The establishment on the islands of São Tomé and Príncipe of agricultural colonies specializing in sugar production further stimulated demand, but African slaves were also employed in Iberia itself, mostly as urban servants or artisans: by the mid-1500s 10 percent of Lisbon's population and 7 percent of that of Seville were African in origin and Africans helped crew many sixteenth century trans-Atlantic ships (Saunders 1982).

It was, however, European colonization of the Americas that massively expanded this trade. The devastating effect of European-introduced diseases on Native American populations, the possibility that they might revolt, and the legal protection subsequently extended to survivors by the Spanish Crown necessitated the development of an alternative workforce, especially in labor-intensive industries such as sugar, production of which began in Brazil in the 1520s. The experience of many Africans in working with the kinds of technologies and subsistence economies used by Europeans made them an obvious possibility in this regard. The Gold Coast divers used to seek out pearls in Venezuela and Trinidad and the livestock-experienced Senegambians who worked on sixteenth century cattle ranches on Hispaniola (Thornton 1992) are but two examples of this.

Furthermore, Africans, at least initially, were thought less likely to escape into wholly unknown terrain and always remained racially identifiable (Wolf 1982, 203–4). Later still, as the association of black Africans with slavery became more pronounced in the European mind, the imputation of racial inferiority itself both encouraged and was invoked to justify their enslavement. However, Africans were not only employed in manual labor: domestic servants, artisans, and skilled or supervisory positions on plantations and mines were all roles that they filled. Finally, we should recall that an additional motivation for the slave trade was the revenue governments could raise by licensing and taxing the import of Africans (Thornton 1992, 137). Nowhere was this more true than in Spain's allocation of the *asiento*, the monopoly granted by the Crown for importing slaves to her American colonies. Its extension to Portuguese merchants when the two Iberian monarchies united in 1580 stimulated the growth of slave exports from Angola in particular (J. C. Miller 2002).

Other Europeans, notably the English and French, who established colonies in the Americas in the seventeenth century initially depended on indentured laborers. Recruited from within their own nation-states (and from Ireland and Scotland too for the English colonies), such workers were cheaper than purchased slaves. However, as the wages paid them rose and Caribbean island economies shifted from small-scale tobacco farming to plantation-scale sugar production, indentured laborers became less attractive. Slaves, by contrast, could be held for an indefinite, rather than a finite, term, were inheritable, and could not take legal action against their masters, who were themselves freed from legal restraint against them. Competing with earlier Dutch ventures, the organization of French and English slave-trading companies in the 1670s and 1680s massively expanded exports from the Slave Coast, providing much of the labor required by plantation developments, not just in the Caribbean but also in North America. Through much of the eighteenth century, English merchants dominated the trans-Atlantic slave trade, acquiring the *asiento* in 1713. Varying in importance over time, the main areas from which slaves were now acquired and to which they were delivered were as follows: Benguela and the central highlands of Angola to Pernambuco; Luanda and northern Angola to southern Brazil, Maranhão, and the French West Indies; Loango to southern Brazil, Maranhão, the Dutch West Indies, and British possessions in the Caribbean and the future United States; the Slave and Gold Coasts to Bahia; and Sierra Leone and Liberia to Pará (J. C. Miller 2002).[2] Along with producing sugar in the Caribbean and Brazil, tobacco in the Carolinas, Georgia, and Virginia, and rice in South Carolina, to which Senegambians and Malagasy were specifically imported because of their previous experience with this crop in Africa (H. Thomas 1997, 258), increased demands for slave labor came from the development of Brazil's gold and diamond mines in the late 1600s. But it was the losses sustained when crossing the Atlantic and the poor health conditions of enslaved Africans in the Americas (e.g., Khudabux 1999), coupled with European preference for a predominantly male slave-labor force, that sustained the trade: deaths, to put it bluntly, were almost always on such a scale that slave populations could not be maintained by natural increase but instead required continual imports. Recent investigations of human remains from New York City's former slave cemetery, the African Burial Ground, illustrate this well through their evidence of hard physical labor, high infant mortality rates, early death, and stunted or disrupted growth patterns (Harrington 1996; African Burial Ground 2004).

Declining profits, lower sugar prices, increasing exports of manufactured goods in a global economy, and humanitarian campaigns prompted Britain to prohibit the Atlantic slave trade in 1807. Combined naval and diplomatic pressures saw other European and American governments sign up to the treaty regime ending the export of slaves from Africa during the nineteenth century, but progress was slow, even after Britain outlawed slavery throughout its colonial possessions in 1833. Since interdiction of slave ships took effect more rapidly off the West African coast, deliveries tended to come ever more frequently from Central Africa. They principally sustained the booming production of coffee in Brazil and Cuba, while in the southern United States the plantations that produced the cotton driving Britain's Industrial Revolution came to be supported by a largely indigenous, self-perpetuating slave labor force. In all three countries abolition came only slowly: 1865 in the United States, 1886 in Cuba, and 1888 in Brazil.

African Archaeology in the New World

It has been argued (Mintz and Price 1976) that the conditions of the slave trade and of slavery itself prevented direct cultural transmissions across the Atlantic. Two reasons are cited, first that African cultures were themselves far from homogeneous, and second that sales randomized the distribution of slaves in the Americas. Mortality during the infamous "Middle Passage,"[3] psychological shock, and limited opportunities for establishing family life compounded this situation. Enslaved Africans thus had no alternative but to create a new culture, built substantially from European material and oriented to the norms of their owners. Leaving to one side for the moment the very real and widespread evidence of resistance to the condition of being enslaved, these arguments are overstated. Thornton (1992) shows, for example, that some groups, such as the Mande and Kongo, were strongly present in many slave consignments, that exports came from a fairly small number of ports, which necessarily produced a degree of cultural and ethnic homogeneity, and that these factors in turn limited the success of any deliberate attempts at randomization so that slaves "would typically have no trouble finding members of their own nation with whom to communicate, at least on large estates" (Thornton 1992, 199). Marriage and language could both sustain a sense of cultural identity, especially where, as in Guadeloupe, Suriname, and Barbados, owners attempted to create demographically viable slave communities that did not require constant "topping up" from Africa.

Striving to maintain a sense of continuity from Africa has, however, to be set against a very real set of changed conditions, including different ecologies and social relations, interactions with a much wider range of African individuals, Europeans, and Native Americans, and the adoption of European languages or creoles based on them as linguae francae among ethnolinguistically diverse slave communities. For all these reasons a major theme in diaspora archaeology has been identifying survivals of African practices, or the lack of them, across an increasingly broad range of material culture, while acknowledging the effects of changes over time and continuing recruitment of new slaves from Africa (Singleton 1985, 1995, 1999; Orser 1998). I look at how and where this has been done before examining more specifically the ways in which Africans resisted their enslavement, a trajectory that diaspora archaeology has itself followed (Orser and Funari 2001). Much of the information on which I draw comes from North America and the Caribbean, comparable research within continental Latin America being as yet less developed. Even then, however, there are important differences of emphasis. On Guadeloupe, for example (figure 7.2), early work focused on the industrial archaeology of planta-

Figure 7.2. Excavation of a slave village on a sugar plantation, Guadeloupe.

tion economies, with little study of the slave communities that worked them, despite the existence of rich documentary and archaeological resources that are only now beginning to be explored (Kelly 2002).

Continuities from Africa

There is uncontestable ethnographic and documentary evidence for the survival in the Americas of recognizably African aesthetic codes in art, design,[4] storytelling, and music to give but four examples, all of which argues for the presence of relevant specialists, at least in some slave communities, and the availability of suitable materials or appropriate substitutes. Archaeologically, efforts at recognizing such continuities are complicated by two factors. First is the likelihood that much of the material culture used or made by slaves was organic in nature, and second is the fact that enslaved Africans arrived in the New World with few, if any, material possessions (Haviser and Simmons-Brito 1995; Haviser 1999).

The same points hold true for identifying new, creolized forms of expression produced through interaction among enslaved and enslaving African, European, and Native American populations. The principal focus of archaeologists has therefore been on housing, including the organization of living space, foodways, and pottery. I look at each in turn, along with evidence for the survival of African practices in the fields of metallurgy, burial, and religious beliefs.

Clay-walled houses, often thought to reflect African architectural traditions, are common in the Caribbean and are now also known from excavated plantation sites in the southern United States (Wheaton and Garrow 1985). Many of the latter also show evidence for indoor storage pits for concealing (stolen?) food and valuables, a practice repeatedly prohibited by slave owners. This too has been considered to have African, even specifically Igbo, origins (Kelso 1986; Yentsch 1992) but might as easily reflect simple resistance to owner authority. Examining more subtle spatial relationships, Agorsah (1999) draws attention to the organization of housing in ways that expressed family relationships as a vehicle for maintaining or reconstituting African uses of space. Deetz's (1977) analysis of Parting Ways, Massachusetts, a late eighteenth through nineteenth century free black community, makes the same point: both the clustering of houses to form a small hamlet and the simple, bicameral floor plans, only 40 percent the size of contemporary Anglo-American houses, recall West African forms of settlement organization.

One of the earliest studies of slave foodways was that of Otto (1984), who used patterning in vessel form and faunal evidence to argue that enslaved Africans on Georgia's Cannon's Point Plantation consumed much of their food in the form of stews served in bowls. Though this pattern is found in much of Africa, the fact that it was also identified among overseers at the plantation, suggests that, instead of indicating a continuity across the Atlantic, it may show limited access to cooking utensils and the time needed for collecting and preparing food. This emphasis on "one-pot meals" extends beyond the United States, being recognizable in many Afro-Caribbean ceramic assemblages. In the Bahamas, Farnsworth (1999) amplifies this picture by identifying a surprisingly high usage of tea and coffee wares, especially cups, interpreted in part as reflecting African traditions of serving relishes alongside the main staple. Interestingly, the color choices evident in the ceramics present recall those reported by DeCorse (2001a) for nineteenth century Elmina. Unsurprisingly perhaps, fish and shellfish were important foods for slaves in the Bahamas, but this emphasis on wild foods is common to many studies (e.g., Otto 1984; Reitz et al. 1985) and may in part reflect indigenous African food preferences (Yentsch 1994); certainly, such resources probably contributed significantly to the nutritional quality of slave diets (Gibbs et al. 1980). Supporting this observation, the Gullah language still spoken by people of African descent in the Lowcountry of Georgia and South Carolina retains a large vocabulary of terms for plants, animals, and forest landscape features that have Western Bantu, often specifically KiKongo, origins, a finding that raises the very interesting question of differential gender input into the transmission of African cultural patterns in the diaspora (R. Brown 2002). Differences within the slave community, another important avenue for research, may be indicated by different patterns of food waste within the slave quarters at Thomas Jefferson's Monticello plantation (Crader 1990), although issues of value, cultural preference, and access also need to be considered. Nor should we forget that domesticates of African origin were introduced to the Americas to provide food for enslaved Africans. As Carney (2001) points out, African rice was but one such crop grown principally for local subsistence needs as widely as South Carolina and the Brazilian Amazon. Several others were introduced, with cowpeas, oil palm, okra, pigeon peas, and yams in particular shaping the distinctive cuisines of black and white Americans alike.

I have already mentioned ceramics, and their analysis has spawned a particularly voluminous literature. Much of this centers around the concept of "colonoware," a term invented by Noël-Hume (1962) to describe coarse, unglazed ceramics reminiscent of European forms and found in colonial Virginia. He interpreted this pottery as having been made by Native Americans for exchange with slaves, and specific groups were later identified as possible manufacturers (Baker 1972). A quite different understanding was proposed by Ferguson (1978), for whom slaves were its primary producers. Though this fits its frequent presence on sites where they are known to have lived, there is little that is obviously African, as opposed to non-European, about it (Hill 1987; figure 7.3). Indeed, the criticism has been made that what unifies colonoware as a concept is no more than a presumed association with African diaspora populations (Hauser and DeCorse 2002). Certainly, although some of the marks found on examples from South Carolina might relate to African divination practices (Ferguson 1992), they can also be paralleled in local Native American traditions (Wesler 1998), and perhaps we might best understand this pottery as a product of interaction between individuals of diverse cultural and technological backgrounds (MacDonald et al. 2002–03).

Broadly comparable low-fired earthenwares also occur in South America (Fairbanks 1984), as well as widely in the Caribbean (see figure 7.3). Searching for specific African influences is, however, rendered difficult by the documented diversity of African pottery traditions and

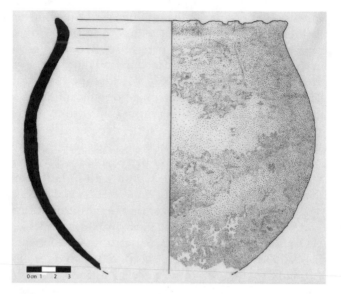

Figure 7.3. Afro-Caribbean cooking pot from St Eustatius, Netherlands Antilles (courtesy and copyright Joanna Gilmore).

slave origins and the sometimes simplistic assumptions made to connect material culture and ethnicity (Hauser and Armstrong 1999). Only rarely can direct parallels be identified, as between pottery found at Spanish Town, Jamaica, and that from seventeenth century sites in Ghana's Shai Hills (Thornton 1992, 230). So-called monkey jars (restricted jars with handles) found in the Caribbean can also be closely matched in West Africa (Petersen et al. 1999, 183). A concentration on cultural-historical issues should, however, be avoided, since it directs attention away from the social dynamics in which African-made pottery was created and used. In the Caribbean, for example, there is ample evidence that pottery was traded. All the earthenwares found on Barbuda, Anguilla, and probably St Kitts Nevis are exotic to those islands (Petersen et al. 1999), while free black communities on the East End of St John traded with plantations elsewhere in the American (formerly Danish) Virgin Islands, as well as with Spain's Caribbean colonies (Hauser and Armstrong 1999).

Metalworking has also been examined. The most detailed study is Goucher's (1993, 1999) work at the John Reader foundry site, Jamaica. Producing both brass and iron, most of the workforce here was African in origin or by descent. Without establishing specific ethnographic parallels, African-derived rituals may nonetheless have been undertaken as part of the metallurgical process since the site produced a bottle, teeth, and cutlass buried beneath the foundry hearth. Dances, rituals, and vocabulary associated with local spirit-possession cults today suggest that metallurgical specialists were accorded religious authority, recalling widespread African associations between iron working and ritual power. Orisha worship in Trinidad and Tobago (Goucher 1999) and postabolition church leadership by skilled metalworkers in Jamaica (Schuler 1980) and the United States (Dickerson 1986) demonstrate the geographical spread of such linkages.

Another area where continuities from previous African experience can be identified is therefore religion. Similarities in belief and practice between Orisha cults in Bahia or Cuba's Santería and southwestern Nigeria, or between Haitian Voudou and traditional religion along West Africa's Slave Coast, have long been identified. Only more recently, however, has it come to be understood how significant the Africanized Catholicism adopted in Kongo from the late fifteenth century was in the acceptance of Christianity among enslaved Africans in the Americas. The extent to which this took place is shown by reports of Christianity's prevalence among free slave communities (Thornton 1992, 269), but more specifically by analyses documenting the many ways in which Kongo-mediated folk Catholicism and pre-Christian Kongo beliefs were instrumental in developing Voudou (MacGaffey 2002; Rey 2002; Vanhee 2002). These studies, and Heywood's (2002) demonstration of the development of syncretic Afro-Christian religious practices in colonial Angola, powerfully support Berlin's (1998) contention that the emergent cultural traditions of New World slave communities had deep roots in earlier European-African interactions on the African side of the Atlantic; they were not (*pace* Mintz and Price 1976) a wholly American phenomenon. Supporting archaeological evidence includes the rosaries and St Christopher medal recovered from excavations at Mosé, a mostly Central African (Kongo) refugee community of free slaves established in then Spanish-controlled Florida in the 1690s (Deagan and MacMahon 1995). Other examples include designs identified as Kongo cosmograms inside broken ceramic bowls found deposited in rivers in South Carolina; their context allows the further link with Kongo beliefs about water being the boundary between the living and the dead (Ferguson 1999). Comparable finds are reported from the Dominican Republic, another area where many slaves were of Kongo origin (Arrom and García Arévalo 1986).

Burial evidence too speaks to religious beliefs, and the burials within houses on Jamaica's late seventeenth through eighteenth century Seville

Plantation suggest links with African practice (Armstrong 1998). On Barbados the Newton cemetery points in the same direction, notably in the form of a ca. 1700 burial of an old man equipped with an elaborate necklace containing cowries, dog canines, and a carnelian bead. Probably African himself by birth, he may have been a religious specialist (Handler 1997). More generally at this site, many burials, though interred in coffins, have their heads turned toward the east (Africa?), contrary to normal Christian practice. This phenomenon, which suggests that conversion was incomplete, can be paralleled elsewhere, including Suriname's mostly nineteenth century Waterloo Plantation (Khudabux 1999). The persistence of beliefs and practices of African origin is also documented in the southern United States, not just in antebellum contexts (Orser 1994a) but also by a mid- to late nineteenth century medicine cache of seashells, bird skulls, chalk, chert scrapers, and other items recovered from the Jordan Plantation, Texas (Brown and Cooper 1990).

Archaeologies of Resistance

It seems unlikely that any of those brought across the Atlantic will have been content with their lot, but archaeologies of resistance were not among the first wave of diaspora studies. Instead, initial attention was directed at demonstrating that it *was* possible to locate and identify the material traces of African and African-descended populations, in opposition to racist, or simply unthinking, assumptions about their supposed lack of importance (Posnansky 1984). Violent resistance to original enslavement either in Africa or onboard ship is well documented (e.g., Rathbone 1996), as is the

---

SIDEBAR 8

Free Blacks, and Other Slave Holders in the Americas

Not all people of African origin or descent in the trans-Atlantic diaspora were slaves. Varying from one European power's colonies to another, manumission was nowhere common, but it did take place, and in some cases freed slaves could amass property, including slaves. Free blacks are, for example, known as plantation owners in Virginia (Berlin 1998), and in Louisiana 18 percent of the black population was free by 1810. With few exceptions (e.g., MacDonald et al. 2002–03; figure 7.4), their archaeology has so far been little studied. Equally rare are archaeological investigations of African-descended communities in the decades following emancipation. Orser's (1988) study of how power relations influenced the size and spatial arrangement of postbellum housing at Millwood Plantation, South Carolina, is one example, but it is not certain that the differences observed reflect class, rather than race (Singleton 1995, 129). Another direction in which research may move is indicated by Andrews and Fenton (2001), who argue that understanding the social and economic relations of slavery as an institution also requires the study of slave owners. Their analysis of ceramics from the Hardin farmstead, Kentucky, and detailed study of associated documentation, underscores how breeding slaves for sale farther south and their use as cheap labor allowed some whites dramatically to raise their socioeconomic position. Not, however, that all slave owners were of European origin: the Cherokee (Perdue 1979) were but one Native American group to hold African slaves, who contributed in important ways to cultural change among them and among other communities, such as the Creek (Dowd 1992).

Figure 7.4. Excavation in progress in 2001 of Melrose Plantation, Cane River, Louisiana, United States (courtesy and copyright Kevin MacDonald).

formation by shipwrecked slaves of free African communities in sixteenth century Panama and São Tomé (Thornton 1992, 284–85). Resistance was, however, less easy once removed to a foreign continent and kept under close supervision. Scott (1990) emphasizes how subtly it may have been shown, and Thornton (1992, 273) distinguishes three forms that it took. At the day-to-day level slowdowns, low morale, and small-scale sabotage are all documentable, to which one must surely add maintaining traditional cultural beliefs and practices or constructing new ones independent of owner preferences (sidebar 8), along the lines we have just considered. Even where, for example, much of the material culture available to enslaved people was not of their making, there is evidence that individuals exercised choice in what they selected for their own use. Wilkie's (1999) study of Clifton Plantation in the Bahamas illustrates this well by demonstrating marked differences between the ceramic assemblages of the owner's house and kitchen and those recovered from slave cabins. The latter emphasize brown and green colors and designs incorporating chevrons, bands, and dots, choices interpreted as reflecting cultural values of ultimately West African origin; the preference for blue glass beads reported from slave contexts in the United States may be another illustration of this principle (Stine et al. 1996).

More pronounced in their effects on the supply of labor, but tolerated by owners with surprising frequency, were acts of so-called *petit marronage*, that is, temporary absences from work. Less common, but attracting perhaps the greatest attention, were acts of *grand marronage*: revolt (most conspicuously, that in Haiti in the 1790s), defection to other European jurisdictions or Native American groups, or escape to already free slave communities. A growing number of archaeological studies have focused on such maroon societies. This is particularly important since, by their very nature, they are likely to feature in colonial documentary sources in quite biased ways, although the need for concealment and isolation may in turn have rendered their archaeological record relatively ephemeral. Generally such maroon communities were small, although there were exceptions, such as those of inland Jamaica (Agorsah 1993). Many were eventually destroyed or reconquered, but, depending on local circumstances, colonial authorities sometimes formally recognized their existence. Well-known examples include that led by Yanga on Mexico's Gulf Coast, San Brasilio near Cartagena, Colombia, and Palmares in Brazil. Already established by 1605, the latter was broadly contemporary with a massive expansion of sugar growing—and hence of slave numbers—in coastal Brazil. Conflict between Portugal and the Netherlands for control of the colony helped prolong its independence, which ended only in 1694. Before then the series of fortified settlements that made up Palmares supported themselves through mixed farming and trade with both Native Americans and European settlers.[5]

Despite its prominence in the literature and an estimated peak population of twenty thousand to thirty thousand, archaeological research at Palmares has been rather limited, consisting mostly of survey work rather than excavation (Orser 1994b; Funari 1995; Allen 1999). Ceramics are sufficiently nondescript as to permit a Native American origin but also resemble Ovimbundu storage jars, hinting at an Angolan connection. Indeed, the term used to describe maroon settlements in Brazil, *quilombo*, itself plausibly derives from the Kimbundu word *kilombo*, meaning house and, by extension, a war band and its camp. Elements of the social and political organization of Palmares and other *quilombos* may have their origins there and, perhaps not coincidentally, Palmares was also known as Angola Janga ("Little Angola"; Orser 1996, 52). Other archaeological finds, including European glazed ceramics and coarser utilitarian earthenwares similar to those found in non-elite Portuguese settler contexts, document some form of exchange with colonial society (Orser and Funari 2001). Rare tobacco pipes found in uncontrolled contexts, but said to be from the main Serra da Barriga site, have also been employed to argue for a complex web of exchanges within and beyond Palmares, with potential parallels noted, perhaps less convincingly, as far afield as the Caribbean (Orser 1996, 129); the pipes themselves may not, however, be properly associated with the Palmares settlement.

Turning back for a moment to less wholesale acts of resistance, it is clear that slave owners frequently went to great trouble to exert close control over their captives. Cuba's nineteenth century coffee plantations provide an extreme example of this: slaves were housed in prison-like barracks that were often locked and guarded at night or kept within high stonewall enclosures (Singleton 2001; figure 7.5). Delle's (1998) work on coffee plantations in Jamaica extends this notion of close control by noting how overseers' houses could be located to allow simultaneous monitoring of both residential and working areas. A more subtle strategy is identified by Pulsipher (1990), who suggests that some owners allowed slaves to tend private gardens and sell their produce as a way of attaching them psychologically and economically to plantations. Archaeology also shows how people contested such close control, for example, by adding backdoors to their houses to provide access to enclosed open spaces as a means of escaping surveillance (Epperson 1990). Keeping house lots "dirty" may have been another means of resisting planters' desires for order and control (McKee 1992), while in Jamaica house-yard arrangements also challenged European-imposed norms (Armstrong 1999).

Figure 7.5. Ruins of the walled enclosure of the slave village at Angerona, a nineteenth century coffee plantation, Cuba (courtesy and copyright Theresa Singleton). Note the bell tower to the left and the iron gate entrance to the right used to control movements in and out of the enclosure.

The Other Diasporas: Europe, the Indian Ocean and Africa

Africans were not only removed across the Atlantic. Some of those sold to Europeans arrived in Europe, mostly as personal servants, but sometimes as freed individuals. They added to a small, but enduring, African presence otherwise constituted by scholars, diplomats, merchants, those obtaining missionary training, and former slaves who had served as British soldiers during the American Revolutionary War (Northrup 2002). This presence has yet to be examined in any systematic way from archaeological sources; one potential strategy would be isotopic analysis of human remains to pinpoint the areas in which individuals had grown up. For different reasons, notably a much greater degree of biological assimilation, locating individuals or communities of trans-Saharan origin in Muslim North Africa is correspondingly problematic.

Among the consequences of the Atlantic slave trade, or rather of its abolition, was the resettlement of freed Africans within Africa. Sierra Leone, for example, became home to ninety-four thousand individuals rescued from slave ships by the Royal Navy between 1815 and 1850 (Northrup 2002). This settlement followed, and in Liberia was paralleled by, the arrival of other individuals freed from slavery in Britain, North America, and the West Indies.[6] Rich textual sources document the adoption of English as a common language, the construction of larger "nations" from previously more disparate groups and, especially in Liberia, the colonization of indigenous populations (Northrup 2002), but all this has yet to be approached archaeologically. Much the same is true of another return movement, that of Yoruba-speaking Muslims deported from, or encouraged to leave, Brazil in the aftermath of failed slave revolts in the 1840s. Many went to southwestern Nigeria or the adjacent areas of Bénin, accelerating the local development of Islam and promoting the evolution of a mixed Yoruba-Brazilian architectural tradition (Khan 1994).

It is, however, in the Indian Ocean that the best evidence survives for diaspora communities outside the Americas (figure 7.6). The export of slaves from East Africa was, as seen in chapter 4, centuries old in this region before 1498, and European traders maintained this pattern, importing slaves to both India and Sri Lanka. Small communities of recognizably African descent survived into the twentieth century in both countries (Basu 2003; Jayasuriya 2003), as well as in Iran (Harris 1971). None has been investigated archaeologically, but, given the possible Indian origins of some African carnelian beads (Insoll and Bhan 2001), it is interesting to note the strong association of African descended Sidi communities in Gujarat with the shrine of an Ethiopian Muslim saint, who is the protector of both the carnelian mines and their workers (Basu 2003).

In the western Indian Ocean we have seen that the Comoros were settled by Africans sometime during the first millennium, and there is also good evidence for a continental African presence on Madagascar, one that grew with increasing Merina demands for soldiers, porters, and plantation workers in the late eighteenth through nineteenth centuries (Newitt 2003). The history of the African diaspora in the more oceanic islands—Seychelles and the Mascarenes (Mauritius, Réunion, Rodrigues)—is discussed by Houbert (2003). In all cases their small size, distance from the African mainland, and isolation from the wind and current systems of greatest interest to sailors help explain why none was settled before the seventeenth or eighteenth centuries: Réunion is 800 km east of Madagascar, Mauritius another 200 km, and Rodrigues 650 km beyond that. Only the much more northerly granitic islands of Seychelles, more than 1,800 km from the African mainland, may have been known to earlier sailors. For the Dutch, who were first to colonize Mauritius (1638), and the French, who settled Réunion (1662) and Seychelles (1770), the primary function of these islands was as supply

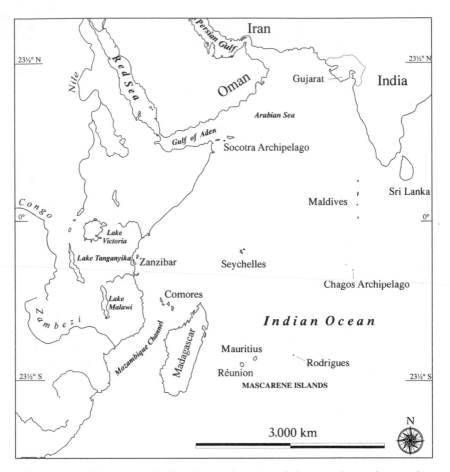

Figure 7.6. The western Indian Ocean: location of places and sites discussed in the text.

bases for ships trading to the East Indies. Mauritius, indeed, was abandoned by the Dutch in 1710 because of competition as a revictualling station from the VOC colony at the Cape of Good Hope, and France annexed it five years later only because of its potentially hostile position leeward of Réunion. Similar reasons led the French to move into Seychelles, occupying them as naval outposts and suppliers of timber and giant tortoises (for meat) for their two larger colonies. Britain seized both Mauritius and Seychelles during the Napoleonic Wars, but left Réunion, with its geostrategically weaker position and lack of a good harbor, to France.

The absence of indigenous inhabitants meant that European settlers had to look elsewhere for a pliant labor force. They found it in Africa, with some 45 percent of slaves, as well as foodstuffs like rice and meat, coming from Madagascar, and some 40 percent from the East African mainland. However, because many of those brought from Madagascar were themselves probably first acquired from East Africa, these figures surely underestimate the African, as opposed to Malagasy, input. Slavery's temporary (1794–1802) abolition during the French Revolution had little effect on island social structures, and imports continued, albeit illegally, for some time after the British slave trade ended in 1807; indeed, on Réunion slavery effectively ceased only in 1860. In all cases the principal employment of slave labor was on plantations raising cash crops. Of these, coffee was important in mid-eighteenth century Réunion, but it was subsequently supplanted by sugar, production of which boomed following France's loss of Haiti to slave rebellions in the 1790s (Hintjens 2003). On all the islands the emphasis on plantation monoculture exacerbated the destructive impact of human settlement on formerly pristine but fragile ecologies[7] and dealt heavy blows at local subsistence self-sufficiency.

The nineteenth and twentieth century histories of the Mascarene Islands and Seychelles followed quite different paths. On Mauritius, and to some extent Réunion, abolition was followed by massive importation of contract Indian labor to work on the sugar plantations, resulting in the former case in the wholesale transformation of island culture. Offering less scope for productive plantation agriculture, Seychelles saw little of this influx. Instead, it became home to several thousand people freed from Omani and Zanzibari slavers off the East African coast. Rodrigues remained even more a largely Creole-populated island, no doubt because of its lack of extensive plantations, while the mid–Indian Ocean Chagos archipelago was settled by former Mauritian and Seychellois slaves employed to work on local coconut plantations until removed to make way for an Anglo-American military base in the 1960s (Hintjens 2003). Today, substantive traces of African cultural traditions are to be found in dance, music, food preparation and preservation techniques, housing styles, and fishing and basketry technologies (Hintjens 2003). In addition, Seychelles and the Mascarenes are home to indigenous Creole languages, greatly modified from French, that first developed on Réunion as a result of close contacts there between slaves and settlers before the establishment of the plantation system (Chaudenson 1995).

Given their relatively small size and lack of wild foodstuffs, none of the islands I have been discussing offered much opportunity for successful large-scale slave resistance. Particularly was this so of Seychelles, where the difficulties created by the small size of individual islands were exacerbated by their rugged terrain (figure 7.7). Archaeologically, most of the work done in this region has focused underwater, investigating European shipwrecks (Lizé 1984; Blake and Green 1986; Von Armin 1998). However, Chowdhury (2004) has recently begun examining escaped slave use of lava tunnels, karst caves, and rock shelters on Mauritius, while Schrire and Floore (1998) have excavated the original Dutch settlement on the island, Fort Frederik Hendrik. More could certainly be done, with Seychelles, in particular, offering opportunities to examine not only the plantation system, but also the cultural impact of later mid-nineteenth century African settlement. Similar possibilities could be pursued with another set of "Creole Islands," those of Africa's Atlantic archipelagos, Cape Verde and the islands of the Gulf of Guinea. As discussed previously, only Bioko was inhabited before European settlement, and even there its population was transformed by immigration from the mainland from the late 1700s.[8] On Cape Verde, São Tomé, and Príncipe, on the other hand, the comparisons are more direct: colonization and disruption of previously uninhabited island ecologies, creation of new communities drawn from both European (in this case Portuguese) and African backgrounds, establishment of slave-

Figure 7.7. Isle Sainte Anne, Seychelles. This, one of the smaller granitic islands in Seychelles, lies just offshore of Mahe, the principal island of the group, and was the base for the first French settlement in 1770. Its rugged terrain is typical of Seychelles's granitic islands.

powered plantation economies, and resistance to enslavement, including the formation of free maroon communities. The comparative archaeological study of all these African islands, a study that might even reach northward to encompass the Canaries, Madeira, and the Azores, awaits.

Conclusion

Archaeological investigations of the recent African diaspora are increasingly numerous and varied. There is, of course, not just a single diaspora to study. Nor, as we have seen, was it invariably involuntary. African experiences in the diaspora also varied. Euro-American domination of the world since the early nineteenth century has frequently obscured the part played by these migrations in constituting the world we see around us today, not only demographically, but also socially and politically. Eric Williams (1944) argued many decades ago that the trans-Atlantic slave trade and the profits from Caribbean and American plantations provided the capital that permitted Britain's take-off into the Industrial Revolution, while British manufacturing was itself stimulated by the need to sell goods to African slavers. It seems likely that this thesis underestimates both European and colonial American markets, but there is no denying the importance of the Atlantic trade in driving British industrial development (Wolf 1982, 200). Recent discussion of the concept of the "Black Atlantic" (Gilroy 1993) reemphasizes the important roles of Africans and people of African descent in building the modern industrial, capitalist world and its ideologies. Historical studies (e.g., Heywood 2002) increasingly stress the relevance of African contributions to these understandings. They also identify a fruitful new research area for archaeologists, namely, collaborative projects between those with specializations in Africa and its diaspora or the extension of fieldwork to one continent by those with previous experience of the other. Work by MacDonald et al. (2002–03) in Louisiana, Agorsah (1993) in Jamaica, Kelly (1997a, 2002) in Bénin and Guadeloupe, and Singleton and DeCorse in Ghana (Singleton 2002) exemplifies this trend, which will surely only grow. One has but to think of the impact of African art on movements such as art deco (Benton et al. 2003) or the origins of contemporary popular music in jazz and blues, to be aware of how far the influence of Africa and its diaspora has reached and of how relevant to us all their archaeological exploration can and should be.

Notes

1. Europeans, mostly but not always of Balkan origin, for example, were used as slaves in late medieval Tuscany and Aragón-Catalunya (Wolf 1982, 202).

2. Note, however, that many captives were given names reflecting the area from which they were exported, which might be different from their area of origin. Hauser and DeCorse (1991), for example, show that many of those shipped from Elmina to the principal Dutch Caribbean slave-trading entrepôt, Curaçao, had, in fact, come from other parts of the West African coast.

3. Disease precipitated by cramped, unsanitary conditions and poor diet, depression, rape, and attempts at suicide or rebellion yielded "average" losses of 20 percent in the sixteenth century, "improving" to 12 percent in the late 1700s, but such figures gloss enormous ship-to-ship variability (Northrup 2002, 118).

4. As one archaeological example, note the white-highlighted stamped and incised motifs found on tobacco pipes produced in seventeenth century Maryland and Virginia (Emerson 1994).

5. That Native Americans were among Palmares's inhabitants is suggested by the fact that three of eleven recorded village names have Tupi origins (Funari 1997).

6. Ironically, other ex-slaves were taken as notionally free but nonetheless indentured servants to the British Caribbean where they "reenergized" the African cultural presence there (Schuler 1980, 2002).

7. The extinction through hunting and habitat destruction of the Mauritian dodo is well known. More tellingly, almost two-thirds of the vertebrates indigenous to Mauritius and more than fifty animal species endemic to Réunion have suffered identical fates, with accompanying destruction of more than half (on Mauritius greater than 95 percent) of the indigenous vegetation through deforestation and overgrazing (Holt-Biddle 1995; Howard 2000). Rodrigues and Seychelles tell comparable stories.

8. The massive nineteenth century settlement of enslaved continental Africans to work plantations on Zanzibar and Pemba calls these islands to mind as another possible comparison.

Reconnecting Africa:
Patterns, Problems,
and Potentials

*Observe how system into systems runs, what other plan-
ets circle other suns.*

—ALEXANDER POPE, 1733,
An Essay on Man, Epistle 1, line 25

N O ONE BOOK can hope to capture the richness of
Africa's past or the complexity of its connections
with other parts of the world. Nor is any single structure able to do this. My choice has been to follow broadly chronological
and geographical lines, based on the conviction that this is probably easiest for those with little familiarity with the continent's archaeology and
of some real worth in delimiting and comparing its extracontinental ties
over time. Other formats are possible, most obviously a thematic one that
would identify and compare particular commodities or institutions across
Africa's different spheres of interaction. The trades in salt and slaves, technologies of transport and communications, adoptions of new religions,
modes of dress and consumption, and introductions and dispersals of new
foodstuffs would all be appropriate topics for such an agenda, and their
comparative study would benefit from more archaeologically enriched
narratives. An alternative format would involve remaining with geography, but inverting the regional framework that I have employed. Why not,

for example, as Sutton (2003) has recently argued, begin with the interior, or with the east coast, and work outward from there, rather than follow a format that, by putting the Nile and the Red Sea before the Indian Ocean, the Sahara, or the Atlantic—and by placing those interfaces in that particular order—might be thought still to privilege contact with Europe, the illumination of the "dark continent" by northern light, the primacy of (early) written sources, and a diffusionist paradigm? I hope to have shown how this would be to oversimplify and misread the picture that archaeological and historical research now describe, but equally that the geographical order that I have followed does, at least in part, reflect the broad flow of historical events and processes connecting Africa and Africans to other parts of the world. Identifying such generalities from the preceding chapters is one of three main themes as I approach the end of this book. A second is to consider how African archaeology can achieve greater prominence in the discipline as a whole. In addition, and as a precondition of achieving this aim, it is appropriate to look briefly at some of the principal challenges facing African archaeology and African archaeologists today and to reflect on how they may be met.

Patterns of Interaction

I hope to have shown that Africa's past has been anything but the static caricature described by Hegel (1965, 246–47) when he declared that "Africa is no historical part of the world; it has no movement or development to exhibit." The path chosen might perhaps be criticized as placing undue emphasis upon Africa's connections with the rest of the world at the expense of developments taking place solely within the continent, but this has been, after all, the unifying theme and rationale of the book. Furthermore, even the longest and most far-reaching of the networks that linked parts of Africa to other regions of the world depended on, indeed grew out of, more local sets of transactions. In chapter 4, for example, we saw how this was the case for the Swahili coast, where trans–Indian Ocean commerce overlay exchanges between individual Swahili towns and between them and communities of hunter-gatherers, pastoralists, and farmers farther inland. As another instance, we saw in chapter 5 how the trans-Saharan trading systems that brought West African gold as far as Europe in the early second millennium were built on multiple intra-African connections. To give but a few examples, and naming only a few commodities, these included the links between Muslim North Africa and the Sahel in flows of manufactured goods, gold, and slaves, between Sahara and Sahel in slaves, foodstuffs, and salt, between the Sahel and the forest zone in all of these commodities, within the Inland Niger Delta and its immediate environs in fish, grain, iron, and other manufactures,[1] and within the Sahara itself through relations between nomads and oasis farmers, including the camel-borne trade in dates. Here, as on the Swahili coast, the "low" commerce of everyday items and consumables (salt, iron, food, textiles) underwrote the movement of the gold, exotic manufactures, and slaves that have historically commanded such great attention. Future research must pursue further the structure and antiquity of smaller-scale exchanges and their part in facilitating the emergence of more complex networks.

A second topic touched on in several of the preceding chapters is that of the relationship between external contacts and trade and the development of more complex political institutions. The African-derived notion of the prestige-goods economy has been frequently invoked as a means whereby elites could enhance their status through cornering access to new items, the very exoticness and scarcity of which endowed them with special significance. But the same examples that can be used to illustrate this point—Meroë, Great Zimbabwe, and Kongo to name but three—also show the vulnerability of those elites to changes in the supply of desirable foreign goods, changing demands on the part of their exchange partners, or simply subversion from junior elites. In few, if any, cases, however, can we identify external, long-distance trade as the sole motor for political change. Even where it looms largest, as in the Zimbabwe Tradition, it is clear that elite power was also founded upon control of land, cattle, and other key resources, including those that moved within purely interior orbits. A similar conclusion can be drawn from that most infamous example of foreign contact, the Atlantic slave trade. As we saw in chapter 6, its initial centuries saw European traders largely dancing to African tunes as far as their supply of goods was concerned. Even later, and well into the nineteenth century, European presence was virtually everywhere either severely limited in number and geographical extent or, where present on a greater scale as in Mozambique and Angola, considerably transformed and Africanized (Heywood 2002). Dutch settlement of the South African interior emphasizes this point by its very uniqueness.

As outlined in chapter 1, it is for reasons such as these that a naïve version of World Systems Theory is insufficient to understand Africa's connections with its neighbors. Though many of Africa's regions undoubtedly supplied primary products (gold, ivory, slaves, etc.) and received largely manufactured goods in return (textiles, beads), this was not invariably the case. Africa too exported manufactured goods, whether in the form of iron and textiles from the Swahili coast (chapter 4) or of textiles and raffia from the Atlantic (chapter 6). Nor were technological and organizational disparities between African populations and those of other regions of the Old World sufficient to turn exchange into exploitation until the nineteenth century. Peripheral to multiple and varying core areas in Eurasia, Egypt, and the Maghreb parts of sub-Saharan Africa may have been, but they were not dependent on them in the sense envisaged by Wallerstein (1974, 1980), nor were their relationships inherently unequal or uniquely expressed through the movement of bulk goods.

On the other hand, it is very likely that several of the key elements in Africa's Holocene history did come from outside the continent. Indeed, it is difficult to contest this for many of them, however much the uses to which they were put and the meanings that they were given were locally defined and locally created. While cattle were very likely domesticated independently in northeastern Africa, goats and sheep were certainly introduced from the Near East, and it was their combination, though with cattle in the symbolic (and often nutritional) lead, that propelled the expansion of livestock keeping across the northern half of the continent (chapter 2). From a subsistence standpoint, domesticated animals were probably valued as important means of countering risk in increasingly arid conditions, and that same aridity limited the expansion in Africa of other Near Eastern domesticates. Only in North Africa, along the Nile, and in Ethiopia-Eritrea, was there any significant adoption of Near Eastern cultigens, and it is precisely there, in areas closest to and most deeply involved with the precociously urbanizing and expanding core regions of Mesopotamia, the Levant, and the Mediterranean, that there was an early development of a mixed farming economy and Africa's first states later emerged. As we saw in chapter 3, one consequence of this was at times to truncate, at others to encourage, the development of other states upstream of the First Cataract of the Nile and in the highlands of Ethiopia-Eritrea.

Returning to the spread of food production, the facts I have just reviewed, coupled with the limited domestication potential of many sub-Saharan species, affected the development of agriculture south of the Sahara. It could not simply take the form—as in Neolithic Europe—of the continuing expansion of an intrusive resource package, but instead had to take shape by working with local food plants for local ends. The antiquity of this process remains in doubt—in part because some of the earliest evidence for its success currently comes from south Asia, not Africa—but much of the continent remained a hunter-gatherer domain as late as the first millennium cal. B.C. Further innovations may have helped transform this situation. One is surely external in origin, even if its mechanism remains frustratingly mysterious (plantains and bananas), the other less certainly so, but equally mired in geographical and chronological haze (iron). If their take-up was not causally connected to the spread of Early

Iron Age farming communities south of the equator, then their broad contemporaneity with its commencement is highly suspicious.

For almost all of sub-Saharan Africa, the adoption of iron can, indeed,
be equated with the development of metallurgy as a whole. With metal
came not only technological advantages in the production of better agricultural and woodworking tools and weapons, but also increased possibilities for the display of status and the accumulation of wealth. Iron's
ubiquity in much of the continent may have directed attention for the latter purposes more toward copper and its alloys, but the process was
nonetheless real, nonetheless widespread. And since even iron was not
universal, and copper and tin much less so, exchange intensified still further, a process encouraged as population levels rose, especially in areas
previously not part of the farming economy. The southern African archaeological record, in particular, shows this situation developing in the first
millennium in a variety of media (iron, copper, pottery, livestock, seashell
ornaments, etc.) and its extension to complex relations between hunter-
gatherers and farmers (see sidebar 2 in chapter 1). In some areas—of which
the Inland Niger Delta is among the best researched—complementary patterns of exchange between communities practicing different subsistence
economies contributed to the emergence of an increasingly complex urban
landscape. For the Sahel and the forests to its south, or indeed for the eastern coasts of Africa and their interior, the existence of local exchange
cycles and the availability of desirable commodities were not by themselves enough to effect substantive links with the wider Eurasian–North
African world. Commodities had to be moved and the connection of
Africa's Saharan and Indian Ocean "coasts" was only possible with
deployment of the appropriate technology and the appropriate demand.
The technological aspect is easier to appreciate—horses and camels in the
first case, seaworthy ships in the second, and knowledge of usable routes[2]
and methods of navigation in both. The demand side is harder to evalu-
ate but may be gauged from the absence of any state-level or urban societies in North Africa until the late first millennium B.C. and their primary
orientation northwards, toward the trade and imperial prospects of the
Mediterranean Sea. Only perhaps as this was transformed in the late third
and fourth centuries, if Garrard's (1982) thesis is correct, did West African
gold begin to arrive in North Africa, just as in the Indian Ocean world
Islam's unification of the Middle East facilitated and encouraged maritime-
borne trade on a scale previously absent (Ray 2003).

Such comments are not meant to ignore the opportunities for increasing social complexity that existed on the basis of local cycles of exchange
and wealth accumulation. However, comparison of the Sahel and the
Swahili world does suggest that in both cases increasing participation in

long-distance trade was strongly associated with the adoption of a new and exotic faith, Islam, taken up in many areas as a means of facilitating that trade and of legitimizing new forms of authority—a process already evident in the earlier spread of Christianity along the Middle Nile and in Ethiopia. The Swahili and the Sahel, both named from the Arabic word for shore (*Sahil*), do indeed form a natural field for comparison. Insoll (2003a, 206) notes as much as regards their export of gold, ivory, and slaves, their shared participation in Islam, and their broad contemporaneity. Sutton (1997) has gone further to highlight the significance of the early fourteenth century peak in the demand for African gold—just before the Black Death—for the political economies of both Mali and Kilwa, and to explore the consequences for both of the global economic downturn that followed. The strength of his paper is his ability to show how both sides of Africa, visited at this time by the same North African traveler, Ibn Battuta (Mackintosh-Smith 2002), were involved in the same world economic system. Not that this meant they were identical—the ethnolinguistic unity of the Swahili world was missing from the Sahel, just as the absence of cavalry, the small scale of Swahili towns and their lack of (inability to maintain?) large flotillas helped preclude the development of anything comparable to the Imperial Tradition represented by Ghana, Mali, Songhay, and the like.[3]

Islam certainly contributed, perhaps more than trade and with longer-lasting effects, to connecting much of Africa to other parts of the Old World. Insoll's (2003a) recent book clearly demonstrates the error made by Trimingham (1968, 37) when he suggested that Muslim Africans were "in touch but in a peripheral way with the developed civilizations of other Islamic peoples," just as Abu-Lughod's (1989) historical analysis confirms Africa's centrality in the medieval Islamic world system. Yet even the incorporation of much of the continent into this system during the late first through early second millennia had its limits. On the eastern side of Africa, for example, state-level societies can only be perceived clearly in the one area able, from flukes of physical and biological geography, to tap several resources of interest to Swahili and overseas traders: the gold, ivory, copper, and tin accessed by the elites of the Zimbabwe Tradition. Social transformations are more dimly evident, at best, in the other areas to which exotic consumables, such as cannabis and rare glass beads, were able to penetrate. Though surely not evident at its outset, it was the opening up of Africa's Atlantic seaboard, and the bringing together of all the world's continents and seas into a single economy that ultimately flowed from this (Fernández-Armesto 2001), that precipitated the engagement of such previously largely isolated regions of Africa with the wider world. Redirection of earlier trading and cultural ties was part of this, something attained more lastingly through the forest zone of West Africa than on the Swahili seaboard (chapter 6), but across western, eastern, central, and southern Africa similar processes can be identified. The take-up of new, often more productive crops, the exchange of goods for desirable exotic manufactures, and the social, political, and economic effects that these processes entailed were, ultimately, profound. Not least among them was the massive and involuntary resettlement of Africans overseas, notably in the Americas, where they forged new connections among themselves and with Europeans and others, connections that in some cases later flowed back into Africa itself.

These paragraphs, and this book, are at best but a preliminary sketch in producing a historical narrative of Africa's connections with the rest of the world from a primarily archaeological standpoint. Such an account, if it is to be coherent, will need to incorporate the structures of geography, the movement of goods and ideas, and the social meanings that those goods embody. Its focus will lie in the development, elaboration, and modification of routes, networks, and flows and the ways in which these were precipitated or encouraged by changes in individual agency, environmental opportunities, and new technologies. The webs of connections so described will in turn most likely be shown to have grown and transformed where synergetic relationships could be built up between potentially complementary systems of exchange (Sherratt 1995). But all externally derived innovations, of whatever kind, will only have been adopted where they made sense to African individuals and could be reworked into African frames of understanding and structures of social relations. Archaeology has already begun to demonstrate the truth of these propositions, but much more remains to be done, with several problems to overcome. I turn now to considering what some of those difficulties are and what kinds of solutions may best resolve them.

Problems of Research

African archaeology is a classic example of too much to do in too little time or, perhaps it would be better to say, with too few resources. Though much has been achieved and much more is currently being investigated, it is but a fraction of the continent's past. In part the poverty of resources devoted to the subject—within and without the continent—is a reflection of Africa's parlous economic state. Limited economic development in colonial times, postindependence political instability, warfare, misgovernment and corruption, overreliance (from a poor negotiating position) on a few commodities and cash crops, adverse environmental circumstances, and, most recently, the dual threats of the AIDS pandemic and accelerating ecological change have reduced many African states and the majority of their inhabitants to among the poorest in the world. Not only does this situation leave understandably little for archaeology, but it also contributes to a dismissal of the continent among Western audiences that extends from the present into its past and is itself colored by the racist stereotypes of the colonial era (Lane 2001). One result may be that foreign archaeologists find it comparatively difficult to obtain sufficient funds to undertake field or laboratory-based research on African topics, but the practical problems confronting archaeologists based in Africa are much greater and well known: too few archaeologists, inadequate funding for research, demoralized staff, insufficient resources for the curation of finds and monuments, lack of training, difficulties in gaining access to journals and books, whether as readers or contributors, and the pillaging of archaeological sites to sell goods on the international "art" market (Kusimba 1996; Schmidt and McIntosh 1996; Shaw 1997). As Kibunjia (1997, 141) points out, a key component of any solution to these problems must lie with sensitizing African governments themselves to the importance of archaeology, but other audiences must also be reached: African populations, rather than just elites; international development funders; and the broader, non-Africanist international academic community.

One positive development in recent years has been the repeated calls made by some leading African politicians for an African renaissance that would ensure a recommitment to effective, sustainable, and democratically based development. Such calls have consistently stressed the value of the continent's past, and specifically its archaeology, in promoting African self-confidence and self-empowerment (Mbeki 1998), provoking debate among archaeologists as a result (e.g., Wadley 2000). The degree to which such rhetoric will carry over into hard money and meaningful economic or political action remains to be seen, but there are two reasons to be positive as regards archaeology. First, some African governments have actively recommitted themselves to supporting initiatives to protect their countries' cultural heritage. Recent examples include cultural sensitization projects undertaken in Mali's Inland Niger Delta (Bedaux and Rowlands 2001) and the efforts made by newly independent Eritrea to develop an indigenous archaeological infrastructure (Schmidt and Curtis 2001). Second, there are the clear economic benefits that can be generated by expanding tourism, especially cultural and ecotourism at the "quality" end of the market. This is not without its problems, which include potential conflicts between increased access to sites and possible damage to them, clashes between tourist requirements and the spiritual values of local people, and the difficulties of striking a balance between the informational and recreational demands of national and international audiences (Ndoro 1994; Pwiti and Ndoro 1999). But these problems are resolvable (e.g., Pwiti and Mvenge 1996). Though it is essential—from an archaeological and a human standpoint—that African societies and their past *not* be presented as standing outside time in some kind of Garden of Eden, the vitality of animal-based tourism in much of Africa and the fact that many key archaeological sites lie close to major parks suggest that archaeology could gain from greater collaboration with wildlife conservation. The growing number of projects sponsored by the Peace Parks Foundation (2004) offers one avenue along which this might proceed, Mabulla's (2000) carefully sketched strategy for cultural heritage management in Tanzania another. But for such projects to work as a means of preserving and investigating Africa's cultural heritage not only must revenue flow back into archaeology, it must also flow back directly into the lives of people living around the sites being protected. Just as with controlling game poaching, community-based initiatives offer the only effective means by which looting can be halted and archaeological sites preserved. The success of community-based museums in Botswana (Phaladi 1998) should serve as an encouraging example in this regard, while Thiaw's (2003b) recent insightful paper on the issues raised by public perceptions of his own fieldwork in Senegal illustrates how emphasizing research on the recent past, one that is still contested and of interest to people today, may provide the greatest scope for building archaeology as a discipline.

Increasing and facilitating access to the past for African communities today is something that has probably received too little attention from professional archaeologists, particularly those working in Africa from bases abroad. The difficulties posed by language, culture, and the demands of a research career that measures success by publications in prestigious journals rather than hours spent communicating to local villagers or townspeople are not to be underestimated, yet such communication is essential for protecting Africa's cultural heritage and for facilitating the growth of a widespread, informed indigenous voice that demands such protection.[4] Linking to this question is the form in which archaeological projects funded from overseas take shape in Africa. How far is collaboration with local institutions or colleagues more than perfunctory? How far does it extend to equality of input into project direction and management? How far does it provide for training and study opportunities for local scholars or technicians? How far does it lead to literature or exhibitions being made available locally or in indigenous languages? The answer, sadly, is still not always, although examples can readily be cited of best practice to the contrary, among them recent excavations at Aksum (D. Phillipson 2000), the Swedish-funded Urban Origins Project (Sinclair 1999), and collaboration between Western and African scholars in Senegal (R. McIntosh 1996b). Where development projects such as roads or dams are constructed with external funding and bring in non-African scholars, this too should be made to provide an excellent opportunity to further such cooperation, although the past history of many such projects illustrates that archaeology is scarcely at the forefront of donor concern (MacEachern 2001). Here, then, there is a need for more productive lobbying of Western or Western-dominated political institutions to effect desired changes, but we can also point to the welcome and increasing scope for cooperation between scholars operating within different parts of the African continent. South Africa's recent democratization, for example, has created wider access to its radio-carbon dating and stable-isotope analysis facilities, as well as paving the way for sharing skills and training in the fields of rock-art research and conservation (Mguni 2002). Training of African archaeologists through to doctoral level and beyond within Africa rather than outside it (Schmidt 1995), and building local publication outlets for archaeological research[5] are other ways in which this may be done.

Potentials for Research

A further strategy for developing African archaeological research lies in increasing awareness of the richness and significance of Africa's past beyond the continent. One element of this has to be for Africanist archaeologists to contribute more frequently and with greater effect to journals, books, and conferences that reach beyond Africanist audiences. Instead of preaching only to the converted, we need to identify ways in which our research and Africa's past can contribute to archaeology and human history as a whole. By way of conclusion, let us briefly examine some of the ways through which this goal might be advanced. One, which was outlined at the beginning of the book, is to combat the prevalence of oversimplified evolutionary models drawn from a narrow range of archaeological or ethnographic instances that straitjacket our understanding of the past. Demonstrating the presence and antiquity of particular social formations or sets of knowledge (cereal cultivation, intensive agriculture, metallurgy, towns, states) had a part to play in building African pride immediately after decolonization and in combating racist reconstructions or denigrations of Africa's past. But we can do more. First, ethnography and archaeology attest to an enormous variability in how precolonial African societies were constructed. Some patterns, notably the development and expansion of livestock keeping in complete independence from cultivation or exchange relations with cereal farmers (Hassan 2002) and the absence of recognizable elites in the clearly urban context of the early first millennium Inland Niger Delta (S. McIntosh 1999c), stand in sharp contrast to the expectations of neoevolutionary thinking. Their identification challenges the norms drawn from elsewhere in the Old World and underlines the inadequacies of simplistic stadial models that downplay or ignore variation in favor of thinking about the past in terms of unified monolithic blocks of space and time (Andah 1995).

Secondly, we can direct attention away from cataloguing increasing complexity and toward examining relations between societies of different scales (Stahl 1999a). The connections between urban centers and their hinterlands, between polities able to project themselves over hundreds of kilometers and smaller, more local communities or between mobile herders and sedentary cultivators, are obscured when research is concentrated at single sites rather than across landscapes or focused on seeking origins instead of processes. Exploring different scales of interaction should reinforce the importance of developing explanations for change framed in terms of more than just increasing caloric output or the simple availability of new domesticates or technologies. Rather, we should think in terms of the socially motivated decisions that led people to obtain, consume, and display new forms of gaining or enhancing prestige and status, remembering that the new is very often the exotic, the distant, even the (originally) extracontinental (Sherratt 1995).

Thirdly, we should critically reassess our use of the "ethnographic present" as a basis for understanding the archaeological past. Those African societies studied by anthropologists have been formed through a long-extended historical process that, for most of them and especially over the last several centuries, has involved the working out of the consequences of Africa's connections with other continents. Whether in considering the impact of New World crops or the Atlantic slave trade, the expansion of Islam or the trans-Indian Ocean export of gold and ivory, African communities have not been divorced from the rest of the world or static in relation to it. Thus, to assume that we can simply project a crystallized "ethnographic present" back in time is fallacious. Instead, our ethnographic knowledge needs to be contextualized historically, a process best done by working from the known (in this case today and the very recent past) back into the unknown (the more remote past). Stahl's (2001a) historical archaeological work at Banda, Ghana, is a prime example of this approach, the Kalahari debate over the "pristineness" of Bushman hunter-gatherers another. Quarrying previously neglected archives, for example, in the former Ottoman Empire and the Maghreb or in private collections in Saharan towns like Timbuktu and Walata (cf. Reichmuth 2000), should become as much a part of this contextualization as anthropological critique, recording oral histories or archaeological excavation.

Common to all the themes I have just identified is a fourth, the importance of breaking out of traditional frameworks of study. In the African context one of the most critical of these has been the compartmentalization of archaeological research into overdistinct regional units. The long-standing Egyptological domination of Nubian archaeology is one example that has, until recently, hindered the development of perspectives that place Kerma, Kush, or Nubia's medieval kingdoms within a broader African comparative context (Edwards 1996). Pharaonic Egypt's own incorporation into a Middle Eastern or Mediterranean-centered world of study at the expense of investigating its connections with Cyrenaica or the wider Sudan is another (O'Connor 1990). Elsewhere, political instability or differences of language or research structure have tended to keep apart the archaeologies of regions such as Nigeria and the Nile Valley or prevented investigation of areas critical to the expansion of farming or the development of states and long-distance exchange networks: southern Sudan, the Central African Republic, Angola, southern Congo-Kinshasa, and the Algerian Sahara all fall within this category. While some projects have deliberately set out to compare developments across a wide area (Sinclair 1999; Breunig and Neumann 2002), the very complexity of African prehistory makes it difficult for any single person to develop a broad competence that spans regions. Yet it is exactly this kind of bridging research of which African archaeology stands in need, most critically perhaps within the Sahara as a complement to recent work in Fezzan (Mattingly 2003), but also east–west across the Sahel.[6] Only when we have a better grasp of connections within Africa shall we be able to trace more fully the flow and impact of the connections linking Africa with the rest of the world.

Asserting the strength, durability, and import of those connections is one means of bringing African archaeology more fully into the center of the discipline. Examples that could be cited from the earlier chapters of this book include the chronological feasibility for domesticated cattle and knowledge of pottery having been able to spread from Africa into the Levant; the northeast African homeland of the Afroasiatic language family (which includes Hebrew, Aramaic, Arabic, Babylonian, Assyrian, and Akkadian); the African origins of several key crops, including sorghum and pearl millet, already important in south Asia in the second millennium cal. B.C.; the likelihood that the precious metal extracted from West African goldfields helped underpin the economy of Roman North Africa in the fourth and fifth centuries; the dependence of both the Muslim and European worlds on the same sources and those of the Zimbabwe Plateau during the late first through early second millennia; the essential role of African scholars, monks, and priests in the development of Christian doctrine and monasticism; the importance for the westward flow of spices from Pharaonic to Ottoman times of trading systems in which Africa's Red Sea hinterland and Indian Ocean coasts played crucial roles; the enduring employment of African slaves in the workforces of the Mediterranean, the Middle East, and India long before the opening up of the Atlantic; and finally the trans-Atlantic slave traffic that, from the sixteenth century, fuelled much of western Europe's (and later North America's) economic growth and eventual take-off into industrialization. Africans and African connections were instrumental in all of these and any understanding of them that excludes their African dimension can only be flawed.

Beyond these historical connections there is also another way in which African archaeology can be foregrounded within the discipline as a whole, and that is through exploring how a knowledge of the African past can extend and enhance the study of the past in other parts of the world. I have already touched on this when discussing how African archaeology may challenge aspects of neoevolutionary thinking, but other possibilities can be suggested. For example, it is a commonplace of the African literature that both iron smelting and the working of other metals were symbolically charged activities (Herbert 1984; Schmidt 1997). How far has such evidence been adequately sought or investigated by archaeologists of Europe's Bronze or Iron Ages? Might not a greater awareness of the rich African evidence on this subject encourage such research? To take another example, might not there be much to be gained from a systematic comparison of how and why first Christianity and then Islam spread in Africa and how and why Christianity expanded across northern Europe in the mid-to-late first and early second millennia (Fletcher 1997)? And might not their study, but particularly perhaps that of the spread of Islam along eastern Africa's coasts, be enhanced if considered alongside that of first Hinduism and then Islam through peninsular and island Southeast Asia (cf. Kratz 1989; Ray 2003)? The swift, pioneering expansion of Early Iron Age farmers across much of subequatorial Africa too calls out for comparison, in this case perhaps with the similarly rapid expansion of Linearbandkeramik (LBK) settlement in Neolithic Europe (Whittle 1996). Indeed, Bogucki (1995) has already called upon Kopytoff's (1987) study of African frontier societies to help understand the cultural conservatism of LBK settlers. To cite only two of several more possibilities, why should not the development of more complex societies linked to Greek, Phoenician (or Punic), and Roman metropoles be investigated in comparative fashion across both northern *and* southern margins of the Mediterranean, and why should the relations between those same Mediterranean powers and their hinterlands not also invite comparison with the connections linking eastern Africa's Swahili towns and their interior trading partners?[7] The popularity in European prehistory of Ekholm's (1972) Kongo-derived analysis of prestige-goods systems, Trigger's (2003) magisterial survey of early civilizations, which includes the Yoruba and Pharaonic Egypt as African examples, and the revolutionary impact on global rock art studies of the Bushman-inspired research of David Lewis-Williams (2002) all illustrate the productivity of broadening comparisons to incorporate African data and theory.

Finally, we need to consider how far a distinctively African school of archaeological theory might be developed. Insofar as archaeological writings are drawn upon by Afrocentric scholars such as Diop (1967), Asante (1987), or Van Sertima (1992) the answer is that one such school already exists, but on the margins of mainstream (Western) scholarship. The wider point has been made that African scholars depend for their professional legitimization upon subscribing to accepted norms of academic discourse, paradigms, and epistemologies that are largely of Euro-American construction (Andah 1995; Schmidt 1995). The point might equally be made, of course, that this is also true of Euro-American scholars themselves, the claims of some postprocessual archaeologists notwithstanding. It does nonetheless raise the issue of whether the ways in which archaeology is undertaken and presented within Africa may conflict with African ways of structuring and understanding time and space. There is certainly scope for exploring these issues in archaeological research and in acknowledging the significance of such modes of thought for how people lived their lives and how they act today in relation to the past (e.g., Schmidt 1997). But archaeology, though it counts such questions as part of its agenda, is also a historical and anthropological discipline that must subscribe to what is loosely called scientific method if it is to develop intellectually credible and robust interpretations of how the world came to be as it is. Distinctively African themes of research are certainly possible within this, as Andah (1995) has forcefully argued. Such themes may well resonate better with the general public than some of those to which archaeologists have previously given emphasis—one thinks, for example, of the respective merits in this regard of the archaeology of farming or slave communities in contemporary South Africa compared with studies of Pleistocene hominids and hunter-gatherers. Abandoning obsessions with origins and with evolutionary thought, emphasizing more contextually nuanced views of ethnic and regional variety, working ever more closely with historical (including oral history) and anthropological data, researching past and present cultural landscapes are all other ways of doing this (Andah 1995). So too is an increased concern for studying the past lives and experiences of ordinary people (Stahl 2001a). Focusing on that level, as well as on the elite plane, can but reinforce and invigorate archaeological studies of the material and social effects of Africa's connections with other continents for "neither African nor non-African culture constitutes a closed system so long as it is a *human* product" (Andah 1995, 154). As Desmond Clark (1974) saw 30 years ago, a better grasp of this reality will only enhance global recognition of Africa's importance in both the present and the past, in the world of today and in that of the future.

Notes

1. Sherratt's (1995, 17–18) comments on the importance of adding value to exchangeable goods through manufacturing them and of taking advantage of a geographically crucial position between potentially complementary exchange networks could have been written about the Inland Niger Delta as readily as about Proto-Dynastic Sumer. The rapidity with which textile manufacture was taken up here and in other parts of the Sahel once cotton and weaving were introduced, the significance of this local technology in supplying West African needs and the suitability of textiles for propagating values and practices of consumption—not least when linked to religion (Islam)—also resonate in the African as much as in the Mesopotamian context (see chapter 5 for more extended discussion).

2. For the Sahara, in particular, this obviously includes a suitably permissive climate (Brooks 1998).

3. Curtin (1984, 39) makes the telling point that a single dhow could carry the equivalent of one thousand camel loads three times as fast and using just one crew member for several metric tons instead of half a metric ton or less. His figures document the advantages of waterborne transport over land-based methods in the preindustrial era, but it is unclear whether the extent of trade between East Africa and the Indian Ocean was correspondingly greater than across the Sahara and what the wider social, political, and economic implications of this would have been; more detailed comparative studies are needed.

4. Of locally based but externally funded institutions, the British Institute in Eastern Africa plays a particularly important role here through funding graduate scholarships for African and British archaeology students, supporting research by local scholars, and hosting workshops, seminars, and conferences.

5. Noteworthy examples include the *West African Journal of Archaeology* and, in eastern Africa, recent edited volumes by Chami et al. (2001) and Chami and Pwiti (2002).

6. Thus far it is work in Sudan's Wadi Howar, which extends westward from the Nile almost to the Chad border, that is particularly important in this regard (Jesse 2003; Keding 2000).

7. Comparison might well be extended to include the relations between European traders and their African partners on the continent's Atlantic and Indian Ocean seaboards from the late fifteenth century.

References

Abdu, B., and R. Gordon. 2004. Iron artifacts from the land of Kush. *Journal of Archaeological Science* 31:979–98.

Abir, M. 1965. "Salt, trade and politics in Ethiopia in the Zamara Mesafint." *Journal of Ethiopian Studies* 4:1–10.

Abrahams-Willis, G. 1998. "Archaeology and local cuisine: signatures of the Cape around 1750." *Annals of the South African Cultural History Museum* 10:1–66.

———. 2000. "Slave Lodge to become a major tourism magnet: preliminary report on year 2000 excavations." *Quarterly Bulletin of the National Library of South Africa* 54(4):134–43.

Abu-Lughod, J. 1989. *Before European Hegemony: The World System A.D. 1250–1350*. New York: Oxford University Press.

Abulafia, D., ed. 2003. *The Mediterranean in History*. London: Thames and Hudson.

Adams, B., and R. F. Friedman. 1992. "Imports and influences in the Predynastic and Protodynastic settlement and funerary assemblages at Hierakonpolis." In *The Nile Delta in Transition: 4th–3rd Millennium B.C.*, E. C. M. van den Brink, ed. (317–38). Tel Aviv: Israel Exploration Society.

Adams, W. M., A. S. Goudie, and A. R. Orme. 1996. *The Physical Geography of Africa*. Oxford: Oxford University Press.

Adams, W. Y. 1977. *Nubia, Corridor to Africa*. London: Allen Lane.

Adelaar, K. A. 1989. "Malay influence on Malagasy: linguistic and culture-historical implications." *Oceanic Linguistics* 28:1–46.

Afolayan, F. 1998. "Zanj slave revolts (*c.* 689–883)." In *The Historical Encyclopedia of World Slavery*, J. P. Rodriguez, ed. (713). Santa Barbara: ABC Clio.

African Burial Ground. 2004. http://www.africanburialground.com (accessed 8 September 2004).

Agorsah, E. K. 1993. "Archaeology and resistance history in the Caribbean." *African Archaeological Review* 11:175–96.

———. 1999. "Ethnoarchaeological consideration of social relationship and settlement patterning among Africans in the Caribbean Diaspora." In *African*

Sites Archaeology in the Caribbean, J. B. Haviser, ed. (38–64). New York: Markus Wiener.

Akyeampong, E. 1996. *Drink, Power and Cultural Change: A Social History of Alcohol in Ghana, c. 1800 to Recent Times.* Portsmouth: Heinemann.

Alaoui, F.-Z. S., and S. Searight. 1997. "Rock art in Morocco." *Proceedings of the Prehistoric Society* 63:87–102.

Alexander, J. 1988. "The Saharan divide: the evidence from Qasr Ibrim." *African Archaeological Review* 6:73–90.

———. 1997. "Salt production and the salt trade." In *Encyclopedia of Precolonial Africa*, J. O. Vogel, ed. (535–39). Walnut Creek: AltaMira Press.

———. 2001. "Islam, archaeology and slavery in Africa." *World Archaeology* 33:44–60.

Allen, S. J. 1999. "A cultural mosaic at Palmares? Grappling with the historical archaeology of a seventeenth-century Brazilian quilombo." In *Cultura Material e Arqueologia Histórica*, P. P. A. Funari, ed. (141–78). Campinas: Instituto de Filosofia e Ciêcias Humanas da UNICAMP.

Allibert, C. 1990. *Textes Anciens sur la Côte Est de l'Afrique et l'Océan Indien Occidental.* Paris: INALCO.

———. 1991–92. "Cités-états et têtes de pont dans l'archipel des Comores." *Omaly sy Anio* 33-6:115–32.

Allibert, C., A. Argant, and J. Argant. 1990. "Le site de Dembeni (Mayotte, Archipel des Comores) Mission 1984." *Etudes Océan Indien* 11:63–172.

Alpern, S. B. 1992. "The European introduction of crops into West Africa in precolonial times." *History in Africa* 19:13–43.

———. 1995. "What Africans got for their slaves: a master list of European trade goods." *History in Africa* 22:5–43.

Alvarez Delgado, J. 1977. "Leyenda erudita sobre la población de Canarias con Africanos de lenguas cortados." *Anuario de Estudios Atlánticos* 23:51–81.

Amblard, S. 1996. "Agricultural evidence and its interpretation on the Dhars Tichitt and Oualata, south-eastern Mauritania." In *Aspects of African Archaeology*, G. Pwiti and R. Soper, eds. (421–28). Harare: University of Zimbabwe Press.

Ambrose, S. H., and M. J. De Niro. 1986. "Reconstruction of African human diet using bone collagen carbon and nitrogen isotope ratios." *Nature* 319:321–24.

Andah, B. W. 1979. "Iron Age beginnings in West Africa: reflections and suggestions." *West African Journal of Archaeology* 9:135–50.

———. 1993. "Identifying early farming traditions of West Africa." In *Archaeology of Africa: Food, Metals and Towns*, T. Shaw, P. J. J. Sinclair, B. W. Andah, and A. Okpoko, eds. (240–54). London: Routledge.

———. 1995. "Studying African societies in cultural context." In *Making Alternative Histories: The Practice of Archaeology and History in Non-Western Settings*, P. R. Schmidt and T. C. Patterson, eds. (149–81). Santa Fe: SAR Press.

Anderson, D. M. 2002. *The Politics of Ecology in Baringo, Kenya, 1890–1963.* Oxford: James Currey.

Andrews, S. C., and J. P. Fenton. 2001. "Archaeology and the invisible man: the role of slavery in the production of wealth and social class in the Bluegrass region of Kentucky, 1820 to 1870." *World Archaeology* 33:115–36.

Ankermann, B. 1905. "Kulturkreise und Kulturschichten in Afrika." *Zeitschrift für Ethnologie* 37:54–84.

Anquandah, J. 1992a. "Archaeological investigations at Fort St Jago, Elmina, Ghana." *Archaeology in Ghana* 3:38–45.

———. 1992b. "A preliminary report on archaeological investigations at Adwuku Hill, Shai, Ghana, 1990." *Archaeology in Ghana* 3:33–37.

———. 1993. "Urbanization and state formation in Ghana during the Iron Age." In *Archaeology of Africa: Food, Metals and Towns*, T. Shaw, P. J. J. Sinclair, B. W. Andah, and A. Okpoko, eds. (642–51). London: Routledge.

Appadurai, A., ed. 1986. *The Social Life of Things: Commodities in Cultural Perspective.* Cambridge: Cambridge University Press.

Appiah, K. A. 1995. "Why Africa? Why art?" In *Africa: The Art of a Continent*, T. Phillips, ed. (21–26). London: Royal Academy of Arts.

———. 1997. "Europe upside down: fallacies of the new Afrocentrism." In *Perspectives on Africa: A Reader in Culture, History, and Representation*, R. R. Grinker and C. B. Steiner, eds. (728–31). Oxford: Blackwells.

Arazi, N. 2003. "Islam and alternative religious practices during the second millennium A.D. in the Inland Niger Delta of Mali." In *Researching Africa's Past: New Contributions from British Archaeologists*, P. J. Mitchell, A. Haour, and J. H. Hobart, eds. (89–95). Oxford: Oxford University School of Archaeology.

Arkell, J. A. 1961. *A History of the Sudan from the Earliest Times to 1821.* London: Athlone Press.

Armstrong, D. V. 1998. "Cultural transformation within enslaved labourer communities in the Caribbean." In *Studies in Culture Contact: Interaction, Culture Change and Archaeology*, J. Cusick, ed. (378–401). Carbondale: Centre for Archaeological Investigation.

———. 1999. "Archaeology and ethnohistory of the Caribbean plantation." In *I, Too, Am America: Archaeological Studies of African-American Life*, T. A. Singleton, ed. (173–92). Charlottesville: University of Virginia Press.

Arqueonautas. 2004. http://www.arq.de (accessed 8 September 2004).

Arrom, J. J., and M. A. García Arévalo. 1986. *Cimarrón.* Santo Domingo: Fundación García Arévalo.

Asante, M. K. 1987. *The Afrocentric Idea.* Philadelphia: Temple University Press.

Aubet, M. E. 2001. *The Phoenicians and the West: Politics, Colonies and Trade.* Cambridge: Cambridge University Press.

Auret, C., and T. M. O'C. Maggs. 1982. "The Great Ship *São Bento*: remains from a mid-sixteenth century Portuguese wreck on the Pondoland coast." *Annals of the Natal Museum* 25:1–39.

Austen, R. A. 1979. "The trans-Saharan slave trade: a tentative census." In *The Uncommon Market: Essays in the Economic History of the Atlantic Slave Trade*, H. A. Gemery and J. S. Hogendorn, eds. (23–76). New York: Academic Press.

Ayalon, D. 1977. *Studies on the Mamluks of Egypt. 1250–1517.* London: Variorum.

Bahuchet, S. 1993. "History of the inhabitants of the central African rain forest: perspectives from comparative linguistics." In *Tropical Forests, People and*

Food: Biocultural Interactions and Applications to Development, C. Hladik, ed. (37–54). Paris: MAB-UNESCO.

Bailey, R., G. Head, M. Jenike, B. Owenn, R. Rechtman, and E. Zechenter. 1989. "Hunting and gathering in tropical rain forest: is it possible?" *American Anthropologist* 91:261–85.

Baines, J. 1995. "Origins of Egyptian kingship." In *Ancient Egyptian Kingship*, D. O'Connor and D. Silverman, eds. (95–156). Leiden: E.J. Brill.

Baker, S. G. 1972. "Colono-Indian pottery from Cambridge, South Carolina, with comments on the historic Catawba pottery trade." *Institute of Archaeology and Anthropology Notebook* 4(1):3–30.

Barakat, H., and A. Fahmy, el-Din. 1999. "Wild grasses as 'Neolithic' food resources in the Eastern Sahara: a review of the evidence from Egypt." In *The Exploitation of Plant Resources in Ancient Africa*, M. van der Veen, ed. (33–46). New York: Kluwer Academic/Plenum Publishers.

Bard, K. A. 2000. "The emergence of the Egyptian state (*c.* 3200–2686 B.C.)." In *The Oxford History of Ancient Egypt*, I. Shaw, ed. (61–88). Oxford: Oxford University Press.

Bard, K. A., and R. Fattovich. 1995. "The I.U.O./B.U. excavation at Bieta Giyorgis (Aksum): an interim report." *Nyame Akuma* 44:25–27.

———. 1997. "The 1997 I.U.O./B.U. excavations at Bieta Giyorgis, Aksum: a preliminary report." *Nyame Akuma* 48:22–28.

Bard, K. A., M. C. Di Blasi, R. Fattovich, A. Manzo, C. Perlingieri, and L. Crescenzi. 1996. "The B.U./I.U.O. archaeological excavations at Bieta Giyorghis (Aksum, Ethiopia): a preliminary report on the 1996 field season." *Nyame Akuma* 46:21–23.

Barich, B. E. 1992. "The botanical collections from Ti-n-Torha/Two Caves and Uan Muhuggiag (Tadrart Acacus, Libya)—an archaeological commentary." *Origini* 16:109–23.

Barker, G. W. W. 1988. "Cows and kings: models for zimbabwes." *Proceedings of the Prehistoric Society* 54:223–39.

———. 1989. "From classification to interpretation: Libyan prehistory 1959–1989." *Libyan Studies* 20:31–43.

———. 2003. "Transitions to farming and pastoralism in North Africa." In *Examining the Farming/Language Dispersal Hypothesis*, A. C. Renfrew and K. A. Boyd, eds. (151–62). Cambridge: McDonald Institute for Archaeological Research.

Barker, G. W. W., and T. Rasmussen. 1998. *The Etruscans*. Oxford: Blackwell Publishers.

Barnett, T. 1999. *The Emergence of Food Production in Ethiopia*. Oxford: British Archaeological Reports International Series S763.

Barthelme, J. 1985. *Fisher-Hunters and Neolithic Pastoralists in East Turkana, Kenya*. Oxford: British Archaeological Reports International Series S254.

Bar-Yosef, O. 1987. "Pleistocene connexions between Africa and Southwest Asia: an archaeological perspective." *African Archaeological Review* 5:29–38.

Bar-Yosef, O., and A. Belfer-Cohen. 1989. "The origins of sedentism and farming communities in the Levant." *Journal of World Prehistory* 3:447–98.

Bass, G. F., C. Pulak, D. Collon, and J. Weinstein. 1989. "The Bronze Age shipwreck at Ulu Burun: 1986 campaign." *American Journal of Archaeology* 83:1–29.

Bassani, E., and W. Fagg. 1988. *Africa and the Renaissance: Art in Ivory.* New York: Centre for African Arts.

Basu, H. 2003. "Slave, soldier, trader, faqir: fragments of African histories in western India (Gujarat)." In *The African Diaspora in the Indian Ocean*, S. de S. Jayasuriya and R. Pankhurst, eds. (223–50). Trenton: Africa World Press.

Beach, D. 1994. *The Shona and their Neighbours.* Oxford: Blackwells.

Bedaux, R. M. A, K. C. MacDonald, A. Person, J. Polet, K. Sanogo, A. Schmidt, and S. Sidibé. 2001. "The Dia archaeological project: rescuing cultural heritage in the Inland Niger Delta (Mali)." *Antiquity* 75:837–48.

Bedaux, R. M. A., and M. J. Rowlands. 2001. "The future of Mali's past." *Antiquity* 75:872–76.

Begley, V., ed. 1996. *The Ancient Port of Arikamedu: New Excavations and Researches 1989–1992. Volume 1.* Pondicherry: Ecole Française d'Extrême Orient.

Ben-Amos, P. 1980. *The Art of Benin.* London: Thames and Hudson.

Bender, M. L. 1996. *The Nilo-Saharan Languages: A Comparative Essay.* Munich: Lincom Europa.

Bennison, A. K. 2001. "Liminal states: Morocco and the Iberian frontier between the twelfth and nineteenth centuries." In *North Africa, Islam and the Mediterranean World: From the Almoravids to the Algerian War.* J. Clancy-Smith, ed. (11–28). London: Frank Cass.

Bent, T. 1892. *The Ruined Cities of Mashonaland.* London: Longman.

Benton, C., T. Benton, and G. Wood, eds. 2003. *Art Deco 1910–1939.* London: Victoria and Albert Publications.

Berchem, J. 1989–90. "Sprachbeziehungen im Bereich des Kulturwortschatzes zwischen den Bantusprachen und dem Malagasy." *Sprache und Geschichte in Afrika* 10/11:9–169.

Berdan, F. 1975. "Trade, tribute and market in the Aztec Empire." Ph.D. diss., University of Texas, Austin.

Berg, G. M. 1985. "The sacred musket: Tactics, technology and power in eighteenth century Madagascar." *Comparative Studies in Society and History* 27:261–79.

Berlin, I. 1998. *Many Thousands Gone: The First Two Centuries of Slavery in North America.* Cambridge: Harvard University Press.

Bernal, M. 1987. *Black Athena. The Afroasiatic Roots of Classical Civilization. Vol. I: The Fabrication of Ancient Greece, 1785–1985.* New Brunswick: Rutgers University Press.

———. 1991. *Black Athena. The Afroasiatic Roots of Classical Civilization. Vol. II: The Archaeological and Documentary Evidence.* New Brunswick: Rutgers University Press.

Bernus, S., and P. Cressier. 1991. *La Région d'In Gall—Teggida n Tesemt (Niger)—Programme Archéologique d'Urgence 1977–1981. Azelik-Takadda et l'Implantation Sédentaire Médiévale.* Niamey: Institut de Recherches en Sciences Humaines.

Berthier, S. 1997. *Recherches Archéologiques sur la Capitale de l'Empire de Ghana: Etude d'un Secteur d'Habitat à Koumbi Saleh, Mauritanie.* Oxford: British Archaeological Reports International Series S680.

Binder, D. 1999. *Into the Temple Courts: The Place of the Synagogue in the Second Temple Period.* Atlanta: The Society for Biblical Literature.

Bisson, M. S. 1975. "Copper currency in central Africa: the archaeological evidence." *World Archaeology* 6:276–92.

———. 2000. "Precolonial copper metallurgy: sociopolitical context." In *Ancient African Metallurgy: The Socio-Cultural Context*, J. O. Vogel, ed. (83–146). Walnut Creek: AltaMira Press.

Blake, W., and J. Green. 1986. "A mid-16th century Portuguese wreck in the Seychelles." *International Journal of Nautical Archaeology and Underwater Exploration* 15:1–23.

Blanton, R., and G. Feinman. 1984. "The Mesoamerican world system." *American Anthropologist* 86:673–82.

Blanton, R., G. Feinman, S. Kowalewski, and P. Peregrine. 1996. "A dual-processual theory for the evolution of Mesoamerican civilization." *Current Anthropology* 37:1–14.

Blench, R. M. 1993a. "Ethnographic and linguistic evidence for the prehistory of African ruminant livestock, horses and ponies." In *Archaeology of Africa: Food, Metals and Towns*, T. Shaw, P. J. J. Sinclair, B. W. Andah, and A. Okpoko, eds. (71–103). London: Routledge.

———. 1993b. "Recent developments in African language classification and their implications for prehistory." In *Archaeology of Africa: Food, Metals and Towns*, T. Shaw, P. J. J. Sinclair, B. W. Andah, and A. Okpoko, eds. (126–38). London: Routledge.

———. 2000a. "A history of donkeys, wild asses and mules in Africa." In *The Origins and Development of African Livestock: Archaeology, Genetics, Linguistics and Ethnography*, R. M. Blench and K. C. MacDonald, eds. (339–54). London: UCL Press.

———. 2000b. "A history of pigs in Africa." In *The Origins and Development of African Livestock: Archaeology, Genetics, Linguistics and Ethnography*, R. M. Blench and K. C. MacDonald, eds. (355–67). London: UCL Press.

Blumler, M. 1992. "Seed weight and environment in Mediterranean-type grasslands in California and Israel." Ph.D. diss., University of California, Berkeley.

Blust, R. 1995. "The prehistory of the Austronesian-speaking peoples: a view from language." *Journal of World Prehistory* 9:453–510.

Boardman, J. 1999. *The Greeks Overseas: Their Early Colonies and Trade.* London: Thames and Hudson.

Boardman, S. 1999. "The agricultural foundation of the Aksumite Empire: an interim report." In *The Exploitation of Plant Resources in Ancient Africa*, M. van der Veen, ed. (137–48). New York: Kluwer Academic/Plenum Publishers.

Bocquet-Appel, J.-P., and P. Y. Demars. 2000. "Neanderthal contraction and modern human colonization of Europe." *Antiquity* 74:544–52.

Bogucki, P. 1995. "The Linear Pottery Culture of Central Europe: conservative colonists?" In *The Emergence of Pottery—Technology and Innovation in*

Ancient Societies, W. K. Barnett and T. W. Hoopes, eds. (87–97). Washington: Smithsonian Institution.

Bohannan, P. 1959. "The impact of money on an African subsistence economy." *Journal of Economic History* 19:491–503.

Bolland, R., ed. 1991. *Tellem Textiles: Archaeological Finds from Burial Caves in Mali's Bandiagara Cliff*. Amsterdam: Royal Tropical Institute.

Bonnet, C. 1992. "Excavations at the Nubian royal town of Kerma: 1975–91." *Antiquity* 66:611–25.

BOSTID (Board on Science and Technology for International Development, National Research Council). 1996. *Lost Crops of Africa, I: Grains*. Washington, D.C.: National Academy Press.

Bourriau, J. 1991. "Relations between Egypt and Kerma during the Middle and New kingdoms." In *Egypt and Africa: Nubia from Prehistory to Islam*, W. V. Davies, ed. (129–44). London: British Museum.

———. 2000. "The Second Intermediate Period (*c.* 1650–1550 B.C.)." In *The Oxford History of Ancient Egypt*, I. Shaw, ed. (184–217). Oxford: Oxford University Press.

Bower, J. 1991. "The Pastoral Neolithic of East Africa." *Journal of World Prehistory* 5:49–82.

Bowman, A. K. 1996. *Egypt After the Pharaohs*. London: British Museum.

Bradbury, J. 1996. "*Kpn*-boats, Punt trade and a lost emporium." *Journal of the American Research Centre in Egypt* 33:37–60.

Bradley, D. G., and R. T. Loftus. 2000. "Two eves for *taurus*? Bovine mitochondrial DNA and African cattle domestication." In *The Origins and Development of African Livestock: Archaeology, Genetics, Linguistics and Ethnography*, R. M. Blench and K. C. MacDonald, eds. (244–50). London: UCL Press.

Bradley, D. G., D. E. MacHugh, E. P. Cunningham, and R. T. Loftus. 1996. "Mitochondrial diversity and the origins of African and European cattle." *Proceedings of the National Academy of Sciences, USA* 93:5131–35.

Bradley, J. 1987. *Evolution of the Onondaga Iroquois*. Syracuse: Syracuse University Press.

Braudel, F. 1972. *The Mediterranean and the Mediterranean World in the Age of Philip II*. London: William Collins.

———. 1981. *The Structures of Everyday Life: The Limits of the Possible*. London: William Collins and Sons Co.

Braumann, R. 1995. "Islamic spirits and African artistry in trans-Saharan perspective." In *Islamic Art and Culture in Sub-Saharan Africa*, K. Adahl and B. Sahlström, eds. (57–69). Uppsala: Uppsala University Press.

Bredwa-Mensah, Y. 1994. "Historical-archaeological investigations at the Bibease plantation site near Abokobi, Eastern Accra Plains, Ghana." *Nyame Akuma* 42:2–6.

Breton, J.-F. 1991. "Le site et la ville de Shabwa." *Syria* 68:59–75.

Brett, M. 1978. "The Arab conquest and the rise of Islam in North Africa." In *The Cambridge History of Africa Vol. 2 c. 500 B.C.–A.D. 1050*, J. D. Fage, ed. (490–555). Cambridge: Cambridge University Press.

Brett, M., and E. Fentress. 1996. *The Berbers*. Oxford: Blackwells.

Breuil, H. 1948. "The White Lady of the Brandberg, South West Africa, her companions and her guards." *South African Archaeological Bulletin* 3:2–11.

———. 1949. "Some foreigners in the frescoes on rocks in southern Africa." *South African Archaeological Bulletin* 4:39–50.

Breunig, P. 1996. "The 8,000-year-old dugout canoe from Dufuna (NE Nigeria)." In *Aspects of African Archaeology*, G. Pwiti and R. Soper, eds. (461–68). Harare: University of Zimbabwe Press.

Breunig, P., and K. Neumann. 2002. "Continuity or discontinuity: the 1st millennium B.C. crisis in West African prehistory." *Africa Praehistorica* 14:491–505.

Breunig, P., K. Neumann, and W. van Neer. 1996. "New research on the Holocene settlement and environment of the Chad Basin in Nigeria." *African Archaeological Review* 13:111–46.

Brewer, D. J., D. B. Redford, and S. Redford. 1994. *Domestic Plants and Animals: The Egyptian Origins*. Warminster: Aris and Phillips.

Brill, R. H. 1995. "Chemical analysis of some glasses from Jenné-jeno." In *Excavations at Jenné-jeno, Hambarketolo and Kaniana (Inland Niger Delta, Mali). The 1981 Season*, S. K. McIntosh, ed. (252–56). Berkeley: University of California Press.

Brink, Y. 1993. "The octagon: an icon of Willem Adriaan van der Stel's aspirations?" *South African Archaeological Society Goodwin Series* 7:92–97.

———. 1997. "Figuring the landscape: land, identity and material culture at the Cape in the eighteenth century." *South African Archaeological Bulletin* 52:105–12.

Brooks, G. E. 1998. "Climate and history in West Africa." In *Transformations in Africa: Essays on Africa's Later Past*, G. Connah, ed. (139–59). Leicester: Leicester University Press.

———. 2003. *Eurafricans in Western Africa: Commerce, Social Status, Gender and Religious Observance from the Sixteenth to the Eighteenth Century*. Oxford: James Currey.

Brown, H. 1988. "Siyu: town of the craftsmen." *Azania* 23:101–14.

Brown, K., and D. Cooper. 1990. "Structural continuity in an African-American slave and tenant community." *Historical Archaeology* 24(4):7–19.

Brown, R. M. 2002. "'Walk in the Feenda': West-Central Africans and the forest in the South Carolina-Georgia Lowcountry." In *Central Africans and Cultural Transformations in the American Diaspora*, L. M. Heywood, ed. (289–318). Cambridge: Cambridge University Press.

Bulliet, R. W. 1992. *The Camel and the Wheel*. Cambridge: Harvard University Press.

Burney, D. A., , L. P. Burney, L. R. Godfrey, W. L. Jungers, S. M. Goodman, H. T. Wright, and A. J. T. Jull. 2004. "A chronology for late prehistoric Madagascar." *Journal of Human Evolution* 47:25–63.

Butzer, K. W. 1981. "The rise and fall of Axum, Ethiopia: a geoarchaeological interpretation." *American Antiquity* 40:471–95.

Butzer, K. W., and H. B. S. Cooke. 1982. "The palaeo-ecology of the African continent: the physical environment of Africa from the earliest geological to Later

Stone Age times." In *Cambridge History of Africa Volume I: From the Earliest Times to c. 500 B.C.*, J. D. Clark, ed. (1–69). Cambridge: Cambridge University Press.

Calvert, N. G. 1978–79. "Water mills on the *levadas* of Madeira." *Industrial Archaeological Review* 3:43–53.

Camps, G. 1982. "Beginnings of pastoralism and cultivation in north-west Africa and the Sahara: origins of the Berbers." In *The Cambridge History of Africa, Vol. 1 From the Earliest Times to c. 500 B.C.*, J. D. Clark, ed. (548–623). Cambridge: Cambridge University Press.

Caneva, I., M. Frangipane, and A. Palmieri. 1987. "Predynastic Egypt: new data from Maadi." *African Archaeological Review* 5:105–14.

———. 1989. "Recent excavations at Maadi (Egypt)." In *Late Prehistory of the Nile Basin and the Sahara*, L. Krzyzaniak and M. Kobusiewicz, eds. (287–93). Poznán: Archaeological Museum of Poznán.

Cappers, R. 1999. "Trade and subsistence at the Roman port of Berenike, Red Sea coast, Egypt." In *The Exploitation of Plant Resources in Ancient Africa*, M. van der Veen, ed. (185–98). New York: Kluwer Academic/Plenum Publishers.

Caraman, P. 1985. *The Lost Empire: The Story of the Jesuits in Ethiopia*. London: Sigdwick and Jackson.

Carney, J. A. 2001. "African rice in the Columbian exchange. " *Journal of African History* 42:377–396.

Casson, L. 1989. *The Periplus Maris Erythraei: Text with Introduction, Translation and Commentary*. Princeton: Princeton University Press.

Caton-Thompson, G. 1931. *The Zimbabwe Culture: Ruins and Reactions*. Oxford: Clarendon Press.

———. 1934. "The camel in dynastic Egypt." *Man* 34:21.

Cavalli-Sforza, L. L., P. Menozzi, and A. Piazza. 1994. *History and Geography of Human Genes*. Princeton: Princeton University Press.

Cazzella, A. 2001. "The Mediterranean: From the beginnings of food production to early forms of social stratification." In *Archaeology: The Widening Debate*, B. W. Cunliffe, W. Davies, and A. C. Renfrew, eds. (414–20). Oxford: Oxford University Press.

Cervicek, P. 1979. "Some African affinities of Arabian rock art." *Rassegna di Studi Etiopici* 27:5–12.

Chami, F. A. 1994. *The Tanzania Coast in the First Millennium A.D.* Uppsala: Uppsala University Press.

———. 1998. "A review of Swahili archaeology." *African Archaeological Review* 15:199–218.

———. 1999a. "The Early Iron Age on Mafia island and its relationship with the mainland." *Azania* 34:1–10.

———. 1999b. "Roman beads from the Rufiji Delta, Tanzania: first incontrovertible archaeological link with the *Periplus*." *Current Anthropology* 40:237–41.

———. 2000. "Further archaeological research on Mafia island." *Azania* 35:208–14.

————. 2001a. "Chicken bones from Neolithic limestone cave site, Zanzibar." In *People, Contacts and the Environment in the African Past*, F. A. Chami, G. Pwiti, and C. Radimilahy, eds. (84–97). Dar es-Salaam: DUP Press.

————. 2001b. "The archaeology of the Rufiji Region since 1987 to 2000." In *People, Contacts and the Environment in the African Past*, F. A. Chami, G. Pwiti, and C. Radimilahy, eds. (7–20). Dar es-Salaam: DUP Press.

Chami, F. A., and A. Kwekason. 2003. "Neolithic pottery traditions from the islands, the coast and the interior of East Africa." *African Archaeological Review* 20:65–80.

Chami, F. A., and P. J. Msemwa. 1997. "A new look at culture and trade on the Azanian coast." *Current Anthropology* 38:673–77.

Chami, F. A., and G. Pwiti, eds. 2002. *Southern Africa and the Swahili World*. Dar es-Salaam: DUP Press.

Chami, F. A., G. Pwiti, and C. Radimilahy, eds. 2001. *People, Contacts and the Environment in the African Past*. Dar es-Salaam: DUP Press.

Champion, T. C., ed. 1989. *Centre and Periphery: Comparative Studies in Archaeology*. London: Unwin Hyman.

Chang, K.-S. 1971. "Ming maritime enterprise and China's knowledge of Africa." *Terrae Incognitae* 3:33–44.

Chaudenson, R. 1995. *Les Créoles*. Paris: PUF.

Chaudhuri, K. N. 1985. *Trade and Civilization in the Indian Ocean: An Economic History from the Rise of Islam to 1750*. Cambridge: Cambridge University Press.

Cherry, J. F. 1990. "The first colonization of the Mediterranean Islands: a review of recent research." *Journal of Mediterranean Archaeology* 3:145–221.

Chikwendu, V. E., P. T. Cradock, E. M. Farquhar, T. Shaw, and A. C. Umeji. 1989. "Nigerian sources of copper, lead and tin for the Igbo-Ukwu bronzes." *Archaeometry* 31:27–36.

Chilardi, S., D. W. Frayer, P. Giola, R. Macchiarelli, and M. Mussi. 1996. "Fontana Nuova di Ragusa (Sicily, Italy): southernmost Aurignacian site in Europe." *Antiquity* 70:553–63.

Chittick, H. N. 1974. *Kilwa: An Islamic Trading City on the East African Coast*. Nairobi: British Institute in Eastern Africa.

————. 1977. "The East Coast, Madagascar and the Indian Ocean." In *The Cambridge History of Africa, Volume 3 c. 1050–c. 1600*, R. Oliver, ed. (183–231). Cambridge: Cambridge University Press.

————. 1984. *Manda: Excavations at an Island Port on the Kenya Coast*. Nairobi: British Institute in Eastern Africa.

Choudhury, K. A., and M. Buth. 1971. "Cotton seeds from the Neolithic in Egyptian Nubia and the origin of the Old World cotton." *Biological Journal of the Linnaean Society* 3:303–13.

Chowdhury, A. 2004. "Survival strategies of fugitive slaves in Mauritius: 1640–1835." Abstract of paper presented at the Fifth World Archaeological Congress, Washington, June 2003. www.godot.unisa.edu.au/wac/session.php?session=155 (accessed 8 September 2004).

Clark, J. D. 1962. "Africa south of the Sahara." In *Courses Towards Urban Life*, R. Braidwood and G. Willey, eds. (1–33). New York: Wenner-Gren Foundation.

———. 1974. "Africa in prehistory: peripheral or paramount?" *Man* 10:175–98.

———. 1978. "The legacy of prehistory: an essay on the background to the individuality of African cultures." In *The Cambridge History of Africa Vol. 2 from c. 500 B.C. to A.D. 1050*, J. D. Fage, ed. (11–86). Cambridge: Cambridge University Press.

Clark, J. D., and M. A. J. Williams. 1978. "Recent archaeological research in southeastern Ethiopia (1974–5): some preliminary results." *Annales d'Ethiopie* 11:19–44.

Cleuziou, S., and L. Constantini. 1980. "Premiers éléments sur l'agriculture protohistorique de l'Arabie orientale." *Paléorient* 6:245–51.

Clist, B. 1995. *Gabon: 100,000 Ans d'Histoire*. Libreville: Centre Culturel Français.

———. 1998. "Nouvelles données archéologiques sur l'histoire ancienne de la Guinée-Equatoriale." *L'Anthropologie* 102:213–17.

Close, A. E. 1990. "Living on the edge: Neolithic herders in the eastern Sahara." *Antiquity* 64:79–96.

———. 1995. "Few and far between: early ceramics in North Africa." In *The Emergence of Pottery: Technology and Innovation in Ancient Societies*, W. K. Barnett and J. W. Hoopes, eds. (23–37). Washington: Smithsonian Institution.

———. 2002. "Sinai, Sahara, Sahel: the introduction of domestic caprines to Africa." *Africa Praehistorica* 14:459–69.

Close, A. E., and F. Wendorf. 1990. "North Africa at 18 000 B.P." In *The World at 18 000 B.P. Vol. 2 Low Latitudes*, C. Gamble and O. Soffer, eds. (41–57). London: Unwin Hyman.

———. 1992. "The beginnings of food production in the eastern Sahara." In *Transitions to Agriculture in Prehistory*, A. B. Gebauer and T. D. Price, eds. (63–72). Madison: Prehistory Press.

Clutton-Brock, J. 1997. "Animal domestication in Africa." In *Encyclopedia of Precolonial Africa*, J. O. Vogel, ed. (418–24). Walnut Creek: AltaMira Press.

———. 2000. "Cattle, sheep and goats south of the Sahara: an archaeozoological perspective." In *The Origins and Development of African Livestock: Archaeology, Genetics, Linguistics and Ethnography*, R. M. Blench and K. C. MacDonald, eds. (30–37). London: UCL Press.

Cohen, A. 1969. *Custom and Politics in Urban Africa: A Study of Hausa Migrants in Yoruba Towns*. Berkeley: University of California Press.

Cole, S. 1954. *The Prehistory of East Africa*. Harmondsworth: Penguin.

Connah, G. 1996. *Kibiro: The Salt of Bunyoro, Past and Present*. Nairobi: British Institute in Eastern Africa.

———. 2001. *African Civilizations*. Cambridge: Cambridge University Press.

———. 2004. *Forgotten Africa. An Introduction to its Archaeology*. London: Routledge.

Conrad, D. C. 1994. "A town called Dakajalan: the Sunjata tradition and the question of ancient Mali's capital." *Journal of African History* 35:355–77.

Conrad, D. C., and H. J. Fisher. 1982. "The attack that never was: Ghana and the Almoravids." *History in Africa* 9:53–98.

Constantini, L. 1984. "The beginning of agriculture in the Kaachi Plain the evidence from Mergharh." In *South East Asian Archaeology*, B. Allchin, ed. (29–33). Cambridge: Cambridge University Press.

———. 1990. "Ecology and farming of the protohistoric communities in the central Yemeni highland." In *The Bronze Age Cultures of Hawlan At-Tyial and Al-Hada*, A. De Maigre, ed. (187–204). Rome: Ismeo.

Coombes, A. E. 1997. *Reinventing Africa*. New Haven: Yale University Press.

Coquery-Vidrovitch, C. 1969. "Recherches sur un mode de production africain." *La Pensée* 144:61–78.

Cordell, D. 1985. *Dar al-Kuti and the Last Years of the Trans-Saharan Slave Trade*. Madison: University of Wisconsin Press.

Coulson, D., and A. C. Campbell. 2001. *African Rock Art: Paintings and Engravings on Stone*. New York: H. N. Abrams.

Cox, G., J. C. Sealy, C. Schrire, and A. G. Morris. 2001. "Stable carbon and nitrogen isotopic analyses of the underclass at the colonial Cape of Good Hope in the eighteenth and nineteenth centuries." *World Archaeology* 33:73–97.

Craddock, P. T., J. Ambers, D. R. Hook, R. M. Farquhar, V. E. Chikwendu, A. C. Umeji, and T. Shaw. 1997. "Metal sources and the bronzes from Igbo-Ukwu, Nigeria." *Journal of Field Archaeology* 24:405–29.

Crader, D. C. 1990. "Slave diet at Monticello." *American Antiquity* 55:690–717.

Cremaschi, M., and S. Di Lernia. 1999. "Holocene climatic changes and cultural dynamics in the Libyan Sahara." *African Archaeological Review* 16:211–38.

———. 2001. "Environment and settlements in the Mid-Holocene palaeo-oasis of Wadi Tanezzuft (Libyan Sahara)." *Antiquity* 75:815–24.

Creswell, K. A. C. 1952–59. *Muslim Architecture of Egypt*. Oxford: Clarendon Press.

Crockford, S. J., ed. 2000. *Dogs through Time: An Archaeological Perspective*. Oxford: British Archaeological Reports International Series S889.

Crosby, A. W. 1986. *Ecological Imperialism: The Biological Expansion of Europe, 900–1900*. Cambridge: Cambridge University Press.

Crossland, Z. 2001. "Time and the ancestors: landscape survey in the Andrantsay region of Madagascar." *Antiquity* 75:825–36.

Cummings, R. 1973. "A note on the history of caravan porters in East Africa." *Kenya Historical Review* 1:109–38.

Cunliffe, B. W. 1997. *The Ancient Celts*. Oxford: Oxford University Press.

———. 2001. *Facing the Ocean: The Atlantic and its Peoples*. Oxford: Oxford University Press.

Curtin, P. D. 1975. *Economic Change in Precolonial Africa: Senegambia in the Era of the Slave Trade*. Madison: University of Wisconsin Press.

———. 1984. *Cross-Cultural Trade in World History*. Cambridge: Cambridge University Press.

Cutler, A. 1985. *The Craft of Ivory: Sources, Techniques and Uses in the Mediterranean World* A.D. 200–1400. Washington: Dumbarton Oaks.

Dahl, O. C. 1977. "La subdivision de la famille Barito et la place du Malgache." *Acta Orientalia* 38:77–134.

D'Andrea, A. C., M. Klee, and J. Casey. 2001. "Archaeobotanical evidence for pearl millet (*Pennisetum glaucum*) in sub-Saharan West Africa." *Antiquity* 75:341–48.

D'Andrea, A. C., D. Lyons, M. Halle, and A. Butler. 1999. "Ethnoarchaeological approaches to the study of prehistoric agriculture in the highlands of Ethiopia." In *The Exploitation of Plant Resources in Ancient Africa*, M. van der Veen, ed. (101–22). New York: Kluwer Academic/Plenum Publishers.

———. 1988. "Bantu substratum in Malagasy." *Etudes Océan Indien* 9:91–132.

Daniels, C. M. 1989. "Excavation and fieldwork amongst the Garamantes." *Libyan Studies* 20:45–61.

Darling, P. J. 1984. *Archaeology and History in Southern Nigeria*. Oxford: British Archaeological Reports International Series S215.

Darwin, C. 1871 *The Descent of Man, and Selection in Relation to Sex*, London: John Murray.

Davidson, B. 1991. *African Civilization Revisited: From Antiquity to Modern Times*. Trenton: Africa World Press.

Davies, O. 2003. "Kush in Egypt: a new historical inscription." *Sudan and Nubia* 7:52–54.

Deagan, K., and D. MacMahon. 1995. *Fort Mosé: America's Fortress of Freedom*. Gainesville: University of Florida Press.

De Barros, P. 2000. "Iron metallurgy: sociocultural context." In *Ancient African Metallurgy: The Socio-Cultural Context*, J. O. Vogel, ed. (147–98). Walnut Creek: AltaMira Press.

———. 2001. "The effect of the slave trade on the Bassar ironworking society, Togo." In *West Africa During the Atlantic Slave Trade: Archaeological Perspectives*, C. R. DeCorse, ed. (59–80). Leicester: Leicester University Press.

DeCorse, C. R. 1989. "Material aspects of Limba, Yalunka and Kuranko ethnicity: archaeological research in northeastern Sierra Leone." In *Archaeological Approaches to Cultural Identity*, S. J. Shennan, ed. (125–40). London: Unwin Hyman.

———. 1992. "Culture contact, continuity and change on the Gold Coast, A.D. 1400–1900." *African Archaeological Review* 10:163–96.

———. 1993. "The Danes on the Gold Coast: culture change and the European presence." *African Archaeological Review* 11:149–74.

———. 1994. "An archaeological reconnaissance of Bunce Island, Sierra Leone." (Abstract). *Nyame Akuma* 42:36.

———. 2001a. *The Archaeology of Elmina*. Washington: Smithsonian Institution.

———,.ed. 2001b. *West Africa during the Atlantic Slave Trade: Archaeological Perspectives*. Leicester: Leicester University Press.

———. 2001c. "Introduction." In *West Africa During the Atlantic Slave Trade: Archaeological Perspectives*, C. R. DeCorse, ed. (1–13). Leicester: Leicester University Press.

DeCorse, C. R., F. G. Richard, and I. Thiaw. 2003. "Toward a systematic analysis of archaeological beads? A view from the Lower Falemme, Senegal." *Journal of African Archaeology* 1:77–110.

Deetz, J. 1977. *In Small Things Forgotten: The Archaeology of Early American Life*. New York: Doubleday.

Del Arco Aguilar, M. C., M. Jiménez Gómez, and J. F. Navarro Mederos. 1992. *La Arqueología en Canarias: Del Mito a la Ciencia*. Santa Cruz de Tenerife: Ediciones Canarias.

Delafosse, M. 1912. *Haut-Sénégal-Niger*. Paris: Larose.

De Langhe, E., and P. De Maret. 1999. "Tracking the banana: its significance in early agriculture." In *The Prehistory of Food*, C. Gosden and J. Hather, eds. (377–96). London: Routledge.

De Langhe, E., R. Swennen, and D. Vuylsteke. 1994–95. "Plantain in the early Bantu world." *Azania* 29/30:147–60.

Delle, J. 1998. *An Archaeology of Social Space: Analyzing Coffee Plantations in Jamaica's Blue Mountains*. New York: Plenum Press.

De Maret, P. 1986. "The Ngovo Group: an industry with polished stone tools and pottery in Lower Zaire." *African Archaeological Review* 4:103–33.

———. 1999. "The power of symbols and the symbols of power through time: probing the Luba past." In *Beyond Chiefdoms: Pathways to Complexity in Africa.*, S. K. McIntosh, ed. (151–65). Cambridge: Cambridge University Press.

Denbow, J. R. 1990. "Congo to Kalahari: data and hypotheses about the political economy of the western stream of the Early Iron Age." *African Archaeological Review* 8:139–75.

———. 1999. "Material culture and the dialectics of identity in the Kalahari: A.D. 700–1700." In *Beyond Chiefdoms: Pathways to Complexity in Africa*, S. K. McIntosh, ed. (110–23). Cambridge: Cambridge University Press.

Devisse, J., ed. 1983. *Tegdaoust III: Recherches sur Aoudaghost (Campagnes 1960–1965)*. Paris: APDF.

———. 1992. "Trade and trade routes in West Africa." In *UNESCO General History of Africa. Vol. 3 Africa from the Seventh to the Eleventh Century (abridged edition)*, I. Hrbek, ed. (190–215). London: James Currey.

———. 1993. "L'or." In *Vallées du Niger*, J. Devisse, ed. (344–57). Paris: Editions de la Réunion des Musées Nationaux.

Dewar, R. E. 1984. "Extinctions in Madagascar: the loss of the subfossil fauna." In *Quaternary Extinctions*, P. Martin and R. G. Klein, eds. (574–93). Tucson: University of Arizona Press.

———. 1996. "The archaeology of the early settlement of Madagascar." In *The Indian Ocean in Antiquity*, J. Reade, ed. (471–86). London: British Museum.

Dewar, R. E., and H. T. Wright. 1993. "The culture history of Madagascar." *Journal of World Prehistory* 7:417–66.

Diamond, J. 1997. *Guns, Germs and Steel*. London: Jonathan Cape.

Dickerson, D. 1986. *Out of the Crucible: Black Steelworkers in Western Pennsylvania, 1875–1980*. Albany: SUNY Press.

Dickinson, O. 1994. *The Aegean Bronze Age*. Cambridge: Cambridge University Press.

Di Lernia, S. 2002. "Dry climatic events and cultural trajectories: adapting Middle Holocene pastoral economy of the Libyan Sahara." In *Droughts, Food and*

Culture: Ecological Change and Food Security in Africa's Later Prehistory, F. A. Hassan, ed. (225–50). New York: Kluwer Academic/Plenum Publishers.

Diop, C. A. 1967. *Antériorité des Civilisations Nègres*. Paris: Présence Africaine.

———. 1981. "Origins of the Ancient Egyptians." In *UNESCO General History of Africa, Volume II Ancient Civilizations of Africa*, G. Mokhtar, ed. (10–38). Paris: UNESCO.

Doebley, J. 1990. "Molecular evidence and the evolution of maize." *Economic Botany* 44 (supplement):6–27.

Donley, L. W. 1987. "Life in the Swahili town house reveals the symbolic meaning of spaces and artefact assemblages." *African Archaeological Review* 5:181–92.

Donley-Reid, L. W. 1990. "A structuring structure: the Swahili house." In *Domestic Architecture and the Use of Space*, S. Kent, ed. (114–26). Cambridge: Cambridge University Press.

Dowd, G. E. 1992. *A Spirited Resistance: The North American Indian Struggle for Unity, 1745–1815*. Baltimore: John Hopkins University Press.

Duarte, R. T. 1993. *Northern Mozambique in the Swahili World*. Uppsala: Uppsala University Press.

Dupuy, C. 1988. Evolution iconographique de trois stations de gravures rupestres de l'Aïr méridional (Niger). *Cahiers des Sciences Humaines (FRA)* 24:303–15.

Dupuy, C., P. Fluzin, A. Ploquin, A. Durand, and C. Rolando. 2001–02. "Nouvelles données sur l'Age ancien des métaux au Mali." *Sahara* 13:61–90.

Du Toit, B. 1976. "Man and cannabis in Africa: a study of diffusion." *African Economic History* 1:17–35.

Duyvendak, J. J. L. 1949. *China's Discovery of Africa*. London: A. Probsthain.

Eddy, M. R. 1994. "Towards a context for the Canary Islands Guanches." *Sahara* 6:115–20.

Edens, C., and T. J. Wilkinson. 1998. "Southwest Arabia during the Holocene: recent archaeological developments." *Journal of World Prehistory* 12:55–119.

Edwards, D. N. 1996. *The Archaeology of the Meroitic State: New Perspectives on its Social and Political Organisation*. Oxford: British Archaeological Reports International Series S640.

———. 1999. "Christianity and Islam in the Middle Nile: towards a study of religion and social change in the long term." In *Case Studies in the Archaeology of World Religion*, T. A. Insoll, ed. (94–104). Oxford: British Archaeological Reports International Series S755.

———. 2003. "Ancient Egypt in the Sudanese Middle Nile: a case of mistaken identity?" In *Ancient Egypt in Africa*, D. O'Connor and D. A. M. Reid eds. (137–50). London: UCL Press.

Effah-Gyamfi, K. 1985. *Bono Manso: An Archaeological Study into Early Akan Urbanism*. Calgary: University of Calgary Press.

Eggert, M. 1993. "Central Africa and the archaeology of the equatorial rainforest: reflections on some major topics." In *Archaeology of Africa: Food, Metals and Towns*, T. Shaw, P. J. J. Sinclair, B. W. Andah, and A. Okpoko, eds. (289–329). London: Routledge.

Ehret, C. 1979. "On the antiquity of agriculture in Ethiopia." *Journal of African History* 20:161–77.

———. 1982. "The first spread of food production to southern Africa." In *The Archaeological and Linguistic Reconstruction of African History*, C. Ehret and M. Posnansky, eds. (158–81). Berkeley: University of California Press.

———. 1993. "Nilo-Saharans and the Saharo-Sudanese Neolithic." In *The Archaeology of Africa: Food, Metals and Towns*, T. Shaw, P. J. J. Sinclair, B. Andah, and A. Okpoko, eds. (104–25). London: Routledge.

———. 1998. *An African Classical Age: Eastern and Southern Africa in World History, 1000 B.C. to A.D. 400*. Oxford: James Currey.

———. 2002. *The Civilizations of Africa: A History to 1800*. Oxford: James Currey.

Eisenmann, V. 1995. "L'origine des ânes: questions et réponses paléontologiques." *Ethnozootechnie* 56:5–26.

Ekeh, P. 1990. "Social anthropology and two contrasting uses of tribalism in Africa." *Comparative Studies in Society and History* 32:660–700.

Ekholm, K. 1972. *Power and Prestige: The Rise and Fall of the Kongo Kingdom*. Uppsala: Skriv Service.

Elenga, H., D. Schwartz, and A. Vincens. 1994. "Pollen evidence of Late Quaternary vegetation and inferred climatic changes in Congo." *Palaeogeography, Palaeoclimatology, Palaeoecology* 109:345–56.

Elphick, R. 1985. *Khoikhoi and the Founding of White South Africa*. Johannesburg: Ravan Press.

Elphick, R., and R. C.-H. Shell. 1989. "Intergroup relations." In *The Shaping of South African Society, 1652–1840*, E. Elphick and H. Giliomee, eds. (184–239). Cape Town: Maskew Miller Longman.

Eltis, D. 1987. *Economic Growth and the Ending of the Transatlantic Slave Trade*. New York: Oxford University Press.

Emerson, M. 1994. "Decorated clay tobacco pipes from the Chesapeake: an African connection." In *Historical Archaeology of the Chesapeake*, P. Shackel and B. J. Little, eds. (35–49). Washington: Smithsonian Institution.

Emery, W. B. 1961. *Archaic Egypt*. Harmondsworth: Penguin.

Epperson, T. W. 1990. "Race and the disciplines of the plantation." *Historical Archaeology* 24(4):29–36.

Fagan, B. M. 2001. *People of the Earth*. New York: HarperCollins.

Fagan, B. M., D. W. Phillipson, and S. G. H. Daniels. 1969. *Iron Age Cultures in Zambia (Dambwa, Ingombe Ilede and the Tonga)*. London: Chatto and Windus.

Fage, J. D. 1969. *A History of West Africa*. Cambridge: Cambridge University Press.

———. 1977. "Upper and Lower Guinea." In *The Cambridge History of Africa, Vol. 3. c. 1050–c. 1600*, J. D. Fage, ed. (463–518). Cambridge: Cambridge University Press.

Fairbanks, C. H. 1984. "The plantation archaeology of the southeastern coast." *Historical Archaeology* 18:1–14.

Farias, de Moraes, P. F. 1990. "The oldest extant writing in West Africa." *Journal des Africanistes* 60:65–113.

Farnsworth, P. 1999. "From the past to the present: an exploration of the formation of African-Bahamian identity during enslavement." In *African Sites Archaeology in the Caribbean*, J. B. Haviser, ed. (94–130). Princeton: Markus Wiener.

Fattovich, R. 1991. "At the periphery of the Empire: the Gash Delta (Eastern Sudan)." In *Egypt and Africa: Nubia from Prehistory to Islam*, W. V. Davies, ed. (40–48). London: British Museum.

———. 1996. "The Gash Group: a complex society in the lowlands to the east of the Nile." *Actes de la VIIIe Conférence Internationale des Etudes Nubiennes* 1:191–200.

———. 1997. "The Near East and Eastern Africa: their interaction." In *Encyclopedia of Precolonial Africa*, J. O. Vogel, ed. (479–84). Walnut Creek: AltaMira Press.

Fattovich, R., A. E. Marks, and A. Mohammed-Ali. 1984. "The archaeology of the eastern Sahel, Sudan: preliminary results." *African Archaeological Review* 2:173–88.

Feinberg, H. M. 1989. "Africans and Europeans in West Africa: Elmina and Dutchmen on the Gold Coast during the eighteenth century." *Transactions of the American Philosophical Society* 79(7):1–186.

Ferguson, L. 1978. "Looking for the "Afro-" in Colono-Indian pottery." *Confederate Historical Site Archaeology Papers* 12:68–86.

———. 1992. *Uncommon Ground: Archaeology and Colonial African America, 1650–1800*. Washington: Smithsonian Institution.

———. 1999. "'The cross is a magic sign': marks on eighteenth-century bowls from South Carolina." In *I, Too, Am America: Archaeological Studies of African-American Life*, T. A. Singleton, ed. (116–31). Charlottesville: University of Virginia Press.

Fernandez, V., and J. J. Tresseras. 2000. "New data on intensive plant processing and beer brewing in the Mesolithic and Neolithic periods of central Sudan." (Abstract). *Nyame Akuma* 54:42.

Fernández-Armesto, F. 2001. *Civilizations*. London: Pan Macmillan.

Filipowiak, W. 1979. *Etudes Archéologiques sur la Capitale Médiévale du Mali*. Szczecin: Muzeum Nardowe.

Finneran, N. 2002. *The Archaeology of Christianity in Africa*. Stroud: Tempus Publishing.

Fisher, H. J. 1977. "The eastern Maghrib and the central Sudan." In *The Cambridge History of Africa Vol. 3 c. 1050–c. 1600*, R. Oliver, ed. (232–330). Cambridge: Cambridge University Press.

Fletcher, R. 1997. *The Conversion of Europe from Paganism to Christianity 371–1386 A.D.* London: HarperCollins.

Flury, S. 1922. "The Kufic inscription of Kizimkazi Mosque, Zanzibar, A.D. 1107." *Journal of the Royal Asiatic Society* 21:257–64.

Foley, R. A. 2001. "Parallel tracks in time: human evolution and archaeology." In *Archaeology: The Widening Debate*, B. W. Cunliffe, W. Davies, and A. C. Renfrew, eds. (3–42). Oxford: Oxford University Press.

R E F E R E N C E S

Foley, R. A., and M. M. Lahr. 1997. "Mode 3 technologies and the evolution of modern humans." *Cambridge Archaeological Journal* 7:3–36.

Folorunso, C. A. 2003. "Views of Ancient Egypt from a West African perspective." In *Ancient Egypt in Africa*, D. O'Connor and D. A. M. Reid, eds. (77–92). London: UCL Press.

Forsythe, W., R. Quinn, and C. Breen. 2003. "Subtidal archaeological investigations in Mombasa's Old Port." In *Researching Africa's Past: New Contributions from British Archaeologists*, P. J. Mitchell, A. Haour, and J. H. Hobart, eds. (133–38). Oxford: Oxford University School of Archaeology.

Francaviglia, V. 1985. "In search of the ancient Arabian obsidian sources." *East and West* 35:373.

Frankenstein, S., and M. J. Rowlands. 1978. "The internal structure and regional context of Early Iron Age society in south-western Germany." *Bulletin of the Institute of Archaeology, London* 15:73–112.

Frankfort, H. 1948. *Kingship and the Gods*. Chicago: University of Chicago Press.

Freeman-Grenville, G. S. P. 1962. *The East African Coast: Select Documents from the First to the Earlier Nineteenth Century*. London: Clarendon Press.

———. 1988. "The Portuguese on the Swahili Coast: buildings and language." In *The Swahili Coast: Second to Nineteenth Centuries*, G. S. P. Freeman-Grenville, ed., chapter 11. London: Variorum.

Frend, W. H. C. 1978. "The Christian period in Mediterranean Africa, *c.* A.D. 200 to 700." In *The Cambridge History of Africa Vol. 2 c. 500 B.C.–A.D. 1050*, J. D. Fage, ed. (410–89). Cambridge: Cambridge University Press.

Friedman, J., and M. J. Rowlands. 1978. "Notes towards an epigenetic model of the evolution of 'civilisation'." In *The Evolution of Social Systems*, J. Friedman and M. J. Rowlands, eds. (201–76). London: Duckworth.

Frobenius, L. 1913. *The Voice of Africa*. London: Hutchinson.

Fuller, D. Q. 1997. "The confluence of history and archaeology in Lower Nubia: scales of continuity and change." *Archaeological Review from Cambridge* 14:105–28.

———. 2001. "Harappan seeds and agriculture: some considerations." *Antiquity* 75:410–13.

———. 2003. "African crops in prehistoric South Asia: a critical review." *Africa Praehistorica* 15:239–71.

Funari, P. P. A. 1995. "The archaeology of Palmares and its contribution to the understanding of the history of African American culture." *Historical Archaeology in Latin America* 7:1–41.

———. 1997. "Archaeology, history and historical archaeology in South America." *International Journal of Historical Archaeology* 1:189–206.

Gabriel, B. 1987. "Palaeoecological evidence from neolithic fireplaces in the Sahara." *African Archaeological Review* 5:93–104.

Gabunia, L., A. Vekua, D. Lordkipanidze, C. C. Swsiher, R. Ferring, A. Justus, M. Nioradze, M. Tvalchrelidze, S. C. Antón, G. Bosinski, O. Jöris, M.-A. de Lumley, G. Majsuradze, and A. Mouskhelishvili. 2000. "Earliest Pleistocene hominid cranial remains from Dmanisi, Republic of Georgia: taxonomy, geological setting and age." *Science* 288:1019–25.

Gado, B. 1993. "'Un village des morts' à Bura en République du Niger." In *Vallées du Niger*, J. Devisse, ed. (320–33). Paris: Editions de la Réunion des Musées Nationaux.

Galand. L. 1994. "A la recherche du Canarien." *Sahara* 6:109–11.

Gardiner, A. H. 1961. *Egypt of the Pharaohs: An Introduction*. Oxford: Oxford University Press.

Garlake, P. S. 1966. *The Early Islamic Architecture of the East African Coast*. Nairobi: British Institute in Eastern Africa.

———. 1967. "Seventeenth century Portuguese earthworks in Rhodesia." *South African Archaeological Bulletin* 21:157–70.

———. 1973. *Great Zimbabwe*. London: Thames and Hudson.

Garrard, T. 1982. "Myth and metrology: the early trans-Saharan gold trade." *Journal of African History* 23:443–61.

Gast, M. 1968. *Alimentation des Populations de l'Ahaggar, Etude Ethnographique*. Algiers: Centre de Recherches Anthropologiques, Préhistoriques et Ethnographiques (Conseil de la Recherche Scientifique en Algérie).

Gaussen, J., and M. Gaussen. 1988. *Le Tilemsi Préhistorique et ses Abords: Sahara et Sahel Maliens*. Paris: CNRS.

Gautier, A. 1987. "Prehistoric men and cattle in North Africa: a dearth of data and a surfeit of models." In *Prehistory of Arid North Africa*, A. E. Close, ed. (163–87). Dallas: Southern Methodist University Press.

———. 2002. "The evidence for the earliest livestock in North Africa: or adventures with large bovids, ovicaprids, dogs and pigs." In *Droughts, Food and Culture: Ecological Change and Food Security in Africa's Later Prehistory*, F. A. Hassan, ed. (195–208). New York: Kluwer Academic/Plenum Publishers.

Gepts, P. 1990. "Biochemical evidence bearing on the domestication of *Phaseolus* (Fabaceae) beans." *Economic Botany* 44 (supplement):28–38.

Gerharz, R. 1994. *Jebel Moya*. Berlin: Akademie.

Gibb, H. A. R. 1972. *The Travels of Ibn Battuta* A.D. *1325–54. Volume 3*. London: Hakluyt Society.

Gibb, H. A. R., and C. Beckingham. 1994. *The Travels of Ibn Battuta* A.D. *1325–54. Volume 4*. London: Hakluyt Society.

Gibbs, T., K. Cargill, L. S. Lieberman, and E. J. Reitz. 1980. "Nutrition in a slave population: an anthropological examination." *Medical Anthropology* 4:175–262.

Gifford-Gonzalez, D. 1998. "Early pastoralists in East Africa: ecological and social dimensions." *Journal of Anthropological Archaeology* 17:166–200.

———. 2000. "Animal disease challenges to the emergence of pastoralism in sub-Saharan Africa." *African Archaeological Review* 17:95–139.

Gilman, A. 1975. *A Later Prehistory of Tangier, Morocco*. Cambridge: Peabody Museum.

Gilroy, P. 1993. *The Black Atlantic: Modernity and Double Consciousness*. Cambridge: Harvard University Press.

Goiten, S. D. 1967–88. *A Mediterranean Society: The Jewish Communities of the Arab World as Portrayed in the Documents of the Cairo Geniza. Volumes 1–5*. Berkeley: University of California Press.

Gomez, M. A. 1990. "Timbuktu under imperial Songhay: a reconsideration of autonomy." *Journal of African History* 31:5–24.

González Antón, R., and A. Tejera Gaspar. 1990. *Los Aborigenes Canarios: Gran Canaria y Tenerife*. Oviedo: Colegio Universitario de Ediciones Istmo.

Goodwin, A. J. H., and C. van Riet Lowe. 1929. "The Stone Age cultures of South Africa." *Annals of the South African Museum* 27:1–289.

Goody, J. 1971. *Technology, Tradition and the State in Africa*. Cambridge: Cambridge University Press.

Goucher, C. 1993. "African metallurgy in the Atlantic world." *African Archaeological Review* 11:197–216.

———. 1999. "African-Caribbean metal technology: forging cultural survivals in the Atlantic World." In *African Sites Archaeology in the Caribbean*, J. B. Haviser, ed. (143–56). Princeton: Markus Wiener.

Grant, M. R. 1999. "The sourcing of southern African tin artefacts." *Journal of Archaeological Science* 26:1111–17.

Gray, R., and D. Birmingham. 1970. *Pre-Colonial African Trade*. Oxford: Oxford University Press.

Grébénart, D. 1988. *Les Premiers Métallurgistes en Afrique Occidentale*. Abidjan: Nouvelles Editions Africaines.

———. 1993. "Marandet." In *Vallées du Niger*, In J. Devisse, ed. (375–77). Paris: Editions de la Réunion des Musées Nationaux.

Green, K. L. 1986. "Dyula and Sonongui rôles in the Islamisation of the region of Kong." *Asian and African Studies* 20:103–23.

Greenlaw, J. P. 1995. *The Coral Buildings of Suakin Islamic Architecture, Planning, Design and Domestic Arrangements in a Red Sea Port*. London: Kegan Paul.

Grigson, C. 2000. *Bos africanus* (Brehm)? Notes on the archaeozoology of the native cattle of Africa. In *The Origins and Development of African Livestock: Archaeology, Genetics, Linguistics and Ethnography*, R. M. Blench and K. C. MacDonald, eds. (38–60). London: UCL Press.

Gronenborn, D. 2001. "Kanem-Borno: a brief summary of the history and archaeology of an empire of the central *bilad al-sudan*." In *West Africa during the Atlantiuc Slave Trade: Archaeological Perspectives*, C. R. DeCorse, ed. (101–30). Leicester: Leicester University Press.

Guelke, L. 1989. "Freehold farmers and frontier settlers, 1657–1780." In *The Shaping of South African Society, 1652–1840*, E. Elphick and H. Giliomee, eds. (66–108). Cape Town: Maskew Miller Longman.

Guyer, J. 1991. "Female farming in anthropology and African history." In *Gender at the Crossroads of Knowledge: Feminist Anthropology in the Postmodern Era*, M. di Leonardo, ed. (257–77). Berkeley: University of California Press.

Haaland, R. 1980. "Man's role in the changing habitat of the Méma during the period of the old Kingdom of Ghana." *Norwegian Archaeological Review* 13:31–46.

———. 1992. "Fish, pots and grain: Early and Mid-Holocene adaptations in the Central Sudan." *African Archaeological Review* 10:43–64.

———. 1996. "A socio-economic perspective on the transition from gathering to cultivation and domestication: a case study of sorghum in the middle Nile region." In *Aspects of African Archaeology*, G. Pwiti and R. Soper, eds. (391–400). Harare: University of Zimbabwe Press.

Haaland, R., and C. S. Msuya. 2000. "Pottery production, iron working and trade in the Early Iron Age: the case of Dakawa, east-central Tanzania." *Azania* 35:75–106.

Hall, M. 1987. *The Changing Past: Farmers, Kings and Traders in Southern Africa, 200–1860*. Cape Town: David Philip.

———. 2002. "Timeless time: Africa and the world." In *Archaeology: The Widening Debate*, B. W. Cunliffe, W. Davies, and A. C. Renfrew, eds. (439–64). Oxford: Oxford University Press.

Hall, M., Y. Brink, and A. Malan. 1988. "Onrust 87/1: an early colonial farm complex in the western Cape." *South African Archaeological Bulletin* 43:91–99.

Hall, R. N., and W. Neal. 1902. *The Ancient Ruins of Rhodesia*. London: Methuen.

Hall, S. L. 1997. "Material culture and gender correlations: the view from Mabotse in the late nineteenth century." In *Our Gendered Past: Archaeological Studies of Gender in Southern Africa*, L. Wadley, ed. (209–20). Johannesburg: Witwatersrand University Press.

Hambolu, M. O. 1996. "Recent excavations along the Yobe valley." In *Vorträge Internationales Symposium–SFB 268–Frankfurt/Main Vol. 8*, G. Nagel, ed. (215–30). Frankfurt-am-Main Berichte des Sonderforschungsbereichs.

Handler, J. S. 1997. "An African-type healer/diviner and his grave goods: a burial from a plantation slave cemetery in Barbados, West Indies." *International Journal of Historical Archaeology* 1:91–130.

Hanisch, E. 1981. "Schroda: a Zhizo site in the northern Transvaal." In *Guide to Archaeological Sites in the Northern and Eastern Transvaal*, E. A. Voigt, ed. (37–53). Pretoria: Southern African Association of Archaeologists.

Haour, A. 2003. *Ethnoarchaeology in the Zinder Region, Republic of Niger: The Site of Kufan Kanawa*. Oxford: British Archaeological Reports International Series S1133.

Harding, A. F. 2001. "Western Eurasia." In *Archaeology: The Widening Debate*, B. W. Cunliffe, W. Davies, and A. C. Renfrew, eds. (363–84). Oxford: Oxford University Press.

Harlan, J. R. 1971. "Agricultural origins—centers and non-centers." *Science* 174:468–74.

———. 1982. "The origins of indigenous African agriculture." In *The Cambridge History of Africa, Vol. 1 From the Earliest Times to c. 500 B.C.*, J. D. Clark, ed. (624–57). Cambridge: Cambridge University Press.

———. 1989. "Wild-grass seed harvesting in the Sahara and Sub-Sahara of Africa." In *Foraging and Farming: The Evolution of Plant Exploitation*, D. R. Harris and G. C. Hillman, eds. (79–97). London: Unwin Hyman.

———. 1993. "The tropical African cereals." In *Archaeology of Africa: Food, Metals and Towns*, T. Shaw, P. J. J. Sinclair, B. W. Andah, and A. Okpoko, eds. (53–60). London: Routledge.

Harlow, M., and W. Smith. 2001. "Between fasting and feasting: the literary and archaeobotanical evidence for monastic diet in Late Antique Egypt." *Antiquity* 75:758–68.

Harrington, S. 1996. "An African cemetery in Manhattan." In *Eyewitness to Discovery*, B. Fagan, ed. (324–33). London: Oxford University Press.

Harris, J. E. 1971. *The African Presence in Asia: Consequences of the East African Slave Trade*. Evanston: Northwestern University Press.

Harrison, R. J., and A. Gilman. 1977. "Trade in the second and third millennia B.C. between the Maghreb and Iberia." In *Ancient Europe and the Mediterranean: Studies Presented in Honour of Hugh Hencken*, V. Markotic, ed. (90–104). Warminster: Aris and Phillips.

Haslip-Viera, G., B. Ortiz de Montellano, and W. Barbour. 1997. "Robbing Native American cultures: Van Sertima's Afrocentricity and the Olmecs." *Current Anthropology* 38:419–41.

Hassan, F. A. 1988. "The Predynastic of Egypt." *Journal of World Prehistory* 2:135–85.

———. 1997. "Egypt: beginnings of agriculture." In *Encyclopedia of Precolonial Africa*, J. O. Vogel, ed. (405–9). Walnut Creek: AltaMira Press.

———. 2000. "Climate and cattle in North Africa: a first approximation." In *The Origins and Development of African Livestock: Archaeology, Genetics, Linguistics and Ethnography*, R. M. Blench and K. C. MacDonald, eds. (61–86). London: UCL Press.

———. 2002. "Palaeoclimate, food and culture change in Africa: an overview." In *Droughts, Food and Culture: Ecological Change and Food Security in Africa's Later Prehistory*, F. A. Hassan, ed. (11–26). New York: Kluwer Academic/Plenum Publishers.

Hastings, A. 1994. *The Church in Africa 1450–1950*. Oxford: Clarendon Press.

Hather, J. 1991. "The identification of charred archaeological remains of vegetative parenchymatous tissues." *Journal of Archaeological Science* 18:661–75.

Hauser, M., and D. V. Armstrong. 1999. "Embedded identities: piecing together relationships through compositional analysis of low-fired earthenwares." In *African Sites Archaeology in the Caribbean*, J. B. Haviser, ed. (65–93). Princeton: Markus Wiener.

Hauser, M., and C. R. DeCorse. 2002. "Low fired earthenwares in the African diaspora: prospects and problems." (Abstract). *Nyame Akuma* 57:54.

Haviser, J. B. 1999. "Identifying a post-emancipation (1863–1940) African-Curaçaoan material culture assemblage." In *African Sites Archaeology in the Caribbean*, J. B. Haviser, ed. (221–63). Princeton: Markus Wiener.

Haviser, J. B., and N. Simmons-Brito. 1995. "Excavations at the Zuurzak site: a possible 17th-century Dutch slave camp on Curaçao, Netherlands Antilles." In *Proceedings of the 15th International Congress of Caribbean Archaeology*, R. Alegria and M. Rodriguez, eds. (380–407). San Juan: Centro de Estudios Avanzados de Puerto Rico y el Caribe.

Hayes, J. W. 1997. *Handbook of Mediterranean Roman Pottery*. Norman: University of Oklahoma Press.

Hayes, W. C. 1964. *Most Ancient Egypt*. Chicago: University of Chicago Press.

Hayward, L. G. 1990. "The origin of the raw elephant ivory used in Greece and the Aegean during the Late Bronze Age." *Antiquity* 64:103–9.

Headland, T. N. 1987. "The wild yam question: how well could independent hunter-gatherers live in a tropical rainforest environment?" *Human Ecology* 15:463–91.

Hegel, F. W. 1965. *La Raison dans l'Histoire: Introduction à la Philosophie de l'Histoire*. Paris: Plon.

Hein, E., and B. Kleidt. 1999. *Ethiopia—Christian Africa: Art, Churches and Culture*. Frankfurt: Melina Verlag.

Helm, R. 2000. "Conflicting Histories: The Archaeology of Iro S. de S. Jayasuriya and R. Pankhurst, eds., nworking, Farming Communities in the Central and Southern Coast Region of Kenya." Ph.D. diss., University of Bristol.

Herbert, E. W. 1984. *The Red Gold of Africa*. Madison: University of Wisconsin Press.

———. 1993. *Iron, Gender and Power: Rituals of Transformation in African Societies*. Bloomington: University of Indiana Press.

Hess, A. 1978. *The Forgotten Frontier: A History of the 16th Century Ibero-African Frontier*. Chicago: Chicago University Press.

Heyerdahl, T. 1972. *The Ra Expeditions*. Harmondsworth: Penguin.

Heywood, L. M. 2002. "Portuguese into African: the eighteenth-century Central African background to Atlantic Creole cultures." In *Central Africans and Cultural Transformations in the American Diaspora*, L. M. Heywood, ed. (91–113). Cambridge: Cambridge University Press.

Hill, M. H. 1987. "Ethnicity lost? Ethnicity gained? Information functions of "African ceramics" in West Africa and North America." In *Ethnicity and Culture*, R. Auger, M. Glass, S. MacEachern, and P. McCartney, eds. (135–59). Calgary: Archaeological Association, University of Calgary.

Hilton, A. 1985. *The Kingdom of Kongo*. Oxford: Clarendon Press.

Hintjens, H. 2003. "From French slaves to citizens: the African Diaspora on the Réunion Island." In *The African Diaspora in the Indian Ocean*, (99–122). Trenton: Africa World Press.

Hiscock, P. 1996. "Transformations of Upper Palaeolithic implements in the Dabba industry from Haua Fteah (Libya)." *Antiquity* 70:657–64.

Hoffman, M. A. 1982. *The Predynastic of Hierakonpolis—An Interim Report*. Giza: Cairo University Herbarium.

Hogendorn, J., and M. Johnson. 1986. *The Shell Money of the Slave Trade*. Cambridge: Cambridge University Press.

Holl, A. F. C. 1985. "Subsistence patterns of the Dhar Tichitt Neolithic, Mauritania." *African Archaeological Review* 3:151–62.

———. 1998. "Livestock husbandry, pastoralisms and territoriality: the West African record." *Journal of Anthropological Archaeology* 17:143–65.

———. 2000. "Metals and precolonial African society." In *Ancient African Metallurgy: The Socio-Cultural Context*, J. O. Vogel, ed. (1–81). Walnut Creek: AltaMira Press.

Holt-Biddle, D. 1995. "Réunion: paradise found, or paradise lost?" *Africa Environment and Wildlife* 3(1):41–47.

Hopkins, A. G. 1973. *An Economic History of West Africa*. London: Longmans.

Horden, P., and N. Purcell. 2000. *The Corrupting Sea: A Study of Mediterranean History*. Oxford: Blackwells.

Horton, M. C. 1987a. "Early Muslim trading settlements on the East African coast: new evidence from Shanga." *Antiquaries Journal* 67:290–323.

———. 1987b. "The Swahili corridor." *Scientific American* 257(3):76–84.

———. 1990. "The *Periplus* and East Africa." *Azania* 25:95–99.

———. 1996a. "Early maritime trade and settlement along the coasts of East Africa." In *The Indian Ocean in Antiquity*, J. Reade, ed. (439–59). London: British Museum.

———. 1996b. *Shanga: The Archaeology of a Muslim Trading Community on the Coast of East Africa*. Nairobi: British Institute in Eastern Africa.

———. 1997. "Eastern African historical archaeology." In *Encyclopedia of Precolonial Africa*, J. O. Vogel, ed. (549–54). Walnut Creek: AltaMira Press.

Horton, M. C., H. W. Brown, and W. A. Oddy. 1986. "The Mtambwe hoard." *Azania* 21:115–23.

Horton, M. C., and C. Clark. 1985. "Archaeological survey of Zanzibar." *Azania* 20:167–71.

Horton, M. C., and J. Middleton. 2000. *The Swahili*. Oxford: Blackwells.

Houbert, J. 2003. "Creolisation and decolonisation in the changing geopolitics of the Indian Ocean." In *The African Diaspora in the Indian Ocean*, S. de S. Jayasuriya and R. Pankhurst, eds. (123–88). Trenton: Africa World Press.

Hourani, G. F. 1995. *Arab Seafaring*. Princeton: Princeton University Press.

Howard, V. 2000. "Mauritius: star and key of the Indian Ocean." *Africa Environment and Wildlife* 8(1):80–88.

Hrbek, I. 1977. "Egypt, Nubia and the Eastern Deserts." In *The Cambridge History of Africa, Volume 3, c. 1050–c. 1600*, R. Oliver, ed. (109–97). Cambridge: Cambridge University Press.

Hrbek, I., and M. El-Fasi. 1992. "Stages in the development of Islam and its dissemination in Africa." In *UNESCO General History of Africa, Volume III: Africa from the Seventh to the Eleventh Century* (abridged edition), I. Hrbek ed. (31–49). London: Heinemann.

Huard, P., and C. Bacquié. 1964. "Un établissement islamique dans le désert tchadien." *Bullétin de l'Institut Français d'Afrique Noire (B)* 26:1–20.

Hublin, J.-J. 2001. "Northwestern African Middle Pleistocene hominids." In *Human Roots: Africa and Asia in the Middle Pleistocene*, L. S. Barham and K. Robson-Brown, eds. (99–122). Bristol: Western Academic and Specialist Press.

Huffman, T. N. 1971. "Cloth from the Iron Age in Rhodesia." *Arnoldia* 5(14):1–19.

———. 1986. "Iron Age settlement patterns and the origins of class distinction in southern Africa." *Advances in World Archaeology* 5:291–338.

———. 1989. "Ceramics, settlements and Late Iron Age migrations." *African Archaeological Review* 7:155–82.

———. 1996a. "Archaeological evidence for climatic change during the last 2,000 years in southern Africa." *Quaternary International* 33:55–60.

———. 1996b. *Snakes and Crocodiles: Power and Symbolism in Ancient Zimbabwe.* Johannesburg: Witwatersrand University Press.

———. 2000. "Mapungubwe and the origins of the Zimbabwe culture." *South African Archaeological Society Goodwin Series* 8:14–29.

Huntingford, G. W. B. 1933. "The Azanian civilization of Kenya." *Antiquity* 7:153–65.

Hunwick, J. 1985. *Shari'a in Songhay: The Replies of Al-Maghili to the Questions of Askia Al-Hajj Muhammad.* Oxford: Oxford University Press.

Iliffe, J. 1995. *Africans, the History of a Continent.* Cambridge: Cambridge University Press.

Insoll, T. A. 1994. The external creation of the Western Sahel's past: use and abuse of the Arabic sources. *Archaeological Review from Cambridge* 13:39–50.

———. 1995. "A cache of hippopotamus ivory at Gao, Mali: and a hypothesis of its use." *Antiquity* 69:327–36.

———. 1996. *Islam, Archaeology and History: Gao Region (Mali) ca.* A.D. *900–1250.* Oxford: British Archaeological Reports International Series S647.

———. 1997a. "An archaeological reconnaissance made to Dahlak Kebir, the Dahlak Islands, Eritrea: preliminary observations." In *Ethiopia in Broader Perspective: Papers of the Thirteenth International Conference of Ethiopian Studies, Volume I,* K. Fukui, E. Kurimoto, and M. Shigeta, eds. (383–88). Kyoto: Shokado Book Sellers.

———. 1997b. "Ngandu and Ngambezi: sites on the nineteenth-century trade route around Lake Victoria, and Speke's expedition of 1861–63." *Azania* 32:109–12.

———, ed. 2000. *Urbanism, Archaeology and Trade: Further Observations on the Gao Region (Mali). The 1996 Fieldseason Results.* Oxford: British Archaeological Reports International Series S829.

———. 2003a. *The Archaeology of Islam in Sub-Saharan Africa.* Cambridge: Cambridge University Press.

———. 2003b. "Timbuktu the less mysterious." In *Researching Africa's Past: New Contributions from British Archaeologists,* P. J. Mitchell, A. Haour, and J. H. Hobart, eds. (81–88). Oxford: Oxford University School of Archaeology.

Insoll, T. A., and K. Bhan. 2001. "Carnelian mines in Gujarat." *Antiquity* 75:495–96.

Insoll, T. A., and M. R. MacLean. 1995. "Prehistoric North-West Africa." In *Africa: The Art of a Continent,* T. Phillips, ed. (535–36). Munich: Presetl.

Insoll, T. A., and T. Shaw. 1997. "Gao and Igbo-Ukwu: beads, interregional trade and beyond." *African Archaeological Review* 14:9–23.

Irstam, T. 1944. *The King of Ganda.* Stockholm: Ethnographic Museum.

Jayasuriya, de S. S. 2003. "The African Diaspora in Sri Lanka." In *The African Diaspora in the Indian Ocean,* S. de S. Jayasuriya and R. Pankhurst, eds. (251–88). Trenton: Africa World Press.

Jesse, F. 2000. "Early Khartoum ceramics in the Wadi Howar (northeast Sudan)." In *Recent Research into the Stone Age of Northeastern Africa,* L. Krzyzaniak, K. Kroeper, and M. Kobusiewicz, eds. (77–87). Poznán: Poznán Archaeological Museum.

————. 2003. "New archaeological work in the Lower Wadi Howar (Northern Sudan): a preliminary report on the 2002 field season." *Nyame Akuma* 60:43–48.

Johnson, M. 1977. "Cloth strips and history." *West African Journal of Archaeology* 7:169–78.

Jones, P. 1984. "Mobility and migration in traditional African farming and Iron Age models." In *Frontiers: Southern African Archaeology Today*, M. Hall, G. Avery, D. M. Avery, M. L. Wilson, and A. J. B. Humphreys, eds. (289–96). Oxford: British Archaeological Reports International Series S207.

Jourdan, S. C., C. Schrire, and D. Miller. 1999. "Petrography of locally produced pottery from the Dutch Colonial Cape of Good Hope, South Africa." *Journal of Archaeological Science* 26:1327–38.

Juma, A. 1996. "The Swahili and the Mediterranean worlds: pottery of the late Roman period from Zanzibar." *Antiquity* 70:148–54.

Kadra, F. K. 1983. 1993. *Les Djedars: Monuments Funéraires Berbères de la Région de Frenda*. Algiers: Editions SNED.

Kea, R. A. 1982. *Settlements, Trade and Politics in the Seventeenth Century Gold Coast*. Baltimore: John Hopkins University Press.

Keding, B. 2000. "New data on the Holocene occupation of the Wadi Howar region." In *Recent Research into the Stone Age of Northeastern Africa*, L. Krzyzaniak, K. Kroeper, and M. Kobusiewicz, eds. (89–104). Poznán: Poznán Archaeological Museum.

Kelly, K. G. 1997a. "The archaeology of African-European interaction: investigating the social roles of trade, traders and the use of space in the 17th and 18th century *Hueda* kingdom, Republic of Bénin." *World Archaeology* 28:351–69.

————. 1997b. "Using historically informed archaeology: seventeenth and eighteenth century Hueda/European interaction on the coast of Bénin." *Journal of Archaeological Method and Theory* 28:77–95.

————. 2001. "Change and continuity in coastal Bénin." In *West Africa during the Atlantic Slave Trade: Archaeological Perspectives*, C. R. DeCorse, ed. (81–100). Leicester: Leicester University Press.

————. 2002. "African Diaspora archaeology in Guadeloupe, French West Indies." *Antiquity* 76:333–34.

Kelso, W. M. 1986. "The archaeology of slave life at Thomas Jefferson's Monticello: 'A wolf by the ears'." *Journal of New World Archaeology* 6(4):5–20.

Kemp, B. J. 1989. *Ancient Egypt: Anatomy of a Civilisation*. London: Routledge.

Khan, H.-U. 1994. "A contemporary view of mosques." In *The Mosque*, M. Frishman and H.-U. Khan eds. (247–72). London: Thames and Hudson.

Khudabux, M. R. 1999. "Effects of life conditions on the health of a Negro slave community in Suriname." In *African Sites Archaeology in the Caribbean*, J. B. Haviser, ed. (291–312). Princeton: Markus Wiener.

Kibunjia, M. 1997. "The management of archaeological collections and resources in Africa." *African Archaeological Review* 14:137–42.

Killick, D. 2004. Review essay. What do we know about African iron working? *Journal of African Archaeology* 2:97–112.

Killick, D., N. J. van der Merwe, R. Gordon, and D. Grébénart. 1988. "Reassessment of the evidence for early metallurgy in Niger, West Africa." *Journal of Archaeological Science* 15:367–94.

Kinahan, J. 1996. "The archaeology of social rank among eighteenth century nomadic pastoralists in southern Namibia." *African Archaeological Review* 13:225–46.

Kinahan, J. H. A. 2000. *Cattle for Beads: The Archaeology of Historical Contact and Trade on the Namib Coast.* Windhoek: Namibia Archaeological Trust.

Kirkman, J. S. 1954. *The Arab City of Gedi: Excavations at the Great Mosque. Architecture and Finds.* Oxford: Oxford University Press.

———. 1974. *Fort Jesus: A Portuguese Fortress on the East African Coast.* Nairobi: British Institute in Eastern Africa.

Kirwan, L. P. 1986. "Rhapta, Metropolis of Azania." *Azania* 21:99–104.

Kitchen, K. A. 1993. "The land of Punt." In *The Archaeology of Africa: Food, Metals and Towns,* T. Shaw, P. J. J. Sinclair, B. W. Andah, and A. Okpoko, eds. (586–608). London: Routledge.

Kiyaga-Mulindwa, D. 1982. "Social and demographic changes in the Birim Valley, southern Ghana, c. 1450 to c. 1800." *Journal of African History* 23:63–82.

Klee, M., and B. Zach. 1999. "The exploitation of wild and domesticated food plants at settlement mounds in north-east Nigeria (1800 cal. B.C. to today)." In *The Exploitation of Plant Resources in Ancient Africa,* M. van der Veen, ed. (89–100). New York: Kluwer Academic/Plenum Publishers.

Klein, R. G. 1999. *The Human Career.* Chicago: University of Chicago Press.

Klein, R. G., and K. Scott. 1986. "Re-analysis of faunal assemblages from the Haua Fteah and other Late Quaternary archaeological sites in Cyrenaican Libya." *Journal of Archaeological Science* 13:515–42.

Klose, J. 1992–93. "Excavated oriental ceramics from the Cape of Good Hope: 1630–1830." *Transactions of the Oriental Ceramic Society* 57:69–81.

Kopytoff, I. 1987. "The internal African frontier: the making of African political culture." In *The African Frontier: The Reproduction of Traditional African Societies,* I. Kopytoff, ed. (3–84). Bloomington: Indiana University Press.

Kraeling, E. G. 1953. *The Brooklyn Museum Aramaic Papyri.* New Haven: Yale Unversity Press.

Kratz, E. 1989. "Islam in Indonesia." In *Islam,* P. Clarke, ed. (119–49). London: Routledge.

Krzyzaniak, L. 1991. "Early farming in the middle Nile basin recent discoveries at Kadero (central Sudan)." *Antiquity* 65:515–32.

Krzyzkowska, O. 1984. "Ivory from hippopotamus tusk in the Aegean Bronze Age." *Antiquity* 58:123–25.

Kubiak, W. B. 1987. *Al-Fustat: Its Foundation and Early Development.* Cairo: American University in Cairo Press.

Kuhlmann, K. P. 2002. "The 'Oasis Bypath' or the issue of desert trade in Pharaonic times." *Africa Praehistorica* 14:125–70.

Kuper, R. 2001. "By donkey train to Kufra?—How Mr Meri went west." *Antiquity* 75:801–2.

Kusimba, C. M. 1996. "Archaeology in African museums." *African Archaeological Review* 13:165–70.

———. 1999. *The Rise and Fall of Swahili States*. Walnut Creek: AltaMira Press.

Kusimba, C. M., and D. Killick. 2003. "Ironworking on the Swahili Coast of Kenya." In *East African Archaeology: Foragers, Potters, Smiths and Traders*, C. M Kusimba and S. B. Kusimba, eds. (99–116). Philadelphia: University of Pennsylvania Press.

Kusimba, C. M., and S. B. Kusimba. 2000. "Hinterlands and cities: archaeological investigations of economy and trade in Tsavo, southeastern Kenya." *Nyame Akuma* 54:13–24.

Lambourn, E. 1999. "The decoration of Fakhr-al-Din Mosque in Mogadishu and other pieces of Gujarati marble carving on the East African coast." *Azania* 34:61–86.

Lane, P. J. 1993. "Tongwe Fort." *Azania* 28:133–41.

———. 2001. "Introduction to special section on African archaeology today." *Antiquity* 75:793–96.

Lanfranchi, R., and B. Clist, eds. 1990. *Aux Origines de l'Afrique Centrale*. Libreville: Centres Culturels Français d'Afrique Centrale.

Larguèche, A. 2001. "The city and the sea: evolving forms of Mediterranean cosmopolitanism in Tunis, 1700–1881." In *North Africa, Islam and the Mediterranean World: From the Almoravids to the Algerian War*, J. Clancy-Smith, ed. (117–28). London: Frank Cass.

Lavachery, P. 2001. "The Holocene archaeological sequence of Shum Laka Rock Shelter (Grassfields, western Cameroon)." *African Archaeological Review* 18:213–48.

LaViolette, A. 2000. "Swahili archaeology on Pemba Island, Tanzania: Pujini, Bandari ya Faraji and Chwaka, 1997–1998." *Nyame Akuma* 53:50–63.

Law, R. C. C. 1967. "The Garamantes and trans-Saharan enterprise in Classical times." *Journal of African History* 8:181–200.

———. 1978. "North Africa in the period of Phoenician and Greek colonization, c. 800 to 323 B.C." In *The Cambridge History of Africa, Vol. 2 c. 500 B.C.–A.D. 1050*, J. D. Fage, ed. (87–147). Cambridge: Cambridge University Press.

———. 1980. *The Horse in West African History: The Role of the Horse in the Societies of Pre-Colonial West Africa*. Oxford: Oxford University Press.

———. 2000. "Ouidah: A pre-colonial urban centre in coastal West Africa 1727–1892." In *Africa's Urban Past*, D. M. Anderson and R. Rathbone, eds. (85–97). Oxford: James Currey.

Lawrence, A. W. 1963. *Trade Castles and Forts in West Africa*. London: Jonathan Cape.

Lefkowitz, M., and G. M. Rogers, eds. 1996. *Black Athena Revisited*. Chapel Hill: University of North Carolina Press.

Leighton, R. 1999. *Sicily before History*. London: Duckworth.

Lenoble, P., and N. D. M. Sharif. 1992. "Barbarians at the gates? The royal mounds of El Hobagi and the end of Meroë." *Antiquity* 66:626–35.

REFERENCES

Lepsius, C. R. 1848–59. *Denkmäler aus Agypten und Aethiopien.* Berlin.
Levtzion, N. 1973. *Ancient Ghana and Mali.* London: Methuen.
————. 1977. "The western Maghrib and Sudan." In *The Cambridge History of Africa Vol. 3 c. 1050–c. 1600,* R. Oliver, ed. (331–462). Cambridge: Cambridge University Press.
————. 1978. "The Sahara and the Sudan from the Arab conquest of the Maghrib to the rise of the Almoravids." In *The Cambridge History of Africa Vol. 2 c. 500 B.C.–A.D. 1050,* J. D. Fage, ed. (637–84). Cambridge: Cambridge University Press.
————. 1985. "The early states of the western Sudan to 1500." In *History of West Africa, Volume 1,* J. Ajayi and M. Crowder, eds. (129–66). Harlow: Longmans.
Levtzion, N., and J. F. P. Hopkins. 2000. *Corpus of Early Arabic Sources for West African History.* Princeton: Markus Wiener.
Lewis-Williams, J. D. 2002. *The Mind in the Cave.* London: Thames and Hudson.
Lewthwaite, J. 1989. "Isolating the residuals: The Mesolithic basis of man-animal relationships in the Mediterranean islands." In *The Mesolithic in Europe,* C. Bonsall, ed. (541–55). Edinburgh: John Donald.
Lhote, H. 1951. "Sur l'emplacement de la ville de Tadmekka, antique capitale des Berberes soudanais." *Notes Africaines* 51:65–69.
L'Hour, M., L. Long, and E. Reith. 1989. *Le Mauritius: La Mémoire Engloutée.* Paris: Casterman.
Lihoreau, M. 1993. *Djorf Torba: Nécropole Saharienne Antéislamique.* Paris: Karthala.
Liverani, M. 2000a. "The Garamantes: a fresh approach." *Libyan Studies* 31:17–28.
————. 2000b. "Looking for the southern frontier of the Garamantes." *Sahara* 12:31–44.
Lizé, P. 1984. "Wreck of the pirate ship *Speaker* on Mauritius." *International Journal of Nautical Archaeology and Underwater Exploration* 13:121–32.
Loubser, J. N. H. 1991. "The ethnoarchaeology of Venda-speakers in South Africa." *Navorsinge van die Nasionale Museum (Bloemfontein)* 7:146–464.
————. 1993. "Ndondonwane: the significance of features and finds from a ninth-century site on the lower Thukela River, Natal." *Natal Museum Journal of Humanities* 5:109–51.
Lovejoy, P. E. 1986. *Salt of the Desert Sun: A History of Salt Production and Trade in the Central Sudan.* Cambridge: Cambridge University Press.
————. 2000. *Transformations in Slavery: A History of Slavery in Africa.* Cambridge: Cambridge University Press.
Lubell, D., P. Sheppard, and A. Gilman. 1992. "The Maghreb: 20,000–4000 B.P." In *Chronologies in Old World Archaeology, Volume 2,* R. W. Ehrich, ed. (257–67). Chicago: University of Chicago Press.
Mabulla, A. Z. P. 2000. "Strategy for cultural heritage management (CHM) in Africa: a case study." *African Archaeological Review* 17:211–34.
MacDonald, K. C. 1995. "Analysis of the mammalian, avian and reptilian remains." In *Excavations at Jenné-jeno, Hambarketolo, and Kaniana (Inland*

Niger Delta, Mali), the 1981 Season, S. K. McIntosh, ed. (291–318). Berkeley: University of California Press.

———. 1996. "The Windé Koroji complex: evidence for the peopling of the eastern Inland Niger Delta (2100–500 B.C.)." *Préhistoire Anthropologie Méditerranéenes* 5:147–65.

———. 1997. "Kouronkorokalé revisited: the *Pays Mande* and the West African microlithic technocomplex." *African Archaeological Review* 14:161–200.

———. 1998a. "Archaeology, language and the peopling of West Africa: a consideration of the evidence." In *Archaeology and Language II: Archaeological Data and Linguistic Hypotheses*, R. Blench and M. Spriggs, eds. (33–66). London: Routledge.

———. 1998b. "Before the Empire of Ghana: pastoralism and the origins of complexity in the Sahel." In *Transformations in Africa: Essays on Africa's Later Past*, G. Connah, ed. (71–103). Leicester: Leicester University Press.

———. 1999a. "Invisible pastoralists: an inquiry into the origins of nomadic pastoralism in the West African Sahel." In *The Prehistory of Food*, C. Gosden and J. Hather, eds. (333–49). London: Routledge.

———. 1999b. "More forgotten tells of Mali: an archaeologist's journey from here to Timbuktu." *Archaeology International* 1:40–42.

———. 2003. "Cheikh Anta Diop and Ancient Egypt in Africa." In *Ancient Egypt in Africa*, D. O'Connor and D. A. M. Reid, eds. (93–106). London: UCL Press.

MacDonald, K. C., and D. N. Edwards. 1993. "Chickens in Africa: the importance of Qasr Ibrim." *Antiquity* 67:584–90.

MacDonald, K. C., and R. H. MacDonald. 2000. "The origins and development of domesticated animals in arid West Africa." In The *Origins and Development of African Livestock: Archaeology, Genetics, Linguistics and Ethnography*, R. M. Blench and K. C. MacDonald, eds. (127–62). London: UCL Press.

MacDonald, K. C., D. Morgan, and F. Handley. 2002–03. "Cane River: the archaeology of 'free people of colour' in colonial Louisiana." *Archaeology International* 6:52–55.

MacDonald, K. C., R. Vernet, D. Fuller, and J. Woodhouse. 2003. "New light on the Tichitt Tradition: a preliminary report on survey and excavation at Dhar Néma. 2003." In *Researching Africa's Past: New Contributions from British Archaeologists*, P. J. Mitchell, A. Haour, and J. H. Hobart, eds. (73–80). Oxford: Oxford University School of Archaeology.

MacEachern, S. 1993. "Selling the iron for their shackles: Wandala-*Montagnard* interactions in northern Cameroon." *Journal of African History* 34:247–70.

———. 2000. "Genes, tribes and African history." *Current Anthropology* 41:357–84.

———. 2001. "Cultural resource management and Africanist archaeology." *Antiquity* 75:866–71.

MacEachern, S., C. Bourges, and M. Reeves. 2001. "Early horse remains from northern Cameroon." *Antiquity* 75:62–67.

MacGaffey, W. 2002. "Twins, simbi spirits and lwas in Kongo and Haiti." In *Central Africans and Cultural Transformations in the American Diaspora*, L. M. Heywood, ed. (211–26). Cambridge: Cambridge University Press.

MacGinty, G. 1983. "The influence of the desert fathers on early Irish monasticism." *Monastic Studies* 14:85–91.

Mackintosh-Smith, T. 2002. *The Travels of Ibn Battuta*. London: Macmillan.

MacLean, M. R., and T. A. Insoll. 2003. "Archaeology, luxury and the exotic: examples from Islamic Gao (Mali) and Bahrain." *World Archaeology* 34:558–70.

Mack, J. 1986. *Madagascar: Island of the Ancestors*. London: British Museum.

———. 2000. *Africa: Arts and Cultures*. London: British Museum.

Maggs, T. M. O'C. 1976. *Iron Age Communities of the Southern Highveld*. Pietermaritzburg: Natal Museum.

———. 1982. "Mgoduyanuka: Terminal Iron Age settlement in the Natal grassland." *Annals of the Natal Museum* 25:85–113.

———. 1984. "The Great Galleon *São João*: remains from a mid-sixteenth century wreck on the Natal South Coast." *Annals of the Natal Museum* 26:173–86.

Maggs, T. M. O'C., and D. Miller. 1995. "Sandstone crucibles from Mhlopeni, KwaZulu-Natal: evidence of precolonial brassworking." *Natal Museum Journal of Humanities* 7:1–16.

Magnavita, S. 2003. "The beads of Kissi, Burkina Faso." *Journal of African Archaeology* 1:127–38.

Manning, P. 1990. *Slavery and African Life Occidental, Oriental and African Slave Trades*. Cambridge: Cambridge University Press.

Manzi, G. 2001. "The earliest diffusion of the genus *Homo* toward Asia and Europe: a brief overview." In *Humanity from African Naissance to Coming Millennia*, P. V. Tobias, M. A. Raath, J. Moggi-Cecchi, and G. A. Doyle, eds. (117–24). Firenze: University of Firenze Press.

Manzo, A. 1999. *Echanges et Contacts le Long du Nil et de la Mer Rouge dans L'Epoque Protohistorique (IIIe et II Millénaires avant J.-C.): Une synthèse Préliminaire*. Oxford: British Archaeological Reports International Series S782.

Mapunda, B. 1995. "An Archaeological View of the History and Variation of Ironworking in Southwestern Tanzania." Ph.D. diss., University of Florida, Gainesville.

———. 1997. "Patching up evidence for ironworking in the Horn." *African Archaeological Review* 14:107–24.

Marinatos, S. 1974. *Excavations at Thera VI*. Athens: University of Athens.

Markell, A. B. 1993. "Building on the past: the architecture and archaeology of Vergelegen." *South African Archaeological Society Goodwin Series* 7:71–83.

Markell, A. B., M. Hall, and C. Schrire. 1995. "The historical archaeology of Vergelegen, an early farmstead at the Cape of Good Hope." *Historical Archaeology* 29:10–34.

Markoe, G. E. 2000. *The Phoenicians*. London: Thames and Hudson.

Marks, A. E. 1987. "Terminal Pleistocene and Holocene hunters and gatherers in the eastern Sudan." *African Archaeological Review* 5:79–92.

Markus, R. 1990. *The End of Ancient Christianity*. Cambridge: Cambridge University Press.

Marshall, F. 1990. "Origins of specialized pastoral production in East Africa." *American Anthropologist* 92:873–94.

———. 2000. "The origins and spread of domestic animals in East Africa." In *The Origins and Development of African Livestock: Archaeology, Genetics, Linguistics and Ethnography*, R. M. Blench and K. C. MacDonald, eds. (191–221). London: UCL Press.

Marshall, F., and E. Hildebrand. 2002. "Cattle before crops: the beginnings of food production in Africa." *Journal of World Prehistory* 16:99–143.

Marshall, F., K. Stewart, and J. Barthelme. 1984. "Early domestic stock at Dongodien in northern Kenya." *Azania* 19:120–27.

Martin del Molino, A. 1989. "Prehistoria de Guinea Ecuatorial." *Africa 2000* 4:4–21.

Masonen, P. 1995. "Conquest and authority: Ghana and the Almoravids in West African historiography." *Saharan Studies Newsletter* 3:4–9.

Mathew, G. 1966. "The Christian background." In *The Cambridge Medieval History. Volume IV The Byzantine Empire. Part I: Byzantium and its Neighbours*, J. M. Hussey, ed. (43–60). Cambridge: Cambridge University Press.

Matthews, R. 2002. "Zebu: harbingers of doom in Bronze Age western Asia?" *Antiquity* 76:438–46.

Mattingly, D. J. 1995. *Tripolitania*. London: Batsford.

———. ed. 2003. *The Archaeology of Fazzan: Volume 1, Synthesis*. London: Society for Libyan Studies.

Mauny, R. 1978. "Trans-Saharan contacts and the Iron Age in West Africa." In *The Cambridge History of Africa Vol. 2, c. 500 B.C.–A.D. 1050*, J. D. Fage, ed. (272–341). Cambridge: Cambridge University Press.

Mazrui, A. 1986. *The Africans: A Triple Heritage*. London: BBC Publications.

Mbeki, T. 1998. *Africa: The Time Has Come*. Cape Town: Government Printer.

Mbida, C., W. van Neer, H. Doutrelepont, and L. Vrydaghs. 2000. "Evidence for banana cultivation and animal husbandry during the first millennium B.C. in the forest of southern Cameroon." *Journal of Archaeological Science* 27:152–62.

McCall, D. F. 1998. "The Afroasiatic language phylum: African in origin, or Asian?" *Current Anthropology* 39:139–44.

McDonald, M. M. A. 1998. "Early African pastoralism: view from Dakhleh Oasis (south central Egypt)." *Journal of Anthropological Archaeology* 17:124–42.

McIntosh, R. J. 1996a. "Just say shame: excising the rot of cultural genocide." In *Plundering Africa's Past*, P. R. Schmidt and R. J. McIntosh, eds. (45–62). London: James Currey.

———. 1996b. "Research strategies, topics and African heritage." *African Archaeological Review* 13:11–15.

———. 1998. *The Peoples of the Middle Niger*. Oxford: Blackwells.

McIntosh, R. J., and S. K. McIntosh. 1981. "The Inland Niger Delta before the empire of Mali: evidence from Jenné-jeno." *Journal of African History* 22:1–22.

McIntosh, S. K. 1981. "A reconsideration of Wangara/Palolus, Island of Gold." *Journal of African History* 22:145–58.

———. ed. 1995. *Excavations at Jenné-jeno, Hambarketolo and Kaniana (Inland Niger Delta, Mali). The 1981 Season.* Berkeley: University of California Press.

———. ed. 1999a. *Beyond Chiefdoms: Pathways to Complexity in Africa.* Cambridge: Cambridge University Press.

———. 1999b. "Pathways to complexity: an African perspective." In *Beyond Chiefdoms: Pathways to Complexity in Africa*, S. K. McIntosh, ed. (1–30). Cambridge: Cambridge University Press.

———. 1999c. "Modeling political organization in large-scale settlement clusters: a case study from the Inland Niger Delta." In *Beyond Chiefdoms: Pathways to Complexity in Africa*, S. K. McIntosh, ed. (66–79). Cambridge: Cambridge University Press.

———. 2001. "Tools for understanding transformation and continuity in Senegambian society: 1500–1900." In *West Africa during the Atlantic Slave Trade: Archaeological Perspectives*, C. R. DeCorse, ed. (14–37). Leicester: Leicester University Press.

McIntosh, S. K., and H. Bocoum. 2000. "New perspectives on Sincu Bara, a first millennium site in the Senegal valley." *African Archaeological Review* 17:1–44.

McIntosh, S. K., D. Gallagher, and R. J. McIntosh. 2003. "Tobacco pipes from excavations at the Museum Site, Jenne, Mali." *Journal of African Archaeology* 1:171–200.

McIntosh, S. K., and R. J. McIntosh. 1980. *Prehistoric Investigations in the Region of Jenné, Mali.* Oxford: British Archaeological Reports International Series S89.

———. 1986a. "Recent archaeological research and dates from West Africa." *Journal of African History* 27:413–42.

———. 1986b. "Archaeological reconnaissance in the region of Timbuktu." *National Geographic Research* 2:302–19.

———. 1988. "From stone to metal: new perspectives on the later prehistory of West Africa." *Journal of World Prehistory* 2:89–133.

McIntosh, S. K., R. J. McIntosh, and H. Bocoum. 1992. "The Middle Senegal Valley Project: preliminary results from the 1990–91 field season." *Nyame Akuma* 38:47–60.

McKee, L. W. 1992. "The ideals and realities behind the design and use of 19th century Virginia slave cabins." In *The Art and Mystery of Historical Archaeology: Essays in Honour of Jim Deetz*, A. Yentsch and M. C. Beaudry, eds. (195–213). Boca Raton: CRC Press.

Meeks, D. 2003. "Locating Punt." In *Mysterious Lands*, D. O'Connor and S. Quirke, eds. (53–80). London: UCL Press.

Meillassoux, C. 1991. *The Anthropology of Slavery.* Chicago: University of Chicago Press.

Mercader, J., S. Rovira, and P. Gómez-Ramos. 2000. "Shared technologies: forager-farmer interaction and ancient iron metallurgy in the Ituri rainforest, Democratic Republic of Congo." *Azania* 35:107–22.

Merrick, H. V., and F. H. Brown. 1984. "Obsidian sources and patterns of source utilization in Kenya and northern Tanzania: some initial findings." *African Archaeological Review* 2:129–52.

Messier, R. A. 1974. "The Almoravids: West African gold and the gold currency of the Mediterranean Basin." *Journal of the Economic and Social History of the Orient* 17:31–47.

————. 2001. "Re-thinking the Almoravids, re-thinking Ibn Khaldun." In *North Africa, Islam and the Mediterranean World: From the Almoravids to the Algerian War*, J. Clancy-Smith, ed. (59–80). London: Frank Cass.

Meyer, A. 1998. *The Archaeological Sites of Greefswald*. Pretoria: University of Pretoria Press.

Meyer, A., and V. Esterhuizen. 1994. "Skerwe uit die verlede: handel tussen Mapungubwe en China." *South African Journal of Ethnology* 17:103–8.

Meyer, C., J. Markley Todd, and C. W. Beck. 1993. "From Zanzibar to Zagros: a copal pendant from Eshnunna." *Near Eastern Studies* 50:289–99.

Mguni, S. 2002. "The Rock Art Research Institute, School of Geography, Archaeology and Environmental Studies, University of the Witwatersrand." *Before Farming* 1:248–52.

Michalowski, K. 1967. *Faras: Die Kathedrale aus dem Wustensand*. Zürich: Benziger.

Midant-Reynes, B. 2000. "The Naqada Period (*c.* 4000–3200 B.C.)." In *The Oxford History of Ancient Egypt*, I. Shaw, ed. (44–60). Oxford: Oxford University Press.

Mies, S., and I. Kopytoff, eds. 1977. *Slavery in Africa: Historical and Anthropological Perspectives*. Madison: University of Wisconsin Press.

Miller, J. A. 2001. "Trading through Islam: the interconnections of Sijilmasa, Ghana and the Almoravid movement." In *North Africa, Islam and the Mediterranean World: From the Almoravids to the Algerian War*, J. Clancy-Smith, ed. (29–58). London: Frank Cass.

Miller, J. C. 2002. "Central Africa during the era of the slave trade, *c.* 1490s–1850s." In *Central Africans and Cultural Transformations in the American Diaspora*, L. M. Heywood, ed. (21–70). Cambridge: Cambridge University Press.

Miller, J. N. 1969. *The Spice Trade of the Roman Empire: 29 B.C. to A.D. 641*. Oxford: Clarendon Press.

Milliken, S. 2002. "Out of Africa and out of Asia? New light on early hominid dispersals." *The Review of Archaeology* 23:21–35.

Mintz, S. W., and R. Price. 1976. *An Anthropological Approach to the Afro-American Past: A Caribbean Perspective*. Philadelphia: Institute for the Study of Human Issues.

Miracle, M. P. 1965. "The introduction and spread of maize in Africa." *Journal of African History* 6:39–55.

Mitchell, P. J. 1996. "Prehistoric exchange and interaction in southeastern southern Africa: marine shells and ostrich eggshell." *African Archaeological Review* 13:35–76.

———. 1999. "Pressure-flaked points in Lesotho: dating, distribution and diversity." *South African Archaeological Bulletin* 54:90–96.

———. 2002a. *The Archaeology of Southern Africa*. Cambridge: Cambridge University Press.

———. 2002b. "Catalogue of Stone Age Artefacts from Southern Africa in The British Museum." *The British Museum Occasional Papers* 108:1–232.

———. 2003. "The archaeological study of epidemic and infectious disease." *World Archaeology* 35:171–79.

Mongin, P., and M. Plouzeau. 1984. "Guinea-fowl." In *Evolution of Domesticated Animals*, I. L. Mason, ed. (322–25). London: Longman.

Monod, T. 1940. "Nouvelles remarques sur Teghaza (Sahara Occidentale)." *Bulletin de l'Institut Français d'Afrique Noire* 2:248–54.

———. 1969. "Le 'Ma'den Ijâfen': une épave caravanière ancienne dans la Majâbat Al-Koubrâ." *Actes du Ier Colloque International d'Archéologie Africaine, 1966* (286–320). Fort Lamy.

———, ed. 1975. *Pastoralism in Tropical Africa*. London: International African Institute.

Monroe, J. C. 2002. "The archaeology of pre-colonial diplomacy: political legitimacy and the development of a West African kingdom." (Abstract). *Nyame Akuma* 57:63.

Morkot, R. 2001. "Egypt and Nubia." In *Empires: Perspectives from Archaeology and History*, S. E. Alcock, T. N. D'Altroy, K. D. Morrison, and C. M. Sinopoli, eds. (227–51). Cambridge: Cambridge University Press.

Mortelmans, G., and R. Monteyne. 1962. "La grotte peinte de Mbafu, témoinage iconographique de la première évangélisation du Bas-Congo." *Actes du IVème Congrès Panafricain de Préhistoire et de l'Etude du Quaternaire* (457–86). Tervuren: Musée Royal de l'Afrique Centrale.

Morwood, M. J., F. Aziz, Nasruddin, D. R. Hobbs, P. O'Sullivan, and A. Raza. 1999. "Archaeological and palaeontological research in central Flores, east Indonesia: results of fieldwork 1997–98." *Antiquity* 73:273–86.

Mudimbe, V. Y. 1988. *The Invention of Africa: Gnosis, Philosophy, and the Order of Knowledge*. Bloomington: Indiana University Press.

———. 1994. *The Idea of Africa*. Bloomington: Indiana University Press.

Muhammed, I. M. 1993. "Iron technology in the middle Sahel/Savanna: with emphasis on central Darfur." In *The Archaeology of Africa: Food, Metals and Towns*, T. Shaw, P. J. J. Sinclair, B. W. Andah, and A. Okpoko, eds. (459–67). London: Routledge.

Munro-Hay, S. C. 1991. *Aksum: An African Civilisation of Late Antiquity*. Edinburgh: Edinburgh University Press.

———. 1993. "State development and urbanism in Ethiopia." In *The Archaeology of Africa: Food, Metals and Towns*, T. Shaw, P. J. J. Sinclair, B. W. Andah, and A. Okpoko, eds. (609–21). London: Routledge.

————. 2002. *Ethiopia: The Unknown Land. A Cultural and Historical Guide.* London: I. B. Tauris Publishers.

Munro-Hay, S. C., and B. Juel-Jensen. 1995. *Aksumite Coinage.* London: Spink.

Munson, P. J. 1980. "Archaeology and the prehistoric origins of the Ghana empire." *Journal of African History* 21:457–66.

Munson, P. J., and C. A. Munson. 1969. "Nouveaux chars à boeufs rupestres du Dhar Tichitt (Mauritanie)." *Notes Africaines* 122:62–63.

Mutoro, H. W. 1998. "Precolonial trading systems of the African interior." In *Transformations in Africa: Essays on Africa's Later Past*, G. Connah, ed. (186–203). Leicester: Leicester University Press.

Muzzolini, A. 1986. *L'Art Rupestre Préhistorique des Massifs Centraux Sahariens.* Oxford: British Archaeological Reports International Series S318.

————. 1989. "La 'néolithisation' du Nord de l'Afrique et ses causes." In *Néolithisations: Proche et Moyen Orient, Méditerranée Orientale, Nord de l'Afrique, Europe Méridionale, Chine, Amérique du Sud*, O. Aurenche and J. Cauvin, eds. (145–86). Oxford: British Archaeological Reports International Series S516.

————. 1993. "The emergence of a food-producing economy in the Sahara." In *Africa: Archaeology of Africa: Food, Metals and Towns*, T. Shaw, P. J. J. Sinclair, B. W. Andah, and A. Okpoko, eds. (227–39). London: Routledge.

————. 2000. "Livestock in Saharan rock art." In *The Origins and Development of African Livestock: Archaeology, Genetics, Linguistics and Ethnography*, R. M. Blench and K. C. MacDonald, eds. (87–110). London: UCL Press.

Nachtigal, G. 1967: *Sahara und Sudan: Ergebnisse Sechsjähriger Reisen in Afrika I.* Graz: Akademische Druck-und Verlagsanstalt.

Naumkin, V. V., and A. V. Sedov. 1993. "Socotra." *Topoi* 3(2):569–623.

Ndong, A. A. 2002. "Synthèse des données archéologiques récentes sur le peuplement à l'Holocène de la Réserve de Faune de la Lopé, Gabon." *L'Anthropologie* 106:135–58.

Ndoro, W. 1994. "The preservation and presentation of Great Zimbabwe." *Antiquity* 68:616–23.

Neumann, K. 1989. "Holocene vegetation of the eastern Sahara: charcoal from prehistoric sites." *African Archaeological Review* 7:97–116.

————. 1999. "Early plant food production in the West African Sahel: new evidence." In *The Exploitation of Plant Resources in Ancient Africa*, M. van der Veen, ed. (81–88). New York: Kluwer Academic/Plenum Publishers.

Newby, J. E. 1984. "Large mammals." In *The Sahara*, L. Cloudsley-Thompson, ed. (277–90). Oxford: Pergamon Press.

Newitt, M. D. D. 2003. "Madagascar and the African Diaspora." In *The African Diaspora in the Indian Ocean*, S. de S. Jayasuriya and R. Pankhurst, eds. (81–98). Trenton: Africa World Press.

Newitt, M. D. D., and P. S. Garlake. 1967. "The 'aringa' at Massangano." *Journal of African History* 8:133–56.

Nibbi, A. 1993. "A geographical note on the Libyans so-called." *Discussions in Egyptology* 25:43–62.

Noël-Hume, I. 1962. "An Indian ware of the colonial period." *Quarterly Bulletin of the Archaeological Society of Virginia* 17:2–14.

Nogwaza, T. 1994. "Early Iron Age pottery from Canasta Place, East London district." *Southern African Field Archaeology* 3:103–6.

North, J. A. 2003. "Attributing colour to the Ancient Egyptians: reflections on Black Athena." In *Ancient Egypt in Africa*, D. O'Connor and D. A. M. Reid, eds. (31–38). London: UCL Press.

Northrup, D. 2002. *Africa's Discovery of Europe 1450–1850*. Oxford: Oxford University Press.

Nurse, D. 1983. "A linguistic reconsideration of Swahili origins." *Azania* 18:127–50.

Nurse, D., and T. Spear. 1985. *The Swahili: Reconstructing the History and Language of an African Society, 800–1500*. Philadelphia: Pennsylvania University Press.

Nzewunwa, N. 1980. *The Niger Delta: Aspects of its Prehistoric Economy and Culture*. Oxford: British Archaeological Reports International Series S75.

O'Connor, D. 1987. "The location of Irem." *Journal of Egyptian Archaeology* 73:99–136.

———. 1990. "Egyptology and archaeology: an African perspective." In *A History of African Archaeology*, P. T. Robertshaw, ed. (236–51). London: Routledge.

———. 1993a. "Urbanism in Bronze Age Egypt and northeast Africa." In *Archaeology of Africa: Food, Metals and Towns*, T. Shaw, P. J. J. Sinclair, B. W. Andah, and A. Okpoko, eds. (570–86). London: Routledge.

———. 1993b. *Ancient Nubia: Egypt's Rival in Africa*. Philadelphia: University of Pennsylvania Press.

O'Connor, D., and D. A. M. Reid, eds. 2003. *Ancient Egypt in Africa*. London: UCL Press.

Ogedengbe, A. Y. 1998. "An historical archaeology of Zungeru colonial settlement: a case study." In *Historical Archaeology in Nigeria*, K. W. Wesler, ed. (273–310). Trenton: Africa World Press.

Ohadike, D. C. 1981. "The influenza pandemic of 1918–19 and the spread of cassava cultivation in the Lower Niger." *Journal of African History* 22:379–91.

Okafor, E. E. 1993. "New evidence on early iron-smelting from southeastern Nigeria." In *Archaeology of Africa: Food, Metals and Towns*, T. Shaw, P. J. J. Sinclair, B. W. Andah, and A. Okpoko, eds. (432–48). London: Routledge.

Oliver, R. 1966. "The problem of the Bantu expansion." *Journal of African History* 7:361–76.

Oliver, R., and A. Atmoore. 2001. *Medieval Africa 1250–1800*. Cambridge: Cambridge University Press.

Onrubia Pintado, J. 1987. "Les cultures préhistoriques des Iles Canaries: état de la question." *L'Anthropologie* 91:653–78.

Orser, C. E. 1988. *The Material Basis of the Postbellum Tenant Plantation: Historical Archaeology in the South Carolina Piedmont*. Athens: University of Georgia Press.

———. 1994a. "The archaeology of African-American slave religion in the antebellum South." *Cambridge Archaeological Journal* 4:33–45.

———. 1994b. "Toward a global historical archaeology: an example from Brazil." *Historical Archaeology* 28:5–22.

———. 1996. *A Historical Archaeology of the Modern World*. New York: Plenum Press.

———. 1998. "The archaeology of the African Diaspora." *Annual Review of Anthropology* 27:63–82.

Orser, C. E., and P. P. A. Funari. 2001. "Archaeology and slave resistance and rebellion." *World Archaeology* 33:61–72.

Otto, J. S. 1984. *Cannon's Point Plantation, 1794–1860: Living Conditions and Status Patterns in the Old South*. Orlando: Academic Press.

Ouzman, S., and J. N. H. Loubser. 2000. "Art of the Apocalypse." *Discovering Archaeology* November–December: 39–42.

Ozanne, P. D. 1962. "Notes on the early historic archaeology of Ghana." *Transactions of the Historical Society of Ghana* 6:51–70.

———. 1969. "The diffusion of smoking in West Africa." *Odu* 2:29–42.

———. 1971. "Ghana." In *The African Iron Age*, P. L. Shinnie, ed. (36–65). Oxford: Clarendon Press.

Pagels, E. 1979. *The Gnostic Gospels*. New York: Random House.

Pakenham, T. 1991. *The Scramble for Africa*. London: Weidenfeld and Nicholson.

Pankhurst, R. 2003. "The Ethiopian Diaspora to India: the role of Habshis and Sidis from Medieval times to the end of the eighteenth century." In *The African Diaspora in the Indian Ocean*, S. de S. Jayasuriya and R. Pankhurst, eds. (189–222). Trenton: Africa World Press.

Paribeni, R. 1907. "Ricerche nel luogo dell'antica Adulis." *Monumenti Antichi, Reale Accademia dei Lincei* 18:438–572.

Paris, F. 1996. *Les Sépultures du Sahara Nigérien du Néolithique à l'Islamisation*. Paris: ORSTOM.

Parker Pearson, M. 1997. "Close encounters of the worst kind: Malagasy resistance and colonial disasters in southern Madagascar." *World Archaeology* 28:393–417.

Parker Pearson, M., and K. Godden. 2002. *In Search of the Red Slave: Shipwreck and Captivity in Madagascar*. Stroud: Sutton Publishing.

Peace Parks Foundation. 2004. Website: www.peaceparks.org (accessed 8 September 2004).

Peacock, D. P. S., and V. A. Maxfield. 1997. *Mons Claudianus: Survey and Excavation*. Cairo: Institut Français d'Archéologie Orientale.

Pearson, M. N. 1998. *Port Cities and Intruders: The Swahili Coast, India and Portugal in the Early Modern Era*. Baltimore: John Hopkins University Press.

Peltenburg, E., S. Colledge, P. Croft, A. Jackson, C. McCartney, and M. A. Murray. 2000. "Agro-pastoralist colonization of Cyprus in the 10th millennium B.P.: initial assessments." *Antiquity* 74:844–53.

Perdue, T. 1979. *Slavery and the Evolution of Cherokee Society 1540–1866*. Knoxville: University of Tennessee Press.

Petersen, J. B., D. R. Watters, and D. V. Nicholson. 1999. "Continuity and syncretism in Afro-Caribbean ceramics from the Northern Lesser Antilles." In *African Sites Archaeology in the Caribbean*, J. B. Haviser, ed. (157–95). Princeton: Markus Wiener.

Petit-Maire, N., and J. Risier. 1983. *Sahara ou Sahel? Quaternaire Récent de Bassin de Taoudeni (Mali)*. Paris: CNRS.

Petraglia, M. D., and A. Alsharekh. 2003. "The Middle Palaeolithic of Arabia: implications for modern human origins, behaviour and dispersals." *Antiquity* 77:671–85.

Phaladi, S. 1998. "The organisation of archaeology." In *Ditswa Mmung: The Archaeology of Botswana*, P. J. Lane, D. A. M. Reid, and A. K. Segobye, eds. (233–39). Gaborone: The Botswana Society.

Phillips, J. 1997. "Punt and Aksum: Egypt and the Horn of Africa." *Journal of African History* 38:423–57.

Phillips, J. R. S. 1988. *The Medieval Expansion of Europe*. Oxford: Oxford University Press.

Phillipson, D. W. 1989. "The first South African pastoralists and the Early Iron Age." *Nsi* 6:127–34.

———. 1993a. *African Archaeology*. Cambridge: Cambridge University Press.

———. 1993b. "The antiquity of cultivation and herding in Ethiopia." In *The Archaeology of Africa: Food, Metals and Towns*, T. Shaw, P. J. J. Sinclair, B. W. Andah, and A. Okpoko, eds. (344–57). London: Routledge.

———. 1998. *Ancient Ethiopia*. London: British Museum.

———. ed. 2000. *Archaeology at Aksum, Ethiopia, 1993–7*. London: Society of Antiquaries/Nairobi: British Institute in Eastern Africa.

———. 2001. "Aksum: an African civilisation in its world contexts." *Proceedings of the British Academy* 111:23–59.

———. 2003. "Aksum: an archaeological introduction and guide." *Azania* 39:1–68.

Phillipson, L. 2000. "Aksumite lithic industries." *African Archaeological Review* 17:49–63.

Pichler, W. 1995. "The decoding of the 'Latino-Canarian' inscriptions from Fuerteventura, Canary Islands." *Sahara* 7:116–18.

———. 1996. "The decoding of the Libyco-Berber inscriptions of the Canary Islands." *Sahara* 8:104–7.

Picton, J., and J. Mack. 1989. *African Textiles*. London: British Museum.

Pikirayi, I. 2001. *The Zimbabwe Culture: Origins and Decline of Southern Zambezian States*. Walnut Creek: AltaMira Press.

Piperno, D. R. 1988. *Phytolith Analysis: An Archaeological and Geological Perspective*. London: Academic Press.

Plug, I., and E. Voigt. "Archaeozoological studies of Iron Age communities in southern Africa." *Advances in World Archaeology* 4:189–238.

Politis, G. G. 2002. "South America: in the garden of forking paths." In *Archaeology: The Widening Debate*, B. W. Cunliffe, W. Davies, and A. C. Renfrew, eds. (193–244). Oxford: Oxford University Press.

Porter, R. 1997. *The Greatest Benefit to Mankind: A Medical History of Humanity from Antiquity to the Present*. London: HarperCollins.

Portères, R. 1955. "L'introduction du maïs en Afrique." *Journal d'Agriculture Tropicale et de Botanie Appliquée* 2:221–31.

———. 1962. "Berceaux agricoles primaires sur le continent africain." *Journal of African History* 3:195–210.

Posnansky, M. 1976. "Archaeology and the origins of Akan society." In *Problems in Economic and Social Archaeology*, G. de Sieveking, I. H. Longworth, and K. E. Wilson, eds. (49–59). London: Duckworth.

———. 1984. "Toward an archaeology of the Black Diaspora." *Journal of Black Studies* 15:195–202.

———. 1987. "Prelude to Akan civilization." In *The Golden Stool: Studies of the Asante Center and Periphery*, E. Schildkrout, ed. (14–22). New York: American Museum of Natural History.

Posnansky, M., and A. van Dantzig. 1976. "Fort Ruchaver rediscovered." *Sankofa* 2:7–18.

Poumailloux, P. 2003. "Une carte chinoise de l'Afrique de la fin du XIVème siècle." *Azania* 39:188–90.

Pouwels, R. L. 1987. *Horn and Crescent: Cultural Change and Traditional Islam on the East African Coast, 800–1900*. Cambridge: Cambridge University Press.

Pradines, S. 2003. "Islamization and urbanization on the coast of East Africa: recent excavations at Gedi, Kenya." *Azania* 39:180–82.

PRISM Project Members. 1995. "Middle Pliocene paleoenvironments of the Northern Hemisphere." In *Paleoclimate and Evolution, with Emphasis on Human Origins*, E. S. Vrba, G. M. Denton, T. C. Partridge, and L. M. Burkle, eds. (197–212). New Haven: Yale University Press.

Pulsipher, L. M. 1990. "They have Saturdays and Sundays to feed themselves: slave gardens in the Caribbean." *Expedition* 35(2):24–33.

Purseglove, J. W. 1969. *Tropical Crops: Dicotyledons*. London: Longmans.

———. 1976. "The origins and migration of crops in tropical Africa." In *Origins of African Plant Domestication*, J. R. Harlan, M. J. De Wet, and A. B. L. Stemler, eds. (291–309). The Hague: Mouton.

Pwiti, G., and G. Mvenge. 1996. "Archaeologists, tourists and rainmakers: problems in the management of rock art sites in Zimbabwe: a case study of Domboshava national monument." In *Aspects of African Archaeology*, G. Pwiti and R. Soper, eds. (817–24). Harare: University of Zimbabwe Press.

Pwiti, G., and W. Ndoro. 1999. "The legacy of colonialism: perceptions of the cultural heritage in southern Africa, with special reference to Zimbabwe." *African Archaeological Review* 16:143–54.

Radimilahy, C. 1998. *Mahilaka: An Archaeological Investigation of an Early Town in Northwestern Madagascar*. Uppsala: University of Uppsala Press.

Rakotozafy, L. M. A. 1996. "Etude de la constitution du régime alimentaire des habitants du site de Mahilaka du XIè au XIVè Siècle à partir des produits de fouilles archéologiques." Thèse de Doctorat de 3è Cycle des Sciences Naturelles, University of Antananarivo.

Randall-MacIver, D. 1906. *Medieval Rhodesia*. London: Macmillan.

Rathbone, R. 1996. "Resistance to enslavement in West Africa." In *Slave Traders, 1500–1800: Globalization of Forced Labour*, P. Manning, ed. (183–94). Aldershot: Variorum.

Raven, S. 1993. *Rome in Africa*. London: Routledge.

Ray, H. P. 2003. *The Archaeology of Seafaring in Ancient South Asia*. Cambridge: Cambridge University Press.

Reader, J. 1998. *Africa: A Biography of the Continent*. London: Penguin.

Redman, C. 1986. *Qsar es Seghir: An Archaeological View of Medieval Life*. New York: Academic Press.

Reese, D. S. 1991. "The trade in Indo-Pacific shells into the Mediterranean basin and Europe." *Oxford Journal of Archaeology* 10:159–96.

Reichmuth, S. 2000. "Islamic education and scholarship in sub-Saharan Africa." In *The History of Islam in Africa*, N. Levtzion and R. Pouwels, eds. (419–40). Oxford: James Currey.

Reid, D. A. M. 1996. "Ntusi and the development of social complexity in southern Uganda." In *Aspects of African Archaeology*, G. Pwiti and R. Soper, eds. (621–28). Harare: University of Zimbabwe Press.

Reid, D. A. M., P. Lane, A. K. Segobye, L. Borjeson, N. Mathibidi, and P. Sekgarametso. 1997. "Tswana architecture and responses to colonialism." *World Archaeology* 28:370–92.

Reid, D. A. M., and A. K. Segobye. 2000. "An ivory cache from Botswana." *Antiquity* 74:326–31.

Reitz, E. J., T. Gibbs, and T. Rathbun. 1985. "Archaeological evidence for subsistence on coastal plantations." In *The Archaeology of Slavery and Plantation Life*, T. A. Singleton, ed. (163–91). Orlando: Academic Press.

Renfrew, A. C. 1973. *Before Civilization*. Harmondsworth: Penguin.

———. 1975. "Trade as action at a distance: questions of integration and communication." In *Ancient Civilization and Trade*, J. Sabloff and C. Lamberg-Karlovsky, eds. (3–59). Albuquerque: University of New Mexico Press.

Renfrew, A. C., and J. F. Cherry, J. F., eds. 1986. *Peer Polity Interaction and Socio-Political Change*. Cambridge: Cambridge University Press.

Rey, T. 2002. "Kongolese Catholic influences on Haitian popular Catholicism: a sociohistorical explanation." In *Central Africans and Cultural Transformations in the American Diaspora*, L. M. Heywood, ed. (265–85). Cambridge: Cambridge University Press.

Reygasse, M. 1950. *Monuments Funéraires Préislamiques de l'Afrique du Nord*. Paris: Arts et Métiers Graphiques.

Richardson, S. 2000. "Libya domestica: Libyan trade and society on the eve of the invasions of Egypt." *Journal of the American Research Centre in Egypt* 36:149–64.

Rightmire, G. P. 2001. "Morphological diversity in Middle Pleistocene *Homo*." In *Humanity from African Naissance to Coming Millennia*, P. V. Tobias, M. A. Raath, J. Moggi-Cecchi, and G. A. Doyle, eds. (135–40). Firenze: University of Firenze Press.

Robert, D., S. Robert, and J. Devisse, eds. 1970. *Tegdaoust: Recherches sur Aoudaghost, Vol. I.* Paris: Arts et Métiers Graphiques.

Robertshaw, P. T. 1987. "Prehistory in the Upper Nile Basin." *Journal of African History* 28:177–89.

———. 1993. "The beginnings of food production in southwestern Kenya." In *The Archaeology of Africa: Food, Metals and Towns,* T. Shaw, P. J. J. Sinclair, B. W. Andah, and A. Okpoko, eds. (358–71). London: Routledge.

———. 1997. "Munsa earthworks: a preliminary report." *Azania* 32:1–20.

———. 1999. "Seeking and keeping power in Bunyoro-Kitara, Uganda." In *Beyond Chiefdoms: Pathways to Complexity in Africa,* S. K. McIntosh, ed. (124–35). Cambridge: Cambridge University Press.

———. 2003. "Explaining the origins of the state in East Africa." In *East African Archaeology: Foragers, Potters, Smiths and Traders,* C. M. Kusimba and S. B. Kusimba, eds. (149–66). Philadelphia: University of Pennsylvania Press.

Robertshaw, P. T., M. D. Glassick, M. Wood, and R. S. Popelka. 2003. "Chemical analysis of ancient African glass beads: a very preliminary report." *Journal of African Archaeology* 1:139–46.

Rodney, W. 1972. *How Europe Underdeveloped Africa.* New York: Howard University Press.

Rodrigues, N. M. L. 1997. "Cape Verde: site and archaeological heritage conservation at Cidade Velha." In *Museums and Archaeology in West Africa,* C. D. Ardouin, ed. (98–104). Oxford: James Currey.

Rossel, G. 1994–95. "*Musa* and *Ensete* in Africa: taxonomy, nomenclature and uses." *Azania* 29/30:130–46.

Rossignol-Strick, M. 2002. "Holocene climatic changes in the eastern Mediterranean and the spread of food production from Southwest Asia to Egypt." In *Droughts, Food and Culture: Ecological Change and Food Security in Africa's Later Prehistory,* F. A. Hassan, ed. (157–70). New York: Kluwer Academic/Plenum Publishers.

Roubet, C. 1979. *Economie Pastorale Préagricole en Algérie Orientale: Le Néolithique de Tradition Capsienne.* Paris: CNRS.

Rowlands, M. J., Larsen, M., and Kristiansen, K., eds. 1987. *Centre and Periphery in the Ancient World.* Cambridge: Cambridge University Press.

Rowley-Conwy, P. 1986. "Between cave painters and crop planters: aspects of the Temperate European Mesolithic." In *Hunters in Transition: Mesolithic Societies of Temperate Eurasia and the Transition to Farming,* M. Zvelebil, ed. (17–32). Cambridge: Cambridge University Press.

———. 1988. "The camel in the Nile Valley: new radiocarbon accelerator (AMS) dates from Qasr Ibrim." *Journal of Egyptian Archaeology* 74:245–48.

———. 1989. "Nubia A.D. 9–550 and the 'Islamic' agricultural revolution: preliminary botanical evidence from Qasr Ibrim, Egyptian Nubia." *Archéologie du Nil Moyen* 3:131–38.

Rowley-Conwy, P., W. Deakin, and C. H. Shaw. 1999. "Ancient DNA from sorghum: the evidence from Qasr Ibrim, Egyptian Nubia." In *The Exploitation of Plant Resources in Ancient Africa,* M. van der Veen, ed. (55–61). New York: Kluwer Academic/Plenum Publishers.

Sadr, K. 1991. *The Development of Nomadism in Ancient Northeastern Africa.* Philadelphia: University of Pennsylvania Press.

———. 1997. "Kalahari archaeology and the Bushman debate." *Current Anthropology* 38:104–12.

———. 1998. "The first herders at the Cape of Good Hope." *African Archaeological Review* 15:101–32.

Sadr, K., A. Castiglioni, and G. Negro. 1994. "Archaeology in the Nubian Desert." *Sahara* 6:69–75.

Sallares, R. 2002. *Malaria and Rome: A History of Malaria in Ancient Italy.* Oxford: Oxford University Press.

Sampson, C. G. 1994. "Ostrich eggs and Bushman survival on the north-east frontier of the Cape Colony, South Africa." *Journal of Arid Environments* 26:383–99.

Saraguti, I., and N. Goren-Inbar. 2001. "The biface assemblages from Gesher Benot Ya'aqov, Israel: illuminating patterns in "Out of Africa" dispersal." *Quaternary International* 75:85–89.

Sassoon, H. 1981. "The Portuguese frigate wrecked in front of Fort Jesus." In *Fort Jesus, Mombasa,* J. S. Kirkman, ed. (25–29). Mombasa: National Museum of Kenya.

Saunders, A. C. de C. M. 1982. *A Social History of Black Slaves and Freedmen in Portugal, 1441–1555.* Cambridge: Cambridge University Press.

Savage, E. 1992. "Berbers and blacks: Ibadi slave traffic in eighth-century North Africa." *Journal of African History* 33:351–68.

Sayce, A. H. 1912. "Second interim report on the excavations at Meroë in Ethiopia: Part 2 The historical results." *Liverpool Annals of Archaeology and Anthropology* 4:53–65.

Sayed, A. M. A. H. 1983. "New light on the recently discovered port on the Red Sea shore." *Chronique d'Egypte* 58:23–37.

Scanlon, G. T. 1994. "Al-Fustât: the riddle of the earliest settlement." In *The Byzantine and Early Islamic Near East II: Land Use and Settlement Patterns,* G. R. D. King and A. Cameron, eds. (171–79). Princeton: Princeton University Press.

Schlanger, N. 2002. "Making the past for South Africa's future: the prehistory of Field-Marshal Smuts (1920s–1940s)." *Antiquity* 76:200–209.

Schmidt, P. R. 1989. "Early exploitation and settlement in the Usambara Mountains." In *Forest Conservation in the East Usambara Mountains Tanzania,* A. C. Hamilton and R. Bensted-Smith, eds. (75–78). Cambridge: IUCN Tropical Forest Programme.

———. 1995. "Using archaeology to remake history in Africa." In *Making Alternative Histories: The Practice of Archaeology and History in Non-Western Settings,* P. R. Schmidt and T. C. Patterson, eds. (119–47). Santa Fe: School of American Research Press.

———. ed. 1996. *The Culture and Technology of African Iron Production.* Gainesville: University of Florida Press.

———. 1997. *Iron Technology in East Africa: Symbolism, Science and Archaeology.* London: James Currey.

Schmidt, P. R., and M. C. Curtis. 2001. "Urban precursors in the Horn: early 1st-millenium B.C. communities in Eritrea." *Antiquity* 75:849–59.

Schmidt, P. R., and R. J. McIntosh, eds. 1996. *Plundering Africa's Past.* London: James Currey.

Schneider, J. 1977. "Was there a pre-capitalist world system?" *Peasant Studies* 6:20–29.

Schoenbrun, D. L. 1998. *A Green Place, a Good Place: Agrarian Change, Gender, and Social Identity in the Great Lakes Region to the 15th Century.* Oxford: James Currey.

Schortman, E. M., and P. A. Urban. 1987. "Modelling interregional interaction in prehistory." *Advances in Archaeological Method and Theory* 11:37–95.

Schrire, C., and P. M. Floore. 1998. *Historisch-Archeologisch Onderzoek van de VOC-Nederzetting (1598–1710) op Mauritius (Indische Oceaan).* Amsterdam: University of Amsterdam Press.

Schuler, M. 1980. *Alas, Alas, Kongo: A Social History of Indentured African Immigrants into Jamaica, 1841–1845.* Baltimore: John Hopkins University Press.

———. 2002. "Liberated Central Africans in nineteenth-century Guyana." In *Central Africans and Cultural Transformations in the American Diaspora,* L. M. Heywood, ed. (319–52). Cambridge: Cambridge University Press.

Schwartz, D. 1992. "Assèchement climatique vers 3000 B.P. et expansion Bantu en Afrique centrale atlantique: quelques réflexions." *Bulletin de la Société Géologique de France* 163:353–61.

Scott, J. C. 1990. *Domination and the Arts of Resistance: Hidden Transcripts.* New Haven: Yale University Press.

Scott, P. E., and J. Deetz. 1990. "Buildings, furnishings and social change in early Victorian Grahamstown." *Social Dynamics* 16:76–89.

Sealy, J. C., A. G. Morris, R. Armstrong, A. B. Markell, and C. Schrire. 1993. "An historical skeleton from the slave lodge at Vergelegen." *South African Archaeological Society Goodwin Series* 7:84–91.

Segal, R. 2002. *Islam's Black Slaves: A History of Africa's Other Black Diaspora.* London: Atlantic Books.

Seidensticker, W. 1981. "Bornu and the east. Notes and hypotheses on the technology of burnt bricks." In *Proceedings of the Nilo-Saharan Conference—Leiden 1980,* T. Schadeberg and M. L. Bender, eds. (239–50). Dordrecht: Foris.

Seligman, C. G. 1930. *Races of Africa.* Oxford: Oxford University Press.

Serjeant, R. B. 1966. "South Arabia and Ethiopia—African elements in the South Arabian population." *Proceedings of the Third International Conference of Ethiopian Studies* (25–33). Addis Ababa: Institute of Ethiopian Studies.

Serpico, M., and R. White. 2000. "The botanical identity and transport of incense during the Egyptian New Kingdom." *Antiquity* 74:884–98.

Sestieri, A. M. B. 2002. "Mediterranean interaction in the second and early first millennia B.C." In *Archaeology: The Widening Debate,* B. W. Cunliffe, W. Davies, and A. C. Renfrew, eds. (420–29). Oxford: Oxford University Press.

Shaw, B. D. 1979. "The camel in Roman North Africa and the Sahara: history, biology and human economy." *Bulletin de l'Institut Fondamental d'Afrique Noire* 41, Ser. B (4):663–721.

Shaw, I. 2000. "Egypt and the outside world." In *The Oxford History of Ancient Egypt*, I. Shaw, ed. (314–29). Oxford: Oxford University Press.

Shaw, T. 1977. *Unearthing Igbo-Ukwu: Archaeological Discoveries in Eastern Nigeria*. Ibadan: Oxford University Press.

———. 1978. *Nigeria: Its Archaeology and Early History*. London: Thames and Hudson.

———. 1997. "The contemporary plundering of Africa's past." *African Archaeological Review* 14:1–8.

Shaw, T. , P. J. J. Sinclair, B. Andah, and A. Okpoko, eds. 1993. *The Archaeology of Africa: Food, Metals and Towns*. London: Routledge.

Sheppard, P. J. 1990. "Soldiers and bureaucrats: the early history of prehistoric archaeology in the Maghreb." In *A History of African Archaeology*, P. T. Robertshaw, ed. (173–88). London: James Currey.

Sherratt, A. G., ed. 1980. *The Cambridge Encyclopedia of Archaeology*. Cambridge: Cambridge University Press.

———. 1993. "What would a Bronze Age world system look like? Relations between temperate Europe and the Mediterranean in later prehistory." *Journal of European Archaeology* 1:1–57.

———. 1995. "Reviving the grand narrative: archaeology and long-term change." *Journal of European Archaeology* 3:1–32.

———. 1999. "Cash-crops before cash: organic consumables and trade." In *The Prehistory of Food*, C. Gosden and J. Hather, eds. (13–34). London: Routledge.

Shinnie, P. L. 1960. "Socotra." *Antiquity* 34:100–110.

———. 1985. "Iron working at Meroe." In *African Iron Working: Ancient and Traditional*, R. Haaland and P. L. Shinnie, eds. (28–35). New York: Norwegian University Press.

Shinnie, P. L., and F. J. Kense. 1989. *Archaeology of Gonja, Ghana: Excavations at Daboya*. Calgary: University of Calgary Press.

Shinnie, P. L., and A. Shinnie. 1995. *Early Asante*. Calgary: University of Calgary Press.

Sidebotham, S. E., and W. Z. Wendrich. 2001–02. "Berenike: archaeological fieldwork at a Ptolemaic-Roman port on the Red Sea coast of Egypt 1999–2001." *Sahara* 13:23–50.

Simoons, F. J. 1973. "The determinants of dairying and milk use in the Old World: ecological, physiological and cultural." *Ecology of Food Nutrition* 2:83–90.

Sinclair, P. J. J. 1991. "Archaeology in eastern Africa: an overview of current chronological issues." *Journal of African History* 32:179–219.

———. 1995. "The origins of urbanism in East and southern Africa: a diachronic perspective." In *Islamic Art and Culture in Sub-Saharan Africa*, K. Aadahl and B. Sahlström, eds. (99–109). Uppsala: Uppsala University Press.

———. 1999. "The development of urbanism from a global perspective." http://www.arkeologi.uu.se/afr/projects/BOOK/default.htm (accessed 8 September 2004).

Singleton, T. A., ed. 1985. *The Archaeology of Slavery and Plantation Life*. Orlando: Academic Press.

———. 1995. "The archaeology of slavery in North America." *Annual Review of Anthropology* 24:119–40.

———. ed. 1999. *I, Too, Am America: Archaeological Studies of African-American Life.* Charlottesville: University of Virginia Press.

———. 2001. "Slavery and spatial dialectics on Cuban coffee plantations." *World Archaeology* 33:98–114.

———. 2002. "An Americanist perspective on African archaeology: toward an archaeology of the Black Atlantic." In *West Africa During the Atlantic Slave Trade: Archaeological Perspectives*, C. R. DeCorse, ed. (179–84). Leicester: Leicester University Press.

Slayman, A. L. 1997. "Roman trade with the Canary Islands." *Archaeology* 50(3): 22.

Smith, A. B. 1986a. "Cattle domestication in North Africa." *African Archaeological Review* 4:197–203.

———. 1986b. "Excavations at Plettenberg Bay, South Africa, of the camp-site of the survivors of the wreck of the *São Gonçalo*, 1630." *The International Journal of Nautical Archaeology and Underwater Exploration* 15:53–63.

———. 1989. "Khoikhoi susceptibility to virgin soil epidemics in the 18th century." *South African Medical Journal* 75:25–26.

———. 1992. *Pastoralism in Africa: Origins and Development Ecology.* London: Hurst.

Smith, B. 1998. *The Emergence of Agriculture.* New York: Scientific American.

Smith, G. 1984. "Climate." In *The Sahara*, L. Cloudsley-Thompson, ed. (17–30). Oxford: Pergamon Press.

Smith, H. S. 1992. "The making of Egypt: a review of the influence of Susa and Sumer on Upper Egypt and Lower Nubia in the 4th millennium B.C." In *The Followers of Horus: Studies Dedicated to Michael Allen Hoffman*, R. Friedman and B. Adams, eds. (235–46). Oxford: Oxbow Publications.

Smith, M. C., and H. T. Wright. 1988. "The ceramics from Ras Hafun in Somalia: notes on a Classical maritime site." *Azania* 23:115–41.

Smith, R. S. 1989. *Warfare and Diplomacy in Pre-Colonial West Africa.* London: James Currey.

Snape, S. 2003. "The emergence of Libya on the horizon of Egypt." In *Mysterious Lands*, D. O'Connor and S. Quirke, eds. (93–106). London: UCL Press.

Snowden, F. 1970. *Blacks in Antiquity: Ethiopians in the Greco-Roman Experience.* Cambridge: Cambridge University Press.

Solway, J. S., and R. B. Lee. 1990. "Foragers, genuine or spurious? Situating the Kalahari San in history." *Current Anthropology* 31:109–46.

Souville, G. 1958–59. "La peche et la vie maritime au Néolithique en Afrique du Nord." *Bulletin Archéologique du Maroc* 3:314–44.

Spring, C. 1993. *African Arms and Armour.* London: British Museum.

Stahl, A. B. 1984. "A history and critique of investigations into early African agriculture." In *From Hunters to Farmers: The Causes and Consequences of Food-Production in Africa*, J. D. Clark and S. A. Brandt, eds. (9–21). Berkeley: University of California Press.

———. 1994. "Innovation, diffusion and culture contact: the Holocene archaeology of Ghana." *Journal of World Prehistory* 8:51–112.

———. 1999a. "Perceiving variability in time and space: the evolutionary mapping of African societies." In *Beyond Chiefdoms: Pathways to Complexity in Africa*, S. K. McIntosh, ed. (39–55). Cambridge: Cambridge University Press.

———. 1999b. "The archaeology of global encounters viewed from Banda, Ghana." *African Archaeological Review* 16:5–82.

———. 2001a. *Making History in Banda: Anthropological Visions of Africa's Past*. Cambridge: Cambridge University Press.

———. 2001b. "Historical process and the impact of the Atlantic slave trade on Banda, Ghana, c. 1800–1920." In *West Africa During the Atlantic Slave Trade: Archaeological Perspectives*, C. R. DeCorse, ed. (38–58). Leicester: Leicester University Press.

———. ed. 2004. *African Archaeology: A Critical Introduction*. Oxford: Blackwells.

Starkey, P. 2000. "The history of working animals in Africa." In *The Origins and Development of African Livestock: Archaeology, Genetics, Linguistics and Ethnography*, R. M. Blench and K. C. MacDonald, eds. (478–502). London: UCL Press.

Stemler, A. B. L. 1984. "The transition from food collecting to food production in northern Africa." In *From Hunters to Farmers: The Causes and Consequences of Food Production in Africa*, J. D. Clark and S. A. Brandt, eds. (127–31). Berkeley: University of California Press.

Stemler, A. B. L., and R. H. Falk. 1981. "SEM of archaeological plant specimens." *Scanning Electron Microscopy 1981*, Part III: 191–96.

Stengroome, C. 2000. "The faunal remains from Gadei (excluding fish)." In *Urbanism, Archaeology and Trade: Further Observations on the Gao Region (Mali). The 1996 Fieldseason Results*, T. A. Insoll, ed. (56–61). Oxford: British Archaeological Reports International Series S829.

Sténuit, R. 1977. "Le *Witte Leeuw*: fouilles sousmarines sur l'épave d'un navire de la V.O.C. coulé en 1613 à l'ile de Sainte Hélène. De schipbrack van een schip van de VOC in 1613 en het onderwateronderzoek naar het wrak in 1976" *Bulletin van het Rijksmuseum* 25:165–78.

Stewart, C. 2002. "Monasticism." In *The Early Christian World Volume I*, P. Esler, ed. (344–66). London: Routledge.

Stiles, D. 1992. "The ports of East Africa, the Comores and Madagascar: their place in Indian Ocean trade from 1–1500 A.D." *Kenya Past and Present* 24:27–36.

Stine, L., M. Cabah, and M. Groover. 1996. "Bluebeads as African-American cultural symbols." *Historical Archaeology* 30(3):44–75.

Stuiver, M., P. J. Reimer, E. Bard, J. W. Beck, G. S. Burr, K. A. Hughen, B. Kromer, G. McCormac, J. van der Plicht, and M. Spurk. 1998. "INTCAL98 radiocarbon age calibration 24000-0 cal B.P." *Radiocarbon* 40:1041–83.

Sutton, J. E. G. 1974. "The aquatic civilization of Middle Africa." *Journal of African History* 15:527–46.

————. 1982. "Archaeology in West Africa: a review of recent work and a further list of radiocarbon dates." *Journal of African History* 23:291–313.

————. 1991. "The international factor at Igbo-Ukwu." *African Archaeological Review* 9:145–60.

————. ed. 1994–95. "The growth of farming communities in Africa from the Equator southwards." *Azania* 29–30:1–338.

————. 1997. "The African lords of the intercontinental gold trade before the Black Death: al-Hasan bin Sulaiman of Kilwa and Mansa Musa of Mali." *Antiquaries Journal* 77:221–42.

————. 1998a. "Kilwa: a history of the ancient Swahili town with a guide to the monuments of Kilwa Kisiwani and adjacent islands." *Azania* 33:113–69.

————. 1998b. "Engaruka: an irrigation agricultural community in northern Tanzania before the Maasai." *Azania* 33:1–38.

————. 1998c. "Ntusi and Bigo: farmers, cattle-herders and rulers in western Uganda, A.D. 1000–1500." *Azania* 33:39–72.

————. 2001. "Igbo-Ukwu and the Nile." *African Archaeological Review* 18:49–62.

————. 2003. "Review of: G. Connah, African Civilizations: an archaeological perspective." *Azania* 39:199–202.

Swan, L. 1994. *Early Gold Mining on the Zimbabwean Plateau.* Uppsala, Sweden: Uppsala University Press.

Takamiya, I. 1994. "Egyptian pottery in A-Group cemeteries, Nubia: towards an understanding of pottery production and distribution in pre-dynastic and early-dynastic Egypt." Masters thesis, University of Cambridge.

Talhami, G. H. 1977. "The Zanj rebellion reconsidered." *International Journal of African Historical Studies* 10(3):443–61.

Tamrat, T. 1977. "Ethiopia, the Red Sea and the Horn." In *The Cambridge History of Africa Vol. III c. 1050–c. 1600*, R. Oliver, ed. (98–182). Cambridge: Cambridge University Press.

Taylor, C. C. 1999. *Sacrifice as Terror: The Rwandan Genocide of 1994.* Oxford: Berg.

Taylor, J. 2000. "The Third Intermediate Period (1069–664 B.C.)." In *The Oxford History of Ancient Egypt*, I. Shaw, ed. (330–68). Oxford: Oxford University Press.

Tchernov, E. 1992. "Biochronology, paleoecology and dispersal events of hominids in the southern Levant." In *The Evolution and Dispersal of Modern Humans in Asia*, T. Akazawa, K. Aoki, and T. Kimura, eds. (149–88). Tokyo: Hokusen-Sha.

Teixeira da Mota, A., and P. E. H. Hair. 1988. *East of Mina: Afro-European Relations on the Gold Coast in the 1550s and the 1560s.* Madison: University of Wisconsin-Madison African Studies Program.

Tejera Gaspar, A., and E. Aznar Vallejo. 1992. "Lessons from the Canaries: the first contact between Europeans and Canarians c. 1312–1477." *Antiquity* 66:120–29.

Thiaw, I. 2001. "Processes of change in the Falemme: A.D. 500–1900." In *West Africa during the Atlantic Slave Trade: Archaeological Perspectives*, C. R. DeCorse, ed. (29–31). Leicester: Leicester University Press.

————. 2002. "Archaeological reconnaissance in Gorée Island (Sénégal): preliminary results." (Abstract). *Nyame Akuma* 57:74.

————. 2003a. "The Gorée archaeological project (GAP): preliminary results. *Nyame Akuma* 60:27–35.

————. 2003b. "Archaeology and the public in Senegal: reflections in doing fieldwork at home." *Journal of African Archaeology* 1:215–26.

Thomas, H. 1997. *The Slave Trade: The History of the Atlantic Slave Trade 1440–1870*. New York: Simon and Schuster.

Thomas, N. 1991. *Entangled Objects: Exchange, Material Culture and Colonialism in the Pacific*. Oxford: Polity Press.

Thornton, J. 1992. *Africa and Africans in the Making of the Atlantic World, 1400–1680*. Cambridge: Cambridge University Press.

————. 2000. "Mbanza Kongo/São Salvador: Kongo's holy city." In *Africa's Urban Past*, D. M. Anderson and R. Rathbone, eds. (67–84). Oxford: James Currey.

Togola, T. 1996. "Iron Age occupation in the Méma Region, Mali." *African Archaeological Review* 13:91–110.

Török, L. 1995. "Nubia." In *Africa: The Art of a Continent*, T. Phillips, ed. (46–51). Munich: Prestel.

Tostain, S. 1998. "Le mil, une longue histoire: hypothèses sur sa domestication et ses migrations." In *Plantes et Paysages d'Afrique—Une Histoire à Explorer*, M. Chastenet, ed. (461–90). Paris: Editions Karthala.

Trevor-Roper, H. 1963. "The rise of Christian Europe." *The Listener* 28 November.

Trigger, B. G. 1969. "The myth of Meroe and the African Iron Age." *African Historical Studies* 2:23–50.

————. 1989. *A History of Archaeological Thought*. Cambridge: Cambridge University Press.

————. 2003. *Understanding Early Civilizations*. Cambridge: Cambridge University Press.

Trimingham, J. S. 1949. *Islam in the Sudan*. London: Oxford University Press.

————. 1968. *The Influence of Islam Upon Africa*. London: Longmans.

Trinkaus, E. 1981. "Neanderthal limb proportions and cold adaptation." In *Aspects of Human Evolution*, C. B. Stringer, ed. (187–224). London: Taylor and Francis.

Tylecote, R. F. 1975. "The origin of iron smelting in Africa." *West African Journal of Archaeology* 5:1–9.

Ullendorf, E. 1956. "Hebraic-Jewish elements in Abyssinian monophysite Christianity." *Journal of Semitic Studies* 1:216–56.

————. 1960. *The Ethiopians*. Oxford: Oxford University Press.

Vaillancourt, R. E., and N. F. Weeden. 1992. "Chloroplast DNA polymorphism suggests Nigerian centre of domestication for the cowpea, *Vigna unguiculata*, Leguminosae." *American Journal of Botany* 79:1194–99.

Van Beek, G. W. 1969. *Hajar bin Humeid: Investigations at a Pre-Islamic Site in South Arabia*. Baltimore: John Hopkins University Press.

Van Dantzig, A. 1980. *Forts and Castles of Ghana*. Accra: Sedco Publishing Ltd.

Van der Veen, M. 1992. "Garamantian agriculture: the plant remains from Zinchecra, Fezzan." *Libyan Studies* 23:7–39.

———. 2003. "Trade and diet at Roman and medieval Quseir al-Qadim, Egypt. A preliminary report." *Africa Praehistorica* 15:207–12.

Van Grunderbeck, M.-C., E. Roche, and H. Doutrelepont. 1983. *Le Premier Age du Fer au Rwanda et au Burundi*. Brussels: IFAQ.

Vanhee, H. 2002. "Central African popular Christianity and the making of Haitian Vodou religion." In *Central Africans and Cultural Transformations in the American Diaspora*, L. M. Heywood, ed. (243–64). Cambridge: Cambridge University Press.

Van Neer, W. 2000. "Domestic animals from archaeological sites in Central and West-Central Africa." In *The Origins and Development of African Livestock: Archaeology, Genetics, Linguistics and Ethnography*, R. M. Blench and K. C. MacDonald, eds. (163–90). London: UCL Press.

Van Noten, F. 1978. *Rock Art of the Jebel Uweinat*. Graz: Akademische Drük und Verlaganstalt.

Van Schalkwyk, L. O. 1994–95. "Settlement shifts and socio-economic transformations in early agriculturist communities in the lower Thukela Basin." *Azania* 29–30:187–98.

Van Sertima, I. 1976. *They Came Before Columbus: The African Presence in Ancient America*. New York: Random House.

———. ed. 1992. *African Presence in Early America*. New Brunswick: Transaction Books.

Vansina, J. 1962. "Long-distance trade-routes in central Africa." *Journal of African History* 3:375–90.

———. 1990. *Paths in the Rainforests: Toward a History of Political Tradition in Equatorial Africa*. London: James Currey.

———. 1994–95. "A slow revolution: farming in subequatorial Africa." *Azania* 29/30:1–14.

———. 1995. "New linguistic evidence on the expansion of Bantu." *Journal of African History* 36:173–95.

———. 2003. "Bananas in Cameroon c. 500 B.C.E.? Not proven." *Azania* 38:174–76.

Vérin, P. 1986. *The History of Civilization in North Madagascar*. Rotterdam: A.A. Balkema.

Vérin, P., C. Kottak, and P. Gorlin. 1970. "The glottochronology of Malagasy speech communities." *Oceanic Linguistics* 8:26–81.

Verlinden, C. 1977. *L'Esclavage dans l'Europe Médiévale*. Ghent: Rijksuniversiteit te Gent.

Vermeeren, C. 1999. "The use of imported and local wood species at the Roman port of Berenike, Red Sea coast, Egypt." In *The Exploitation of Plant Resources in Ancient Africa*, M. van der Veen, ed. (199–204). New York: Kluwer Academic/Plenum Publishers.

Vermeersch, P. M. 2001. "'Out of Africa' from an Egyptian point of view." *Quaternary International* 75:103–12.

Vermeersch, P. M., P. van Peer, J. Moeyersons, and W. van Neer. 1996. "Neolithic occupation of the Sodmein area, Red Sea Mountains, Egypt." In *Aspects of African Archaeology*, G. Pwiti and R. Soper, eds. (411–20). Harare: University of Zimbabwe Press.

Vernet, R. 1986. *La Mauritanie des Origines au Début de l'Histoire*. Nouakchott: Centre Culturel Français A. de St Exupéry.

Vernet, T. 2003. "Le commerce des esclaves sur la côte swahili, 1500–1750." *Azania* 39:69–97.

Vinnicombe, P. 1976. *People of the Eland*. Pietermaritzburg: University of Natal Press.

Vivian, B. C. 1992. "Sacred to secular: transitions in Akan funerary customs." In *An African Commitment: Papers in Honour of Peter Lewis Shinnie*, J. Sterner and N. David, eds. (157–67). Calgary: University of Calgary Press.

Vogel, J. O. 1971. *Kumadzulo: An Early Iron Age Village in Southern Zambia*. Lusaka: Oxford University Press.

Voigt, E. 1983. *Mapungubwe: An Archaeozoological Interpretation of an Iron Age Community*. Pretoria: Transvaal Museum.

Von Armin, Y. 1998. "The wreck of the 5th rated British frigate *HMS Sirius* (1797) in Mauritius." *Bulletin of the Australian Institute for Maritime Archaeology* 22:35–44.

Von der Way, T. 1987. "Tell el-Fara'in-Buto. 2. Bericht." *Mitteilungen des Deutschen Archäologischen Instituts, Abteilung Kairo* 43:241–57.

Wadley, L. 2000. "South African archaeology, gender and the African renaissance." *South African Historical Journal* 43:81–95.

Waldren, W. H., and J. A. Ensenyat, eds. 2002. *World Islands in Prehistory: International Insular Investigations*. Oxford: British Archaeological Reports International Series S1095.

Wallerstein, I. 1974. *The Modern World-System I*. New York: Academic Press.

———. 1980. *The Modern World-System II*. New York: Academic Press.

Ward, C. 2001. "The Sadana Island shipwreck: an eighteenth-century A.D. merchantman off the Red Sea coast of Egypt." *World Archaeology* 32:368–82.

Ward, G. M., T. M. Sutherland, and J. M. Sutherland. 1980. "Animals as an energy source in Third World agriculture." *Science* 208:571–74.

Wasylikowa, K., J. Mitka, F. Wendorf, and R. Schild. 1997. "Exploitation of wild plants by the early Neolithic hunter-gatherers of the Western Desert, Egypt: Nabta Playa as a case-study." *Antiquity* 71:932–41.

Watson, A. M. 1983. *Agricultural Innovation in the Early Islamic World*. Cambridge: Cambridge University Press.

Webb, J. A. 1995. *Desert Frontier: Ecological and Economic Change along the Western Sahel 1600–1850*. Madison: University of Wisconsin Press.

Weber, S. 1998. "Out of Africa: the initial impact of millets in South Asia." *Current Anthropology* 40:267–74.

———. 2001. "Seeds of urbanism revisited." *Antiquity* 75:413–14.

Welsby, D. A. 1996. *The Kingdom of Kush*. London: British Museum.

———. 1998. *Soba II. Renewed Excavations within the Metropolis of the Kingdom of Alwa in Central Sudan*. Nairobi: British Institute in Eastern Africa.

————. 2002. *The Medieval Kingdoms of Nubia.* London: British Museum.

Welsby, D. A., and C. M. Daniels. 1991. *Soba. Archaeological Research at a Medieval Capital on the Blue Nile.* Nairobi: British Institute in Eastern Africa.

Wendorf, F., and R. Schild. 1980. *The Prehistory of the Eastern Sahara.* New York: Academic Press.

————. 1994. "Are the Early Holocene cattle in the eastern Sahara domestic or wild?" *Evolutionary Anthropology* 3:118–28.

————. 1998. "Nabta Playa and its role in Northeastern African prehistory." *Journal of Anthropological Archaeology* 17:97–123.

————. 2002. "The role of storage in the Neolithic of the Egyptian Sahara." *Africa Praehistorica* 41–49.

Wengrow, D. 2003. "Landscapes of knowledge, idioms of power: the African foundations of Ancient Egyptian civilization reconsidered." In *Ancient Egypt in Africa,* D. O'Connor and D. A. M. Reid, eds. (121–36). London: UCL Press.

Wenke, R. J. 1999. *Patterns in Prehistory: Humankind's First Three Million Years.* Oxford: Oxford University Press.

Werz, B. E. J. S. 1999. *Diving up the Human Past: Perspectives on Maritime Archaeology, with Special Reference to Developments in South Africa until 1996.* Oxford: British Archaeological Reports International Series S749.

Wesler, K. W. 1983. "Trade politics and native polities in Iroquoia and Asante." *Comparative Studies in Society and History* 25:641–60.

————. 1998. "Cross-cultural archaeology: Nigerian perspectives on North American research problems." In *Historical Archaeology in Nigeria,* K. W. Wesler, ed. (311–52). Trenton: Africa World Press.

Wheaton, T., and P. Garrow. 1985. "Acculturation and the archaeological record in the Carolina lowcountry." In *The Archaeology of Slavery and Plantation Life,* T. A. Singleton, ed. (232–59). Orlando: Academic Press.

Whitcomb, D. 1988. *Aqaba: Port of Palestine on the China Sea.* Chicago: Oriental Institute.

White, D. 2002. *Marsa Matruh.* Oxford: INSTAP Academic Press.

Whitelaw, G. 1994–95. "Towards an Early Iron Age worldview: some ideas from KwaZulu-Natal." *Azania* 29–30:37–50.

Whittle, A. 1996. *Europe in the Neolithic: The Creation of New Worlds.* Cambridge: Cambridge University Press.

Widgren, M., and J. E. G. Sutton, eds. 2003. *Islands of Agricultural Intensification in Eastern Africa.* Oxford: James Currey.

Wiessner, P. 1982. "Risk, reciprocity and social influence on !Kung San economics." In *Politics and History in Band Societies,* E. Leacock and R. B. Lee, eds. (61–84). Cambridge: Cambridge University Press.

Wigboldus, J. S. 1994–95. "The spread of crops into sub-equatorial Africa during the Early Iron Age." *Azania* 29/30:121–29.

Wilding, R. 1989. "The pottery." In *Excavations at Aksum,* S. C. Munro-Hay, ed. (235–316). Nairobi: British Institute in Eastern Africa.

Wilkie, L. A. 1999. "Evidence of African continuities in the material culture of Clifton Plantation, Bahamas." In *African Sites Archaeology in the Caribbean*, J. B. Haviser, ed. (264–75). Princeton: Marlus Wiener.

Wilkinson, J. C. 1981. "Oman and East Africa: new light on early Kilwan history from the Omani sources." *International Journal of African Historical Studies* 14:272–305.

Wilkinson, T. A. H. 1999. *Early Dynastic Egypt*. London: Routledge.

———. 2003. *Genesis of the Pharaohs*. London: Thames and Hudson.

Wilks, I. 1962. "A medieval trade-route from the Niger to the Gulf of Guinea." *Journal of African History* 3:337–41.

———. 1982. "Wangara, Akan and Portuguese in the fifteenth and sixteenth centuries." *Journal of African History* 23:333–49 and 23:563–72.

Williams, B. B. 1986. *Excavations Between Abu Simbel and the Sudan Frontier. The A-Group Royal Cemetery at Qustul: Cemetery L*. Chicago: The Oriental Institute of the University of Chicago.

Williams, E. 1944. *Capitalism and Slavery*. Chapel Hill: University of North Carolina Press.

Wilmsen, E. N., and J. R. Denbow. 1990. "Paradigmatic history of San-speaking peoples and current attempts at revision." *Current Anthropology* 31:489–524.

Wilson, A. 2003. "Irrigation technologies: *foggaras*, wells and field systems." In *The Archaeology of Fazzan Volume I, Synthesis*, D. J. Mattingly, ed. (235–78). London: Society for Libyan Studies.

Wilson, T. H., and A. L. Omar. 1997. "Archaeological investigations at Pate." *Azania* 32:31–76.

Winer, M., and J. Deetz. 1990. "The transformation of British culture in the Eastern Cape, 1820–1860." *Social Dynamics* 16:55–75.

Witt, R. 1971. *Isis in the Graeco-Roman World*. London: Thames and Hudson.

Wolf, E. 1982. *Europe and the People without History*. Berkeley: University of California Press.

Wolska-Conus, W. 1968–73. *Cosmas Indicopleustes: Topographie Chrétienne*. Paris: Sources Chrétiennes.

Wood, M. 2000. "Making connections: relationships between international trade and glass beads from the Shashe-Limpopo area." *South African Archaeological Goodwin Society Series* 8:78–90.

Woodhouse, J. 1998. "Iron in Africa: metal from nowhere." In *Transformations in Africa: Essays on Africa's Later Past*, G. Connah, ed. (160–85). Leicester: Leicester University Press.

Wright, H. T. 1984. "Early seafarers of the Comoro Islands: the Dembeni Phase of the IXth–Xth centuries A.D." *Azania* 19:13–59.

———. 1992. "Early Islam, oceanic trade and town development on Nzwani: the Comorian Archipelago in the XIth–XVth centuries A.D." *Azania* 27:81–128.

———. 1993. "Trade and politics on the eastern littoral of Africa, A.D. 800–1300." In *Archaeology of Africa: Food, Metals and Towns*, T. Shaw, P. J. J. Sinclair, B. W. Andah, and A. Okpoko, eds. (658–72). London: Routledge.

Yajima, H. 1996. "Some problems on the formation of the Swahili world and the Indian Ocean maritime world." *Essays in Northeast African Studies Senri Ethnological Studies* 43:319–54.

Yentsch, A. 1992. "Gudgeons, mullet and proud pigs: historicity, black fishermen and southern myth." In *The Art and Mystery of Historical Archaeology: Essays in Honour of Jim Deetz,* A. Yentsch and M. C. Beaudry, eds. (283–314). Boca Raton: CRC Press.

———. 1994. *A Chesapeake Family and Their Slaves: A Study in Historical Archaeology.* Cambridge: Cambridge University Press.

Young, R., and J. Thompson. 1999. "Missing plant foods? Where is the archaeobotanical evidence for sorghum and finger millet in East Africa?" In *The Exploitation of Plant Resources in Ancient Africa,* M. van der Veen, ed. (63–72). New York: Kluwer Academic/Plenum Publishers.

Zachernuk, P. S. 1994. "Of origins and colonial order: southern Nigerian historians and the 'Hamitic Hypothesis' c. 1870–1970." *Journal of African History* 35:427–55.

Zarins, J. 1990. "Obsidian and the Red Sea trade: prehistoric aspects." In *South Asian Archaeology 1987,* I. M. Taddei and P. Cawen, eds. (507–41). Rome: ISMEO.

———. 1996. "Obsidian in the larger context of Predynastic/Archaic Egyptian Red Sea trade." In *The Indian Ocean in Antiquity,* J. E. Reade, ed. (89–106). London: British Museum.

Zarins, J., A. Murad, and K. al-Yish. 1981. "The comprehensive archaeological survey programme. The second preliminary report on the Southwest Province." *Atlatl* 5:9–42.

Zilhão, J. 2000. "From the Mesolithic to the Neolithic in the Iberian peninsula." In *Europe's First Farmers,* T. D. Price, ed. (144–82). Cambridge: Cambridge University Press.

Zohary, D. 1996. "The mode of domestication of the founder crops of Southwest Asian agriculture." In *The Origin and Spread of Agriculture and Pastoralism in Eurasia,* D. R. Harris, ed. (142–58). London: UCL Press.

Index

About the Author

PETER MITCHELL first encountered African archaeology as an undergraduate in Cambridge in 1982–83. From there he moved to Oxford, completing a doctorate on the Pleistocene Later Stone Age of southern Africa in 1987. Tenure of a British Academy Post-doctoral Research Fellowship supported a major program of fieldwork in western Lesotho, which was extended to the Lesotho highlands when he held a second post-doctoral research fellowship at the University of Cape Town. Both projects focused on the archaeology of Middle and Later Stone Age hunter-gatherers and on obtaining data relevant to the reconstruction of late Quaternary paleoenvironments. After having taught at the University of Cape Town in 1990 and at the University of Wales, Lampeter, from 1993 to 1995, he returned to Oxford in 1995. There he combines the position of University Lecturer in African Prehistory with a Tutorial Fellowship in Archaeology at St Hugh's College and the post of Curator of African Archaeology at the Pitt Rivers Museum. He continues to investigate the Later Stone Age archaeology of Lesotho and is also actively researching the history of southern African archaeology. Recent publications include *The Archaeology of Southern Africa* (2002) and a volume coedited with two former research students, Anne Haour and John Hobart, *Researching Africa's Past: Contributions from British Archaeologists* (2003), along with numerous journal articles and chapters in edited books. He serves on the Governing Council of the British Institute in Eastern Africa and is a member of the editorial boards of *African Archaeological Review, Antiquity, Before Farming*, the *Journal of African History*, the *South African Archaeological Bulletin, Southern African Humanities*, and *World Archaeology*. From 2004–2006 he is also President of the Society of Africanist Archaeologists.